■ Trust in Social Dilemmas

Series in Human Cooperation

Series Editor
PAUL A. M. VAN LANGE

Reward and Punishment in Social Dilemmas
Edited by Paul A.M. Van Lange, Bettina Rockenbach, and Toshio Yamagishi

Trust in Social Dilemmas
Edited by Paul A.M. Van Lange, Bettina Rockenbach, and Toshio Yamagishi

Trust in Social Dilemmas

EDITED BY

Paul A. M. Van Lange
Bettina Rockenbach
Toshio Yamagishi

OXFORD
UNIVERSITY PRESS

OXFORD
UNIVERSITY PRESS

Oxford University Press is a department of the University of Oxford. It furthers
the University's objective of excellence in research, scholarship, and education
by publishing worldwide. Oxford is a registered trade mark of Oxford University
Press in the UK and certain other countries.

Published in the United States of America by Oxford University Press
198 Madison Avenue, New York, NY 10016, United States of America.

© Oxford University Press 2017

Library of Congress Cataloging-in-Publication Data
Names: Lange, Paul A. M. van, editor. | Rockenbach, Bettina, editor. |
Yamagishi, Toshio, 1948– editor.
Title: Trust in social dilemmas / edited by Paul A.M. Van Lange, Bettina
Rockenbach, Toshio Yamagishi.
Description: New York, NY : Oxford University Press, [2017] |
Series: Series in human cooperation | Includes bibliographical references and index.
Identifiers: LCCN 2016054088 | ISBN 9780190630782 (jacketed hardcover : alk. paper)
Subjects: LCSH: Trust—Social aspects. | Cooperativeness. | Social problems.
Classification: LCC BF575.T7 T7935 2017 | DDC 158—dc23
LC record available at https://lccn.loc.gov/2016054088

9 8 7 6 5 4 3 2 1
Printed by Sheridan Books, Inc., United States of America

■ CONTENTS

PART III ■ **Trust in Different Cultures**

■ PREFACE

Social dilemmas pose a key challenge to human society. Conflicts between self-interest and collective interests are inherently complex. Global warming and depletion of natural resources, such as rainforest, fish, or threatened species all share important social dilemma features. Likewise, how can we make most or all people feel committed to contribute to important public goods, such as going beyond the call of duty at the workplace to realize important goals or simply paying tickets when enjoying public transportation. Besides their obvious societal relevance, social dilemmas constitute an important scientific topic as it relates to the study of human cooperation. Social dilemmas bring to the forefront motives such as selfishness, egalitarianism, and retaliation or emotions such as empathy, guilt, or shame. It is a "rich" situation that has, predictably, drawn the scientific curiosity of many scientists working in various disciplines, such as anthropology, biology, economics, management science, political science, psychology, and sociology.

One of the most basic "states" that is relevant to social dilemmas is trust. We do not know of any scientist who would not agree about the importance of trust for understanding cooperation in social dilemmas. Some might even go so far as to say that cooperation without trust is hardly possible at all, in that trust is a considered a necessary, albeit not sufficient, ingredient in cooperation. Others would note that cooperation is still possible without trust but nevertheless agree that trust is one of the most important keys to promoting and maintaining cooperation. And empirically, the correlation between expectations regarding cooperative behavior by others and own cooperation has been observed in many types of social dilemmas and is relative to other variables, large in magnitude. In short, trust matters in social dilemmas.

The concept of trust has received immense attention from various scientists. It has been proven useful in understanding the functioning of societies, organizations, groups, and relationships. For example, numerous studies in sociology and political science have been conducted under the label of "social capital" to understand how and why trust and social connection are important to well-functioning societies. Likewise, in the smaller contexts, such as organizations and teams, the concept of trust has been shown to play a key role in predicting outcomes such as motivation and performance, citizenship behaviors, and absenteeism. And in the context of close relationships, trust is one of the key predictors of happiness and relationship stability.

The broad attention of trust has yielded a wealth of findings that have contributed to theorizing about the functioning of collectives, whether they be relationships, organizations, or societies at large. Needless to say, while past research has answered many questions, it has also energized new questions. One emerging topic is connected to understanding the biology and human development of trust. For example, what are the neuroscientific underpinnings of trust? Do people become more (or less) trusting over a lifetime, and if so, why? There are indeed many mysteries regarding trust even at the level of the individual. These issues are captured in Part I, titled "Biology and Development of Trust." There are also new developments in how trust unfolds in the context of dyads, groups, and organizations. The focus here is on social interaction and on the functions that trust may serve in organized settings. These issues are captured in Part II, titled "Trust in Dyads, Groups, and Organizations." Finally, one especially novel area of research operates at the level of culture. Recent empirical approaches examine economic games to explore cultural similarities and differences among societies. Also, there is now more attention on societies that are clearly understudied and that may inform us about the various roots of trust and distrust in differing societies, as well as how cooperation can be maintained and promoted in differing societies. These issues are captured in Part III, titled "Trust in Different Cultures."

Accordingly, we have used three broad themes as an organizing framework for the chapters on trust: the biological and developmental approaches to trust; trust in dyads, groups, and organizations; and trust in different cultures. This book benefits from contributions of scientists that are all highly distinguished, active researchers on the topic of trust in social dilemmas and related economic games. Because the contributors differ in their scientific backgrounds, be it anthropology, economics, neuroscience, political science, or psychology, the chapters complement each other in various ways. Indeed, this book series was inspired by two general ideas. First, we wanted a topic, within the social dilemma literature, that is key to understanding human cooperation and that has generated considerable research. Second, we believe that for many broad topics in social dilemmas, it takes the expertise from scientists working in different fields and disciplines to make scientific progress in understanding how exactly cooperation can be promoted. For such reasons, we invited researchers working from different perspectives and backgrounds but who in the final analysis all seek to answer the question about how trust can promote cooperation to contribute to this book project. And we were fortunate that nearly all of the scientists we invited were happy to contribute.

This is the second volume in the series on human cooperation. As in the first volume, which focused on reward and punishment in social dilemmas, we hope to reach a broad audience of scientists in various fields and disciplines, as well as the interested reader or practitioner who is committed to managing and resolving social dilemmas in various domains of social life. We should add that this book is primarily aimed at the scientific community of researchers interested in the question of human cooperation. After all, the book provides an up-to-date overview of many of the key issues in trust in social dilemmas. As such, the book should be especially informative to students and faculty working in these areas. At the same time, our view, perhaps slightly biased, is also that the book should also be relevant to scientists and practitioners in areas such as conflict resolution, management, morality, fairness, negotiation, and public policy. Trust in social dilemmas is at heart of these issues, as one could also infer from the programs of research that are covered in this book. As such, we hope the book will be helpful to a relatively broader field of students, faculty, and professionals working in areas that are importantly linked to social dilemmas.

We would like to extend our gratitude to a number of people for making valuable contributions to this book project. To begin with, we wish to thank the community of all social dilemma researchers who collectively have contributed to this interesting, and important, theme. Moreover, this book grew out of the biannual international conferences on social dilemmas. The first conference was held in Groningen, the Netherlands, in 1984, and the most recent conference was held in Hong Kong in 2015. In between there were conferences in the United States, the Netherlands, Japan, Australia, Germany, Israel, Poland, Sweden, and Switzerland, a period during which the community of social dilemma researchers that attend these conferences grew from around 15 in 1984 to about 150 scientists in more recent years. These scientists work in various disciplines, adopt diverse theoretical perspectives, address complementary topics in social dilemmas, and work in different parts of the world. It was not only the topic as such but also the increasing popularity and breadth of social dilemma research that our publisher seems to appreciate. Indeed, we want to thank Abby Gross, who has expressed her genuine enthusiasm and commitment from the very beginning at a meeting of the Society and Personality and Social Psychology and throughout the six years after that meeting while we edited this book (and our previous book). The help and support of Courtney McCarroll is also strongly appreciated.

Finally, we hope that you will enjoy reading this book—as a student, fellow academic, teacher, and perhaps practitioner, or member of the general public—and that it makes a meaningful difference, even if only a small difference, in how you think about your next step in research on human cooperation, in your theoretical work on social dilemmas, or in the ways in which you effectively promote cooperation in your everyday lives and society at large.

The Editors, January 2016

■ CONTRIBUTORS

René Bekkers
Faculty of Social Sciences
VU University
Amsterdam, the Netherlands

Iris Bohnet
John F. Kennedy School of
  Government
Harvard University
Cambridge, MA

Nancy Buchan
Darla Moore School of Business
University of South Carolina
Columbia, SC

Erwin Bulte
Development Economics Group
Wageningen University
Wageningen, the Netherlands;
Department of Economics
Utrecht University
Utrecht, the Netherlands

Karen S. Cook
Department of Sociology
Stanford University
Stanford, CA

Carsten K. W. De Dreu
Department of Psychology
Center for Experimental Economics
  and Political Decision Making
University of Amsterdam
Amsterdam, the Netherlands

Bart de Jong
Centre for Sustainable HRM and
  Well-being
Australian Catholic University
Melbourne, Australia

Peter Thisted Dinesen
Department of Political Science
University of Copenhagen
Copenhagen, Denmark

David Dunning
Department of Psychology
Cornell University
Ithaca, NY

Jan Engelmann
Centre for Cognitive Neuroimaging
Radboud University
Nijmegen, the Netherlands

Anthony M. Evans
Department of Social Psychology
Tilburg University
Tilburg, the Netherlands

Ernst Fehr
Department of Economics
University of Zurich
Zurich, Switzerland

Detlef Fetchenhauer
Department of Economic and Social
  Psychology
University of Cologne
Köln, Germany

Michael Giffin
Department of Psychology
University of Amsterdam
Amsterdam, the Netherlands

Patrick R. Heck
Department of Cognitive, Linguistic,
  and Psychological Sciences
Brown University
Providence, RI

Benedikt Herrmann
School of Economics
University of Nottingham
Nottingham, United Kingdom

Paul Hofman
Development Economics Group
Wageningen University
Wageningen, the Netherlands

Martin Kocher
Department of Economics
University of Munich
Munich, Germany

David P. Kroon
Department of Management and
  Organization
VU University
Amsterdam, the Netherlands

Joachim I. Krueger
Department of Cognitive, Linguistic,
  and Psychological Sciences
Brown University
Providence, RI

Maliheh Paryavi
John F. Kennedy School of
  Government
Harvard University
Cambridge, MA

Bettina Rockenbach
Faculty of Management, Economics
  and Social Sciences
University of Cologne
Köln, Germany

Robert Rolfe
Darla Moore School of Business
University of South Carolina
Columbia, SC

Oliver Schilke
Department of Management and
  Organizations
University of Arizona
Tucson, AZ

Thomas Schlösser
Department of Economic and Social
  Psychology
University of Cologne
Köln, Germany

Bogdan State
Department of Sociology
Stanford University
Stanford, CA

Christian Thöni
Département D'économétrie et
  D'économie Politique
University of Lausanne
Lausanne, Switzerland

Anh Tran
School of Public and Environmental
  Affairs
Indiana University Bloomington
Bloomington, IN

Paul A. M. Van Lange
Department of Psychology
VU University
Amsterdam, the Netherlands

Maarten Voors
Development Economics Group
Wageningen University
Wageningen, the Netherlands;
Department of Land Economy
University of Cambridge
Cambridge, England, UK

Toshio Yamagishi
Department of Behavioral Science
Graduate School of Letters
Hokkaido University
Hokkaido Prefecture, Japan

Richard Zeckhauser
John F. Kennedy School of
  Government
Harvard University
Cambridge, MA

1 Trust

Introduction and Trending Topics

■ PAUL A. M. VAN LANGE,
BETTINA ROCKENBACH,
AND TOSHIO YAMAGISHI

One might debate about when exactly research on social dilemmas truly began to flourish, whether it was around 1960 or even earlier. But there is clear consensus that it was much later that the concept of *social dilemmas* was introduced. Indeed, as far as we know, the integrative concept of social dilemmas was first described and defined by Robyn Dawes (1980). There is now, several decades later, little doubt that social dilemmas as a concept will be used as theoretical construct in summarizing research on how people deal with conflicts between self-interest and collective interests. But the seminal paper by Dawes did much more. It also advanced a broad hypothesis about human cooperation, as the following quote illustrates:

> Thus, three important ingredients for enhancing cooperation in social dilemma situations may be: knowledge, morality, and trust. These ancient virtues were not discovered by the author or by the United States Government, which invested millions of dollars in research grants over the years to have subjects play experimental games. But the above analysis indicates that they may be the particular virtues relevant to the noncoercive (and hence efficient) resolution of the social dilemmas we face. (Dawes, 1980, p. 191)

It is not completely clear how to assess the importance of knowledge and morality. Indeed, the ingredients of knowledge and morality are in need of more research to evaluate their central importance to social dilemmas. But especially since 1980, the central importance of trust in social dilemmas has been demonstrated in various disciplines. In fact, most would agree that it is quite a challenge to maintain or promote cooperation in the absence of trust. And most would agree even more that trust is especially important when thinking of "noncoercive resolutions of the social dilemmas we face."

This is already sufficient reason to devote a special volume of social dilemmas to the topic of trust. Besides the fact that trust has been shown important to understanding cooperation in social dilemmas, there are more reasons. One is empirical: trust has been one of the most widely studied concepts across the various disciplines—in anthropology, biology, economics, neuroscience, political science, psychology, and sociology. Another is general and perhaps even more important. Trust has been shown to be essential in social dilemmas, as well as in various situations that go beyond social dilemmas. Trust has been shown to be crucial to understanding personality differences (dispositional trust), social relations (relational trust), organizations (organizational trust), institutions or politics (institutional trust), as well as trust in specific others (particularized trust) or others in general (general or generalized trust). Also, trust is key to understanding how people process social information, such as judgments of others' faces, emotions, and behavior. And many have noted before us that it takes trust, although often unconscious, to eat out at a restaurant, to initiate a business relation with another party, or in the present era: for example, whether to respond to an email from a stranger.

■ TRUST IN SOCIAL DILEMMAS AND BEYOND

Trust is often defined in terms of the intention to accept vulnerability based upon the positive expectations or beliefs regarding the intentions or behavior of another person or other people in general (Rotter, 1967; Rousseau, Sitkin, Burt, & Camerer, 1998). Yet other definitions of trust emphasize expectations, predictability, and confidence in others' behavior (e.g., Dasgupta, 1988; McAllister, 1995; Sitkin & Roth, 1993). And there are definitions that emphasize that trust involves expectations of other's benevolent motives in situations that involve a conflict of interests (e.g., Mayer, Davis, & Schoorman, 1995; Yamagishi, 2011). This book captures a mixture of these definitions, especially that the defining feature of trust originates in the expectation or beliefs of benevolent motives of a particular other or others in general (Balliet & Van Lange, 2013 a). Behaviorally, trust becomes manifest in accepting vulnerability, which is based on these such "benevolent beliefs." Although there may be different bases of trust, such as competence-based trust or integrity-based trust, our treatment of trust will often be focused on benevolence-based trust. This approach is most suitable to how the issue of trust is examined in the context of various social dilemmas or situations closely related to social dilemmas—such as the trust game, the ultimatum game, and the like.

We have already noted that trust is relevant to both social dilemmas as well as many situations other than social dilemmas. This underlines the general importance of trust across many social situations. But perhaps even more importantly, in most social interaction situations, where the past and especially the future matters, trust may well be one of the most vital constructs that gives direction to one's behavior. Trust is often described as "social glue" to relationships, groups, and societies, in that it connects people, and facilitates thoughts, motives, and behaviors that promote collective goals (Van Lange, 2015). It is no overstatement that with trust, relationships fare better, organizations perform better, and societies function better (e.g., Holmes & Rempel, 1989; Fehr & Rockenbach, 2003; Kramer, 1999; Simpson, 2007; Putnam, 1993; Yamagishi, 2011). One might speculate that these benefits of trust are ultimately linked to the specific social dilemmas that people face in relationships, organizations, and societies at large.

It is also important to note that trust serves important functions for not only collectives, such as relationships, organizations, and societies, but also for individuals themselves. For example, individuals with high (versus low) trust in other people are more likely to sustain volunteering activities, have greater perspective-taking skills, report greater life satisfaction, exhibit greater physical health, and even live longer (e.g., Balliet & Van Lange, 2013a; Barefoot, Beckham, Brummet, & Maynard, 1998; Bekkers, 2012, Carter & Weber, 2010). Some theories, such as attachment theory, have emphasized the importance of trust, in the form of secure attachment, for human development. For example, there is a close association between early secure attachment and later quality of social relations, cognitive ability, and emotional stability (e.g., Mikulincer, 1998; Simpson, 2007). As such, the importance of trust for collectives and individuals alike seems difficult to overestimate.

■ TRUST: FROM BIOLOGY TO CULTURE

The broad attention of trust has yielded a wealth of findings, which have contributed to theorizing about the functioning of collectives, whether they be relationships, organizations, or societies at large. However, while past research has answered many questions, it has also energized new questions. One emerging topic is connected to understanding the biology and human development of trust. In particular, recent research has focused on the neuroscience of trust, to understand the processing of information that is relevant to trust (e.g., Adolph, 2002). Likewise, the function of hormonal responses has captured the interest of many researchers (De Dreu et al., 2010; Kosfeld, Heinrichs, Zak, Fischbacher, & Fehr, 2005). A complementary topic focuses on the development of trust over the life course. For example, do people become more (or less) trusting over a life time, and if so, why? There are indeed many mysteries regarding trust even at the level of the individual. These issues are captured in Part I, titled "Biology and Development of Trust."

A second important innovation in research on trust operates at the interpersonal, group, and organizational level. This is the level where trust often is shaped by face-to-face interactions or through social media in small groups. It is a context where individuals respond to one another's actions and where there often is a fairly strong (and direct) connection between how people interact in social settings. And in groups and formal organizations, communication styles, leadership, and justice are important to trust. As alluded to earlier, this is also the level where trust is strongly linked to social functioning. For example, because there is often an awareness that people seek to get a grip on one another's trustworthiness, people may use heuristics and norms (or norms as heuristics) in dealing with the complexities of situations. And although trust has received considerable attention in teams and organizations, many thorny issues exist. For example, the complexities of trust also operate at the level of relationships between units or teams. These issues are captured in Part II, titled "Trust in Dyads, Groups, and Organizations."

A third and final important innovation is the emerging trend toward understanding trust at the level of culture. There is already strong evidence that cultural influences should be quite pervasive. The evidence obtained in the World Values Survey shows immense differences among countries in their levels of generalized trust. More recent approaches examine economic games to explore cultural similarities and differences. Also, there is now more attention for societies that are clearly understudied, and that may inform us about the various roots of trust and distrust in differing societies, as well as how cooperation can be maintained and promoted in differing societies. These issues are captured in Part III, titled "Trust in Different Cultures."

■ OVERVIEW OF THE BOOK

The major themes and puzzles discussed here are central to contemporary research on trust in social dilemmas—although there are several other puzzles that can be addressed as well. The themes we highlighted cut across scientific fields and disciplines, and together they should provide the bigger picture on the workings and the functions of trust in facing challenges and opportunities of social life at the level of the individual, the dyad or organization, or the society at large. Although many chapters can be categorized in a variety of ways, we have decided to organize the book around three complementary topics: (a) biology and development of trust (Part I); (b) trust in dyads, groups, and organizations (Part II); and (c) trust in different cultures (Part III).

Before the thematic sections, this book includes a brief introduction and "trending topics" (this chapter) as well as a selective review of trust and social dilemmas by Karen S. Cook and Bogdan State (Chapter 2). In combination, these chapters serve as broad introductions to trust in social dilemmas (and beyond). We should also note that there are already several brief or comprehensive reviews of trust (e.g., Cook, Hardin, & Levi, 2005; Simpson, 2007; Van Lange, 2015; Yamagishi, 2011), social dilemmas (e.g., Parks et al., 2013; Van Lange, Joireman, Parks, & Van Dijk, 2013), as well as trust in social dilemmas (e.g., Balliet & Van Lange, 2013; Ostrom, 1998; Weber, Kopelman, & Messick, 2004). If desired, we believe that the readers could consult these sources to familiarize themselves with trust, social dilemmas, or both in combination.

The first section of this book, titled "Biology and Development of Trust," addresses the key questions about the biology and development of trust. In Chapter 3, economists Jan B. Engelmann and Ernst Fehr discuss the neurobiology of trust and cooperation. In doing so, they draw attention to the neuroscience of approach and aversive emotions in understanding trust and cooperation. In Chapter 4, psychologists Carsten K. W. de Dreu and Michael Giffin focus on the neuroendocrine pathways to trust in groups, with a particular emphasis on the challenges and threats of intergroup conflict. While Chapters 3 and 4 focus on the biology of trust, Chapters 5 and 6 focus on the development of trust. In Chapter 5, Peter Thisted Dinesen and René Bekkers provide a state of the art regarding the key determinants relevant to the development of trust. In Chapter 6, economist Martin G. Kocher discusses empirical research addressing the important yet under-addressed issue of how trust may develop over a lifetime.

In Part II we focus on trust as a key variable to social decision-making and interaction. The section is labeled "Trust in Dyads, Groups, and Organizations." In Chapter 7, Joachim I. Krueger, Anthony M. Evans, and Patrick R. Heck discuss the instrumental, or perhaps pragmatic value, of trust. The inviting title "Let Me Help You Help Me" should trigger the curiosity of anyone who (realistically) believes or seeks to challenge that assumed similarity and assumed reciprocity underlie trust and human cooperation. One step further, in Chapter 8, Detlef Fetchenhauer, David Dunning, and Thomas Schlösser discuss the mystery of trust: Can trusting too little and trusting too much go together? In Chapter 9 Christian Thöni focuses on normative influences on cooperation, but especially on antisocial punishment, in an attempt to understand why people might seek to punish those who contribute to collective welfare or public good dilemmas. Last, Bart A. de Jong, David P. Kroon, and Oliver Schilke provide a systematic, content-analytic review of research on trust in organizations, outlining various avenues for future developments of various issues, including how trust can be maintained or promoted in organizations.

The final section, titled "Trust in Different Cultures," is perhaps the most novel section. After all, there is not much research in trust in non-Western societies, but insights from these societies, small or not, might help us understand many societal issues that are classic, timely, or both. In Chapter 11, Toshio Yamagishi discusses pros and cons of the rule of law as a determinant of trust in various societies. In particular, do people with weak ties in their immediate proximity seek out opportunities of exchange in the broader world? If so, does general trust matter? In Chapter 12, Nancy R. Buchan and Robert Rolfe examine the influence of globalization and ethnic fractionalization on cooperation. Sometimes, ethnic roots and identification may undermine the role of globalization on cooperation. How can we replace local identities with global ones? The final two chapters focus on two particular cultures. In Chapter 13, Iris Bohnet, Benedikt Herrmann, Maliheh Paryavi, Anh Tran, and Richard Zeckhauser examine differences and similarities among the participants living in Oman, the United States, and Vietnam, uncovering striking similarities in principals' tendencies to avoid risks and play it safe—with the implication that they do not benefit from communicating trust to the members they represent. In the final chapter, Paul Hofman, Erwin Bulte, and Maarten Voors examine rural Sierra Leone as a relative unique society in which exchange in agriculture and farming plays a key role. Their findings uncover that people are somewhat less trusting than we may witness among strangers in trust games, but there are similarities in terms of trustworthiness.

▪ **CONCLUSION**

Trust represents a classic theme in research on social dilemmas. Historically, trust has been one of the key variables in research on prisoner's dilemma and early theory theorizing on human cooperation. After an explosion of research on trust during the past two decades in particular, scientists are now "en route" to examining basic issues revolving around the biology and development of trust, how and why trust precisely grows (or not) in social settings, including dyads and organizations, and how trust is shaped in various societies, including societies that have received relatively little empirical attention. These are exciting times, because the topic of trust is classic and fundamental—there is little doubt that trust is an effective tool to promote cooperation, even if cooperation without trust is possible under certain circumstances. The past decade has also increasingly revealed emerging themes, new theoretical developments, intriguing questions, and a challenging debate revolving around the evolution, as well as strengths and limitations, of trust in social dilemmas and other situations of interdependence. Of course, living in the era of migration, the issue of intergroup trust becomes an urgent issue. Why is it that we tend to approach individuals with a healthy dose of trust but tend to be suspicious of other groups—or even individual members of other groups? Some scientists make the claim that it is ultimately trust—or rather the lack of it—that undermines intergroup relations. One of the next challenges is to examine the workings of trust and how best to organize a system that exploits the opportunities of trust within groups and between groups in contemporary society. We hope this book provides a state of the art of this literature and that the themes discussed in this book will indeed become prominent ones in future research on trust in social dilemmas—whether they operate at the level of interpersonal or intergroup relations.

■ REFERENCES

Adolph, R. (2002). Trust in the brain. *Nature Neuroscience*, *5*, 192–193.

Balliet D., & Van Lange, P. A. M. (2013a). Trust, conflict, and cooperation: A meta-analysis. *Psychological Bulletin*, *139*, 1090–1112.

Balliet, D., & Van Lange, P. A. M. (2013b). Trust, punishment, and cooperation across 18 societies: A meta-analysis. *Perspectives on Psychological Science*, *8*, 363–379.

Barefoot, J. C., Maynard, K. E., Beckham, J. C., Brummett, B. H., Hooker, K., & Siegler, I. C. (1998). Trust, health, and longevity. *Journal of Behavioral Medicine*, *21*, 517–626.

Bekkers, R. (2012). Trust and volunteering: Selection or causation? Evidence from a four-year panel study. *Political Psychology*, *32*, 225–247.

Carter, N. L., & Weber, M. (2010). Not Pollyannas: Higher generalized trust predicts lie detection ability. *Social Psychological and Personality Science*, *1*, 274–279.

Cook, K. S., Hardin, R., & Levi, M. (2005). *Cooperation without trust?* New York: Russell Sage Foundation.

Dasgupta, P. (1988). Trust as a commodity. In D. Gambetta (Ed.), *Trust: Making and breaking cooperative relations* (pp. 49–72). New York: Basil Blackwell.

Dawes, R. M. (1980). Social dilemmas. *Annual Review of Psychology*, *31*, 169–193.

De Dreu, C. K. W., Greer, L. L., Handgraaf, M. J. J., Shalvi, S., Van Kleef, G. A., Baas, M., . . . Feith, S. W. (2010). The neuropeptide oxytocin regulates parochial altruism in intergroup conflict among humans. *Science*, *328*, 1408–1411.

Fehr, E., & Rockenbach, B. (2003). Detrimental effects of sanctions on human altruism. *Nature*, *422*(6928), 137–140.

Holmes, J. G., & Rempel, J. K. (1989). Trust in close relationships. In C. Hendrick (Ed.), *Close relationships* (pp. 187–220). Newbury Park, CA: SAGE.

Kosfeld, M., Heinrichs, M., Zak, P. J., Fischbacher, U., & Fehr, E. (2005). Oxytocin increases trust in humans. *Nature*, *435*, 673–676.

Kramer, R. M. (1999). Trust and distrust in organizations: Emerging perspectives, enduring questions. *Annual Review of Psychology*, *50*, 569–598.

Mayer, R. C., Davis, J. H., & Schoorman, F. D. (1995). An integrative model of organizational trust. *Academy of Management Review*, *20*, 709–734.

McAllister, D. J. (1995). Affect- and cognition-based trust as foundations for interpersonal cooperation in organizations. *Academy of Management Journal, 38*, 24–59.

Mikulincer, M. (1998). Attachment working models and the sense of trust: An exploration of interaction goals and affect regulation. *Journal of Personality and Social Psychology, 74*, 1209–1224.

Ostrom, E. (1998). A behavioral approach to the rational choice theory of collective action. *American Political Science Review, 92*, 1–22.

Rousseau, D. M., Sitkin, S. B., Burt, R. S., & Camerer, C. (1998). Not so different after all: A cross-discipline view of trust. *Academy of Management Review, 23*, 393–404.

Rotter, J. B. (1967). A new scale for the measurement of interpersonal trust. *Journal of Personality, 35*, 651–665.

Putnam, R. (1993). *Making democracy work.* Princeton, NJ: Princeton University Press.

Simpson, J. A. (2007). Psychological foundations of trust. *Current Directions in Psychological Science, 16*, 264–268.

Sitkin, S. B., & Roth, N. L. (1993). Explaining the limited effectiveness of legalistic "remedies" for trust/distrust. *Organization Science, 4*, 367–392.

Van Lange, P. A. M. (2015). Generalized trust: Lessons from genetics and culture. *Current Directions in Psychological Science, 24*, 71–76.

Van Lange, P. A. M., Joireman, J., Parks, C. D., & Van Dijk, E. (2013). The psychology of social dilemmas: A review. *Organizational Behavior and Human Decision Processes, 120*, 125–141.

Weber, J. M., Kopelman, S., & Messick, D. M. (2004). A conceptual review of social dilemmas: Applying a logic of appropriateness. *Personality and Social Psychology Review, 8*, 281–307.

Yamagishi, T. (2011) *Trust: The evolutionary game of mind and society.* New York: Springer.

2 Trust and Social Dilemmas

A Selected Review of Evidence and Applications

■ KAREN S. COOK AND BOGDAN STATE

■ INTRODUCTION

From pollution, corruption, and taxation to providing schools, bridges, and general public goods, research on social dilemmas gives us important insights into the challenges that human societies face in solving a class of problems in which individual and collective goals are by definition in conflict. Social dilemmas are ubiquitous and often seemingly intractable. They lie at the nexus of interactions between the micro and macro levels of social analysis, and their solutions are typically seen as central to social order. Trust is an important mechanism through which social dilemmas can be resolved; however, the range of such dilemmas that are solved based solely on trust is limited. Cooperation often occurs in the absence of trust (see Cook, Hardin, & Levi, 2005). While researchers have focused a lot of attention on social dilemmas and trust during the past few decades, often in separate streams of work, the problems groups and larger communities face of securing the grounds for trust and ensuring cooperation remain far from resolved.

■ UNDERSTANDING SOCIAL DILEMMAS

Broadly speaking, social dilemmas can be defined as situations in which individual interests conflict with the long-run collective interest of those involved. This conflict between individual and group-level interests is at the core of the definition provided by Van Lange, Balliet et al. (2014, p. 8), who understand *social dilemmas* as

> situations in which a non-cooperative course of action is (at times) tempting for each individual in that it yields superior (often short-term) outcomes for self, and if all pursue this non-cooperative course of action, all are (often in the longer-term) worse off than if all had cooperated.

This general definition provides a clear indication of the types of situations covered by the term *social dilemma* and the nature of the conflict involved.

Game theory has been used to represent social dilemmas in terms of variations in the nature of the interdependencies between the choices the parties can make and the associated payoffs, such as mutual cooperation or mutual noncooperation (or defection), among other choices. A number of reviews have been written that characterize the types of situations that can be represented this way, including those most frequently examined in the experimental literature. These include the game of chicken, the assurance game, and social dilemmas such as those involved in the provision of public goods and the protection of common resource pools (see Dawes, 1980; Kollock, 1998, among others). For our purposes we also include a brief discussion of the trust (or investment) game as well, given that it is a form of an assurance game.

Perhaps the most general game-theoretical understanding of a social dilemma is as the N-person prisoner's dilemma (PD; Hamburger, 1973; Dawes, 1980), a generalized version of the canonical two-party PD game (Luce & Raiffa, 1957). Trust is typically represented in experimental settings by the trust game (also referred to as the investment game; Berg, Dickhaut, & McCabe, 1995). In the typical trust game, one player (the investor) makes a decision to entrust a certain amount of his or her resources to another player (the recipient) who must then decide whether or not to return those resources in order for both to obtain a positive outcome. The trustee can simply walk away with the resources that have been entrusted to him or her in an act of defection, thus exploiting the trustor; herein lies the dilemma for each player in the trust game.

A key difference between trust games and the typical PD is that in the PD the decisions of both players are made simultaneously and the players do not know what action each will take. Hence their assessment of the intentions of the other party to cooperate or defect is central to their own decision to cooperate or not, and they do not know what the other person will do. This is the source of the uncertainty in the situation, and the risk involved is the risk of being exploited. However, in the standard trust game the first player who commits to transfer her resources to the other party is placing her trust in him to return the favor and to prove himself trustworthy with respect to her. The initial "investment" of one party in another serves as a "signal" that she views the other party as potentially trustworthy. This act lowers the uncertainty in the setting but not the risk involved in making the choice to cooperate, since the other person may not return the favor.

In the typical PD there is no opportunity for such signaling, thus the players are wholly dependent on the assumptions they make about the possible cooperativeness or trustworthiness of the other party (or the possibility that he will defect and end up exploiting her). In our selective review of relevant research we include studies based on both paradigms, but it should be noted that the underlying decision structures are significantly different in ways that affect the degree to which trust matters (see also Cook and Cooper, 2003).

In addition to important differences in their dyadic instantiations, the N-person generalization of the trust game and the PD offer a more complex picture of situations that fall under the category of social dilemmas. The key distinction in the multiplayer case arguably concerns the simultaneity of decision-making and the opportunity for signaling. The N-person PD game was conceptualized as one in which players make their decisions simultaneously (Dawes, 1980; Hamburger, 1973). Conversely, a generalized trust game typically has some individuals deciding asynchronously whether to cooperate (repay the trust placed in them), as noted earlier.

Even in a stylized form, a generalized trust game poses complicated issues if we remove the requirement that entrustment/cooperation decisions be made simultaneously (as they are in a PD). We can imagine important ramifications associated, say, with a player being the first or the last to make the cooperation decision and with details such as whether the order is changed between rounds. Furthermore, in real-world situations, we can expect individuals to have imperfect information about the behavior of others, a situation that may further permit "free riding." There has been some research (e.g., Kollock 1993) in settings in which "noise" has been added to the standard paradigm in such a way as to make it unclear at times whether or not the partner has cooperated (or intends to cooperate), a factor that makes the experimental paradigm more realistic as a reflection of the conditions under which individuals often have to make decisions.

Note that many social dilemmas require the existence of a group-level exchange structure (Ekeh, 1974; Yamagishi & Cook, 1993). That is, players must contribute to and draw from a group pool of resources, rather than conducting dyadic exchanges with one another in a type of generalized exchange. Trust has been shown to play an important role in both group and network generalized exchange structures, and its effect is tempered in group generalized exchange structures since free riding is more likely. Yamagishi and Cook present findings indicating that there is greater cooperation in network generalized exchange structures than in group generalized exchange in part because there is less diffusion of responsibility for making a contribution in the network structure involving unilateral reciprocity. Their findings also suggest that trust is more important in some social dilemmas than in others, which may not simply be a function of group or network size. The type of social structure in which the dilemma is embedded matters.

■ THE ROLE OF TRUST AND OTHER KEY FACTORS

Several relatively standard factors are key to understanding the role of trust in social dilemmas and decisions to cooperate more generally. These factors include the perceived efficacy of one's contributions, the asymmetry of the contributions, the excludability of those who fail to contribute, and the number of contributions required to provide the public good (or to preserve it when it can be depleted by overuse). In addition, a major concern of those who do contribute is the extent to which others will free ride on the efforts of those who do contribute, especially when excludability of noncontributors is not possible, allowing some to enjoy the benefit without paying the cost of helping to provide the public good.

Social dilemma situations as we have noted come in varying forms. However, in each situation it is fair to say perceived efficacy of one's contribution is central to the decision of whether to cooperate. In reviews of the research on this topic we find that this factor is key especially in situations in which a critical mass can provide the public good and individuals can assess the impact of their contribution on the eventual provisioning of the public good. In addition, when noncontributors can be excluded from receiving the benefits once the public good is provided, it is well known that others are more likely to contribute. In this case, trust in others facilitates contributions, which may be enhanced if individuals are members of the same in-group.

If noncontributors cannot be excluded, a large literature suggests that sanctioning can help. In fact, sanctions are often the most prevalent solution to social dilemmas (see review in Van Lange, Rockenback, & Yamagishi 2014). Sanctions can increase the cost of failing to contribute (negative sanctions) as well as increase the reward (positive sanctions) for those who do contribute. But, as Yamagishi (1986, 1988b) first indicated, the imposition of a sanctioning system also represents a social dilemma, identified as the *second-order social dilemma*. Who will contribute to the provision of the sanctioning system? Once a sanctioning system is established, research reveals that individuals are less likely to free ride and that this solution is especially effective in low trust societies in which people are more fearful of being taken advantage of.

■ THE EFFECTS OF PARTICULAR AND GENERAL TRUST ON COOPERATION IN SOCIAL DILEMMAS

A large number of studies have focused on cross-cultural variations in general trust. Using items from the World Values Survey (WVS) and the General Social Survey (GSS), for example, researchers have identified wide differences in the tendency of people to view strangers they might encounter as trustworthy. Typical survey items include "Do you think most people can be trusted or you can't be too cautious in dealing with them?" The validity of the WVS and GSS questions as unambiguous measures of individuals' general dispositions to trust strangers has come into question (Delhey, Newton, & Welzel, 2011; Miller & Mitamura, 2003; van Hoorn, 2014). Miller and Mitamura, for example, in a critique of the survey question used most frequently, argue that it is best considered a measure of cautiousness in dealing with strangers, rather than a measure of the extent to which they are trusted. Despite its flaws, however, it remains the most commonly used measure of generalized trust collected at a cross-country level to date. This factor is important since the success (or failure) of various solutions to securing cooperation in social dilemma situations depends not only on the nature of the interpersonal relations involved at the local level but also on the extent to which they are embedded in a general culture of trust or distrust.

In a meta-analysis of trust and cooperation Balliet and Van Lange (2013) find that various types of trust matter in predicting cooperation in social dilemmas. They distinguish between "state" and "dispositional" trust. Dispositional trust (Rotter 1980) is the general tendency of individuals to be trusting of others, and it has typically been measured by various general trust scales. They refer to state trust as a belief in the other person's cooperativeness in a specific setting as in a PD (e.g., will my partner cooperate and not turn state's evidence?). Other investigators have called this form of local trust particular (or particularized) trust.

In an effort to identify the specific conditions under which trust (of either type referred to as state versus dispositional, or as particular versus general) affects cooperation, Balliet and Van Lange (2013) review several studies focusing on the level of conflict between individual and collective interests. Importantly, they conclude that the evidence supports the claim that trust matters most when the conflict between individual and collective interests is highest. When there is a lesser degree of conflict, it appears that other factors may be just as important in determining the degree of cooperation that emerges, perhaps because the risk of defection or noncooperation is lower. Where these risks are high, it would make sense that trust comes into play, as indicated in the classic PD—the prototypical dilemma in which mutual cooperation is much preferred to mutual defection (resulting in the worst outcome—e.g., prison for both parties). Trust is generally more important in higher risk settings in which exploitation is possible.

With respect to level of conflict between individual and collective interests, an additional important finding revealed in the meta-analysis of studies of cooperation and trust conducted by Balliet and Van Lange (2013) is that the finding that trust matters most when the conflict is highest holds primarily for interpersonal relations and less so for intergroup relations. This finding has significant implications for the extent to which various solutions to social dilemmas are effective in these two contexts. Building bases for trust appears to be more helpful when the conflict between individual and collective interests is relatively high in interpersonal relations. This may in part be a result of the fact that it is less difficult to assess the trustworthiness of another person over time than it is to assess the trustworthiness of a larger group of people—a matter of scale.

■ IDENTITY, SOCIAL DILEMMAS, AND COLLECTIVE ACTION

Other solutions, less reliant on assessments of trustworthiness, may be more effective when the conflict is high between individual level interests and what is good for the collective in the domain of intergroup relations. Research by Tyler, Boeckmann, Smith, and Huo (1997), for example, implies that trust between groups is harder to build especially when the groups have had a history of negative interactions, or active distrust. They suggest that creating an overarching identity as members of a larger community or entity is one of the more promising techniques for reducing both the intergroup conflict and the conflict between perceived individual level interests and what is in their collective interest. It is not yet clear how much this work gives us insights into possible solutions to the social dilemmas most relevant to global environmental issues such as reducing CO_2 and its effects on global warming, for example. Identifying with a larger entity is thus one important factor in motivating action that is in the collective interest, but it is not at all clear how to generate commitment to such an overarching identity, especially when general trust is low.

Identification with another person or group is predicted to affect the extent to which actors will take the interests of that person or group into account when deciding whether to cooperate or defect in a PD (the dyadic form) or a social dilemma involving a larger number of actors whose fates are interdependent (e.g., Dawes, van de Kragt, & Orbell, 1988; DeCremer & Stanten, 2003). Identity has been treated as a group-level resource that can be called upon to motivate people to contribute to the group or to engage in collective action (often in the form of social movements large and small) on behalf of the group. It may also serve as a resource that enables effective recruitment into a social movement (Brewer & Silver, 2000; Klandermans & de Weerd, 1999; Kollock, 1998; Snow & McAdam, 2000). Lawler and Yoon (1996) found that identification with the group increases social cohesion and decreases tolerance for inequality in outcomes. This effect is similar to what has been called *inequity aversion* in the social dilemmas literature by Fehr and Gachter (2000), among others. In addition, identity similarity may increase trust (e.g. Cook, Hardin, & Levi, 2005).

An interesting feature of many of the early social dilemma experiments is that the individuals involved have typically been structurally equal. There were no power or status inequalities between those engaged in the experimental games; the major decision was only whether or not to cooperate (and, in some cases, whether to "exit" and not play the game altogether; Yamagishi, 1988a). Recent work has begun to explore the effects of inequality and power differences among the potential contributors to the public good. There is also some work on the relationship between power inequality and trust (e.g., Cook, 2005; Reimann, Schilke, & Cook, 2015). Power differences and inequality in contributions often inhibit cooperation and collective identification.

Identification, however, makes individuals more aware of their interdependencies and the extent to which mutual cooperation will pay off if those who identify with one another are prone to trust those they identify with in the sense that they develop a sense of shared fate and "encapsulated interest." Identity serves to embed economic transactions in deeper social structures such as those created by family ties or friendship relations (Granovetter 1985). Evidence suggests that group-level identification can serve as a basis for trust and thus mitigate some social dilemmas that arise, for example, among the Orthodox Jews in New York engaged in diamond trading (Coleman, 1988; Richman, 2006). As Simpson and Macy (2004, p. 1377) point out, Coleman (1990, p. 158) sees identification as the "process through which 'one actor has adopted, or taken up, the other's interest.'" When this occurs, trust is more likely to occur between the individuals involved on the encapsulated interest account of trust (Cook, Hardin, & Levi, 2005; Hardin, 2002). It cannot be assumed, however, that shared identity (e.g., based on shared attributes) simply activates group-level collective orientation. In the next few sections we explore various domains of activity in which trust is said to matter in resolving significant social dilemmas before we comment on other factors (beyond trust) that often provide grounds for cooperation.

■ TRUST AND REAL-WORLD SOCIAL DILEMMAS

Trust and cooperation are important topics to study because they are essential elements of a wide range of social interactions from dyads and small groups to communities and large societies. Trust and cooperation can be seen at work not only in the laboratory, the locus of much of the existing research, but also in many real-world settings. Social movements, for example, rise and fall based on their successes or failures to generate collective action on behalf of a specific goal or mission. As Olson

(1965) famously noted, social mobilization itself can be conceptualized as a free rider problem, a generalized social dilemma. Interpersonal trust between the movement participants (or at least the belief that others will continue to cooperate for the benefit of the group) is often the *sine qua non* of the movement's success. Indeed, there are countless studies in the social movement literature showing the importance of social ties for the success of social movements (e.g., Gould, 1991; see Poletta & Jasper [2001] for a more in-depth discussion), not to mention recruitment to the cause.

■ CORRUPTION

Corruption provides another example of a social dilemma in which trust is often involved. Arguably, a corrupt, patronage-based state or organization creates economic inefficiencies and thus provides a Pareto-suboptimal, but nonetheless stable, outcome in which many transactions are "taxed" by various officials who appropriate a share of the material flows available by means of their government positions. Taken in isolation, corruption does not create a social dilemma: there are no necessary conflicts between individual and group incentives in a state that functions on a system of patronage. However, corruption has been shown to lead to suboptimal economic outcomes at both the macro (Mauro, 1995) and micro (Fisman and Svensson, 2007) levels. Corruption thus presents an implicit social dilemma, in which members of the polity would likely be better off, *ceteris paribus,* living in a system without corruption than in a corrupt political system (della Porta & Vannucci, 1999; Kingston, 2008).

The implicit social dilemma inherent in political corruption can be made explicit when states undertake anticorruption efforts. In such efforts, paying and taking bribes can be reframed from simply being "the cost of doing business" to being an anticivic and possibly criminal practice. Anticorruption projects often create a clear social dilemma. While it may be immediately apparent (to citizens and officials alike) that a country's economy and political system would be better off without corruption, not engaging in corruption on one's own would appear foolish and ineffectual (Rothstein, 2011). In such cases solving the problem of trust in government is coupled with the problem of corruption itself. The government can be trusted only to the extent that it is not corrupt, but, due to the social dilemma inherent in anticorruption efforts, it cannot succeed at eliminating corruption if it cannot be trusted. Recent work (Persson, Rothstein, & Teorell, 2013; Rothstein, 2011) has identified an important consequence of the theoretical framing of corruption: because corruption has been traditionally conceptualized as a principal-agent problem, gradualist policy prescriptions have tended to dominate, often proving themselves ineffective. Instead, Rothstein and collaborators argue for a "big-bang" approach to anticorruption that is cognizant of the inherent stability of the social dilemma situation created by political corruption.

■ TAX COMPLIANCE

Low levels of tax compliance constitute another issue that afflicts countries with high levels of corruption, creating another type of social dilemma. As Rothstein

(2000) notes, differences in tax compliance between countries such as Sweden and Russia are staggering, as are differences in generalized trust between these two countries (cf. Bjørnskov, 2008). This is arguably not incidental, as trust in others and in the government have been found to be important determinants of taxpayers' willingness to comply with taxation demands (Rothstein, 2000; Rotter, 1980; Scholz & Lubell, 1998), and, more broadly, of citizens' willingness to comply with the demands of the state (Levi, 1997; Levi & Stoker, 2000). Generally speaking, taxpayers would be willing to pay their taxes, but only under conditions of fairness and trust: the taxpayer must believe that (a) other taxpayers will themselves pay their share, (b) the money will not be misused by corrupt or incompetent government officials, and (c) the fiscal burden has an equitable distribution. These issues have become increasingly acute in the wake of the Greek tax crisis, for instance, which scholars have directly connected to low levels of trust in government (Kaplanoglou & Rapanos, 2013).

All three of these requirements create social dilemmas of their own. If individuals believe that no one pays their taxes, then the natural incentive of fairness would dictate noncompliance. Paying one's taxes would essentially translate into letting others free ride. Perhaps trust in government and the state apparatus presents the most important social dilemma: taxpayers would like to pay their taxes *if* the government could be trusted with their money. But the very reasons why government offices come to be appropriated for personal gain is arguably intimately tied up with the syndrome that produces low trust in government in the first place. A state that collects few taxes is by definition weak: it cannot afford to pay its officials much, and neither can it afford to sanction their transgressions.

The third requirement, of an equitable fiscal burden, produces its own dilemma, though in a manner that is perhaps less well appreciated. We could conceive of both tax collector and taxpayer as players in a repeated "tax game" (Pickhardt & Prinz, 2014) in which there are potentially two strategies for each of the players. The collector has to decide whether to demand a reasonable or an onerous payment from the payer. In turn, the payer may choose to honor the tax payment or attempt to cheat on taxes, with some probability of success. An onerous tax demand will induce the payer to cheat on taxes in the future (Feld & Frey, 2002; Kirchler, Hoelzl, & Wahl, 2008). Thus a virtuous Pareto optimum is expected to exist, where the taxpayer honors reasonable tax obligations set by the collector in each round. However, assume that, for some reason such as an external shock or an increase in the payer's cheating propensity, the taxpayer does not render any payments for a number of rounds. In that case, the collector may become convinced of the payer's ill intentions and begin demanding onerous payments. Because of the patent unfairness of the payment demands, the taxpayer may become convinced of the collector's ill intent: the game is expected to settle into an equilibrium of low tax collection and onerous tax demands.

Here research based on the slippery slope framework (Kirchler, Hoelzl, & Wahl, 2008) for tax compliance is extremely promising. In a survey of Italian taxpayers Kastlunger, Lozza, Kirchler, and Schabmann (2013) found trust to be positively related to *voluntary* tax compliance. Only power perceived as legitimate (as measured by questionnaire items) was found to be positively associated with trust, whereas perceptions of coercive power[1] were associated with distrust in the authorities but also with more *coerced* tax compliance (the latter understood as compliance with fiscal demands out of fear of reprisals). This last point further brings out the dilemma policymakers themselves face. If a state's demands are perceived as illegitimate, it is nonetheless possible for the state to collect more money from taxes by means of coercion. This is a strategy that may work well in the short run but will likely further undermine citizens' trust in government, leading to even less tax compliance. Reliance on coercion and heavy sanctioning has even been demonstrated in laboratory research to undermine cooperation (e.g., Mulder et al., 2006).

While generalized trust and trust in government have both received a great deal of scientific attention, we believe the issue of lawmakers' and officials' trust in the public has been insufficiently studied (but see Yang [2005] for an important exception). As the hypothetical "tax game" proposed previously highlights, trust operates both ways in the citizen–state relationship. Our suspicion is that, as in many other situations, citizens' trust in the state and the officials' trust in citizens are correlated and reinforce one another (here we echo the conclusions of Feld and Frey, 2002).

■ HEALTH-RELATED SOCIAL DILEMMAS

Recently, the spread of measles in the United States after a number of people were exposed to the virus at Disneyland in southern California highlights the type of social dilemma Van Lange et. al. (2012) discuss in the health domain. We would all be better off if everyone vaccinated their children since in that way the virus would be unlikely to spread. However, for religious reasons, in some instances, and for beliefs that vaccinations can occasionally (but very rarely) cause severe health problems, some people refuse to vaccinate their children. (Such views may also be linked to low trust in science.) In small communities (e.g., Marin, California, and Vashon Island, Washington) where noncompliance with vaccination is rampant, the risk of the spread of diseases like the measles, once thought to be eradicated in the United States, is quite high.

The refusal to vaccinate one's child, in this case because one believes it is in his or her best interest to avoid complications or rare side effects, sets up the dilemma because it is also important not to contract the disease. Thus at the same time one does not have one's own child vaccinated, one prefers that others will in fact vaccinate their children to lower the risk of disease for everyone, including one's own unvaccinated child. Solutions to this particular health-related social dilemma vary. Some states require vaccination (i.e., Kentucky, where the vaccination rate is now about 93% for measles and other common childhood diseases) and thus rely on a central authority to manage the social dilemma and provide relevant sanctions. In other states, public schools require vaccination, so the only way to avoid it is to enroll one's child in private schools, if they do not require a health record that substantiates vaccination for application and/or attendance.

Many social dilemmas, as Ostrom and her collaborators' (e.g., 1990) work indicates, can be resolved either by deference to a central authority such as that provided by state law or the rules of the relevant organizations (often backed by law or another form of regulation), as in the cases mentioned previously. In these situations the public has abdicated their role in solving the social dilemma locally to an authority that can impose sanctions and force compliance to create a more disease-free environment for children. What matters most then is trust in the authorities (e.g., the state or the school administration) rather than interpersonal trust. We explore these alternative mechanisms later in this chapter.

More social dilemmas in the health domain clearly exist especially in a world in which the environment of viruses is constantly changing, many becoming "super-bugs" over time and resistant to treatment as in the recently reported problem with endoscopes (tubes used for endoscopy procedures for examination of the digestive tract) in US hospitals. In this case failure to fully sterilize instruments led to a number of life-threatening illnesses, and the problem was not isolated to one medical setting. Managing to protect everyone from exposure to such viruses and bacteria that are hard to eradicate on the surfaces we touch will require creative efforts to motivate individuals to do what is best for all. If the current debates over vaccination are any clue to the future, short of a statewide mandate that can be legally enforced, it may be difficult to provide the kinds of protection from disease that would be beneficial to all. In addition, with widespread travel across the globe, containing outbreaks, as we have learned from the Ebola case, will be increasingly difficult. Asking people to voluntarily quarantine themselves if exposed, for example, proved hard to monitor, and enforcement mechanisms were barely in existence. These issues will clearly need further research in the very near future.

■ TRUST, SOCIAL DILEMMAS, AND THE ENVIRONMENT

The modern description of a commons dilemma (a more general class of which social dilemmas are an instance) dates back to a 1968 *Science* article by Garett Hardin. In his examination Hardin used examples tied to overpopulation, resource depletion, and pollution. This connection is not happenstance: the relationship between humans and the environment is often based on structures of common property rights or on processes that generate negative environmental externalities and thus create typical social dilemma situations (Van Vugt & Samuelson, 1999).

Climate change offers perhaps one of the most consequential global exercises in generalized distrust in the context of a social dilemma. At the intergovernmental level, repeated, yearly rounds of negotiation have resulted in gridlock, due to issues of perceived inequity and distrust. In democratic societies the decline in citizens' trust in government (Hetherington, 1998; Twenge, Campbell, & Carter, 2014) has arguably further shifted politicians' incentives away from compromise. Furthermore, a decrease in the trust individuals have in science and scientists (Gauchat, 2012) has for some time eroded even the credibility of the threat posed by climate change.

Trust likewise affects the resolution of less impactful social dilemmas than those posed by climate change. Van Lange, Van Vugt, Meertens, and Ruiter (1998) found a stronger preference for commuting by public transit—which poses another environmentally salient social dilemma—among high-trust individuals. Similarly, using a survey of consumers, Gupta and Ogden (2009) established a link between the likelihood to buy energy-efficient products and individuals' direct trust in others' environmentally friendly behavior. In an experimental setting, Sonderskov (2011) found that individuals with higher levels of generalized trust are more likely to recycle. A more nuanced finding was established recently by Irwin and Berigan (2013), who found that in the low-trust US South, individuals with high and low generalized trust were equally unlikely to support environmental protection, while high trusters were significantly more likely to be in favor of environmental protection than low trusters were. We believe a focus on identifying the mediators of the trust–cooperation relationship will be extremely important as the policy implications of this field of research develop further.

■ SOCIAL DILEMMAS AND TRUST IN THE SHARING ECONOMY

The Internet has not been immune to social dilemmas. Some of the earliest (and still very relevant) examples concern the creation of free online resources by voluntary contributors. Here we count nonprofit efforts such as Open Source projects (e.g., the ecosystem around the Linux Operating System), encyclopedias such as Wikipedia, or open online datasets such as the one created by OpenStreetMap. There is a clear social dilemma in these cases, having to do with the *free rider problem*: because the common good—access to an online encyclopedia or an open-source download—is typically freely available for all to take, the rational incentive for users is to avail themselves of the content and not to contribute to the collective open-source effort. This is a rather unambiguous example of the "tragedy of the commons."

Trust plays an arguably more muted role in the case of online communities. It is hard to imagine how others' noncontributing to Wikipedia would have the same kind of effect on a contributor as, say, others' failure to pay their taxes would have on a taxpayer or others' failed mobilization would have on a would-be social movement participant. Perhaps this is because it is far more difficult for one to frame a contribution to a distant online community as a loss than it is for a taxpayer who feels like he or she is made to bear an unjust fiscal burden by the many noncooperators in the system. Contribution disparities may also be linked to the differential costliness of the behaviors involved. This is not to say that trust does not figure into this kind of online social dilemma, however. Rather than others' cooperation being a direct concern, users and potential contributors to online resources are concerned with the reliability of the resource and the ongoing support provided by the community. Indeed, Hsu et al. (2007) found that individuals who had more trust in their fellow contributors and the platform itself were more likely to contribute to virtual communities. Antin and Cheshire (2010) explore the reasons contributions to Wikipedia have been declining, indicating an increase in free riding (and/or saturation) even though use of Wikipedia in the form of reading has increased, which they treat as a form of participation. In earlier work

Cheshire (2007) examined other social psychological reasons related to self-regard and status that sometimes motivate participation in such communities.

A more recent development in the Internet sphere concerns the emergence of the "sharing economy" (Botsman & Rogers, 2010), an organizational field comprised of platforms that facilitate peer-to-peer interactions such as home rentals (e.g., AirBnB) or car sharing (e.g., Lyft or Zimride). Interpersonal and platform trust are core mechanisms through which the sharing economy functions: a full review of trust in the sharing economy lies beyond the scope of this chapter. A subset of the sharing economy is of particular interest to us: in addition to the now well-known (and highly valued) companies that facilitate the exchange of goods or services in return for payment, the sharing economy also features a number of platforms where payment is not expected and even sometimes prohibited. The main examples here are the goods exchange platform Freecycle and hospitality exchange platforms such as CouchSurfing or BeWelcome.

As in the case of knowledge exchange and open-source platforms, a social dilemma is apparent in the case of moneyless sharing economy systems. One could arguably choose to free ride on the contributions of others and act solely as a "surfer" (a guest) on CouchSurfing or as a receiver of resources on Freecycle. Of course, if this were the case, the systems would eventually collapse. Their continuation is an interesting puzzle that informs our understanding of the conditions under which social dilemmas are resolved by a combination of interpersonal and organizational solutions. The fact that these systems continue to be functional has also elicited the fascination of countless media outlets and social scientists alike. Trust is arguably a key component of the puzzle concerning the continuing survival of nonmonetary sharing economy platforms, especially in the face of monetary competitors. Here reputation mechanisms seem to play a crucial role, as they may incentivize individual contributions (Lauterbach et al., 2009; State, Abrahao, & Cook, 2012; Willer, 2009).

■ WHAT ALTERNATIVE MECHANISMS LEAD TO COOPERATION WHEN TRUST IS NOT POSSIBLE?

In social dilemma situations, trust shapes individuals' expectations of other participants' behavior. In high-trust situations, participants in a social dilemma can side-step the problem of incentives. Acting under the expectation that others will cooperate allows players to assume the best about their partners. Furthermore, recent research into the *social exchange heuristic* (Sonderskov, 2011) has lent further credence to the idea that most individuals are *conditional cooperators*, having a preference for cooperation when assured that others will likewise cooperate. Of course, the key problem is determining when such assurance exists.

As the previous case studies we have discussed reveal, though an important solution to social dilemmas, trust is not always available for their resolution. The absence of trust, however, does not necessarily translate into the lack of cooperation between individuals. As Ostrom's (1990) work demonstrates, there are many ways in which communities create mechanisms to solve social dilemmas that do not depend on interpersonal trust. Cook, Hardin, and Levi (2005), in their book titled *Cooperation without Trust?*, explore the mechanisms, other than trust, societies rely on to create the conditions that ensure and maintain cooperation. These mechanisms range from informal social norms and reputations to more formal arrangements such as professional associations, legal strategies including enforceable contracts, and regulatory regimes, among others. An example of reliance on legal strategies is provided in a unique study of national constitutions, Bjørnskov and Voigt (2014) find that countries with lower levels of social trust are also likely to have more verbose constitutions providing potential evidence for the reliance on overly specified contracts in low-trust societies.

Incentives is a topic of research that has received a great deal of attention in the past decade, specifically the role of rewards and punishment in social dilemmas (for a recent review see Van Lange, Rockenback, et al. 2014). Yamagishi (1986a, 1988a) introduced the study of sanctioning systems as one mechanism groups and societies use to facilitate cooperation, especially when individuals are reluctant to engage in cooperation in the face of limited trust (if any). This is perhaps the most direct mechanism for groups to extricate themselves from social dilemma situations: change the incentives so as to align individual and group interests. Doing so is not always easy and typically requires that what is termed the "second-order" social dilemma is resolved first: who will reward the contributors and punish the defectors or free riders?

Identity appears both as a mediator of and a substitute for trust in social dilemmas. We have already discussed how group identity can represent a basis on which trust is grounded. But identity can also be understood as the source of *commitment* to a set of values or a cause. Committed individuals may act prosocially not because they trust that others will do the same but simply because they believe in the intrinsic worthiness of their contribution. The role of identity and commitment is a mainstay of social movement theory (Friedman & McAdam, 1992; Hirsch, 1990; Poletta and Jasper, 2001), but the importance of this mechanism should not be neglected in other social dilemma situations. For instance, Lakhani and Wolf (2003) find that strong identification with the community motivates the work of open-source contributors.

Status is another alternative mechanism to trust in the resolution of social dilemmas that has recently received increased attention. The stylized form of the theory has individuals contributing not because they trust others will do the same but because contributors tend to be held in esteem by others. Willer (2009) finds a two-way association between status and contributions to collective action: in an experimental setting, contributors were rewarded with higher status by their peers, while higher status individuals were found more likely to contribute to collective action. This finding is echoed in the results reported by State, Abrahao, and Cook (2012), who found that contributors (hosts) on the CouchSurfing. org hospitality platform were likely to receive higher ratings than resource users ("surfers"). It is important to note that status should not be conflated here with reputation. Whereas concern for one's reputation represents a powerful incentive against free riding, status is its own reward for prosocial behavior. While reputational concerns may hinder outright selfish actions, status is received as a reward for one's perceived altruism. The same conclusion is echoed in a different setting by Griskevicius, Tybur, and Van den Bergh (2010) who found that the activation of status in an experimental setting led to increased preference for environmentally friendly products.

While the status mechanism is fundamental, it should not be considered a perfect substitute for trust. For one reason, *what* is held in high esteem is a highly contextualized variable that may itself be influenced by trust. There are no guarantees, for instance, that noncompliant taxpayers would hold an obstinate contributor in high esteem. The difference between abnegation and foolishness is in this case a matter of semantics, likely to be colored by citizens' trust in government. If the government is trustworthy, a compliant taxpayer is to others somewhere between merely a good citizen and a hero. To someone who sees a government as untrustworthy, the evaluation of the same taxpayer may fall somewhere between being perceived as a sucker and a coward. Status can likewise work against the resolution of social dilemmas in situations such as those created by vaccination campaigns: absent trust in the motives of physicians and scientists, those who choose to vaccinate their children may well be perceived as recklessly endangering their progeny. Finally, trust and status are often conflated in real-world settings. For instance, the "vouching" mechanism used on CouchSurfing (Lauterbach et al., 2009) enables participants to express both their trust and their esteem for the other person. Clarifying the relationship between trust and reputation as it affects cooperation is an important topic for further research.

■ WHAT ARE THE EFFECTS OF SOCIAL DILEMMA SITUATIONS ON TRUST AND DISTRUST IN SOCIETY?

Moving beyond the main focus of this chapter and the boundaries of the task we set for ourselves we are interested in exploring the ways in which the range of solutions to social dilemmas of various types identified in the existing literature may have implications for the further evolution of trust in those settings or distrust where solutions fail. Future research could explore the longer-term social implications, both positive and negative, of implementing particular strategies for solving real world social dilemmas or the failure to do so.

There is some research that is relevant to answering this important set of questions. For example, several authors have written about the "paradox of sanctioning" and the negative implications of securing cooperation through the use of contracts (Bohnet & Baytelman, 2007; Malhotra & Murnighan, 2002; Mulder et al., 2006) but also at the level of collective action in earlier work by Taylor (1987) in political science and even at the broader level of constitutional design (Frey, 1997). A key concern in much of this research is the extent to which the use of sanctions, for example, to punish those who fail to contribute, further undermines the internal drive to cooperate in the long run —often referred to as the "crowding out" of trust through institutional mechanisms. The same issue arises in the use of selective incentives (originally proposed by Olson, 1965) in the sense that the expectation of extrinsic rewards for making a contribution to the collective good may undermine the intrinsic motivation to do so.

As Malhotra and Murnighan (2002) demonstrate, in their laboratory research on the effects of binding contracts on interpersonal trust, the simple fact that a contract is required limits the development of trust. A clear example is the use of premarital contracts, which often raise doubts in the minds of the parties involved about the long-term commitments being made, especially if one party is the primary source of the pressure to sign such a contract before walking down the aisle. Malhotra and Murnighan's (2002) results suggest that when contracts are binding the parties involved attribute cooperation to the constraints imposed by the contractual nature of the relationship, rather than as a signal that each party is trustworthy given that mutual cooperation is viewed as a reflection of mutual trust. When contracts in their studies were nonbinding there was greater room for trust development given the absence of constraints that were binding on both parties. Their findings also revealed that the removal of contracts lowered trust, indicating the continued negative effect of a contractual orientation on trust levels. They seem to continue to color the assessments of trustworthiness going forward.

This research provides some evidence of a "catch 22" in terms of solutions to social dilemmas. Institutions and organizations can set in motion practices and procedures that alter incentives to contribute or build in contractual elements to assure cooperation and the alignment of individual and collective incentives, but these same mechanisms may undermine the motivation to contribute or cooperate and, in fact, reduce the symbolic value of doing so. There may be no alternative, however, when distrust is deeply embedded in the situation or the fabric of the culture. Careful research on the externalities created by the use of specific mechanisms for generating the grounds for cooperation and trust in various settings is needed, especially longitudinal research.

■ FUTURE DIRECTIONS IN RESEARCH LINKING TRUST AND COOPERATION IN SOCIAL DILEMMAS

Part of what makes both social dilemmas and trust compelling objects of empirical study in the social sciences is precisely the fact that they occur at multiple scales in society. Trust and social dilemmas can be isolated in stylized laboratory studies, or they can be observed at work in a wide variety of real-world situations. A great deal of research on both topics has revealed mechanisms in which suboptimal equibria of generalized distrust and noncooperation are self-sustaining. Investigating the determinants of change is likewise important. Social dilemmas have consequences. Their resolution (or lack thereof) leads to different outcomes for the actors involved. The outcomes themselves then contribute to individuals and groups' experience of the social world. The accumulation of successful or unsuccessful experiences with the resolution of social dilemmas may have important consequences on individuals' future behavior, their beliefs, and, ultimately, the norms and institutions that govern a society.

We consider investigation into the consequences of social dilemmas on trust to be an important direction for future research, at multiple levels of analysis. For instance, we consider it important to understand what (un-)successful cooperation does to a group's cohesion in an experimental setting. Similarly, recent history offers multiple examples of successful and failed attempts at national-level collective action (such as Tunisia's Arab Spring or the Green Revolution in Iran). We consider another important topic for future research to be the investigation of the links between these social movements and changes in the degree to which participants or observers in these movements trust others.

The theoretical shift between individual and society remains a challenging one even a quarter-century after Coleman (1990) famously identified the micro to macro problem, which, indeed, continues to complicate the study of both trust and social dilemmas. Both social networks and group identities emerge as convenient conceptual devices for connecting the individual and social levels of analysis (see, e.g., Simpson & Macy 2004; Yamagishi & Cook, 1993), and research of this type is particularly important to building a more robust theory of social interaction. It also bears noting that the ever-increasing growth of social interaction on Internet platforms offers ever more compelling datasets for the study of trust in situations requiring coordination and cooperation.

■ CONCLUSION

Our review highlights the crucial role that trust may play in the resolution of social dilemmas. Unfortunately, trust is increasingly in short supply in many societies (Hetherington, 1998; Twenge et al., 2014). This development has potentially negative consequences for the future ability of modern societies to solve some of the most complex challenges they face. There are some reasons for optimism, however. For one, as previously discussed, there are other solutions to social dilemmas than those based on trust. In particular, careful institutional design appears to be an important requirement for the successful resolution of large-scale social dilemmas. Especially in settings in which distrust is widespread, there are few other more effective mechanisms, even though building confidence in such institutions is itself a dilemma to be resolved initially.

The successful resolution of social dilemmas (possibly through mechanisms unrelated to trust) may also provide the impetus necessary for the future (re)emergence of social trust. Putnam, Leonardi, and Nanetti (1993), for example, argue that membership in voluntary associations may help improve general social trust. But the evidence on this effect is quite mixed. Stolle (1998) and Paxton (2007) provide some supportive results, but recent longitudinal research by Bekkers (2012) suggests that this association may not hold up under closer scrutiny. Bekkers' findings indicate that, at least in the Netherlands Panel Study on giving, variation in volunteering is not linked to changes in trust; rather it appears that over time those who are low in trust stop volunteering, indicating that while trust may lead people to volunteer, selective attrition may be at work, leaving sustained volunteering to the more trusting. Precisely which factors lead to higher levels of generalized social trust and what causes variations within and between countries is still under debate. Some argue that what matters most is the existence of fair and impartial institutions in which citizens have high confidence. Others point to factors such as income equality and strong social safety nets (which seems to correlate with the higher levels of general social trust in the Scandinavian countries, for example). This broad and important topic should remain on our future research agenda since at its root some of these findings suggest what may be important associations between successful solutions to society-wide social dilemmas and generalized trust. However, rather than a continued focus on the role of civic associations, perhaps a more crucial direction of research will be investigation of the effects of recent social movements on trust and cooperation. In particular, beyond continued work at the institutional level of analysis, it is important to ask, for example, how an increasingly polarized Internet environment (Adamic and Glance, 2005; Conover et al., 2011) is influencing individuals' perceptions of others and their trust in them.

We conclude with a final remark from Ostrom and Cox (2010): there are no panaceas for the resolution of social dilemmas. Social dilemmas occur in complex social systems, which are by definition chaotic and often unpredictable. Thus it would be hubris for social scientists to assume that social dilemmas, especially large-scale ones, can be solved according to any simple recipe. In most cases social dilemmas are not solved by values, institutions, or trust, taken in isolation. What we know from existing research is that all of these factors are important, among others including culture and historical path dependence in specific settings. With respect to trust, research to date in various domains suggests that trust alone is unlikely to be sufficient to lead to solutions to our most pressing collective action problems even though at the micro level it allows for increased cooperation, social cohesion and commitment both to other individuals and to the organizational contexts in which trust emerges (when it does) and is sustained. However, trust often facilitates solutions to social dilemmas by creating the grounds for initial risk-taking that may eventually make other factors more effective, or it may serve as an additive, making these factors more forceful. In the end, it is important to recognize that cooperation occurs in many contexts even in the absence of trust (Cook et al., 2005).

It is clear that solutions to social dilemmas typically emerge as highly contextualized mechanisms with numerous interactions among key factors, and these solutions are not easy to generalize across contexts. On the optimistic side, increasingly detailed data sets about complex social interactions are becoming more readily available each year. The future of our understanding of both trust and cooperation lies at the intersection of new data and new theories constructed to provide fresh insights into long-standing concerns about the perpetual conflicts that exist between individual and collective interests in all societies. Such fundamental conflicts may change in content over time but not in structure or potential impact. Understanding the role of trust in all of this will remain part of our future research agenda because where it does exist it extends cooperation, reduces reliance on sanctioning and other compliance mechanisms, and provides for increased social cohesion of certain values in an increasingly global context in which conflicts have widespread consequences. Even the most pressing of problems including solutions to environmental dilemmas will involve cooperation and even trust on a scale not yet fully imagined.

■ NOTE

1. Here coercive power is understood as the state's perceived ability to extract compliance based on force rather than the taxpayer's agreement with the state's goals. More specifically, Kastlunger et al. (2013, p. 43) indicate that "coercive power was assessed as power to set punishment and to impose severe fines, legitimate power was assessed as the efficacy of the tax authorities' interventions (due to its expertise and ability) in reducing tax crimes."

■ REFERENCES

Adamic, L. A., & Glance, N. (2005). The political blogosphere and the 2004 US election: divided they blog. *Proceedings of the 3rd international workshop on Link discovery.* ACM, 36–43. Vancouver, Canada.

Antin, J., & Cheshire, C. (2010). Readers are not free-riders: reading as a form of participation on Wikipedia. In *Proceedings of the 2010 ACM conference on computer supported cooperative work* (pp. 127–130). New York: ACM.

Balliet, D., & Van Lange, P. A. M. (2013). Trust, conflict, and cooperation: A meta-analysis. *Psychological Bulletin, 139*(5), 1090–1112.

Bekkers, R. (2012). Trust and volunteering: selection or causation? Evidence from a 4-year panel study. *Political Behavior, 34*, 225–247. doi:10.1007/s11109-011-9165-x

Berg, J., Dickhaut, J., & McCabe, K. A. (1995). Trust, reciprocity, and social history. *Games and Economic Behavior, 10*, 122–142.

Bjørnskov, C. (2008). Social trust and fractionalization: A possible reinterpretation. *European Sociological Review, 24*(3), 271–283.

Bjørnskov, C., & Voigt, S. (2014). Constitutional verbosity and social trust. *Public Choice, 161*(1–2), 91–112.

Bohnet, I., & Baytelman, Y. (2007). Institutions and trust: Implications for preferences, beliefs and behavior. *Rationality and Society, 19*(1), 99–135.doi:10.1177/1043463107075110

Botsman, R., & Rogers, R. (2010). *"What's mine is yours." The rise of collaborative consumption.* London: Collins.

Brewer, M. B., & Silver, M. D. (2000). Group Distinctiveness, Social Identity, and Collective Mobilization. In S. Stryker, T. J. Owens, and R. W. White (Eds.), *Self, Identity, and Social Movement.* Minneapolis, Minn.: University of Minnesota.

Cheshire, C. (2007). Selective incentives and generalized information exchange. *Social Psychology Quarterly, 70*(1), 82–100.

Coleman, J. S. (1988). Social capital in the creation of human capital. *American Journal of Sociology, 94*, S95–S120.

Coleman, J. S. (1990). *Foundations of Social Theory.* Cambridge: Harvard University Press.

Cook, K. S., & Cooper, R. (2003). Experimental studies of cooperation, trust, and social exchange. In Elinor Ostrom and James Walker (Eds.), *Trust and reciprocity: Interdisciplinary lessons* (pp. 277–333). New York: Russell Sage Foundation.

Cook, K. S., Hardin, R. & Levi, M. (2005) *Cooperation without trust?* New York: Russell Sage Foundation.

Conover, M., Ratkiewicz, J., Francisco, M., Goncalves, B., Flaminni, A., & Menczer, F. (2011). Political polarization on Twitter. *ICWSM, 133*(26), 89–96.

Dalhey, J., Newton, K., & Welzel, C. (2011). How General is Trust in 'Most People'? Solving the Radius of Trust Problem. *American Sociological Review, 76*(5), 786–807. doi: 10.1177/0003122411420817

Dawes, R. M. (1980). Social dilemmas. *Annual Review of Psychology, 31*(1), 169–193.

Dawes, R. M., van de Kragt, A. J. C., & Orbell, J. M. (1988). Not me or thee but we: The importance of group identity in eliciting cooperation in dilemma situations. *Acta Psychologica, 68*, 83–97.

De Cremer, D., & Stouten, J. (2003). When do people find cooperation most justified: The effect of trust and self-other merging in social dilemmas. *Social Justice Research, 16*(1), 41–52.

della Porta, D., & Vannucci, A. (1999). *Corrupt exchanges: Actors, resources, and mechanisms of political corruption.* Piscataway, NJ: Transaction.

De Weerd, M., & Klandermans, B. (1999). Group identification and political protest: Farmers' protest in the Netherlands. *European Journal of Social Psychology, 29*(8), 1073–1095.

Ekeh, P. P. (1974). *Social exchange theory: The two traditions.* London: Heinemann.

Fehr, E., & Gachter, S. (2000). Cooperation and punishment in public goods experiments. *American Economic Review, 90*, 980–994.

Feld, L. P., & Frey, B. S. (2002). Trust breeds trust: How taxpayers are treated. *Economics of Governance, 3*(2), 87–99.

Fisman, R., & Svensson, J. (2007). Are corruption and taxation really harmful to growth? Firm level evidence. *Journal of Development Economics, 83*(1), 63–75.

Frey, B. S. (1997). A constitution for knaves crowds out civic virtues. *The Economic Journal, 107*(443), 1043–1053.

Friedman, D., & McAdam, D. (1992). Collective identity and activism: Networks, choices and the life of a social movement. In C. Mueller & A. Morris (Eds.), *Frontiers in social movement theory* (pp. 156–173). New Haven, CT: Yale University Press.

Gauchat, G. (2012). Politicization of science in the public sphere: A study of public trust in the United States, 1974 to 2010. *American Sociological Review, 77*(2), 167–187.

Gould, R. V. (1991). Multiple networks and mobilization in the Paris commune, 1871. *American Sociological Review, 56*(6), 716–729. http://www.jstor.org/stable/2096251

Granovetter, M. (1985). Economic action and social structure: The problem of embeddedness. *American Journal of Sociology, 91*(3), 481–510.

Griskevicius, V., Tybur, J. M., & Van den Bergh, B. (2010). Going green to be seen: Status, reputation, and conspicuous conservation. *Journal of Personality and Social Psychology, 98*(3), 392–404.

Gupta, S., & Ogden, D. T. (2009). To buy or not to buy? A social dilemma perspective on green buying. *Journal of Consumer Marketing, 26*(6), 376–391. http://doi.org/10.1108/07363760910988201

Hamburger, H. (1973). The N-person's prisoner's dilemma. *Journal of Mathematical Sociology, 3*, 27–48.

Hardin, G. (1968). The tragedy of the commons. *Science, 162*, 1243–1248.

Hardin, R. (2002). *Trust and trustworthiness.* New York: Russell Sage Foundation.

Hetherington, M. J. (1998). The political relevance of political trust. *The American Political Science Review, 92*(4), 791–808.

Hirsch, E. L. (1990). Sacrifice for the cause: Group processes, recruitment, and commitment in a student social movement. *American Sociological Review, 55*(2), 243–254. http://doi. org/10.2307/2095630

Hsu, M. H., Ju, T. L., Yen, C. H., & Chang, C. M. (2007). Knowledge sharing behavior in virtual communities: The relationship between trust, self-efficacy, and outcome expectations. *International Journal of Human-Computer Studies, 65*(2).

Irwin, K., & Berigan, N. (2013). Trust, culture, and cooperation: A social dilemma analysis of pro-environmental behaviors. *Sociological Quarterly, 54*(3), 424–449. http://doi.org/ 10.1111/tsq.12029

Kaplanoglou, G., & Rapanos, V. T. (2013). Tax and trust: The fiscal crisis in Greece. *South European Society and Politics, 18*(3), 283–304. http://doi.org/10.1080/ 13608746.2012.723327

Kastlunger, B., Lozza, E., Kirchler, E., & Schabmann, A. (2013). Powerful authorities and trusting citizens: The slippery slope framework and tax compliance in Italy. *Journal of Economic Psychology, 34*, 36–45.

Kirchler, E., Hoelzl, E., & Wahl, I. (2008). Enforced versus voluntary tax compliance: The "slippery slope" framework. *Journal of Economic Psychology, 29*(2), 210–225.

Kingston, C. (2008). Social structure and cultures of corruption. *Journal of Economic Behavior and Organization, 67*(1), 90–102.

Kollock, P. (1993). "An eye for an eye leaves everyone blind": Cooperation and accounting systems. *American Sociological Review, 58*, 768–786.

Kollock, P. (1998). Social dilemmas: The anatomy of cooperation. *Annual Review of Sociology, 24*(1), 183–214.

Lakhani, K., & Wolf, R. G. (2003). Why hackers do what they do: Understanding motivation and effort in free/open source software projects. *Social Science Research Network, 49*, 1–27. http://doi.org/10.2139/ssrn.443040

Lauterbach, D., Truong, H., Shah, T., & Adamic, L. (2009). Surfing a web of trust: Reputation and reciprocity on CouchSurfing.com. In *2009 International Conference on Computational Science and Engineering* (pp. 346–353). Aug. 29–31, Vancouver, Canada publisher IEEE.

Lawler, E., & Yoon, J. (1996). Commitment in exchange relations: Test of a theory of relational cohesion. *American Sociological Review, 61*(1), 89–108. http://www.jstor.org/ stable/2096408

Levi, M. (1997). *Consent, dissent and patriorism.* Cambridge, UK: Cambridge University Press.

Levi, M., & Stoker, L. (2000). Political trust and trustworthiness. *Annual Review of Political Science, 3*(1), 475–507.

Luce, R. D., & Raiffa, H. (1957). *Games and decisions: Introduction and critical surveys.* New York: Wiley.

Malhotra, D., & Murnighan, J. K. (2002). The effects of contracts on interpersonal trust. *Administrative Science Quarterly, 47*, 534–559.

Mauro, P. (1995). Corruption and growth. *Quarterly Journal of Economics, 110*(3), 681–712. http://doi.org/10.1007/s12117-997-1097-9

Miller, A. S., & Mitamura, T. (2003). Are surveys on trust trustworthy? *Social Psychology Quarterly, 66*(1), 62–70.

Mulder, L. B., van Dijk, E., De Cremer, D., & Wilke, H. A. M. (2006). Undermining trust and cooperation: The paradox of sanctioning systems in social dilemmas. *Journal of Experimental Social Psychology, 42*(2), 147–162.

Olson, M. (1965). *The logic of collective action*. Cambridge MA.: Harvard University Press.

Ostrom, E. (1990) *Governing the commons: The evolutions of institutions for collective action*. Cambridge, UK: Cambridge University Press.

Ostrom, E., & Cox, M. (2010). Moving beyond panaceas: A multi-tiered diagnostic approach for social-ecological analysis. *Environmental Conservation, 37*(4), 451–463. doi:10.1017/S0376892910000834

Paxton, P. M. (2007). Association memberships and generalized trust: A multilevel model across 31 countries. *Social Forces, 86*(1), 47–76. http://doi.org/10.1353/sof.2007.0107

Pickhardt, M., & Prinz, A. (2014). Behavioral dynamics of tax evasion—A survey. *Journal of Economic Psychology, 40*, 1–19.

Poletta, F., & Jasper, J. M. (2001). Collective identity and social movements. *Annual Review of Sociology, 27*, 283–305.

Putnam, R. D., Leonardi, R., & Nanetti, R. (1993). *Making democracy work: Civic traditions in modern Italy*. Princeton, NJ: Princeton University Press.

Richman, Barak D. (2006). How community institutions create economic advantage: Jewish diamond merchants in New York. *Law & Social Inquiry, 31*(2), 383–420.

Rothstein, B. (2000). Trust, social dilemmas and collective memories. *Journal of Theoretical Politics, 12*(4), 477–501.

Rothstein, B. (2011). Anti-corruption: The indirect "big bang" approach. *Review of International Political Economy, 18*(2), 228–250.

Rothstein, B., & Teorell, J. (2015). Getting to Sweden, Part II: Breaking with Corruption in the Nineteenth Century. *Scandinavian Political Studies, 38*(3), 238–254.

Rotter, J. B. (1980). Interpersonal trust, trustworthiness, and gullibility. *American Psychologist, 35*(1), 1–7.

Scholz, J. T., & Lubell, M. (1998). Trust and Taxpaying: Testing the heuristic approach to collective action. *American Journal of Political Science, 4/1*, 398–417.

Simpson, B., & Macy, M. W. (2004). Power, identity, and collective action in social exchange. *Social Forces, 82*, 1373–1409.

Snow, David A., & McAdam, D. (2000). Identity work processes in the context of social movements: Clarifying the identity/movement nexus. In S. Stryker, T. J. Owens, & R. W. White (Eds.), *Self, identity, and social movements*. Minneapolis: University of Minnesota Press.

State, B., Abrahao, B., & Cook, K. S. (2012). From power to status in online social exchange. *Proceedings of the 4th ACM Conference on Web Science (WebSci)*. Evanston, IL.

Stolle, D. (1998). Bowling together, bowling alone: The development of generalized trust in voluntary associations. *Political Psychology, 19*(3), 497–525.

Sonderskov, K. (2011). Explaining large-N cooperation: Generalized social trust and the social exchange heuristic. *Rationality and Society, 23*(1), 51–74. http://doi.org/10.1177/1043463110396058

Taylor, M. (1987). *The possibility of cooperation*. New York: Cambridge University Press.

Tyler, T. R., Boeckmann, R., Smith, H. J., & Huo, Y. J. (1997). *Social justice in a diverse society*. Denver, CO: Westview.

Twenge, J. M., Campbell, W. K., & Carter, N. T. (2014). Declines in trust in others and confidence in institutions among American adults and late adolescents, 1972–2012. *Psychological Science, 25*(10), 1914–1923.

Van Lange, P.A. M., Balliet, D., Parks, C. D., & Van Vugt, M. (2014). *Social dilemmas: The psychology of human cooperation*. New York: Oxford University Press.

Van Lange, P. A. M., Rockenbach, B., & Yamagishi, T. (2014). *Reward and punishment in social dilemmas.* New York: Oxford University Press.

Van Lange, P. A.M., Van Vugt, M., Meertens, R. M., & Ruiter, R. A. C. (1998). A social dilemma analysis of commuting preferences: The roles of social value orientation and trust. *Journal of Applied Social Psychology, 28,* 796–820.

Van Vugt, M., & Samuelson, C. D. (1999). The impact of metering in a natural resource crisis: A social dilemma analysis. *Personality and Social Psychology Bulletin, 25*(6), 735–750.

Willer, R. (2009). Groups reward individual sacrifice: The status solution to the collective action problem. *American Sociological Review, 74*(1), 23–43. http://doi.org/10.1177/000312240907400102

Yamagishi, T. (1986). The provision of a sanctioning system as a public good. *Journal of Personality and Social Psychology, 51,* 110–116.

Yamagishi, T. (1988a). Exit from the group as an individualistic solution to the free rider problem in the United States and Japan. *Journal of Experimental Social Psychology, 24,* 530–542.

Yamagishi, T. (1988b). The provision of a sanctioning system in the United States and Japan. *Social Psychology Quarterly, 51,* 265–271.

Yamagishi, T., & Cook, K. S. (1993). Generalized Exchange and Social Dilemmas. *Social Psychology Quarterly, 56*(4), 235–248. Published by: American Sociological Association Stable URL: http://www.jstor.org/stable/2786661

Yang, K. (2005). Public administrators' trust in citizens: A missing link in citizen involvement efforts. *Public Administration Review, 65*(3), 273–285.

PART I

Biology and Development of Trust

3 The Neurobiology of Trust and Social Decision-Making

The Important Role of Emotions

■ JAN B. ENGELMANN AND ERNST FEHR

■ THE CENTRAL ROLE OF EMOTIONS IN SOCIAL DECISION-MAKING

Increasing evidence indicates that emotions influence decision-making (Cohn, Engelmann, Fehr, & Maréchal, 2015; Engelmann & Hare, in press; Engelmann, Meyer, Fehr, & Ruff, 2015; Harlé & Sanfey, 2007, 2010; Lerner, Li, Valdesolo, & Kassam, 2015; Loewenstein, Weber, Hsee, & Welch, 2001; Phelps, Lempert, & Sokol-Hessner, 2014). This is consistent with recent results in cognitive and affective neuroscience that blur the traditional distinction between emotional and cognitive processes and underline their interactive nature (Pessoa, 2008; Phelps, 2006). Specifically, it has been shown that cognitive processes, such as attention and memory, rely heavily on emotional information to control goal-directed behavior (e.g., Anderson & Phelps, 2001; Hamann, Ely, Grafton, & Kilts, 1999; Lim, Padmala, & Pessoa, 2009; Vuilleumier, Richardson, Armony, Driver, & Dolan, 2004). Decision-making constitutes one form of goal-directed behavior that is particularly complex and involves multiple component processes. These include, at a minimum, forming a perceptual representation and computing the values of the available choice options, planning and executing an action to obtain the chosen outcomes, and learning about the outcomes of the decision to improve future choices (Rangel, Camerer, & Montague, 2008; Rangel & Hare, 2010; Fehr and Rangel, 2011). Moreover, decisions made in a social context involve considerations of others' well-being and prediction of their actions (Fehr & Camerer, 2007; Sanfey, 2007). These choice processes are subserved by multiple cognitive mechanisms including attention (e.g., Hare, Malmaud, & Rangel, 2011; Lim, O'Doherty, & Rangel, 2011; Rangel, 2010), memory (e.g., Bechara & Martin, 2004; Hinson, Jameson, & Whitney, 2003), learning (e.g., Niv, Edlund, Dayan, & O'Doherty, 2012; Schonberg, Daw, Joel, & O'Doherty, 2007; Schultz, 2002), and, in a social context, perspective taking (Gallagher & Frith, 2003; Saxe, 2006). Given the well-documented interactions between emotions and choice-relevant cognitive processes, in conjunction with the significant overlap in the neural circuitry of these processes (Engelmann & Hare, in press), emotions can be expected to influence choice-related cognitive mechanisms at all stages of the decision process.

Multiple theories of emotion agree that the brain generates behavior, among other things, via two opposing motivational systems, the approach and avoidance system, which mediate behavioral responses to reinforcement and can be linked to different underlying neural circuitry (Alcaro & Panksepp, 2011; Cacioppo & Gardner, 2003; Cloninger, 1987; Davidson, Ekman, Saron, Senulis, & Friesen, 1990; J. A. Gray, 1987; J. R. Gray, 2001; Lang, Bradley, & Cuthbert, 1998; Schneirla, 1959). Approach (appetitive) motivation is responsible for orchestrating behavior that increases the probability of rewarding outcomes and is intimately related to positive affect. Neuroscientific research has identified neural circuitry within the mesolimbic and mesocortical dopamine system that encodes appetitive value across species (the "reward system"), with central projection sites in ventral striatum (VS) and ventromedial prefrontal cortex (VMPFC) (e.g., Bartra, McGuire, & Kable, 2013; Haber & Knutson, 2009; Levy & Glimcher, 2012; McClure, York, & Montague, 2004). Avoidance (aversive) motivation, on the other hand, is responsible for guiding behavior to avoid punishments and threats and is intimately related to negative affect. Aversive value has been shown to be encoded in a network of regions (the "avoidance system") that includes the anterior insula (AI; Nitschke, Sarinopoulos, Mackiewicz, Schaefer, & Davidson, 2006; Paulus & Stein, 2006; Wager, Phan, Liberzon, & Taylor, 2003), lateral orbitofrontal cortex (O'Doherty, Kringelbach, Rolls, Hornak, & Andrews, 2001a; Small, Zatorre, Dagher, vans, & Jones-Gotman, 2001), and amygdala (O'Doherty, Rolls, Francis, Bowtell, & McGlone, 2001b; Phelps & LeDoux, 2005; Wager et al., 2003). Supporting evidence for the consistent and specific involvement of these regions in processing aversive events is provided by quantitative forward and reverse inference analyses conducted in the context of large-scale automated meta-analyses (Yarkoni, Poldrack, Nichols, Van Essen, & Wager, 2011).[1]

Here we integrate recent evidence from the fields of social neuroeconomics and social neuroscience to show that social decision-making, with a focus on trust-taking, relies in important ways on the emotions and behavioral tendencies elicited by the approach and avoidance neural systems. We first review behavioral and neural evidence demonstrating that a particular form of social anxiety, betrayal aversion, influences trust decisions. We show that the importance of social emotions generalizes to decision-making in the context of other social decision-making tasks, such as the ultimatum and prisoner's dilemma (PD) games. Drawing upon recent developments in social neuroscience that underline the role of social emotions in interpersonal interactions, we argue that the anticipation of both approach- and avoidance-related social emotions elicited by the potential pro- and antisocial intentions of other players can influence social decision-making in important ways and in addition to economic considerations concerning monetary outcomes. Together, recent evidence from social neuroscience and social neuroeconomics calls for a more integrated theory of social decision-making that incorporates the influence of emotions.

■ TRUST DECISIONS INVOLVE EMOTIONAL CONSIDERATION

The importance of emotions in social decision-making is best illustrated by a concrete example underlining the role of social anxiety in decisions to trust. Trust is an essential component of human relationships that not only permeates interpersonal interactions but is also an essential building block of economic transactions (Algan & Cahuc, 2013; Knack & Keefer, 1997; Zak & Knack, 2001). Trust has been extensively studied in behavioral economics and social neuroeconomics (Fehr, 2009; Rilling & Sanfey, 2011). A standard way to experimentally assess trust-taking is the trust game (Berg, Dickhaut, & McCabe, 1995). In this game, two players interact by sequentially exchanging monetary amounts. First, the investor (player 1) and the trustee (player 2) receive an identical endowment from the experimenter. The investor can transfer any amount of his endowment to the trustee (player 2). If the investor decides to send a positive amount, the trustee receives the tripled amount of what the investor transferred. Next, the trustee decides whether and how much of his current holdings, which consist of her endowment plus the tripled transfer, to share with the investor. These rules are known by both players and provide an opportunity for mutual gain if the investor transfers a positive amount and the trustee is willing to share part of his resources. The amount sent by the investor reflects trust-taking, while the amount returned by the trustee reflects a willingness to reciprocate trust ("reciprocity").

The trust game thus captures the notion of trust as a behavior that makes an individual (the investor) vulnerable to the actions of another person (the trustee) (Coleman, 1990; Fehr, 2009). The investor's motive for taking this social risk is that mutual cooperation can increase not only his financial well-being (and that of the trustee), but also, as we argue later, that cooperation in itself is rewarding. That the trust game captures complex choice mechanisms, which involve emotions and thereby go beyond simple exchanges of money, has repeatedly been demonstrated. A number of recent behavioral studies have suggested that nonreciprocated trust elicits an emotional reaction associated with betrayal and therefore carries a cost above and beyond the loss of money (e.g., Bohnet & Zeckhauser, 2004; Bohnet, Greig, Herrmann, & Zeckhauser, 2008; Kosfeld, Heinrichs, Zak, Fischbacher, & Fehr, 2005). One of the clearest demonstrations of the involvement of social emotions in trust-taking comes from a series of experiments conducted by Bohnet and Zeckhauser (2004, 2008). The authors investigated betrayal aversion using a modified version of the trust game in which both the investor and the trustee had only two choices: the investor could only decide to trust or not to trust (imagine, for simplicity, that the previously described trust game gives the investor only two choices—to invest nothing or to invest the whole endowment) and the trustee could only decide to send back a very low share or a fair share of his holdings in case that the investor trusted her (imagine, again for simplicity, that the trustee can only send back nothing or equally share her holdings). Many investors and many trustees simultaneously participated in the experiments of Bohnet and Zeckhauser, and they were randomly matched with each other. However, the investors did not know whether they were matched with a trustworthy or a greedy trustee. Nor did they know the share of trustworthy trustees that participated in the experiment. The authors exploit this fact and asked the investors to state the minimum share of trustworthy trustees (i.e., those who share their holdings equally) that need to be present in order to make them willing to trust. The statement of such a minimum share of trustworthy trustees that need to be present basically boils down to making trusting conditional on the existence of a minimum probability of getting trust repaid, a measure that the authors called the "minimum acceptance probability" (MAP). If the actual share of trustworthy trustees was equal to or exceeded the required share (i.e., the MAP), the trusting action was implemented. If the actual share fell below the stated MAP, the nontrusting action was implemented. This procedure is closely related to the Becker-DeGroot-Marschak method (Becker, DeGroot, & Marschak, 1964) and therefore incentive compatible. To assess the specificity of risk attitude in social compared to nonsocial settings, participants played two additional control games: a risk game, in which participants stated their MAP to accept a gamble over a sure outcome (with payoffs for the investor that were exactly identical to the payoffs in the binary trust game described earlier), and a risky dictator game that was identical to the trust game except that the decision to be trustworthy or not was determined by a random mechanism and not by the second player in the game.

Results from an initial investigation indicate significantly greater MAPs in the trust game compared to the risk game (Bohnet & Zeckhauser, 2004). This result has subsequently been replicated across six different countries (Bohnet et al., 2008). Participants are therefore more reluctant to trade a sure payout for a gamble in a social compared to a nonsocial setting, indicating that factors beyond mere risk aversion influence trust-taking. One such factor was revealed by a comparison between MAPs in the trust and risky dictator games. The trust game differed from the risky dictator game only with respect to the mechanism that determines the payout for both players—a trustee that can intentionally behave in an untrustworthy manner in the binary trust game or a random mechanism that lacks intentionality in the risky dictator game. A comparison between the MAPs in the two games therefore controls for outcome-based social preferences and reveals betrayal aversion. Results show significantly greater MAPs in the trust compared to the risky dictator game, reflective of betrayal aversion. Moreover, results were replicated in six different countries (Bohnet et al., 2008), indicating that betrayal aversion is a robust phenomenon across different cultural contexts.

A recent functional magnetic resonance imaging (fMRI) study directly investigated the neural correlates of betrayal aversion (Aimone, Houser, & Weber, 2014). Specifically, participants played two types of trust games in the role of the investor while undergoing scanning: a standard binary trust game, in which a trustee decided payout distributions, and a computer-mediated game, where the payout distribution to the two players was determined by a random mechanism equivalent to the risky dictator game of Bohnet and Zeckhauser (2004). Consistent with prior results (Bohnet et al., 2008; Bohnet & Zeckhauser, 2004), Aimone et al. (2014) observed significantly more trust-taking in the computer-mediated game compared to the standard game, confirming the presence of betrayal aversion.

This effect is reflected at the neural level by increased activity in the AI, both when participants played with a human compared to a computer mediator and when they decided to give compared to withhold trust. Moreover, increasing levels of betrayal aversion were associated with increasing AI activation during trust decisions with human counterparts compared to computer mediators. Together, these results implicate the AI in betrayal aversion. Given the consistent role of the AI in processing negative affect (Kuhnen & Knutson, 2005; Nitschke et al., 2006; Paulus & Stein, 2006), as well as social emotions (Lamm & Singer, 2010), the authors conclude that the heightened insular activity during human interactions is reflective of an emotional warning signal of potential future betrayal of trust.

These results are supported and extended by a series of pharmacological and neuroimaging studies investigating the role of oxytocin (OXT) in trust decisions (Baumgartner, Heinrichs, Vonlanthen, Fischbacher, & Fehr, 2008; Kosfeld et al., 2005; Mikolajczak et al., 2010). OXT is a uniquely mammalian neuropeptide that is synthesized in the hypothalamus and can act as a neurotransmitter within the central nervous system. OXT's action on the brain can influence social behavior, including maternal behavior and pair bonding, as well as social motivation and sexual behavior (for review see Meyer-Lindenberg, Domes, Kirsch, & Heinrichs, 2011; Skuse & Gallagher, 2009) and facilitate social cognition (Domes, Heinrichs, Gläscher, et al., 2007; Domes, Heinrichs, Michel, Berger, & Herpertz, 2007; Guastella et al., 2010; Guastella, Mitchell, & Mathews, 2008; Kirsch et al., 2005). Kosfeld et al. tested the hypothesis that OXT enhances trust by administering the trust game to two groups of participants, the treatment group that received synthetic OXT and the control group that received an inactive placebo. Their results show increased trust-taking in the OXT relative to the control group. Importantly, the effect of OXT was specific for trust-taking, as OXT administration had no effect on transfer rates in the non-social risk game (despite the fact that the choice context was perfectly matched), as well as on trustees' reciprocity. Given prior results demonstrating that hesitation to trust is in part driven by betrayal aversion (Aimone et al., 2014; Bohnet et al., 2008; Bohnet & Zeckhauser, 2004; Kosfeld et al., 2005), in combination with OXT's role in reducing social anxiety (Kirsch et al., 2005; Labuschagne et al., 2010), results from Kosfeld et al. suggest that one mechanisms by which OXT mediates trust-taking is by reducing betrayal aversion.

A neuroimaging investigation by Baumgartner et al. (2008) examined the role of OXT in trust decisions and the underlying neural circuitry involved in OXT's effects on trust-taking. While undergoing fMRI, two groups of participants (OXT and placebo control) played both the trust game and a matched risk game. Importantly, at the halfway point of the experiment participants received negative feedback, revealing that decisions to trust (and take risks) were not returned on half the trials. Behavioral adaptation to feedback was significantly affected by the administration of OXT, such that average postfeedback transfers decreased relative to prefeedback in the placebo group, while an increase in postfeedback average transfers was observed in the OXT group. No differential effect of feedback on choices in the OXT and control group were observed in the risk game, indicating that OXT exerts its behavioral effect in the domain of social risks taken in the trust game. Moreover, neuroimaging findings demonstrate increased activity in the amygdala during trust-taking in the postfeedback (relative to prefeedback) phase in the placebo but not the OXT group. Administration of OXT thus suppressed behavioral and neural adaptation to trust betrayal. Taken together with an extensive literature implicating the amygdala in processing aversive emotions and emotional relevance detection (e.g., Phelps & LeDoux, 2005), as well as studies showing that OXT decreases fear responses by modulating activity in the amygdala (Domes, Heinrichs, Gläscher, et al., 2007; Kirsch et al., 2005; Labuschagne et al., 2010), these findings are consistent with the notion that OXT reduces emotional reactions to trust betrayal by decreasing reactivity of the amygdala. Since such effects are specific to social risk-taking, OXT administration likely leads to a reduction of social anxiety.

Taken together, these results suggest that emotions are important mediators of trust decisions. Specifically, betrayal aversion, which is a form of social anxiety, has been postulated to reduce the propensity to trust relative to matched situations, in which financial loss is not associated with intentional betrayal by another person. These results are supported by recent neuroimaging and pharmacological evidence, indicating that betrayal aversion is processed in a core structure of the avoidance system, the AI, while learning about trustworthiness of another is mediated by a central projection site of the AI (Shi & Cassell, 1998), the amygdala.

▪ SOCIAL DECISIONS ARE INFLUENCED BY ANTICIPATED EMOTIONAL COSTS ABOVE AND BEYOND POTENTIAL MATERIAL LOSSES

There is a large body of behavioral and neuroimaging evidence that supports the notion that, in addition to betrayal, unreciprocated cooperation and unfairness elicit aversive emotions and influence social decisions. The ultimatum game (UG) has been widely employed to investigate emotional reactions in response to unfair treatment. In this game, an endowment (e.g., 10 monetary units [MU]) is given to one player, the proposer, who decides on a division of this money with another player, the responder. The responder can accept the division (e.g., 50/50 split), in which case both players receive their respective amounts, or reject the division, in which case both players receive zero MU. If subjects care only about their own income, they should accept any amount greater than zero MU. This prediction does not match empirical observations, which have repeatedly shown rejections of 20/80 divisions. Rejections of unfair offers are not reconcilable with models of decision-making that assume self-interest maximization and neglect social motives (and the underlying social emotions) such as fairness concerns, as rejections entail a financial loss for the responder and no direct financial benefit in one-shot interactions.

There is now considerable evidence suggesting that social emotions, such as anger, constitute a central motivating factor of costly punishment in the UG. One line of research investigated the role of emotions in costly punishment decisions via self-reports. While this approach has various methodological limitations (e.g., Nisbett & Wilson, 1977), it remains an important means to assess the subjective feeling states associated with social interactions.

In one of the first investigations of the role of emotions in UG decisions (Pillutla & Murnighan, 1996), participants made decisions about whether to accept or reject UG offers in the role of the responder and rated their emotional reactions to each offer. Results indicate that, in a classical UG, in which participants know the exact amount that is being split by the proposer, UG rejections of small offers are associated with feelings of anger and perceptions of unfairness. Interestingly, the UG was played in various conditions, one of which was designed to examine emotional responses to unfairness. Specifically, under conditions in which the responder received a small monetary amount from the experimenter in case he rejected the offer (outside option), other players' proposals that equaled this amount were rejected in almost 75% of the cases, and rejection rates were still high (~40%) when the offer was slightly larger than the outside option. The authors argue that such low offers in conditions of low outside options are a signal of bad intentions, as proposers could use their knowledge about the responder's low alternative income to intentionally reduce their own offer. This notion is supported by the emotional reactions of responders. A large majority of participants who rejected such offers reported feeling angry (72%). Moreover, a subset of participants who accepted unfair offers to avoid financial loss (outside option < offer) still reported feeling angry (21%). Importantly, emotional reactions to unfair offers were associated with actual decisions to reject, as demonstrated in logistic regressions showing that greater levels of anger are predictive of increases in rejection likelihoods.

Results from Tabibnia et al. (2008) show that the unfairness level of UG offers is significantly associated with self-reported contempt. Importantly, their study design employed a modified version of the UG, in which offer size and fairness level were varied independently across trials. This allowed for the dissociation of offer fairness from offer size and thus for investigating the emotional influences on choice above and beyond monetary considerations (see also Crockett, Clark, Tabibnia, Lieberman, & Robbins, 2008; Gradin et al., 2015). For instance, the same offer (e.g., 2MU) could be presented in a fair context (when the proposers' endowment was 4MU), or in an unfair context (when the proposers' endowment was 10MU). The significant relationship between level of unfairness and contempt persisted even after controlling for offer amount, indicating that unfairness can elicit aversive emotions. Another experiment showed that, given the opportunity, participants not only readily verbalize their emotional reactions to unfair UG offers, but such verbalization also reduces rejection rates (Xiao & Houser, 2005). A large number of participants (90%) expressed their negative emotions in response to unfair offers of 20% of the proposer's endowment. Moreover, when comparing rejection rates in a standard UG with a modified version that allowed responders to send unconstrained messages, significantly reduced rejection rates of unfair offers were found in the modified version of the game. These results indicate that participants use costly punishment in the standard UG in which participants have no other way to communicate their emotions. When given the opportunity for alternative ways of expressing their contempt, however, these are preferred over costly punishment.

Emotions also influence decisions in games other than the UG. In one experiment, Rilling et al. (2008) assessed self-reported emotional reactions to unreciprocated cooperation in a PD game. Unreciprocated cooperation was associated with greater self-reports of aversive emotions that include betrayal, anger, envy, irritation, sadness, and disappointment. Finally, punishment of free riders in public goods games is associated with increased negative emotions. Fehr and Gächter (2002) show that participants expressed significant anger toward free riders in a hypothetical public goods game scenario. Moreover, the intensity of self-reported negative emotions toward free riders increased as the average contributions from other players increased. The punishment pattern in the public goods game—that high contributors tend to punish low contributors and the positive correlation between the punishment of free riders and the free riders' deviation from average contribution—suggests that negative emotions are an important proximate factor behind the costly punishment of free riders.

A further way to assess emotional reactions to unfairness is via psychophysiological measures of autonomic nervous system activation, such as Galvanic skin conductance responses (SCR), which reflect emotional arousal (Figner & Murphy, 2011). Using SCRs as a proxy for emotional arousal, van't Wout et al. (2006) show significantly enhanced SCR for unfair compared to fair offers. Importantly, enhanced emotional arousal was specific to interactions with another human player, as it was not observed during an equivalently framed game with a computer proposer. Participants in Civai et al. (2010) played both a classical UG and a third-party UG, in which they made decisions on behalf of another person. Civai and colleagues measured SCR in these two UG games and probed participants' emotional responses. The authors show significant negative emotions for unfair offers and significant positive emotions for fair offers in both game types, with the intensity of the emotional reaction being stronger in the classical UG compared to the third-party UG. Investigating the relationship between SCR and rejections of the most unfair offers, the authors show greater SCR amplitudes for classical UG rejections compared to acceptance but also compared to decisions made in the third-party version of the UG. These results confirm findings from van't Wout and colleagues, showing that aversive emotional reactions to unfair offers, as indexed by SCR responses during decision-making and emotional self-reports, are related to classical UG decisions. Emotional reactions may be weaker as social distance increases (Strombach et al., 2015), for instance during third-party UG decisions when the unfairness is not directed at the self.

Functional neuroimaging studies lend support to the picture that is emerging from behavioral experiments, namely that negative emotions are important drivers of social decision-making. Sanfey et al. (2003) investigated the neural correlates of responder decisions in the UG. Unfair offers elicited greater activation in bilateral AI, dorsolateral prefrontal cortex, and anterior cingulate cortex (ACC). Control and computer offers did not yield responses in these areas, underlining the importance of interactions with another human for insular activation patterns. The involvement of the anterior insula in UG decisions is strengthened by further evidence showing increasing insula activity with increasing unfairness, greater insula activity on trials during which the unfair offer was rejected and an association between rejection likelihood and insula activity. Follow-up studies generally support the involvement of the insula in fairness considerations, with several investigations showing activation of AI during UG decisions (Corradi-Dell'Acqua, Civai, Rumiati, & Fink, 2013; Güroğlu, van den Bos, Rombouts, & Crone, 2010; Güroğlu, van den Bos, van Dijk, Rombouts, & Crone, 2011; Tabibnia, Satpute, & Lieberman, 2008), while another implicates an important projection site of AI, the amygdala, in UG rejections (Gospic et al., 2011). Results demonstrating anger and contempt in response to unfair UG offers (Civai, Corradi-Dell'Acqua, Gamer, & Rumiati, 2010; Pillutla & Murnighan, 1996; Tabibnia et al., 2008) on the one hand, and the involvement of the anterior insula in both UG decisions and negative emotional states on the other (Nitschke et al., 2006; Paulus & Stein, 2006; Wager et al., 2003) provide converging evidence for the hypothesis that insula activation during unfair UG offers may reflect the emotional aspects of UG decisions.[2] This notion is further corroborated by recent results from social neuroscience demonstrating the involvement of anterior insula in aversive emotional reactions to social rejection (Eisenberger, 2012).

■ SOCIAL REJECTION ELICITS AVERSIVE EMOTIONS THAT ARE PROCESSED IN CIRCUITRY RELATED TO PHYSICAL PAIN AND NEGATIVE AFFECT

Humans care deeply about how they are evaluated by others. This fact is well captured in the high prevalence of public speaking anxiety (Pull, 2012), as well as research on social stress showing that social evaluation triggers a strong stress response in a great majority of participants (Dawans, Kirschbaum, & Heinrichs, 2011; Kirschbaum, Pirke, & Hellhammer, 1993). These effects of social evaluation are driven in part by reputation concerns (Fehr & Fischbacher, 2003; Izuma, 2012). Moreover, recent research has demonstrated that social approval can elicit positive emotions and is largely processed in core reward circuitry (Izuma, 2012), while social rejection can elicit aversive emotions and is largely processed in neural circuitry implicated in processing the affective component of pain (Eisenberger, 2012).

Although only a relatively recent research endeavor, great progress has been made in identifying the neural circuitry involved in processing social evaluation. Research investigating the behavioral and neural mechanisms underlying rejection have led to the proposal that social and physical pain share common psychological and neural mechanisms (Pain Overlap Theory; Eisenberger, 2012; Eisenberger & Lieberman, 2004; MacDonald & Leary, 2005). Indeed, behavioral experiments have demonstrated similarities in the psychological responses to physical and social pain. Specifically, participants recalling past episodes of social pain (e.g., betrayal by a close person) reported levels of experienced pain that were statistically indistinguishable from participants recalling past episodes of physical pain (Chen, Williams, Fitness, & Newton, 2008; Riva, Wirth, & Williams, 2011). Both recall and induction of physical pain (via the immersion of one hand in cold water) and social pain (via a virtual computer game of social exclusion outlined in detail later) led to equivalent decreases in feelings of self-esteem and control, as well as increases in negative affect and the desire to aggress (Riva et al., 2011). Moreover, physical pain induction significantly heightened feelings of being ignored and excluded, which are typically associated with social pain, further supporting the emotional overlap between social and physical pain.

In parallel, neuroimaging research on the neural circuitry of social rejection has revealed that social rejection is processed within regions implicated in physical pain processing. In an initial study investigating the neural circuitry of social exclusion (Eisenberger, Lieberman, & Williams, 2003), participants played a virtual ball tossing game (the "Cyberball game," Williams & Jarvis, 2006) with two other human participants. In one condition, virtual players included participants in the game by throwing the ball to participants, while in another, participants were actively excluded by the other two players. Results revealed that explicit social exclusion triggered greater self-reported distress and was associated with enhanced activation in dorsal ACC and anterior insula. Interestingly, both regions have consistently been implicated in processing the affective component of pain. Research on the neural basis of pain emphasizes the presence of distinct neural pathways for processing the somatosensory and affective components of pain (e.g., Bushnell, Čeko, & Low, 2013; Price, 2000; Rainville, Duncan, Price, Carrier, & Bushnell, 1997). Specifically, the brain first needs to represent the sensory aspects of pain, such as its location on the body, as well as its quality and intensity. This information is subsequently employed to assign an aversive emotional value to the painful sensation, which is crucial for motivating protective behavior that terminates the painful stimulation. Imaging studies have shown that distinct, but interacting neural pathways process the sensory and affective components of pain, with primary (S1) and secondary (S2) somatosensory cortices encoding the sensory aspects (e.g., Bushnell et al., 1999; Treede, Kenshalo, Gracely, & Jones, 1999), while anterior insula (AI) and dorsal anterior cingulate cortex (dACC) encode the affective components (e.g., Rainville et al., 1997; Shackman et al., 2011; Wiech et al., 2010). Eisenberger et al. (2003) therefore concluded that regions that process the affective component of pain, such as AI and dACC, are also intimately involved in processing social pain (Eisenberger, 2012).

While results from this initial study suggest the presence of shared circuitry for physical and social pain, a direct demonstration of overlap in the neural circuitry requires assessment of both physical and social pain in the same participants. Kross et al. (2011) addressed this shortcoming and investigated the overlap of physical and social pain in the same sample of participants. Participants who had recently experienced an unwanted relationship break-up viewed photographs of their ex-partner while thinking about being rejected (compared to thinking about a recent positive experience when viewing a photograph depicting a friend) in the social pain task. In the physical pain task, participants experienced noxious (compared to nonnoxious) thermal stimulation. Imaging results confirm that neural circuitry encoding physical and social pain overlapped in the dACC and AI, confirming previous reports. Conjunction analysis also revealed significant overlap between social and physical pain in somatosensory brain systems, which encode the sensory component of pain, including thalamus and secondary somatosensory cortex, as well as the opercular insular region and dorsal posterior insula (see also Fisher, Brown, Aron, Strong, & Mashek, 2010). These results suggest a more extensive overlap in the neural circuitry for social and physical pain under conditions of intense social pain, such as rejection from a loved one.

Correlations between self-reported feelings of distress and neural sensitivity to experienced social exclusion in the AI and dACC can more closely identify the involvement of neural activation patterns in these regions in the affective component of social pain. Indeed, participants reporting greater distress to social exclusion showed greater social exclusion-related activity in the ACC (Eisenberger et al., 2003). More recent studies using the cyberball game further underline the relationship between social rejection-related neural signals in the AI and dACC and self-reported feelings of distress. A number of studies have shown a positive correlation between self-reported feelings of social distress and activity in the dACC (DeWall et al., 2012; Eisenberger et al., 2003; Masten, Telzer, Fuligni, Lieberman, & Eisenberger, 2012), as well as the AI (DeWall et al., 2012; Masten et al., 2012, 2009). These results have been corroborated in a series of studies showing that greater trait sensitivity to social exclusion (e.g., low self-esteem, anxious attachment) has been associated with increased social exclusion related signal in the AI and dACC (DeWall et al., 2012; Onoda et al., 2010), while reduced sensitivity to social exclusion (e.g., social support, avoidant attachment) has been associated with decreased social exclusion related signal in these regions (DeWall et al., 2012; Eisenberger, Taylor, Gable, Hilmert, & Lieberman, 2007; Masten et al., 2012). A recent investigation of felt understanding demonstrates an even closer link between social emotions and brain activity in the AI (Morelli, Torre, & Eisenberger, 2014). Specifically, the authors show that trial-by-trial signal changes in the AI and dorsomedial prefrontal cortex (DMPFC) tracked subjective ratings of feelings of nonunderstanding. Moreover, participants high in rejection sensitivity showed greater activity in the AI when they received negative feedback indicating nonunderstanding. Jointly, these results consistently implicate bold oxygen level dependent (BOLD) signals in the AI and dACC in the affective responses associated with social exclusion.

One consequence of shared neural circuitry for physical and social pain is that analgesics known to reduce physical pain would be expected to similarly influence social pain. Indeed, De Wall et al. (2010) show that, compared to placebo, daily intake of acetaminophen (a physical pain suppressant commonly known as ibuprofen) for a period of three weeks reduced self-reports of social pain during daily life, as well as neural responsivity to social exclusion in the dACC, AI, and amygdala. Interestingly, the analgesic effects of acetaminophen have been shown to be mediated via the cannabinoid system (Mallet et al., 2008), activation of which has been shown to reduce anxiety (Patel & Hillard, 2006), as well as amygdala reactivity to social threat (Phan et al., 2008). Together, these results implicate the amygdala, a structure with a high density of cannabinoid CB1 receptors (Herkenham et al., 1990; Katona et al., 2001), in social pain, which parallels results from social neuroeconomics on the effects of betrayal (e.g., Baumgartner et al., 2008). Furthermore, they suggest an interesting relationship between the cannabinoid system and social pain perception that provides a venue for future research on the neural mechanisms of alleviating social pain and social anxiety.

Taken together, these results provide converging evidence for the notion that aversive social emotions and the affective aspects of physical pain share underlying neural circuitry within the dACC and AI. Moreover, results from social neuroscience provide a putative neural mechanism underlying aversive emotions important for social decisions, such as fear of betrayal, as well as anger and contempt due to unfairness and unreciprocated cooperation. The AI in particular emerges as a neural hub important for aversive emotions in social dilemmas and social situations involving unfairness, as it activates during situations signifying trust betrayal (Aimone et al., 2014) and unfairness (Sanfey, Rilling, Aronson, Nystrom, & Cohen, 2003), as well as in the context of social rejection, where AI activity correlates with feelings of social distress and tracks trial-by-trial changes in social emotions (DeWall et al., 2012; Masten et al., 2009, 2012; Morelli et al., 2014).

■ SOCIAL ACCEPTANCE ELICITS APPROACH EMOTIONS THAT ARE PROCESSED IN CORE REWARD CIRCUITRY

On the flip side, social neuroscience research investigating the neural basis of positive social feedback has demonstrated that different forms of social approval are processed within core reward circuitry in VS and VMPFC, suggesting that social approval has affective properties that resemble primary rewards. Izuma et al. (2008) conducted one of the first studies investigating the behavioral and neural effects of social approval. Participants performed both a simple gambling task, in which outcomes were monetary rewards, as well as a matched social reward task, in which outcomes were positive evaluations of their personality by strangers. Despite the fact that the currency of reward differed, imaging results indicated that positive outcomes in both the monetary and the social domain are processed in overlapping regions of the VS and follow similar activation patterns. Importantly, this was paralleled by behavioral reports, indicating positive social feedback to be desirable and to increase participants' subjective happiness.

Follow-up studies confirm this initial report of overlapping activation patterns in reward circuitry in response to monetary and social rewards. Receiving positive feedback reflective of first impressions from strangers based on participants' appearance in a photograph was associated with activation in core reward regions including the VS and VMPFC (Davey, Allen, Harrison, Dwyer, & Yücel, 2010). Moreover, when positive feedback came from strangers that participants regarded highly, greater activity was observed in the VMPFC and amygdala. In another study (Spreckelmeyer et al., 2009), overlapping regions in the VS also showed enhanced activation during reward anticipation of both monetary and social rewards when comparing brain responses during a standard version of the Monetary Incentive Delay (MID; Knutson, Westdorp, Kaiser, & Hommer, 2000) task to those during a social version of the MID. Moreover, it has repeatedly been shown that activity in the VS parametrically tracks both monetary and social rewards (increasing intensity of happy facial expressions) particularly during reward anticipation (Rademacher, Salama, Gründer, & Spreckelmeyer, 2013; Spreckelmeyer et al., 2009).

Another series of studies employed a social feedback task that allowed for the dissociation of social approval from expectancy violations (Somerville, Heatherton, & Kelley, 2006). Participants viewed pictures of unfamiliar faces and communicated their expectation about whether the depicted individual would like them. After the participants' initial rating, they received feedback about whether the individual accepted or rejected the participant. Social feedback thus varied in terms of congruency with participants' expectations (confirm vs. contradict) and valence (positive vs. negative). Results revealed a neural dissociation between social feedback valence and expectancy, such that positive social feedback was preferentially processed in the VMPFC, while expectancy violations were processed in the dACC. Moreover, anticipation of positive social evaluations from peers was processed in the VS, in addition to the VMPFC, in one follow-up study (Moor, van Leijenhorst, Rombouts, Crone, & Van der Molen, 2010) and the VS and DMPFC in another (Powers, Somerville, Kelley, & Heatherton, 2013). Individuals higher in self-reported rejection sensitivity also showed greater VS and DMPFC responses during anticipation of positive feedback (Powers et al., 2013). Finally, Morelli et al. (2014) show that feeling understood is tracked by signal in the VS. In this study, participants received feedback from strangers about how much they sympathized with a videotaped description of an important and emotional event from the participants' lives. Feeling understood (relative to not feeling understood) activated the VS and middle insula. Importantly, the authors also demonstrate a close relationship between neural signals and social emotions, as activity in the VS and temporoparietal junction also parametrically tracked subjective ratings of felt understanding on a trial-by-trial basis (Morelli et al., 2014; Rademacher et al., 2013; Spreckelmeyer et al., 2009).

Taken together, these studies consistently show that (a) activations in response to social rewards overlap with core reward circuitry in VS and VMPFC; (b) disparate social rewards that include social approval, first impressions, the feeling of being understood, and happy facial expressions are encoded in the VS and VMPFC across different tasks and contexts (Davey et al., 2010; Izuma, Saito, & Sadato, 2008; Moor et al., 2010; Morelli et al., 2014; Powers et al., 2013; Rademacher et al., 2013); and (c) the VS and VMPFC often parametrically track social rewards in a manner that parallels their processing of monetary rewards (Morelli et al., 2014). Moreover, positive social evaluations elicit positive emotions (Izuma et al., 2008). Together, the behavioral and neuroimaging evidence suggests that positive social interactions are rewarding at the psychological and neural level.[3] This is consistent with the view that positive social outcomes are processed by the brain in a manner that parallels the neural processing of primary rewards and money, which supports theories claiming that core reward circuitry encodes subjective values of disparate rewards on a common scale (Montague & Berns, 2002).

■ SOCIAL DECISIONS ARE INFLUENCED BY ANTICIPATED EMOTIONAL BENEFITS ABOVE AND BEYOND POTENTIAL MATERIAL GAINS

These considerations directly translate to social interactions that are commonly investigated experimentally using social decision-making tasks, such as the UG, the PD and the trust game. In particular, the results reviewed earlier predict that cooperation has rewarding properties, by association with positive social feedback and acceptance, above and beyond the monetary outcomes that can be earned from cooperation. Support for this notion would be provided by evidence showing that prosocial actions of interaction partners in social choice tasks elicit (a) approach emotions and (b) activation in core reward circuitry.

Indeed, social neuroeconomic research has repeatedly shown that cooperation in social dilemmas elicits positive emotions and is processed in core reward circuitry. In an initial investigation of cooperative behavior in the context of a social dilemma, Rilling et al. (2002) show that mutual cooperation in a repeated PD was associated with enhanced activations in the VS and VMPFC. Importantly, mutual cooperation showed greater BOLD signals in these regions than trials that led to greater financial outcomes, which is consistent with the view that cooperation was more rewarding than greater financial payoffs. Moreover, greater activity in the VS and VMPFC was obtained when monetary gains were due to social cooperation but not when the same monetary outcome was accomplished in the nonsocial control condition. Further support for the involvement of the VMPFC in cooperation is provided by a study by Decety, Jackson, Sommerville, Chaminade, and Meltzoff (2004), in which participants played a computer game that required the completion of a pattern with help from another player. Even in the absence of monetary payouts, the VMPFC showed prolonged enhanced activation when participants faced a cooperative player compared to a competitive one. Together, these results support the notion that cooperation is associated with activity in core reward circuitry.

Given that brain activation patterns do not necessarily reflect the emotional states of the participants during cooperation (Poldrack, 2006. 2011), it is important to assess actual emotional responses of participants to the different game outcomes. Initial evidence for positive emotional reactions to cooperation comes from interviews conducted by Rilling et al. (2002), which indicate that mutual cooperation was the most personally satisfying outcome. Extending these results, Rilling et al. (2008) assessed emotional reactions to PD outcomes in a questionnaire. Participants reported enhanced positive emotions due to cooperation. Importantly, enhancements of positive emotions that were specific to mutual cooperation outcomes included trust, camaraderie, and happiness (Rilling et al., 2008). The most direct evidence for the strong relationship between cooperation and positive emotions has been provided by a study by Tabibnia et al. (2007), which assessed the relationship between emotions and responder decisions in the UG. The researchers employed a study design that allowed for dissociation of emotional reactions to unfairness from reactions to low offer amounts (see detailed design outline previously). Findings revealed that fairness was associated with greater happiness ratings, a result that persisted even after controlling for offer amount. Neurally, fairness (relative to unfair offers) elicited greater activation in the VS, VMPFC, and amygdala. Again, this relationship persisted even after controlling for the size of the offer, indicating that both emotional reactions and brain responses were specific to fairness considerations and not driven by monetary stake size. Finally, Xiao and Houser (2005) show that participants, when given the opportunity to communicate their emotions about UG offers, express exclusively positive emotions when receiving fair, but not unfair, offers.

The results reviewed here indicate that positive social interactions (a) elicit approach emotions associated with reward above and beyond monetary payoffs and (b) are associated with enhanced brain activity in core regions of reward circuitry, including the VS and VMPFC. Taken together with results from social neuroscience that attribute rewarding properties to social acceptance, emotional reactions to cooperative actions may well reflect inferences about the prosocial intentions of interaction partners and mimic emotions associated with social acceptance.

■ CONCLUSION

Results from two independent streams of research in social neuroeconomics and social neuroscience jointly emphasize the importance of both approach and avoidance emotions in social interactions. The studies reviewed in this chapter provide converging evidence—using multiple methods, which include self-reports of subjective emotional state, choice behavior, psychophysiology, and neuroimaging—that supports the involvement of emotions in social decisions. On the one hand, unsuccessful social interactions in interactive games such as the trust game, UG, and PD have been shown to elicit aversive emotions related to betrayal, unfairness, and unreciprocated cooperation. On the other hand, successful social interactions in these games are associated with approach emotions. Moreover, our review of an independent research stream in social neuroscience identifies a striking overlap in two neural systems, one in core reward circuitry in the VS and VMPFC that processes positive social feedback and successful cooperation and the other in a core structure of the avoidance system, the AI, which emerges as a neural hub important for processing aversive emotions in social decision-making tasks. Anticipatory emotions related to the potential pro- and antisocial actions of interaction partners in these tasks therefore mimic emotional reactions to social acceptance and rejection, both neurally and behaviorally. Jointly, results from social neuroeconomics and social neuroscience suggest that social decision-making partially relies on emotional brain systems that signal the magnitude of positive and negative feelings about the pro- and antisocial intentions of interaction partners above and beyond the material benefits and costs that result from their actions. Importantly, the anticipatory emotions associated with social approval and rejection can have central, but often ignored, influences on social choices. These considerations call for the integration of emotions into theories of social decision-making.

■ NOTES

1. Neurosynth, a tool for conducting large-scale meta-analyses, allows for the quantitative identification of cognitive states from brain activity patterns, commonly referred to as reverse inference. The reverse inference analysis for the term *aversive* identifies a network of regions, which are specifically activated during aversive events and include the right anterior insula (peak voxel at 42, 30, −2), bilateral amygdala (peak voxel at left: −22, −2, −18; right: 28, −4, −18), right lateral orbitofrontal cortex (peak voxel at 42, 46, −14), and dorsal anterior cingulate cortex (peak voxel at −2, 12, 28).

2. Quantitative reverse inference analysis (neurosynth term *aversive*; Yarkoni et al., 2011) that identifies the right anterior insula (peak voxel at 42, 30, −2) and its projection sites in the amygdala (peak voxel at left: −22, −2, −18; right: 28, −4, −18) as regions that are selectively activated during aversive events lend further support to this idea.

3. This notion is further corroborated by quantitative reverse inference analysis (neurosynth term *reward*, Yarkoni et al., 2011) that identifies a network consisting of bilateral ventral striatum (peak voxel at left: −12, 10, −8; right: 10, 12, −6), ventromedial Prefrontal Cortex (peak voxel at 2, 58, −8), and brain stem (peak voxel at 4, −18, −14) to be selectively activated during rewarding events.

■ REFERENCES

Aimone, J. A., Houser, D., & Weber, B. (2014). Neural signatures of betrayal aversion: An fMRI study of trust. *Proceedings of the Royal Society B: Biological Sciences, 281*(1782), 20132127–20132127. http://doi.org/10.1098/rspb.2013.2127

Alcaro, A., & Panksepp, J. (2011). The SEEKING mind: Primal neuro-affective substrates for appetitive incentive states and their pathological dynamics in addictions and depression. *Neuroscience and Biobehavioral Reviews, 35*(9), 1805–1820. http://doi.org/10.1016/j.neubiorev.2011.03.002

Algan, Y., & Cahuc, P. (2013). Trust and growth. *Annual Review of Economics, 5*(1), 521–549. http://doi.org/10.1146/annurev-economics-081412-102108

Anderson, A. K., & Phelps, E. A. (2001). Lesions of the human amygdala impair enhanced perception of emotionally salient events. *Nature, 411*(6835), 305–309. http://doi.org/10.1038/35077083

Bartra, O., McGuire, J. T., & Kable, J. W. (2013). The valuation system: A coordinate-based meta-analysis of BOLD fMRI experiments examining neural correlates of subjective value. *NeuroImage, 76*(C), 412–427. http://doi.org/10.1016/j.neuroimage.2013.02.063

Baumgartner, T., Heinrichs, M., Vonlanthen, A., Fischbacher, U., & Fehr, E. (2008). Oxytocin shapes the neural circuitry of trust and trust adaptation in humans. *Neuron, 58*(4), 639–650. http://doi.org/10.1016/j.neuron.2008.04.009

Bechara, A., & Martin, E. M. (2004). Impaired decision making related to working memory deficits in individuals with substance addictions. *Neuropsychology, 18*(1), 152–162. http://doi.org/10.1037/0894-4105.18.1.152

Becker, G. M., DeGroot, M. H., & Marschak, J. (1964). Measuring utility by a single-response sequential method. *Behavioral Science, 9*(3), 226–232.

Berg, J., Dickhaut, J., & McCabe, K. (1995). Trust, reciprocity, and social history. *Games and Economic Behavior, 10*(1), 122–142. http://doi.org/10.1006/game.1995.1027

Bohnet, I., Greig, F., Herrmann, B., & Zeckhauser, R. (2008). Betrayal aversion: Evidence from Brazil, China, Oman, Switzerland, Turkey, and the United States. *American Economic Review, 98*(1), 294–310. http://doi.org/10.1257/aer.98.1.294

Bohnet, I., & Zeckhauser, R. (2004). Trust, risk and betrayal. *Journal of Economic Behavior & Organization, 55*(4), 467–484. http://doi.org/10.1016/j.jebo.2003.11.004

Bushnell, M. C., Čeko, M., & Low, L. A. (2013). Cognitive and emotional control of pain and its disruption in chronic pain. *Nature Reviews Neuroscience, 14*, 502–511. http://doi.org/10.1038/nrn3516

Bushnell, M. C., Duncan, G. H., Hofbauer, R. K., Ha, B., Chen, J. I., & Carrier, B. (1999). Pain perception: Is there a role for primary somatosensory cortex? *Proceedings of the National Academy of Sciences, 96*(14), 7705–7709. http://doi.org/10.1073/pnas.96.14.7705

Cacioppo, J. T., & Gardner, W. L. (2003). Emotion. Annual Review of Psychology, 50, 1–705. http://doi.org/10.1146/annurev.psych.50.1.191

Chen, Z., Williams, K. D., Fitness, J., & Newton, N. C. (2008). When hurt will not heal: Exploring the capacity to relive social and physical pain. *Psychological Science, 19*(8), 789–795. http://doi.org/10.1111/j.1467-9280.2008.02158.x

Civai, C., Corradi-Dell'Acqua, C., Gamer, M., & Rumiati, R. I. (2010). Are irrational reactions to unfairness truly emotionally driven? Dissociated behavioural and emotional responses in the ultimatum game task. *Cognition, 114*(1), 89–95. http://doi.org/10.1016/j.cognition.2009.09.001

Cloninger, C. R. (1987). A systematic method for clinical description and classification of personality variants: A proposal. *Archives of General Psychiatry, 44*(6), 573–588.

Cohn, A., Engelmann, J., Fehr, E., & Maréchal, M. A. (2015). Evidence for countercyclical risk aversion: An experiment with financial professionals. *American Economic Review, 105*(2), 860–885. http://doi.org/10.1257/aer.20131314

Coleman, J. S. (1990). *Foundations of social theory*. Cambridge, MA: Harvard University Press.

Corradi-Dell'Acqua, C., Civai, C., Rumiati, R. I., & Fink, G. R. (2013). Disentangling self- and fairness-related neural mechanisms involved in the ultimatum game: An fMRI study. *Social Cognitive and Affective Neuroscience, 8*(4), 424–431. http://doi.org/10.1093/scan/nss014

Crockett, M. J., Clark, L., Tabibnia, G., Lieberman, M. D., & Robbins, T. W. (2008). Serotonin modulates behavioral reactions to unfairness. *Science, 320*(5884), 1739–1739. http://doi.org/10.1126/science.1155577

Davey, C. G., Allen, N. B., Harrison, B. J., Dwyer, D. B., & Yücel, M. (2010). Being liked activates primary reward and midline self-related brain regions. *Human Brain Mapping, 31*(4), 660–668. http://doi.org/10.1002/hbm.20895

Davidson, R. J., Ekman, P., Saron, C. D., Senulis, J. A., & Friesen, W. V. (1990). Approach-withdrawal and cerebral asymmetry: Emotional expression and brain physiology. I. *Journal of Personality and Social Psychology, 58*(2), 330–341.

Dawans, von B., Kirschbaum, C., & Heinrichs, M. (2011). The Trier Social Stress Test for Groups (TSST-G): A new research tool for controlled simultaneous social stress exposure in a group format. *Psychoneuroendocrinology, 36*(4), 514–522. http://doi.org/10.1016/j.psyneuen.2010.08.004

Decety, J., Jackson, P. L., Sommerville, J. A., Chaminade, T., & Meltzoff, A. N. (2004). The neural bases of cooperation and competition: An fMRI investigation. *NeuroImage, 23*(2), 744–751. http://doi.org/10.1016/j.neuroimage.2004.05.025

DeWall, C. N., Masten, C. L., Powell, C., Combs, D., Schurtz, D. R., & Eisenberger, N. I. (2012). Do neural responses to rejection depend on attachment style? An fMRI study. *Social Cognitive and Affective Neuroscience*, 7(2), 184–192. http://doi.org/10.1093/scan/nsq107

Domes, G., Heinrichs, M., Gläscher, J., Büchel, C., Braus, D. F., & Herpertz, S. C. (2007). Oxytocin attenuates amygdala responses to emotional faces regardless of valence. *Biological Psychiatry*, 62(10), 1187–1190. http://doi.org/10.1016/j.biopsych.2007.03.025

Domes, G., Heinrichs, M., Michel, A., Berger, C., & Herpertz, S. C. (2007). Oxytocin improves "mind-reading" in humans. *Biological Psychiatry*, 61(6), 731–733. http://doi.org/10.1016/j.biopsych.2006.07.015

Eisenberger, N. I. (2012). The pain of social disconnection: Examining the shared neural underpinnings of physical and social pain. *Nature Reviews Neuroscience*, 13(6), 421–434. http://doi.org/10.1038/nrn3231

Eisenberger, N. I., & Lieberman, M. D. (2004). Why rejection hurts: A common neural alarm system for physical and social pain. *Trends in Cognitive Sciences*, 8(7), 294–300. http://doi.org/10.1016/j.tics.2004.05.010

Eisenberger, N. I., Lieberman, M. D., & Williams, K. D. (2003). Does rejection hurt? An FMRI study of social exclusion. *Science*, 302(5643), 290–292. http://doi.org/10.1126/science.1089134

Eisenberger, N. I., Taylor, S. E., Gable, S. L., Hilmert, C. J., & Lieberman, M. D. (2007). Neural pathways link social support to attenuated neuroendocrine stress responses. *NeuroImage*, 35(4), 1601–1612. http://doi.org/10.1016/j.neuroimage.2007.01.038

Engelmann, J.B. & Hare, T. (in press) Emotions can bias decision-making processes by promoting specific behavioral tendencies. Davidson, R, Shackman, A., Fox, A., Lapate, R. (Eds.) *The Nature of Emotion*, 2nd edition, Oxford University Press.

Engelmann, J. B., Meyer, F., Fehr, E., & Ruff, C. C. (2015). Anticipatory anxiety disrupts neural valuation during risky choice. *Journal of Neuroscience*, 35(7), 3085–3099. http://doi.org/10.1523/JNEUROSCI.2880-14.2015

Fehr, E. (2009). On the economics and biology of trust. *Journal of the European Economic Association*, 7(2–3), 235–266. http://doi.org/10.1162/JEEA.2009.7.2-3.235

Fehr, E., & Camerer, C. F. (2007). Social neuroeconomics: The neural circuitry of social preferences. *Trends in Cognitive Sciences*, 11(10), 419–427. http://doi.org/10.1016/j.tics.2007.09.002

Fehr, E., & Fischbacher, U. (2003). The nature of human altruism. *Nature*, 425(6960), 785–791. http://doi.org/10.1038/nature02043

Fehr, E., & Gächter, S. (2002). Altruistic punishment in humans. *Nature*, 415(6868), 137–140. http://doi.org/10.1038/415137a

Fehr, E., & Rangel, A. (2011). Neuroeconomic Foundations of Economic Choice—Recent Advances. *Journal of Economic Perspectives*, 25(4), 3–30. http://doi.org/10.1257/jep.25.4.3

Figner, B., & Murphy, R. O. (2011). Using skin conductance in judgment and decision making research. In M. Schulte-Mecklenbeck, A. Kuehberger, & R. Ranyard (Eds.), *A handbook of process tracing methods for decision research* (pp. 163–184). New York: Psychology Press.

Fisher, H. E., Brown, L. L., Aron, A., Strong, G., & Mashek, D. (2010). Reward, addiction, and emotion regulation systems associated with rejection in love. *Journal of Neurophysiology*, 104(1), 51–60. http://doi.org/10.1152/jn.00784.2009

Gallagher, H. L., & Frith, C. D. (2003). Functional imaging of "theory of mind." *Trends in Cognitive Sciences, 7*(2), 77–83. http://doi.org/10.1016/S1364-6613(02)00025-6

Gospic, K., Mohlin, E., Fransson, P., Petrovic, P., Johannesson, M., & Ingvar, M. (2011). Limbic justice—amygdala involvement in immediate rejection in the ultimatum game. *PLoS Biology, 9*(5), e1001054–e1001058. http://doi.org/10.1371/journal.pbio.1001054

Gradin, V. B., Pérez, A., MacFarlane, J. A., Cavin, I., Waiter, G., Engelmann, J., . . . Steele, J. D. (2015). Abnormal brain responses to social fairness in depression: an fMRI study using the ultimatum game. *Psychological Medicine, 45*(6), 1241–1251. http://doi.org/10.1017/S0033291714002347

Gray, J. A. (1987). *The psychology of fear and stress* (2nd ed.). Cambridge, UK: Cambridge University Press.

Gray, J. R. (2001). Emotional modulation of cognitive control: Approach-withdrawal states double-dissociate spatial from verbal two-back task performance. *Journal of Experimental Psychology: General, 130*(3), 436–452.

Guastella, A. J., Einfeld, S. L., Gray, K. M., Rinehart, N. J., Tonge, B. J., Lambert, T. J., & Hickie, I. B. (2010). Intranasal oxytocin improves emotion recognition for youth with autism spectrum disorders. *Biological Psychiatry, 67*(7), 692–694. http://doi.org/10.1016/j.biopsych.2009.09.020

Guastella, A. J., Mitchell, P. B., & Mathews, F. (2008). Oxytocin enhances the encoding of positive social memories in humans. *Biological Psychiatry, 64*(3), 256–258. http://doi.org/10.1016/j.biopsych.2008.02.008

Güroğlu, B., van den Bos, W., Rombouts, S. A. R. B., & Crone, E. A. (2010). Unfair? It depends: Neural correlates of fairness in social context. *Social Cognitive and Affective Neuroscience, 5*(4), 414–423. http://doi.org/10.1093/scan/nsq013

Güroğlu, B., van den Bos, W., van Dijk, E., Rombouts, S. A. R. B., & Crone, E. A. (2011). Dissociable brain networks involved in development of fairness considerations: Understanding intentionality behind unfairness. *NeuroImage, 57*(2), 634–641. http://doi.org/10.1016/j.neuroimage.2011.04.032

Haber, S. N., & Knutson, B. (2009). The reward circuit: Linking primate anatomy and human imaging. *Neuropsychopharmacology, 35*(1), 4–26. http://doi.org/10.1038/npp.2009.129

Hamann, S. B., Ely, T. D., Grafton, S. T., & Kilts, C. D. (1999). Amygdala activity related to enhanced memory for pleasant and aversive stimuli. *Nature Neuroscience, 2*(3), 289–293. http://doi.org/10.1038/6404

Hare, T. A., Malmaud, J., & Rangel, A. (2011). Focusing attention on the health aspects of foods changes value signals in vmPFC and improves dietary choice. *Journal of Neuroscience, 31*(30), 11077–11087. http://doi.org/10.1523/JNEUROSCI.6383-10.2011

Harlé, K. M., & Sanfey, A. G. (2007). Incidental sadness biases social economic decisions in the ultimatum game. *Emotion, 7*(4), 876–881. http://doi.org/10.1037/1528-3542.7.4.876

Harlé, K. M., & Sanfey, A. G. (2010). Effects of approach and withdrawal motivation on interactive economic decisions. *Cognition and Emotion, 24*(8), 1456–1465. http://doi.org/10.1080/02699930903510220

Herkenham, M., Lynn, A.D., Little, M.D., Johnson, M.R., Melvin, L.S., de Costa, B.R., & Rice, K.C. (1990). Cannabinoid receptor localization in brain. *Proceedings of the National Academy of Sciences, 87*(5), 1932–1936.

Hinson, J. M., Jameson, T. L., & Whitney, P. (2003). Impulsive decision making and working memory. *Journal of Experimental Psychology: Learning, Memory, and Cognition, 29*(2), 298–306. http://doi.org/10.1037/0278-7393.29.2.298

Izuma, K. (2012). The social neuroscience of reputation. *Neuroscience Research*, 72(4), 283–288. http://doi.org/10.1016/j.neures.2012.01.003

Izuma, K., Saito, D. N., & Sadato, N. (2008). Processing of social and monetary rewards in the human striatum. *Neuron*, 58(2), 284–294. http://doi.org/10.1016/j.neuron.2008.03.020

Katona, I., Rancz, E. A., Acsady, L., Ledent, C., Mackie, K., Hajos, N., & Freund, T. F. (2001). Distribution of CB1 cannabinoid receptors in the amygdala and their role in the control of GABAergic transmission. *Journal of Neuroscience*, 21, 9506–9518.

Kirsch, P., Esslinger, C., Chen, Q., Mier, D., Lis, S., Siddhanti, S., . . . Meyer-Lindenberg A. (2005). Oxytocin modulates neural circuitry for social cognition and fear in humans. *Journal of Neuroscience*, 25(49), 11489–11493. http://doi.org/10.1523/JNEUROSCI.3984-05.2005

Kirschbaum, C., Pirke, K. M., & Hellhammer, D. H. (1993). The "Trier Social Stress Test"—a tool for investigating psychobiological stress responses in a laboratory setting. *Neuropsychobiology*, 28(1–2), 76–81.

Knack, S., & Keefer, P. (1997). Does social capital have an economic payoff? A cross-country investigation. *The Quarterly Journal of Economics*, 112(4), 1251-1288. http://doi.org/10.2307/2951271

Knutson, B., Westdorp, A., Kaiser, E., & Hommer, D. (2000). FMRI visualization of brain activity during a monetary incentive delay task. *NeuroImage*, 12(1), 20–27. http://doi.org/10.1006/nimg.2000.0593

Kosfeld, M., Heinrichs, M., Zak, P. J., Fischbacher, U., & Fehr, E. (2005). Oxytocin increases trust in humans. *Nature*, 435(7042), 673–676. http://doi.org/10.1038/nature03701

Kross, E., Berman, M. G., Mischel, W., Smith, E. E., & Wagner, W. D. (2011). Social rejection shares somatosensory representations with physical pain. *Proc Natl Acad Sci*, 108(15), 6270–6275. http://doi.org/10.1073/pnas.1102693108

Kuhnen, C. M., & Knutson, B. (2005). The neural basis of financial risk taking. *Neuron*, 47(5), 763–770. http://doi.org/10.1016/j.neuron.2005.08.008

Labuschagne, I., Phan, K. L., Wood, A., Angstadt, M., Chua, P., Heinrichs, M., . . . Nathan, P. J. (2010). Oxytocin attenuates amygdala reactivity to fear in generalized social anxiety disorder. *Neuropsychopharmacology*, 35(12), 2403–2413. http://doi.org/10.1038/npp.2010.123

Lamm, C., & Singer, T. (2010). The role of anterior insular cortex in social emotions. *Brain Structure and Function*, 214(5–6), 579–591. http://doi.org/10.1007/s00429-010-0251-3

Lang, P. J., Bradley, M. M., & Cuthbert, B. N. (1998). Emotion, motivation, and anxiety: Brain mechanisms and psychophysiology. *Biological Psychiatry*, 44(12), 1248–1263.

Lerner, J. S., Li, Y., Valdesolo, P., & Kassam, K. S. (2015). Emotion and decision making. *Annual Review of Psychology*, 66, 799–823. http://doi.org/10.1146/annurev-psych-010213-115043

Levy, D. J., & Glimcher, P. W. (2012). The root of all value: A neural common currency for choice. *Current Opinion in Neurobiology*, 22(6), 1027–1038. http://doi.org/10.1016/j.conb.2012.06.001

Lim, S.-L., O'Doherty, J. P., & Rangel, A. (2011). The decision value computations in the vmPFC and striatum use a relative value code that is guided by visual attention. *Journal of Neuroscience*, 31(37), 13214–13223. http://doi.org/10.1523/JNEUROSCI.1246-11.2011

Lim, S.-L., Padmala, S., & Pessoa, L. (2009). Segregating the significant from the mundane on a moment-to-moment basis via direct and indirect amygdala contributions. *Proceedings of the National Academy of Sciences*, 106(39), 16841–16846. http://doi.org/10.1073/pnas.0904551106

Loewenstein, G. F., Weber, E. U., Hsee, C. K., & Welch, N. (2001). Risk as feelings. *Psychological Bulletin, 127*(2), 267–286.

MacDonald, G., & Leary, M. R. (2005). Why does social exclusion hurt? The relationship between social and physical pain. *Psychological Bulletin, 131*(2), 202–223. http://doi.org/10.1037/0033-2909.131.2.202

Mallet, C., Daulhac, L., Bonnefont, J., Ledent, C., Etienne, M., Chapuy, E., . . . Eschalier A. (2008). Endocannabinoid and serotonergic systems are needed for acetaminophen-induced analgesia. *Pain, 139*(1), 190–200. http://doi.org/10.1016/j.pain.2008.03.030

Masten, C. L., Eisenberger, N. I., Borofsky, L. A., Pfeifer, J. H., McNealy, K., Mazziotta, J. C., & Dapretto, M. (2009). Neural correlates of social exclusion during adolescence: Understanding the distress of peer rejection. *Social Cognitive and Affective Neuroscience, 4*(2), 143–157. http://doi.org/10.1093/scan/nsp007

Masten, C. L., Telzer, E. H., Fuligni, A. J., Lieberman, M. D., & Eisenberger, N. I. (2012). Time spent with friends in adolescence relates to less neural sensitivity to later peer rejection. *Social Cognitive and Affective Neuroscience, 7*(1), 106–114. http://doi.org/10.1093/scan/nsq098

McClure, S. M., York, M. K., & Montague, P. R. (2004). The neural substrates of reward processing in humans: The modern role of fMRI. *The Neuroscientist, 10*(3), 260–268. http://doi.org/10.1177/1073858404263526

Meshi, D. (2013). Nucleus accumbens response to gains in reputation for the self relative to gains for others predicts social media use. *Frontiers in Human Neuroscience, 7*, 439. http://doi.org/10.3389/fnhum.2013.00439/abstract

Meyer-Lindenberg, A., Domes, G., Kirsch, P., & Heinrichs, M. (2011). Oxytocin and vasopressin in the human brain: Social neuropeptides for translational medicine. *Nature Reviews Neuroscience, 12*, 524–538. http://doi.org/10.1038/nrn3044

Mikolajczak, M., Gross, J. J., Lane, A., Corneille, O., de Timary, P., & Luminet, O. (2010). Oxytocin makes people trusting, not gullible. *Psychological Science, 21*(8), 1072–1074. http://doi.org/10.1177/0956797610377343

Montague, P. R., & Berns, G. S. (2002). Neural economics and the biological substrates of valuation. *Neuron, 36*(2), 265–284.

Moor, B. G., van Leijenhorst, L., Rombouts, S. A. R. B., Crone, E. A., & Van der Molen, M. W. (2010). Do you like me? Neural correlates of social evaluation and developmental trajectories. *Social Neuroscience, 5*(5–6), 461–482. http://doi.org/10.1080/17470910903526155

Morelli, S. A., Torre, J. B., & Eisenberger, N. I. (2014). The neural bases of feeling understood and not understood. *Social Cognitive and Affective Neuroscience, 9*(12), 1890–1896. http://doi.org/10.1093/scan/nst191

Nisbett, R. E., & Wilson, T. D. (1977). Telling more than we can know: Verbal reports on mental processes. *Psychological Review, 84*(3), 231–259. http://doi.org/10.1037/0033-295X.84.3.231

Nitschke, J. B., Sarinopoulos, I., Mackiewicz, K. L., Schaefer, H. S., & Davidson, R. J. (2006). Functional neuroanatomy of aversion and its anticipation. *NeuroImage, 29*(1), 106–116. http://doi.org/10.1016/j.neuroimage.2005.06.068

Niv, Y., Edlund, J. A., Dayan, P., & O'Doherty, J. P. (2012). Neural prediction errors reveal a risk-sensitive reinforcement-learning process in the human brain. *Journal of Neuroscience, 32*(2), 551–562. http://doi.org/10.1523/JNEUROSCI.5498-10.2012

O'Doherty, J., Kringelbach, M. L., Rolls, E. T., Hornak, J., & Andrews, C. (2001a). Abstract reward and punishment representations in the human orbitofrontal cortex. *Nature Neuroscience, 4*(1), 95–102. http://doi.org/10.1038/82959

O'Doherty, J., Rolls, E. T., Francis, S., Bowtell, R., & McGlone, F. (2001b). Representation of pleasant and aversive taste in the human brain. *Journal of Neurophysiology, 85*(3), 1315–1321.

Onoda, K., Okamoto, Y., Nakashima, K., Nittono, H., Yoshimura, S., Yamawaki, S., . . . Ura, M. (2010). Does low self-esteem enhance social pain? The relationship between trait self-esteem and anterior cingulate cortex activation induced by ostracism. *Social Cognitive and Affective Neuroscience, 5*(4), 385–391. http://doi.org/10.1093/scan/nsq002

Patel, S., & Hillard, C. J. (2006). Pharmacological evaluation of cannabinoid receptor ligands in a mouse model of anxiety: Further evidence for an anxiolytic role for endogenous cannabinoid signaling. *Journal of Pharmacology and Experimental Therapeutics, 318*(1), 304–311. http://doi.org/10.1124/jpet.106.101287

Paulus, M. P., & Stein, M. B. (2006). An insular view of anxiety. *Biological Psychiatry, 60*(4), 383–387. http://doi.org/10.1016/j.biopsych.2006.03.042

Pessoa, L. (2008). On the relationship between emotion and cognition. *Nature Reviews Neuroscience, 9*(2), 148–158. http://doi.org/10.1038/nrn2317

Phan, K. L., Angstadt, M., Golden, J., Onyewuenyi, I., Popovska, A., & de Wit, H. (2008). Cannabinoid modulation of amygdala reactivity to social signals of threat in humans. *Journal of Neuroscience, 28*(10), 2313–2319. http://doi.org/10.1523/JNEUROSCI.5603-07.2008

Phelps, E. A. (2006). Emotion and cognition: Insights from studies of the human amygdala. *Annual Review of Psychology, 57*(1), 27–53. http://doi.org/10.1146/annurev.psych.56.091103.070234

Phelps, E. A., & LeDoux, J. E. (2005). Contributions of the amygdala to emotion processing: From animal models to human behavior. *Neuron, 48*(2), 175–187. http://doi.org/10.1016/j.neuron.2005.09.025

Phelps, E. A., Lempert, K. M., & Sokol-Hessner, P. (2014). Emotion and decision making: Multiple modulatory neural circuits. *Annual Review of Neuroscience, 37*(1), 263–287. http://doi.org/10.1146/annurev-neuro-071013-014119

Pillutla, M. M., & Murnighan, J. K. (1996). Unfairness, anger, and spite: Emotional rejections of ultimatum offers. *Organizational Behavior and Human Decision Processes, 68*(3), 208–224. http://doi.org/10.1006/obhd.1996.0100

Poldrack, R. A. (2006). Can cognitive processes be inferred from neuroimaging data? *Trends in Cognitive Sciences, 10*(2), 59–63. http://doi.org/10.1016/j.tics.2005.12.004

Poldrack, R. A. (2011). Inferring mental states from neuroimaging data: From reverse inference to large-scale decoding. *Neuron, 72*(5), 692–697. http://doi.org/10.1016/j.neuron.2011.11.001

Powers, K. E., Somerville, L. H., Kelley, W. M., & Heatherton, T. F. (2013). Rejection sensitivity polarizes striatal–medial prefrontal activity when anticipating social feedback. *Journal of Cognitive Neuroscience, 25*(11), 1887–1895. http://doi.org/10.1162/jocn_a_00446

Price, D. D. (2000). Psychological and neural mechanisms of the affective dimension of pain. *Science, 288*(5472), 1769–1772. http://doi.org/10.1126/science.288.5472.1769

Pull, C. B. (2012). Current status of knowledge on public-speaking anxiety. *Current Opinion in Psychiatry, 25*(1), 32–38. http://doi.org/10.1097/YCO.0b013e32834e06dc

Rademacher, L., Salama, A., Gründer, G., & Spreckelmeyer, K. N. (2013). Differential patterns of nucleus accumbens activation during anticipation of monetary and social reward in young and older adults. *Social Cognitive and Affective Neuroscience, 9*(6), 825–831. http://doi.org/10.1093/scan/nst047

Rainville, P., Duncan, G. H., Price, D. D., Carrier, B., & Bushnell, M. C. (1997). Pain affect encoded in human anterior cingulate but not somatosensory cortex. *Science*, *277*(5328), 968–971.

Rangel, A. (2010). Visual fixations and the computation and comparison of value in simple choice. *Nature Neuroscience*, *13*(10), 1292–1298. http://doi.org/10.1038/nn.2635

Rangel, A., Camerer, C., & Montague, P. R. (2008). A framework for studying the neurobiology of value-based decision making. *Nature Reviews Neuroscience*, *9*(7), 545–556. http://doi.org/10.1038/nrn2357

Rangel, A., & Hare, T. (2010). Neural computations associated with goal-directed choice. *Current Opinion in Neurobiology*, *20*(2), 262–270. http://doi.org/10.1016/j.conb.2010.03.001

Rilling, J. K., Goldsmith, D. R., Glenn, A. L., Jairam, M. R., Elfenbein, H. A., Dagenais, J. E., ... Panoni, G. (2008). The neural correlates of the affective response to unreciprocated cooperation. *Neuropsychologia*, *46*(5), 1256–1266. http://doi.org/10.1016/j.neuropsychologia.2007.11.033

Rilling, J. K., & Sanfey, A. G. (2011). The neuroscience of social decision-making. *Annual Review of Psychology*, *62*(1), 23–48. http://doi.org/10.1146/annurev.psych.121208.131647

Riva, P., Wirth, J. H., & Williams, K. D. (2011). The consequences of pain: The social and physical pain overlap on psychological responses. *European Journal of Social Psychology*, *41*(6), 681–687. http://doi.org/10.1002/ejsp.837

Sanfey, A. G. (2007). Social decision-making: Insights from game theory and neuroscience. *Science*, *318*(5850), 598–602. http://doi.org/10.1126/science.1142996

Sanfey, A. G., Rilling, J. K., Aronson, J. A., Nystrom, L. E., & Cohen, J. D. (2003). The neural basis of economic decision-making in the ultimatum game. *Science*, *300*(5626), 1755–1758. http://doi.org/10.1126/science.1082976

Saxe, R. (2006). Uniquely human social cognition. *Current Opinion in Neurobiology*, *16*(2), 235–239. http://doi.org/10.1016/j.conb.2006.03.001

Schneirla, T. C. (1959). An evolutionary and developmental theory of biphasic processes underlying approach and withdrawal. In M. R. Jones (Ed.), *Nebraska symposium on motivation* (pp. 1–42). Lincoln: University of Nebraska Press,

Schonberg, T., Daw, N. D., Joel, D., & O'Doherty, J. P. (2007). Reinforcement learning signals in the human striatum distinguish learners from nonlearners during reward-based decision making. *Journal of Neuroscience*, *27*(47), 12860–12867. http://doi.org/10.1523/JNEUROSCI.2496-07.2007

Schultz, W. (2002). Getting formal with dopamine and reward. *Neuron*, *36*(2), 241–263.

Shackman, A. J., Salomons, T. V., Slagter, H. A., Fox, A. S., Winter, J. J., & Davidson, R. J. (2011). The integration of negative affect, pain and cognitive control in the cingulate cortex. *Nature Reviews Neuroscience*, *12*(3), 154–167. http://doi.org/10.1038/nrn2994

Shi, C. J., & Cassell, M. D. (1998). Cortical, thalamic, and amygdaloid connections of the anterior and posterior insular cortices. *Journal of Comparative Neurology*, *399*(4), 440–468. http://doi.org/10.1002/(SICI)1096-9861(19981005)399:4<440::AID-CNE2>3.0.CO;2-1

Skuse, D. H., & Gallagher, L. (2009). Dopaminergic-neuropeptide interactions in the social brain. *Trends in Cognitive Sciences*, *13*(1), 27–35. http://doi.org/10.1016/j.tics.2008.09.007

Small, D. M., Zatorre, R. J., Dagher, A., Evans, A. C., & Jones-Gotman, M. (2001). Changes in brain activity related to eating chocolate: From pleasure to aversion. *Brain*, *124*(Pt. 9), 1720–1733.

Somerville, L. H., Heatherton, T. F., & Kelley, W. M. (2006). Anterior cingulate cortex responds differentially to expectancy violation and social rejection. *Nature Neuroscience*, *9*(8), 1007–1008. http://doi.org/10.1038/nn1728

Spreckelmeyer, K. N., Krach, S., Kohls, G., Rademacher, L., Irmak, A., Konrad, K., . . . Gründer, G. (2009). Anticipation of monetary and social reward differently activates mesolimbic brain structures in men and women. *Social Cognitive and Affective Neuroscience*, *4*(2), 158–165. http://doi.org/10.1093/scan/nsn051

Strombach, T., Weber, B., Hangebrauk, Z., Kenning, P., Karipidis, I. I., Tobler, P. N., & Kalenscher, T. (2015). Social discounting involves modulation of neural value signals by temporoparietal junction. *Proceedings of the National Academy of Sciences*, *112*(5), 1619–1624. http://doi.org/10.1073/pnas.1414715112

Tabibnia, G., Satpute, A. B., & Lieberman, M. D. (2008). The sunny side of fairness: Preference for fairness activates reward circuitry (and disregarding unfairness activates self-control circuitry). *Psychological Science*, *19*(4), 339–347. http://doi.org/10.1111/j.1467-9280.2008.02091.x

Treede, R. D., Kenshalo, D. R., Gracely, R. H., & Jones, A. K. (1999). The cortical representation of pain. *Pain*, *79*(2–3), 105–111. http://doi.org/10.1016/S0304-3959(98)00184-5

van't Wout, M., Kahn, R. S., Sanfey, A. G., & Aleman, A. (2006). Affective state and decision-making in the ultimatum game. *Experimental Brain Research*, *169*(4), 564–568. http://doi.org/10.1007/s00221-006-0346-5

Vuilleumier, P., Richardson, M. P., Armony, J. L., Driver, J., & Dolan, R. J. (2004). Distant influences of amygdala lesion on visual cortical activation during emotional face processing. *Nature Neuroscience*, *7*(11), 1271–1278. http://doi.org/10.1038/nn1341

Wager, T. D., Phan, K. L., Liberzon, I., & Taylor, S. F. (2003). Valence, gender, and lateralization of functional brain anatomy in emotion: A meta-analysis of findings from neuroimaging. *NeuroImage*, *19*(3), 513–531.

Wiech, K., Lin, C. S., Brodersen, K. H., Bingel, U., Ploner, M., & Tracey, I. (2010). Anterior insula integrates information about salience into perceptual decisions about pain. *Journal of Neuroscience*, *30*(48), 16324–16331. http://doi.org/10.1523/JNEUROSCI.2087-10.2010

Williams, K. D., & Jarvis, B. (2006). Cyberball: A program for use in research on interpersonal ostracism and acceptance. *Behavior Research Methods*, *38*(1), 174–180. http://doi.org/10.3758/BF03192765

Xiao, E., & Houser, D. (2005). Emotion expression in human punishment behavior. *Proceedings of the National Academy of Sciences*, *102*(20), 7398–7401. http://doi.org/10.1073/pnas.0502399102

Yarkoni, T., Poldrack, R. A., Nichols, T. E., Van Essen, D. C., & Wager, T. D. (2011). Large-scale automated synthesis of human functional neuroimaging data. *Nature Methods*, *8*(8), 665–670. http://doi.org/10.1038/nmeth.1635

Zak, P. J., & Knack, S. (2001). Trust and growth. *The Economic Journal*, *111*(470), 295–321. http://doi.org/10.1111/1468-0297.00609

4 Neuroendrocrine Pathways to In-Group Bounded Trust and Cooperation

■ CARSTEN K. W. DE DREU
AND MICHAEL GIFFIN

■ INTRODUCTION

People have a lot of trust, and they have to trust a lot. When investing money in a savings account, we have to trust employees on the receiving end to return the money with interest when we need it. When donating to charity, we trust those institutions to put it to the benefit of the charitable cause we so carefully selected. When getting into a cab, we have to trust the driver to take us to our destination quickly and safely. In all these cases, and many others, we put our fate in the hands of others, and we do so without much thought. In fact, once we start thinking carefully and recall those situations in which banks went bankrupt, charity organizations paid their CEOs excessive salaries, or cab drivers deceived passengers, we lose faith and stop acting, and our lives may come to a grinding halt. Trust, it seems, oils our lives and often comes rather automatically. It enables us to negotiate mutually beneficial deals, to benefit others at relatively low cost, and to connect with others and create social bonds that may persist throughout our entire lives. Trust, it seems, is the *sine qua non* of social functioning.

To trust others means that we have a positive expectation that these others will cooperate and not exploit us (Pruitt & Kimmel, 1977). Sometimes, assessments of others' trustworthiness may be based on careful assessments of the risks involved and the possible benefits that outweigh the potential losses (Bohnet & Zeckhauser, 2004; Boon & Holmes, 1991; Houser, Schunk, & Winter, 2010; Lewicki & Bunker, 1995). Oftentimes, however, trust is affect-based (Rousseau, 1989) and derives from a heuristic interpretation of the relationship between trustor and trustee, a relationship that is appraised based on the motivational orientation and the physical and symbolic features of each interaction partner. This affect-based trust arises relatively fast and is grounded in quick and heuristic assessments of other's trustworthiness—rather than knowing whether someone can be trusted, we have some gut feeling that our savings are in good hands, that the charity organization is trustworthy, or that the cab driver knows what he is doing. Indeed, we extend and reciprocate trust when we have prosocial goals and cooperative motivation (De Dreu, Giebels, & Van de Vliert, 1998; De Dreu & Van Lange, 1995), and we see our partner as belonging to a group stereotyped as benign and high in morality, rather than cool-headed and profit-oriented (De Dreu, Yzerbyt, & Leyens, 1995). We make such decision fast and on the basis of quick first impressions (Fetchenhauer & Dunning, 2010; O'Brien, Tumminelli, & Wilson, 2011), relying on self–other similarity (Keltner et al., 2014), and physical features of our interaction partner's facial width (Stirrat & Perrett, 2010), emotion expressions (Van Kleef, De Dreu, & Manstead, 2010), and preinteraction mimicry (Kret, Fischer, & De Dreu, 2015; Swaab, Maddux, & Sinaceur, 2011).

Here we seek to understand the neurobiological underpinnings of such affect-based trust and the fast and intuitive decisions to cooperate with others. Point of departure is evolutionary theory and empirical evidence showing that affect-based trust and cooperation is stronger when interaction partners belong to, or can be reasonably assumed to be part of, one's in-group compared to when they are unfamiliar strangers or members of a rivaling out-group (Balliet, Wu, & De Dreu, 2014; De Dreu et al., 2010, 2011; De Dreu, Balliet, & Halevy, 2014; Rand & Nowak, 2013). This evolutionary thinking implies that humans may have evolved biological preparedness for such in-group bounded trust and cooperation, a possibility that we examine in terms of recent work on two core neurohormones—oxytocin and testosterone. Specifically, we review a selected set of recent research papers suggesting, indeed, that in-group bounded trust and cooperation rests on, and is modulated by, oxytocin and testosterone. Our main conclusion is that oxytocin and testosterone both promote in-group bounded trust and cooperation, yet for very different reasons. Oxytocin facilitates trust and cooperation because it shifts the individual's focus from self-interest to group interests; testosterone facilitates trust and cooperation when and because these tendencies benefit social status and reputation.

▪ BIOLOGICALLY PREPARED FOR IN-GROUP BOUNDED TRUST AND COOPERATION

Humans are group-living, social animals that create cohesive groups and, more than any other species, engage in complex forms of cooperative exchange with unfamiliar and genetically unrelated others (Nowak, Tarnita, & Wilson, 2010). Possibly, humans evolved into such social animals because creating and promoting group life increases individual survival and prosperity probabilities well beyond what individuals could achieve in isolation. It is because humans work hard, contribute accurate information and solid insights to the group, adequately process others' contributions, and stick to agreed-upon rules and regulations that the group avoids disaster, reaches high-quality decisions, and prospers (De Dreu, Balliet, & Halevy, 2014). And being part of such strong, well-functioning, and innovative groups provides fitness functionality to individual members, who thus are more likely to survive, prosper, and reproduce than individuals living in groups where most members lack such cooperative inclinations. In short, individuals in cooperative groups function relatively well, and herein lies a strong motivation for individuals, and their offspring, to contribute to their group and to cooperate with its members (Bowles & Gintis, 2011; Darwin, 1873).

Because of the importance of groups, both in ancestral and contemporary times, humans may have evolved a "group psychology" that includes a propensity to (a) identify with a group and its members; (b) empathize with the needs and interests of fellow group members; (c) self-sacrifice, trust, and cooperate with other group members; and (d) loyally commit and contribute to the functioning of one's group (De Dreu et al., 2014; De Dreu & Kret, 2015). Indeed, infants selectively imitate in-group members over out-group members (Buttelmann, Zmyj, Daum, & Carpenter, 2013) and use self-other similarity as the basis of social categorization and discrimination (Hamlin, Mahajan, Liberman, & Wynn, 2013). Adult humans quickly and automatically assign self and others to social categories (Amodio, 2008; Van Bavel, Packer, & Cunningham, 2011), ground their self-concept in part in their group membership (Turner, Oakes, Haslam, & McGarty, 1994), experience greater empathy for in-group members in need (Hein, Silani, Preuschoff, Batson, & Singer, 2010), and are more likely to cooperate with in-group members than with unfamiliar strangers or members of rivaling out-groups (Balliet, Wu, & De Dreu, 2014). Additionally, these cognitive and motivational processes that result in behavioral discrimination in favor of in-groups appear in cultures around the world (Hruschka & Henrich, 2013; Levine & Campbell, 1972) and recruit the evolutionarily ancient, subcortical circuitry involved in reward processing (Rilling & Sanfey, 2011).

In determining whether or not to trust others, group membership may be a critical cue that can be quickly and effortlessly applied. Those who are familiar, similar to oneself, and with whom we share a common fate are heuristically trusted; those who are unfamiliar and different from oneself cannot be trusted instantly, and decisions to trust and cooperate will require deep thinking and close scrutiny (Mussweiler & Ockenfels, 2013). In addition to reducing cognitive effort during decision-making (Tversky & Kahneman, 1973), such in-group bounded, heuristic trust is functional because trusting in-group members contributes to one's reputation as a reliable, cooperative group member who can be included rather than excluded from potentially beneficial exchanges on future occasions. On the other hand, not automatically extending trust to unfamiliar others, members from rivaling out-groups in particular, adds to one's reputation as being a good patriot that may be ready to help the in-group, be vigilant, and protect against out-group competition (Balliet et al., 2014; Halevy, Weisel, et al., 2012; Yamagishi, Jin, & Kiyonari, 1999; Yamagishi & Mifune, 2009). Second, by heuristically extending trust to in-group members—but not to out-group members—individuals contribute to group efficiency, from which they indirectly reap the benefits, and by making themselves deliberately vulnerable to exploitation and abuse, individuals who display (in-group) trust communicate self-confidence that adds rather than reduces social standing and status. And indeed, displays of in-group trust are rewarded while displays of out-group trust are frowned upon; displays of in-group betrayal are punished, while displays of out-group betrayal are sometimes rewarded (e.g., Halevy, Chou, et al., 2012; also see Boyd & Richerson, 1982). Finally, displays of in-group bounded trust may add to the self-perception that one is a valuable member of a valuable group and thus helps to develop, maintain, and boost a positive social identity (Ellemers & Haslam, 2012; Turner et al., 1994).

These findings suggest that affect-based, in-group bounded trust serves at least two critical functions. It promotes group functioning, and it helps to build and maintain a positive reputation and standing within the group. Because alone and in interaction these two consequences contribute to individual fitness, they may rest on evolved and tractable neurobiological mechanisms. Importantly, such neurobiological mechanisms should modulate in-group bounded trust and cooperation but not (at least to the same extent) affect trust in and cooperation with unfamiliar strangers and out-group members. Such neurobiological mechanisms may involve genetic predispositions (e.g., Ebstein, Israel, Chew, Zhong, & Knafo, 2010), specific brain circuitries (e.g., Aimone, Houser, & Weber, 2014; Delgado, Frank, & Phelps, 2005; McCabe, Houser, Ryan, Smith, & Trouard, 2001; also see Engelmann & Fehr, this volume), and neurohormonal modulators.

Here we examine in-depth the possibility that in-group bounded trust and cooperation is modulated by neurohormonal mechanisms. Neurohormones are the chemicals that oil, fuel, and ignite the brain and body. Neurohormones are secreted into the blood stream for systemic effect (e.g., to regulate stress, sleep, food intake and digestion, lactation, muscle development), but each of these also excites or inhibits specific brain circuitries. Two neurohormones have been studied extensively in relation to trust and cooperation and are the focus of the current review. Our review is, however, deliberatively selective. First, we focus on experimentally manipulated levels of oxytocin and testosterone, although some reference will be made to studies measuring endogenous oxytocin and testosterone from saliva or blood. Second, we focus on those studies that cast trust and cooperation in the context of intergroup comparison and competition, to examine the key hypothesis from evolutionary theory that humans evolved a biological preparedness for in-group bounded trust and cooperation (as opposed to generic, "universal," trust and cooperation).

■ OXYTOCIN PROMOTES IN-GROUP BOUNDED TRUST AND COOPERATION

Oxytocin is a nine-amino acid peptide produced and synthesized primarily in the paraventricular and supraoptic nuclei of the hypothalamus and the posterior pituitary glands (Carter, 2014; Donaldson & Young, 2008). Upon its release from neuronal soma, axons, and dendrites, oxytocin acts as a neuromodulator—it flows through neural tissue by a process termed volume transmission, which allows the oxytocin molecule to quickly modulate social emotional functions of the amygdala and brain stem (Carter, 2014). Thus oxytocin attenuates stress responses at both the bodily and neural level (Bos, Panksepp, Bluthé, & Honk, 2012; Carter, 2014; Neumann, 2008). Specifically, oxytocin in humans reduces cortisol levels after exposure to stressors (Cardoso, Kingdon, & Ellenbogen, 2014), and it inhibits cardiovascular stress responses (Uvnäs-Moberg, 1998).

In addition to its anxiolytic effects, oxytocin modulates neural circuitries involved in reward processing and empathic responding (e.g., Donaldson & Young, 2008). According to the social salience hypothesis (Shamay-Tsoory et al., 2009), oxytocin strengthens general tendencies in social-cognitive processing. What is usually considered positive and interesting becomes more positive and interesting under oxytocin, and what is commonly considered negative and aversive becomes more negative and aversive under oxytocin. Thus, when given oxytocin (versus matching placebo) and asked to recall memories of maternal care and closeness, securely attached males recalled more positive events, while anxiously attached males recalled more negative experiences (Bartz et al., 2010). Also, following an interpersonal competition, oxytocin enhanced feelings of envy when the competition was lost and feelings of schadenfreude (gloating) when the competition was won (Shamay-Tsoory et al., 2009).

Possibly through the combination of fear-dampening and increased social salience, oxytocin (a) acts on the "wanting" mesocorticolimbic circuitry promoting (affiliative) approach, especially when (social) targets or events have positive valence, and (b) acts on the cortico-amygdala circuitry to reduce fear and tendencies to withdraw and move away from (social) threat, thus permitting alternative responses to danger and threat than flight (De Dreu, 2012; De Dreu & Kret, 2015; De Dreu et al., 2014; Kemp & Guastella, 2011; Striepens et al., 2012). Such biased biobehavioral approach-avoidance resonates with a wealth of research showing that, first, oxytocin promotes the social bonds between sexual partners (Holt-Lunstad et al., 2008; Rilling & Young, 2014) and enables positive parent–offspring interactions such as play and caring (Gordon, Zagoory-Sharon, Leckman, & Feldman, 2010). Second, the biased biobehavioral approach-avoidance hypothesis fits evidence showing that oxytocin potentiates startle reactivity to threat stimuli, especially when these are unpredictable (Striepens et al., 2012; Eckstein et al., 2014). This hypothesis also fits the growing evidence that oxytocin prepares for and enables aggressive responding to threat, especially threat to offspring (so-called maternal defense; Bosch, Meddle, Beiderbeck, Douglas, & Neumann, 2005; Hahn-Holbrook et al., 2011).

How such oxytocin-induced biased biobehavioral approach may impact trust and cooperation was revealed in a recent study examining effects of oxytocin on competitive tendencies motivated either by selfish greed or by fear of exploitation (De Dreu, Scholte, Van Winden, & Ridderinkhof, 2014). Both greed and fear block trust and cooperation, and both must be reduced to enable people to extend trust and engage in cooperative exchange (Pruitt & Kimmel, 1977; Van Lange, Liebrand, & Kuhlman, 1990). The experiment disentangled greed and fear as motives underlying competitiveness by using a newly developed, two-player predator–prey game (PPG). The PPG is grounded in the economic theory of predation and economic growth (Carter & Anderton, 2001; Grossman & Kim, 2002) and models the conflict between survival and preservation of the status quo on the one hand and the drive toward appropriation and expansion on the other. In the PPG, one player (the predator) has to decide how much to invest in predation (X) out of a given endowment E (with $0 \leq X \leq E$), while the other player (the prey) simultaneously decides how much to invest in defense (Y) out of an equal endowment E (with $0 \leq Y \leq E$). If $X > Y$ then the predator obtains all of E − Y; added to the remaining endowment E − X, this leads to a total payoff for the predator of: 2E − X − Y, while the prey is left with zero. If $X \leq Y$ then the predator appropriates nothing, leading to a payoff of E − X for the predator and E − Y for the prey. The

PPG is formally equivalent to a contest with as contest success function $f = X^m/(X^m + Y^m)$, where f is the probability that the predator wins, $m \to \infty$ for $X \neq Y$, and $f = 0$ if $Y = X$ (De Dreu et al., 2014; Tullock, 1980). Thus, in the PPG, predator investments index the greedy desire to accumulate personal wealth by subordinating the prey (and lack of cooperative motivation). On the other hand, prey investments index fear of being exploited (and lack of trust) and concomitant defensive aggression (Camerer, 2003; Coombs, 1973).

In the experiment, healthy males were given oxytocin or a placebo and invested as predator to win their prey's endowment or as prey to protect their endowment against predation. Neural activity was registered using 3T-MRI. Human decision-making geared at the inconsiderate accumulation of wealth rests on brain circuitries involved in impulse control, such as the superior frontal gyrus (Fahrenfort, Van Winden, Pelloux, Stallen, & Ridderinkhof, 2012), whereas decisions concerning protection and defense are strongly amygdala-dependent (Baumgartner, Heinrichs, Vonlanthen, Fischbacher, & Fehr, 2008; Delgado, Schotter, Ozbay, & Phelps, 2008; Rilling et al., 2012). Accordingly, analyses of neural activation focused on the prefrontal cortex and on the amygdala. Results showed, indeed, that greed-driven investments in predators were relatively slow and conditioned by neural activation in the superior frontal gyrus; fear-driven investments in prey were relatively fast and conditioned by neural activation in the (right) amygdala. More important, however, oxytocin reduced greed-driven investments in predators but did not affect fear-driven investment in prey.

Results from De Dreu et al. (2014) suggest that oxytocin reduces greed, which resonates with studies showing that oxytocin may increase empathy and cooperation (for reviews, see, e.g., Carter, 2014; De Dreu, 2012). However, results also suggest that oxytocin did not reduce fear of exploitation, which resonates with studies that failed to find reliable correlations between endogenous oxytocin and cooperation in two-person prisoner's dilemma games (e.g., Christensen, Shiyanov, Estepp, & Schlager, 2014; Conlisk, 2011; but see Zak, Kurzban, & Matzner, 2005) as well as studies that found that at both *low* and *high* levels of oxytocin, trust was lower than at intermediate levels (Zhong et al., 2012). It resonates too with pioneering work by Kosfeld and colleagues (2005) and Baumgartner and colleagues (2008) who, across the board, found weak to nonexistent effects of oxytocin on investment behavior in interpersonal trust game decisions. In fact, Mikolajczak and colleagues (2010) showed that "investors" given oxytocin rather than placebo transferred more money to "trustees," who were described prosocial people (e.g., studying philosophy, practicing first aid) but less money to trustees described in less prosocial terms (e.g., studying marketing, practicing violent combat sports). Likewise, Declerck, Boone, and Kiyonari (2010) studied cooperation in an assurance game where the only reason not to cooperate is distrust and found that individuals given oxytocin expected more cooperation and cooperated more but only when they had familiarized themselves with their protagonist. Absent such positive prior interaction, oxytocin actually led to *less* cooperation than placebo.

From In-Group Bounded Cooperation to Aggression Against Out-Groups

Several studies suggest that oxytocin-induced trust and cooperation is not only in-group bounded but may also produce intergroup discrimination. Ten Velden and colleagues (2014) designed an incentivized two-player poker game with either an in-group or out-group protagonist. Seventy-two healthy males received 24IU oxytocin or matching placebo and played four rounds of poker with another individual from either their in-group or a rivaling out-group. Compared to placebo, participants under oxytocin settled more and competed less with an in-group compared to out-group protagonist. These results suggest that oxytocin sensitizes humans to the group membership of their interaction partner, rendering them relatively more benevolent and less competitive toward those seen as in-group.

Other studies reported similar effects, showing that oxytocin increases liking for in-group members relative to out-group members (De Dreu et al., 2011; also see Ma et al., 2014) and rendered people relatively more empathic to in-group rather than out-group members (Luo et al., 2015; Sheng, Liu, Zhou, Zhou, & Han, 2013). In one series of experiments, De Dreu and colleagues gave healthy males intranasal oxytocin or placebo, assigned them to one of two groups, and asked them to make decisions in an intergroup prisoner's dilemma-maximizing differences game (Halevy, Bornstein, & Sagiv, 2008). Each individual received €10 and was allowed to keep it, to invest it in a within-group pool benefitting other in-group members, or in a between-group pool benefitting other in-group members while simultaneously punishing out-group members. Within-group pool investments reflect (personally costly) in-group love, whereas between-group pool investments reflect (personally costly) out-group hate that is symbolic and, if anything, reflective of offensive aggression. Results showed that (a) individuals who received oxytocin rather than placebo were less selfish; (b) in-group love was stronger than out-group hate, especially among individuals given oxytocin; and (c) in-group love but not out-group hate was influenced by oxytocin (also see Israel, Bornstein, Epstein, & Weisel, 2012).

That oxytocin motivates in-group liking and cooperation but not out-group hate may appear inconsistent with animal literatures showing that oxytocin prepares for and enables aggressive responding to threat, especially threat to offspring (so-called maternal defense; Bosch et al., 2005; Hahn-Holbrook et al., 2011). However, out-group hate in the aforementioned works reflect attitudinal preferences rather than behavioral expressions, and out-group hate can be offensive (aimed at subordinating out-groups) or defensive (aimed at protecting oneself and others against out-group threat). Thus, these works suggest that oxytocin neither strengthens nor reduces offensive out-group hate (De Dreu et al., 2010, 2011). There is evidence, however, that oxytocin can increase defensive aggression aimed at protection. In De Dreu et al. (2010, exp. 3; De Dreu et al., 2012), individuals represented their in-group in a competitive interaction with an out-group representative who either had strong or weak power to exploit the in-group (thus creating differential fear for exploitation in the in-group and a need for defensive aggression) or was easy or difficult to exploit (thus creating differential desire in the in-group for greed and offensive aggression; Bornstein, 2003; Coombs, 1973). Oxytocin promoted defensive aggression when out-groups had high (versus low) power to exploit the in-group. These findings resonate with the literature on oxytocin and maternal defense, as well as with studies showing that wild meerkats infused with oxytocin (versus placebo) not only more strongly engage in cooperative behaviors, including digging, food sharing, and attending to offspring, but also spend longer time-on-guard, a particularly risky and personally costly but group-serving behavior (Madden & Clutton-Brock, 2011; also see Shalvi & De Dreu, 2014).

Taken together, accumulating evidence indicates that (a) oxytocin has a non-substantial effect on indiscriminate trust and cooperation; (b) oxytocin-induced trust and cooperation appears strongly contingent upon target characteristics, such as cues signaling benevolence rather than untrustworthiness, familiarity, and, most important, in-group membership so that (c) oxytocin promotes trust and cooperation with individuals belonging to one's in-group and not with individuals belonging to rivaling out-groups, and (d) oxytocin upregulates defense-motivated aggression against rivaling out-groups that threaten the in-group.

■ TESTOSTERONE PROMOTES IN-GROUP TRUST AND COOPERATION

Oxytocin's anxiolytic, fear-dampening effects discussed in the previous section emerge because oxytocin interacts with a key neuroendocrine pathway in the human brain—the hypothalamic–pituitary–adrenal (HPA) axis. The HPA axis consists of three levels, beginning with the paraventricular nucleus of the hypothalamus, which not only produces oxytocin but also the corticotropin-releasing hormone in response to stress. The corticotropin-releasing hormone, in turn, promotes the release of adrenocorticotropic hormone by the pituitary—the second level of the HPA axis. The adrenocorticotropic hormone then stimulates the adrenal cortex, which ultimately leads to the synthesis and release of glucocorticoids (corticosterone in rodents and cortisol in humans). Elevated cortisol in humans thus reflects the presence of either an exogenous stressor (e.g., a risky decision to be made; Michaud, Matheson, Kelly, & Anisman, 2008) or an endogenous stressor (e.g., an internal infection; Zeisberger, Roth, & Kluger, 1994) and enables the individual to cope (Engert et al., 2011). Oxytocin counteracts the production of cortisol and therefore has a downregulating effect on stress.

A second key neuroendocrine system in the human brain is the hypothalamic–pituitary–gonadal (HPG) axis Like the HPA-axis, the HPG axis also consists of three levels, the first two of which are the hypothalamus and the pituitary gland, where gonadotropin releasing hormone and luteinizing hormone together with follicle stimulating hormone are released. These two hormones are transported to the third level of the HPG axis, the gonads, where they are responsible for the production of testosterone, the end product of the HPG axis. And whereas the HPA axis is critical for the regulation of stress, the HPG axis, and testosterone in particular, is key to regulating challenge and dominance (Sapolsky, 1982). Indeed, whereas cortisol has been linked to anxiety disorders, risk aversion, and low social class status (Abbott et al., 2003; Cohen et al., 2006; Heim & Nemeroff, 2001; Putman, Antypa, Crysovergi, & Van Der Does, 2010; Segerstrom, & Miller, 2004), people with high basal testosterone tend to be more dominant and aggressive than individuals with low basal testosterone (Archer, 2006; Archer, Birring, & Wu, 1998; Book Starzyk, & Quinsey, 2001; Mazur & Booth, 1998).

Resonating with animal literatures on the role of testosterone in regulating social behavior, studies looking into trust and cooperation evolved around three complementary theoretical perspectives: the challenge hypothesis, the biosocial model, and the social status hypothesis (Mazur & Booth, 1998; Oliveira & Oliveira, 2014; Wingfield Hegner, Dufty, & Ball, 1990). The challenge hypothesis postulates that testosterone rises in response to threats, so as to facilitate competition and to enable the behaviors necessary for a rise in status (Archer, 2006; Wingfield et al., 1990). Similarly, the biosocial model postulates that testosterone rises to facilitate competition; however, this model further asserts that testosterone has a mutually reinforcing relationship with dominance. That is, dominant individuals have relatively high baseline testosterone, which facilitates status maintenance, and these levels rise in anticipation of competition and then rise in response to victory and fall in response to loss (Mazur & Booth, 1998; Oliveira & Oliveira, 2014; Trumble Smith, O'Connor, Kaplan, & Gurven, 2014). Finally, the social status hypothesis proposes that testosterone is unrelated to social aggression but, instead, relates to status-seeking behavior (Eisenegger Naef, Snozzi, Heinrichs, & Fehr, 2010). It builds off a study by Eisenegger and colleagues (2010) that showed that females given testosterone made fairer offers in an ultimatum bargaining game than those given a placebo. Along similar lines, Van Honk and colleagues (2012) showed that testosterone facilitated cooperation in public goods provision, especially among individuals with low levels of prenatal testosterone (as reflected in the right hand's second-to-fourth-digit ratio [2D:4D]). These findings fit the robust observation that higher testosterone associates with higher status across both animal and human groups (Anderson & Kilduff, 2009; Sapolsky, 2005).

The social status hypothesis is useful in explaining a seemingly inconsistent pattern of findings, namely that testosterone in humans sometimes associates with enhanced distrust and aggression (Mazur & Booth, 1998; Oliveira & Oliveira, 2014; Trumble et al., 2014) and sometimes with stronger tendencies to trust, empathize, and cooperate (e.g., Eisenegger et al., 2010; Van Honk et al., 2012). For example, Bos and colleagues (2010) showed that, compared to placebo, testosterone reduced interpersonal trust yet only among those individuals with a high propensity to trust easily. Accordingly, the authors conclude that testosterone adaptively increases social vigilance to prepare individuals to trust and reciprocate but only when such behavior enables them to maintain and improve social status. On the other hand, testosterone spurs individuals to aggress and dominate when doing so appears most conducive to maintaining and improving social status and within-group dominance. Boksem and colleagues (2013) indeed showed that testosterone, compared to placebo, decreased trust (i.e., investing in trust game) yet increased repaying trust (i.e., sharing revenues from the counterpart's investments). Again, it is concluded that testosterone may increase competitive and aggressive behavior when social challenges and threats need to be considered yet increase prosocial tendencies when these promote high status and a good reputation.

From In-Group Cooperation to Out-Group Oriented Aggression

Both status and reputation considerations matter primarily when individuals are interacting with members of their in-group. Indeed, as noted previously, trust and cooperation (a) have powerful effects on within-group status and reputation (Balliet et al., 2014; Halevy, Chou, et al., 2012) and (b) emerge more readily in interactions with in-group members (De Dreu et al., 2014; Rand & Nowak, 2013). A case in point is a recent study by Diekhof, Wittmer, and Reimers (2014) on testosterone and parochial altruism—cooperative behavior that benefits the in-group and/or hurts rivaling out-groups (Bowles & Gintis, 2011; De Dreu et al., 2014; Rand & Nowak, 2013). In this study 50 male soccer fans with a strong feeling of group coherence were recruited to respond to ultimatum game offers that were either fair or unfair and were proposed by members of their in-group or by fans of one of three other teams (two soccer teams and one cricket team). The ultimatum game was played twice, once with fans of all other teams under the instruction to maximize personal outcome and once under the instruction that cooperation with their fellow group members would maximize group reward and would result in extra points if they outperformed the other groups in the competition. Note that this requires a sacrifice of one's personal reward, since group success could only be achieved if subjects also minimized out-group reward (i.e., by rejecting offers from out-groups and accepting offers from in-groups, regardless of the offer's value to oneself).

Diekhof and colleagues (2014) found, as could be expected, that unfair offers were rejected more frequently than fair offers and that rejection increased with social distance to the outgroups (in-group < neutral out-group < unknown out-group < antagonist out-group). Importantly, endogenous testosterone was associated with lower rejection of in-group offers and with increased rejection of out-group offers especially in the context of explicit intergroup competition. Thus high endogenous testosterone predicts increased prosocial tendencies during interactions with the in-group as well as an escalation of costly out-group hostility in intergroup competition.

■ OXYTOCIN AND TESTOSTERONE: COUNTERACTING OR COMPLEMENTING?

To some extent, the adrenal (HPA) and gonadal (HPG) systems interact antagonistically (Montoya, Terburg, Bos, & Van Honk, 2012; Viau 2002), and, accordingly, oxytocin and testosterone have been argued and shown to operate antagonistically: Oxytocin release inhibits the production of testosterone, and high levels of testosterone limit effects of oxytocin (Bos et al., 2012; Kret & De Dreu, 2013). For example, in a study on prosocial approach tendencies, Kret and De Dreu observed that, compared to placebo, oxytocin increased tendencies to include people into one's group but only among individuals with low prenatal testosterone exposure (as measured by their 2D:4D ratios). Apparently, intranasal oxytocin impacts social behavior less among participants with chronically high testosterone exposure.

That oxytocin and testosterone interact antagonistically creates a puzzle when we also realize, considering the works reviewed earlier, that both oxytocin and testosterone can promote in-group trust and cooperation and drive aggressiveness against rivaling out-groups. Thus, while antagonistic at the neurophysiological level, these two neurohormonal pathways may have similar behavioral implications.

To appreciate this observation, it is important to consider the specific functions underlying trust, cooperation, and out-group aggression. By extending reciprocating trust, the individual contributes to smooth interpersonal relations, aids group efficiency, adheres to social norms, and builds a positive reputation. The same applies to cooperative behavior—by making costly contributions to the group, and by benefitting others at a cost to oneself, the individual both helps the group and his or her personal reputation as a committed and to-be-included group member others can rely on. We conjecture that oxytocin leads individuals to shift from self-interests to group interests and promotes the extension of trust and cooperation when this fits and promotes group goals. Testosterone, in contrast, associates with a drive to seek and expand social status within the group, which requires building and maintaining a solid and positive reputation. When extending trust and cooperating with others secures and promotes a positive reputation and one's social standing, testosterone will be associated with trust and cooperation. Put differently, oxytocin and testosterone both promote in-group bounded trust and cooperation, yet for very different reasons (group efficiency and reputation concerns, respectively).

With regard to out-group rivalry and aggression, a similar reasoning can be applied. As noted, aggressing rivaling out-groups can be motivated by a need to defend the in-group against out-group threat or by a desire to dominate the out-group and subordinate its members. Oxytocin clearly relates to defensive aggression (especially when out-group threat is high), a tendency that strongly resonates with an oxytocin-induced focus on in-group efficiency. Research is less unequivocal with regard to the function of testosterone but suggests that testosterone motivates out-group aggression of a more offensive, dominance-orientated nature. Such would fit the observation that individuals lashing out against out-groups, and subordinate out-groups, gain in-group status and reputation (e.g., Halevy, Chou, et al., 2012). Thus oxytocin and testosterone both promote out-group aggression yet for very different reasons (in-group defense and in-group reputation concerns, respectively).

Most work we relied on looked at oxytocin in males and at testosterone in females. Importantly, accumulated evidence suggests that effects on trust and cooperation for both oxytocin and testosterone are similar, albeit varying in strength, for both males and females. Nevertheless, oxytocin is more abundant in females, and testosterone is more prevalent in males. Although observed in males too (De Dreu et al., 2010, 2011, 2012), oxytocin's tend-and-defend functionality may be stronger in females. And although observed in females (Diekhof et al., 2014; Eisenegger et al., 2010), testosterone's status-seeking functionality may be stronger in males.

■ CONCLUSION

A strong and well-functioning group provides fitness functionality to its individual members, and herein lies a strong motivation for individuals, and their offspring, to contribute to their group, to cooperate with its members, and to aggressively defend the group against outside threat. We reviewed evidence for the possibility, implied by evolutionary theory, that humans may have a biological preparedness for in-group bounded trust and cooperation and that such biological preparedness co-opts core neuroendocrine pathways in sustaining trust and cooperation within groups and aggressive defense against outside threat, human enemies included. Studies linking (in-group bounded, parochial) trust and cooperation to oxytocin suggests that oxytocin promotes trust in, and cooperation toward, in-group members more than toward individuals considered unfamiliar or out-group; oxytocin also enables aggressive defense toward rivaling out-groups especially when these threaten the in-group. Testosterone, in contrast, associates with social status seeking, which in intergroup competitions may manifest itself in within-group cooperation and between-group offensive aggression. Together, these works suggest that oxytocin is co-opted to enable and motivate individuals to fit into their groups and contribute to group efficiency, including defense against out-group threat, whereas testosterone is co-opted to enable and motivate individuals to achieve status within their groups and to lead to aggression aimed at dominating rivaling out-groups.

We started with the observation that we trust a lot, and often do so rather automatically and without much thought. We noted that much of this affect-based trust is limited to those we are familiar with and with whom we share some common fate, and that such tendency may have had strong functionality throughout human evolution. Our review of the accumulating literatures on oxytocin and testosterone suggest that affect-based trust and cooperation may have strong neurobiological underpinnings that set us up to trust and cooperate to enable groups to function and to secure our individual role and position within such well-functioning groups.

■ REFERENCES

Abbott, D. H., Keverne, E. B., Bercovitch, F. B., Shively, C. A., Mendoza, S. P., Saltzman, W., . . . Sapolsky, R. M. (2003). Are subordinates always stressed? A comparative analysis of rank differences in cortisol levels among primates. *Hormones and Behavior, 43*, 67–82.

Aimone, J. A., Houser, D., & Weber, B. (2014). Neural signatures of betrayal aversion: an fMRI study of trust. *Proceedings of the Royal Society B: Biological Sciences, 281*, 2113–2127.

Amodio, D. (2008). The social neuroscience of intergroup relations. *European Review of Social Psychology, 19*, 1–54.

Anderson, C., & Kilduff, G. J. (2009). Why do dominant personalities attain influence in face-to-face groups? The competence-signaling effects of trait dominance. *Journal of Personality and Social Psychology, 96*, 491–503.

Archer, J. (2006). Testosterone and human aggression: An evaluation of the challenge hypothesis. *Neuroscience and Biobehavioral Reviews, 30*, 319–345.

Archer, J., Birring, S. S., & Wu, F. C. W. (1998). The association between testosterone and aggression in young men: Empirical findings and a meta-analysis. *Aggressive Behavior, 24*, 411–420.

Balliet, D., Wu, J., & De Dreu, C. K. W. (2014). Ingroup favoritism in cooperation: A meta-analysis. *Psychological Bulletin, 140*, 1556–1581.

Bartz, J. A., Zaki, J., Bolger, N., Hollander, E., Ludwig, N. N., Kolevzon, A., & Ochsner, K. N. (2010). Oxytocin selectively improves empathic accuracy. *Psychological Science, 21*, 1426–1428.

Baumgartner, T., Heinrichs, M., Vonlanthen, A., Fischbacher, U., & Fehr, E. (2008). Oxytocin shapes the neural circuitry of trust and trust adaptation in humans. *Neuron, 58*, 639–650.

Bohnet, I., & Zeckhauser, R. (2004). Trust, risk and betrayal. *Journal of Economic Behavior and Organization, 55*, 467–484.

Boksem, M. a S., Mehta, P. H., Van den Bergh, B., van Son, V., Trautmann, S. T., Roelofs, K., . . . Sanfey, A. G. (2013). Testosterone inhibits trust but promotes reciprocity. *Psychological Science, 24*, 2306–14.

Book, A. S., Starzyk, K. B., & Quinsey, V. L. (2001). The relationship between testosterone and aggression: A meta-analysis. *Aggression and Violent Behavior, 6*, 579–599.

Boon, S. D., & Holmes, J. G. (1991). The dynamics of interpersonal trust: Resolving uncertainty in the face of risk. In R. A. Hinde & J. Groebel (Eds.), *Cooperation and prosocial behavior* (pp. 190–211). Cambridge, UK: Cambridge University Press.

Bornstein, G. (2003). Intergroup conflict: Individual, group, and collective interests. *Personality and Social Psychology Review, 7*, 129–145.

Bos, P. A., Panksepp, J., Bluthé, R. M., & Honk, J. van. (2012). Acute effects of steroid hormones and neuropeptides on human social-emotional behavior: A review of single administration studies. *Frontiers in Neuroendocrinology, 33*, 17–35.

Bos, P. A., Terburg, D., & van Honk, J. (2010). Testosterone decreases trust in socially naive humans. *Proceedings of the National Academy of Sciences, 107*, 9991–9995.

Bosch, O. J., Meddle, S. L., Beiderbeck, D. I., Douglas, A. J., & Neumann, I. D. (2005). Brain oxytocin correlates with maternal aggression: link to anxiety. *Journal of Neuroscience, 25*, 6807–6815.

Bowles, S., & Gintis, H. (2011). *A cooperative species: Human reciprocity and its evolution.* Princeton, NJ: Princeton University Press.

Boyd, R., & Richerson, P. (1982). Cultural transmission and the evolution of cooperative behavior. *Human Ecology, 10*, 325–351.

Buttelmann, D., Zmyj, N., Daum, M., & Carpenter, M. (2013). Selective imitation of ingroup over out-group members in 14-month-old infants. *Child Development, 84*, 422–428.

Camerer, C. F. (2003). Behavioral game theory: Experiments in strategic interaction. *Journal of Socio-Economics, 32*, 550.

Cardoso, C., Kingdon, D., & Ellenbogen, M.A. (2014). A meta-analytic review of the impact of intranasal oxytocin administration on cortisol concentrations during laboratory tasks: Moderation by method and mental health. *Psychoneuroendocrinology, 49,* 161–170.

Carter, C. S. (2014). Oxytocin pathways and the evolution of human behavior. *Annual Review of Psychology, 65,* 17–39.

Carter, J. R., & Anderton, C. H. (2001). An experimental test of a predator-prey model of appropriation. *Journal of Economic Behavior and Organization, 45,* 83–97.

Christensen, J. C., Shiyanov, P.A, Estepp, J. R., & Schlager, J. J. (2014). Lack of association between human plasma oxytocin and interpersonal trust in a prisoner's dilemma paradigm. *PLoS One.* http://dx.doi.org/10.1371/journal.pone.0116172

Cohen, S., Schwartz, J. E., Epel, E., Kirschbaum, C., Sidney, S., & Seeman, T. (2006). Socioeconomic status, race, and diurnal cortisol decline in the Coronary Artery Risk Development in Young Adults (CARDIA) Study. *Psychosomatic Medicine, 68,* 41–50.

Conlisk, J. (2011). Professor Zak's empirical studies on trust and oxytocin. *Journal of Economic Behavior and Organization, 78,* 160–166.

Coombs, C. (1973). A reparameterization of the prisoner's dilemma game. *Behavioral Science, 18,* 424–428.

Darwin, C. (1873). *The descent of man.* New York: Appleton.

De Dreu, C. K. W. (2012). Oxytocin modulates cooperation within and competition between groups: An integrative review and research agenda. *Hormones and Behavior, 61,* 419–428.

De Dreu, C. K. W., Balliet, D., & Halevy, N. (2014). Parochial cooperation in humans: Forms and functions of self-sacrifice in intergroup competition and conflict. In A. J. Elliot (Ed.), *Advances in motivational science* (Vol. 1, pp. 1–47). New York: Elsevier.

De Dreu, C. K. W., Giebels, E., & Van de Vliert, E. (1998). Social motives and trust in integrative negotiation: The disruptive effects of punitive capability. *Journal of Applied Psychology, 83,* 408–422.

De Dreu, C. K. W., Greer, L. L., Handgraaf, M. J. J., Shalvi, S., Van Kleef, G. A., Baas, M., . . . Feith, S. W. W. (2010). The neuropeptide oxytocin regulates parochial altruism in intergroup conflict among humans. *Science, 328,* 1408–1411.

De Dreu, C. K. W., Greer, L. L., Van Kleef, G. A., Shalvi, S., & Handgraaf, M. J. J. (2011). Oxytocin promotes human ethnocentrism. *Proceedings of the National Academy of Sciences, 108,* 1262–1266.

De Dreu, C. K. W., & Kret, M. E. (2015). Oxytocin conditions intergroup relations through up-regulated in-group empathy, cooperation, conformity, and defense. *Biological Psychiatry, 79*(3), 165–173.

De Dreu, C. K. W., Scholte, H. S., van Winden, F. A. A. M., & Ridderinkhof, K. R. (2015). Oxytocin tempers calculated greed but not impulsive defense in predator-prey contests. *Social Cognitive and Affective Neuroscience, 10,* 721–728.

De Dreu, C. K. W., Shalvi, S., Greer, L. L., Van Kleef, G. A., & Handgraaf, M. J. J. (2012). Oxytocin motivates non-cooperation in intergroup conflict to protect vulnerable in-group members. *Plos One, 7* (11), E46751 doi:10.1371/journal.pone.0046751

De Dreu, C. K. W., & van Lange, P. A. M. (1995). The impact of social value orientations on negotiator cognition and behavior. *Personality and Social Psychology Bulletin, 21,* 1178–1188.

De Dreu, C. K. W., Yzerbyt, V. Y., & Leyens, J.-P. (1995). Dilution of stereotype-based cooperation in mixed-motive interdependence. *Journal of Experimental Social Psychology*, *31*, 575–593.

Declerck, C. H., Boone, C., & Kiyonari, T. (2010). Oxytocin and cooperation under conditions of uncertainty: The modulating role of incentives and social information. *Hormones and Behavior*, *57*, 368–374.

Delgado, M. R., Frank, R. H., & Phelps, E. A. (2005). Perceptions of moral character modulate the neural systems of reward during the trust game. *Nature Neuroscience*, *8*, 1611–1618.

Delgado, M. R., Schotter, A., Ozbay, E. Y., & Phelps, E. A. (2008). Understanding overbidding: Using the neural circuitry of reward to design economic auctions. *Science*, *321*, 1849–1852.

Diekhof, E. K., Wittmer, S., & Reimers, L. (2014). Does competition really bring out the worst? Testosterone, social distance and inter-male competition shape parochial altruism in human males. *PLoS One*, *9*, 0098977

Donaldson, Z. R., & Young, L. J. (2008). Oxytocin, vasopressin, and the neurogenetics of sociality. *Science*, *322*, 900–904.

Ebstein, R. P., Israel, S., Chew, S. H., Zhong, S., & Knafo, A. (2010). Genetics of human social behavior. *Neuron*, *65*, 831–844.

Eckstein, M., Becker, B., Scheele, D., Scholz, C., Preckel, K., Schlaepfer, T. E., . . . Hurlemann, R. (2014). Oxytocin facilitates the extinction of conditioned fear in humans. *Human Brain Mapping*, *35*, 4741–4750.

Eisenegger, C., Naef, M., Snozzi, R., Heinrichs, M., & Fehr, E. (2010). Prejudice and truth about the effect of testosterone on human bargaining behaviour. *Nature*, *463*, 356–359.

Ellemers, N., & Haslam, S. A. (2012). Social identity theory. In P. A. M. van Lange, A. W. Kruglanski, & E. T. Higgins (Eds.), *Handbook of theories of social psychology* (Vol. 2, pp. 379–398). Los Angeles, CA: SAGE.

Engert, V., Vogel, S., Efanov, S. I., Duchesne, A., Corbo, V., Ali, N., & Pruessner, J. C. (2011). Investigation into the cross-correlation of salivary cortisol and alpha-amylase responses to psychological stress. *Psychoneuroendocrinology*, *36*, 1294–302.

Fahrenfort, J. J., van Winden, F., Pelloux, B., Stallen, M., & Ridderinkhof, K. R. (2012). Neural correlates of dynamically evolving interpersonal ties predict prosocial behavior. *Frontiers in Human Neuroscience*, *6*, 28. doi:10.3389/fnins.2012.00028

Fetchenhauer, D., & Dunning, D. (2010). Why so cynical? Asymmetric feedback underlies misguided skepticism regarding the trustworthiness of others. *Psychological Science*, *21*, 189–193.

Gordon, I., Zagoory-Sharon, O., Leckman, J. F., & Feldman, R. (2010). Oxytocin and the development of parenting in humans. *Biological Psychiatry*, *68*, 377–382.

Grossman, H. I., & Kim, M. (2002). Predation and accumulation. *Journal of Economic Growth*, *158*, 393–407.

Hahn-Holbrook, J., Holt-Lunstad, J., Holbrook, C., Coyne, S. M., & Lawson, E. T. (2011). Maternal defense: Breast feeding increases aggression by reducing stress. *Psychological Science*, *22*, 1288–1295.

Halevy, N., Bornstein, G., & Sagiv, L. (2008). "In-group love" and "out-group hate" as motives for individual participation in intergroup conflict: A new game paradigm. *Psychological Science*, *19*, 405–411.

Halevy, N., Chou, E. Y., Cohen, T. R., & Livingston, R. W. (2012). Status conferral in inter-group social dilemmas: Behavioral antecedents and consequences of prestige and dominance. *Journal of Personality and Social Psychology, 102,* 351–366.

Halevy, N., Weisel, O., & Bornstein, G. (2012). "In-group love" and "out-group hate" in repeated interaction between groups. *Journal of Behavioral Decision Making, 25,* 188–195.

Hamlin, J. K., Mahajan, N., Liberman, Z., & Wynn, K. (2013). Not like me = bad: Infants prefer those who harm dissimilar others. *Psychological Science, 24,* 589–94.

Heim, C., & Nemeroff, C. B. (2001). The role of childhood trauma in the neurobiology of mood and anxiety disorders: Preclinical and clinical studies. *Biological Psychiatry, 49,* 1023–1039.

Hein, G., Silani, G., Preuschoff, K., Batson, C. D., & Singer, T. (2010). Neural responses to ingroup and outgroup members' suffering predict individual differences in costly helping. *Neuron, 68,* 149–160.

Holt-Lunstad, J., Birmingham, W. A., & Light, K. C. (2008). Influence of a "warm touch" support enhancement intervention among married couples on ambulatory blood pressure, oxytocin, alpha amylase, and cortisol. *Psychosomatic Medicine, 70,* 976–985.

Houser, D., Schunk, D., & Winter, J. (2010). Distinguishing trust from risk: An anatomy of the investment game. *Journal of Economic Behavior and Organization, 74,* 72–81.

Hruschka, D. J., & Henrich, J. (2013). Economic and evolutionary hypotheses for cross-population variation in parochialism. *Frontiers in Human Neuroscience, 7,* 559.

Israel, S., Weisel, O., Ebstein, R. P., & Bornstein, G. (2012). Oxytocin, but not vasopressin, increases both parochial and universal altruism. *Psychoneuroendocrinology, 37,* 1341–1344.

Keltner, D., Kogan, A., Piff, P. K., & Saturn, S. R. (2014). The sociocultural appraisals, values, and emotions (SAVE) framework of prosociality: Core processes from gene to meme. *Annual Review of Psychology, 65,* 425–460.

Kemp, A. H., & Guastella A. J. (2011). The role of oxytocin in human affect—a novel hypothesis. *Current Directions in Psychological Science, 20,* 222–231.

Kosfeld, M., Heinrichs, M., Zak, P. J., Fischbacher, U., & Fehr, E. (2005). Oxytocin increases trust in humans. *Nature, 435,* 673–676.

Kret, M. E., & De Dreu, C. K. W. (2013). Oxytocin-motivated ally selection is moderated by fetal testosterone exposure and empathic concern. *Frontiers in Neuroscience, 7,* 1.

Kret, M. E., Fischer, A. H., & De Dreu, C. K. W. (2015). Pupil-mimicry correlates with trust in in-group partners with dilating pupils. *Psychological Science, 26*(9), 1401–1410.

LeVine, R. A., & Campbell, D. T. (1972). *Ethnocentrism: Theories of conflict, ethnic attitudes, and group behavior.* New York: Wiley.

Lewicki, R. J., & Bunker, B. B. (1995). Trust in relationships: A model of development and decline. In B. B. Bunker, J. Z. Rubin, and associates (Eds.), *Conflict, cooperation, and justice: Essays inspired by the work of Morton Deutsch* (pp. 133–173). New York: Academic Press.

Luo, S., Li, B., Ma, Y., Zhang, W., Rao, Y., & Han, S. (2015). Oxytocin receptor gene and racial ingroup bias in empathy-related brain activity. *NeuroImage, 110,* 22–31.

Ma, X., Luo, L., Geng, Y., Zhao, W., Zhang, Q., & Kendrick, K. M. (2014). Oxytocin increases liking for a country's people and national flag but not for other cultural symbols or consumer products. *Frontiers in Behavioral Neuroscience, 8,* 1–10.

Madden, J. R., & Clutton-Brock, T. H. (2011). Experimental peripheral administration of oxytocin elevates a suite of cooperative behaviours in a wild social mammal. *Proceedings of the Royal Society B: Biology, 278,* 1189–1194.

Mazur, A., & Booth, A. (1998). Testosterone and dominance in men. *Behavioral and Brain Sciences, 21,* 353–363.

McCabe, K., Houser, D., Ryan, L., Smith, V., & Trouard, T. (2001). A functional imaging study of cooperation in two-person reciprocal exchange. *Proceedings of the National Academy of Sciences, 98,* 11832–11835.

Michaud, K., Matheson, K., Kelly, O., & Anisman, H. (2008). Impact of stressors in a natural context on release of cortisol in healthy adult humans: A meta-analysis. *Stress, 11,* 177–197.

Mikolajczak, M., Gross, J. J., Lane, A., Corneille, O., de Timary, P., & Luminet, O. (2010). Oxytocin makes people trusting, not gullible. *Psychological Science, 21,* 1072–1074.

Montoya, E. R., Terburg, D., Bos, P. A, & van Honk, J. (2012). Testosterone, cortisol, and serotonin as key regulators of social aggression: A review and theoretical perspective. *Motivation and Emotion, 36,* 65–73.

Mussweiler, T., & Ockenfels, A. (2013). Similarity increases altruistic punishment in humans. *Proceedings of the National Academy of Sciences, 110,* 19318–19323.

Neumann, I. D. (2008). Brain oxytocin: A key regulator of emotional and social behaviors in both females and males. *Journal of Neuroendocrinology, 20,* 858–865

Nowak, M. A., Tarnita, C. E., & Wilson, E. O. (2010). The evolution of eusociality. *Nature, 466,* 1057–1062.

O'Brien, D. T., & Wilson, D. S. (2011). Community perception: The ability to assess the safety of unfamiliar neighborhoods and respond adaptively. *Journal of Personality and Social Psychology, 100,* 606–620.

Oliveira, G., & Oliveira, R. (2014). Androgen responsiveness to competition in humans: The role of cognitive variables. *Frontiers in Neuroscience, 8,* 270.

Pruitt, D. G., & Kimmel, M. J. (1977). Twenty years of experimental gaming: Critique, synthesis, and suggestions for the future. *Annual Review of Psychology, 28,* 363–392.

Putman, P., Antypa, N., Crysovergi, P., & Van Der Does, W. A. J. (2010). Exogenous cortisol acutely influences motivated decision making in healthy young men. *Psychopharmacology, 208,* 257–263.

Rand, D. G., & Nowak, M. A. (2013). Human cooperation. *Trends in Cognitive Sciences, 17,* 413–424.

Rilling, J. K., DeMarco, A. C., Hackett, P. D., Thompson, R., Ditzen, B., Patel, R., & Pagnoni, G. (2012). Effects of intranasal oxytocin and vasopressin on cooperative behavior and associated brain activity in men. *Psychoneuroendocrinology, 37,* 447–461.

Rilling, J. K., & Sanfey, A. G. (2011). The neuroscience of social decision making. *Annual Review of Psychology, 62,* 23–48.

Rilling, J. K., & Young, L. J. (2014). The biology of mammalian parenting and its effect on offspring social development. *Science, 345,* 771–776.

Rousseau, D. M. (1989). Psychological and implied contracts in organizations. *Employee Responsibilities and Rights Journal, 2,* 121–139.

Sapolsky, R. M. (1982). The endocrine stress-response and social status in the wild baboon. *Hormones and Behavior, 16,* 279–292.

Sapolsky, R. M. (2005). The influence of social hierarchy on primate health. *Science, 308,* 648–652.

Segerstrom, S. C., & Miller, G. E. (2004). Psychological stress and the human immune system: A meta-analytic study of 30 years of inquiry. *Psychological Bulletin, 130,* 601–630.

Shalvi, S., & De Dreu, C. K. W. (2014). Oxytocin promotes group-serving dishonesty. *Proceedings of the National Academy of Sciences, 111,* 5503–5507.

Shamay-Tsoory, S. G., Fischer, M., Dvash, J., Harari, H., Perach-Bloom, N., & Levkovitz, Y. (2009). Intranasal administration of oxytocin increases envy and schadenfreude (gloating). *Biological Psychiatry, 66,* 864–870.

Sheng, F., Liu, Y., Zhou, B., Zhou, W., & Han, S. (2013). Oxytocin modulates the racial bias in neural responses to others' suffering. *Biological Psychology, 92,* 380–386.

Stirrat, M., & Perrett, D. I. (2010). Valid facial cues to cooperation and trust: Male facial width and trustworthiness. *Psychological Science, 21,* 349–354.

Striepens, N., Scheele, D., Kendrick, K. M., Becker, B., Schafer, L., Schwalba, K., . . . Hurlemann, R. (2012). Oxytocin facilitates protective responses to aversive social stimuli in males. *Proceedings of the National Academy of Sciences, 109,* 18144–18149.

Swaab, R. I., Maddux, W. W., & Sinaceur, M. (2011). Early words that work: When and how virtual linguistic mimicry facilitates negotiation outcomes. *Journal of Experimental Social Psychology, 47,* 616–621.

Ten Velden, F. S., Baas, M., Shalvi, S., Kret, M. E., & De Dreu, C. K. W. (2014). Oxytocin differentially modulates compromise and competitive approach but not withdrawal to antagonists from own vs. rivaling other groups. *Brain Research, 1580,* 172–179.

Trumble, B., Smith, E., O'Connor, K., Kaplan, H., & Gurven MD. (2014). Successful hunting increases testosterone and cortisol in a subsistence population. *Proceedings of the Royal Society Biological Sciences, 281*(1776), 20132876.

Tullock, G. (1980). Efficient rent seeking. In J. M. Buchanan, R. D. Tollison, & G. Tullock (Eds.), *Toward a theory of the rent-seeking society* (pp. 97–112). College Station: Texas A&M University Press.

Turner, J. C., Oakes, P. J., Haslam, S. A., & McGarty, C. (1994). Self and collective: Cognition and social context. *Personality and Social Psychology Bulletin, 20*(5), 454–463.

Tversky, A., & Kahneman, D. (1973). Availability: A heuristic for judging frequency and probability. *Cognitive Psychology, 5*(2), 207–232.

Uvnäs-Moberg, K. (1998). Oxytocin may mediate the benefits of positive social interaction and emotions. *Psychoneuroendocrinology, 23,* 819–835.

Van Bavel, J. J., Packer, D. J., & Cunningham, W. A. (2011). Modulation of the fusiform face area following minimal exposure to motivationally relevant faces: Evidence of in-group enhancement (not out-group disregard). *Journal of Cognitive Neuroscience, 23,* 3343–3354.

Van Honk, J., Montoya, E. R., Bos, P. A., van Vugt, M., & Terburg, D. (2012). New evidence on testosterone and cooperation. *Nature, 485,* E4–E5.

Van Kleef, G. A., De Dreu, C. K. W., & Manstead, A. S. R. (2010). An interpersonal approach to emotion in social decision making: The emotions as social information model. *Advances in Experimental Social Psychology, 42,* 45–96.

Van Lange, P. A., Liebrand, W. B., & Kuhlman, D. M. (1990). Causal attribution of choice behavior in three N-person prisoner's dilemmas. *Journal of Experimental Social Psychology, 26,* 34–48.

Viau, V. (2002). Functional cross-talk between the hypothalamic-pituitary-gonadal and adrenal axes. *Journal of Neuroendocrinology, 14,* 506–513.

Wingfield, J. C., Hegner, R. E., Dufty, Jr., A. M., & Ball, G. F. (1990). The "challenge hypothesis": Theoretical implications for patterns of testosterone secretion, mating systems, and breeding strategies. *The American Naturalist, 136*, 829–846.

Yamagishi, T., Jin, N., & Kiyonari, T. (1999). Bounded generalized reciprocity: Ingroup boasting and in-group favoritism. *Advances in Group Processes, 16*, 161–197.

Yamagishi, T., & Mifune, N. (2009). Social exchange and solidarity: In-group love or out-group hate? *Evolution and Human Behavior, 30*, 229–237.

Zak, P. J., Kurzban, R., & Matzner, W. T. (2005). Oxytocin is associated with human trustworthiness. *Hormones and Behavior, 48*, 522–527.

Zeisberger, E., Roth, J., & Kluger, M. J. (1994). Interactions between the immune system and the hypothalamic neuroendocrine system during fever and endogenous antipyresis. In K. Pleschka & R. Gerstberger (Eds.), *Proceedings integrative and cellular aspects of autonomic functions* (pp. 181–190). Montrouge, France: John Libbey Eurotext.

Zhong, S., Monakhov, M., Mok, H. P., Tong, T., Lai, P. S., Chew, S. H., & Ebstein, R. P. (2012). U-shaped relation between plasma oxytocin levels and behavior in the trust game. *PLoS One, 7*. doi:10.1371/journal.pone.0051095

5 The Foundations of Individuals' Generalized Social Trust

A Review

■ PETER THISTED DINESEN
AND RENÉ BEKKERS

■ INTRODUCTION

Generalized social trust concerns the expectancy about the trustworthiness of strangers, that is, people we do not have any information about (Rotter, 1971). Consequently, generalized social trust is an important heuristic that people use to navigate the numerous daily interactions with unknown others that are characteristic of modern societies. Trust bears consequences for individuals in specific interactions—it may or may not be honored—but perhaps even more importantly, trust has pronounced positive effects in the aggregate through its effect on collective action. When people trust others to a greater extent, they tend to cooperate more with strangers and behave more prosocially (Dawes, McTavish, & Shaklee, 1977; Rönnerstrand, 2013; Sønderskov, 2011b). Societies with higher densities of trusters are therefore characterized by better, more efficient government and higher levels of economic growth (Knack & Keefer, 1997; Knack & Zak, 2002).[1]

Being the ostensible mainspring of many things good in life, the causes of generalized social trust have attracted massive attention across a variety of disciplines including developmental psychology, social psychology, economics, political science, and sociology. Being an individual-level phenomenon in nature, most studies have focused on explaining trust at the micro level, although some have also focused on the causes of macro-level trust across various collective aggregates (typically countries) (e.g., Delhey and Newton, 2005). In line with most research, this review focuses exclusively on trust as a dependent variable at the individual-level.

The purpose of the review is to give an overview of the literature on the causes of generalized social trust at the individual level with a special focus on more recent studies published after the latest review by Nannestad (2008). Moreover, we give special emphasis to the data and methodology utilized in the studies reviewed, specifically with an eye to the potential for drawing causal inference.

■ SCOPE OF THE REVIEW

In addition to narrowing down the focus to causes of individual-level trust, we delimit the scope of the review on three dimensions: conceptually, in terms of measurement, and with regard to the causes of trust in focus.

First, in the interest of keeping a stringent focus, we focus on the concept of generalized social trust as defined previously (i.e., trust in unknown others) rather than broader concepts such as social cohesion or social capital (see, e.g., Portes & Vikstrom [2011] for a review related to social cohesion). Hereby we also avoid the risk of conflating social trust with other related and unrelated phenomena falling under these broader concepts. We also exclude types of trust that are either not "social" (e.g., trust in institutions) or to a reasonable extent "generalized" (e.g., trust in well-known others, such as family or friends, or trust in specific out-groups).

Second, research on trust has mainly employed one of two measurement strategies: behaviors in experimental games and survey-based measures, both of which hold strengths and weaknesses.[2] Here we focus on survey-based research. More specifically, we look at survey questions, which capture the essence of generalized social trust, namely trust in unknown others. In this regard, most research has relied on a subset of the seminal "faith in people" scale developed by Rosenberg (1956); typically either the single item concerning trust ("most people can be trusted" vs. "you cannot be too careful in dealing with people") or a scale composed of this and two items regarding helpfulness and fairness of others.[3] In addition to these questions, we also review studies using related measures regarding trustworthiness of a generic, mostly anonymous group of people (e.g. "strangers" or "co-nationals"), as well as measures focusing on specific actions (e.g., trust in anonymous others giving back a wallet). Finally, to the extent that we found it meaningful, we also include studies that use indicators (scales) of social trust that partially conflate generalized social trust with trust in more specific others.

Third, we exclude studies that focus on the impact of ethnic diversity in various contexts (most important, the residential context; see, e.g., Dinesen & Sønderskov, 2015) on generalized social trust. While contextual ethnic diversity is not inherently different from other explanations of trust, research on this topic has grown—mainly in response to Putnam's (2007) controversial findings on the topic—so explosively over the past few years that it essentially deserves its own review (see Schaeffer [2013] and Van der Meer & Tolsma [2014] for reviews of the effects of ethnic diversity on the wider concept of social cohesion including social trust).

■ GENERIC EXPLANATIONS OF TRUST: GENETIC AND ENVIRONMENTAL FACTORS

Like other human traits, trust can be innate (i.e., shaped by genetic differences), acquired (formed by environmental conditioning), or shaped in an interplay between genes and environment. A number of behavioral genetic analyses have used samples of twins to partition sources of trust into genetic and environmental factors (Hirashi, Yamagata, Shikishima, & Ando, 2008; Oskarsson, Dawes, Johannesson, & Magnusson, 2012; Sturgis, Read, Hatemi, et al., 2010; Van Lange,

Vinkhuyzen, & Posthuma, 2014). The results of these studies vary considerably, but, on average, heritability is estimated to be in the range of 30% to 40%, indicating stronger environmental than genetic influences on trust.[4] Moreover, these studies show that the environmental sources of trust are overwhelmingly of the so-called non-shared kind, that is, unique to the individual and not shared by his or her siblings and therefore not the result of, for example, common socialization in the family.

While the twin studies published thus far are very valuable for our understanding of the generic sources of trust, they speak little to the specific genetic and, particularly, environmental influences shaping trust. As we are mainly interested in the latter source—mostly because, to our knowledge, little research exists on the former—we do not delve more into these analyses here but instead direct our focus toward the analyses that have examined the role of specific—primarily environmental—factors in shaping trust.

■ TWO PERSPECTIVES ON TRUST: DISPOSITIONAL AND EXPERIENTIAL EXPLANATIONS

The literature outlines two broad perspectives on the roots of trust: the dispositional and the experiential perspective. While not mutually exclusive, the two perspectives provide a stylized conception of how trust is formed and develops over the life course.

In the *dispositional* perspective, trust is considered a deep-seated disposition or belief that varies between individuals. After the formative years, the rank order of individuals from low to high trust changes little. In parts of the literature, trust is considered a downstream consequence of proximate dispositions such as personality traits, while in others it is regarded as a facet of personality in its own right. Both, however, stress the dispositional nature of trust. From this perspective, trust (or anteceding dispositions) may be formed by either genetic transmission or early-life socialization, but the key point is that trust in adult life is a stable individual-level disposition, which is not modified much by experience. From this perspective, trust is considered a moral value (Uslaner, 2002), largely independent of environmental conditioning.

The *experiential* perspective, in contrast, considers trust to be malleable through experiences. More specifically, individuals are expected to continuously update their trust in others based on their experiences—good or bad—throughout life (Glanville & Paxton, 2007; Dinesen, 2012a; Uslaner, 2008). Experiences may be understood in both a narrower (i.e., concrete experiences with others) and a broader (i.e., environmental conditioning more generally) sense. Here we conceptualize experiences closer to the latter—mainly to provide a meaningful category contrasting with that of the dispositional perspective.

Again, the two perspectives on the roots of trust are not mutually exclusive (Van Lange, 2015). For example, experiences in childhood may influence trust (or anteceding dispositions), which is then subsequently stable over the adult life course. Similarly, they may also interact. Dispositions such as personality traits may for example influence how certain experiences are perceived and influence trust. That said, we still find the dispositional and the experiential perspective useful for a general classification of explanations of trust and thus structure our review around this distinction.

The Dispositional Perspective

As noted, the key premise underlying the dispositional perspective is that trust is a deeply rooted disposition—either in itself or as a downstream consequence of other "deeper" dispositions—which is stable and only to a limited extent subject to experiential influences after the formative years of adolescence and early adulthood. Emphasizing stability further, trust is often considered stable over generations as a consequence of genetic or social transmission. This assumed stability of trust—over the life course and over generations—has been examined in four distinct lines of empirical research: one focusing on intergenerational transmission of trust, a second on the stability of trust over the life course, a third on the link between trust and various fundamental predispositions, and a fourth investigating stability of trust across individuals from different cultures. We review each of them in turn.

The Intergenerational Transmission of Trust

A number of studies look at the intergenerational transmission of trust by studying parent–child correlations in trust (Dalton, 1980; Dinesen, 2012b; Dohmen, Falk, Huffman, & Sunde, 2012; Stolle & Hooghe, 2004; Stolle & Nishikawa, 2011; Uslaner, 2002). They tie in with the implied stability in the dispositional perspective by looking at how strongly trust is transmitted from one generation to the next. The intergenerational studies typically interpret the parent–child correlation in trust as an indication of familial socialization, although this could in principle also reflect genetic transmission (Dohmen et al., 2012).[5] Independent of the specific transmission mechanism, these studies speak to the rank-order stability of trust. Importantly, this does not imply that children have the same absolute level of trust as their parents[6] but only that parents and children tend to have the same relative placement in the trust distribution in a population. Hence, while trust may be significantly higher or lower in one generation than in the previous as a result of any aggregate level phenomenon that influences trust equally across a population (e.g., increases in living standards or reduced income inequality), this does not influence the transmission of the relative tendency to trust.

The studies generally find indications of an intergenerational transmission of trust (i.e., a positive parent–child correlation) but vary considerably in the detected strength of this transmission. As the exception to the rule, Stolle and Nishikawa (2011) found weak and mostly insignificant correlations between 12- and 13-year-olds and their parents in the United States and Canada in the early 2000s. Conversely, in analyses based on the Niemi-Jennings Youth-Parent Socialization Panel study of high school seniors and their parents in the United States in 1965 (Jennings, Markus, & Niemi, 1991), a moderate (Uslaner, 2002) to weak (Dalton, 1980) transmission is observed. The effect did not linger, however, as a weak and insignificant relation between parents' trust in 1965 and their children's trust in 1982 was observed (Stolle & Hooghe, 2004). In a German sample of parents and children (over 17), who live in the same household, Dohmen et al. (2012) found a significant and relatively strong transmission of trust from both parents (separately) to their children. Interestingly, the transmission from mothers is stronger than that from fathers. Finally, Dinesen (2012b) shows a significant trust transmission from parents to children for young (Grade 7–9) non-Western immigrants and native Danes in Denmark. Importantly, he finds that the transmission is stronger for native Danes than for first- and second-generation immigrants, which is taken as an indication that experiences incongruent with parental trust levels likely weaken the parental transmission of (mis)trust.

In addition to the studies focusing on the direct parental transmission of trust, a number of studies speak to the specific form of social transmission, primarily by examining how parents instill trust in their offspring through the upbringing.[7] In the United States, Uslaner (2002) finds that children who were brought up by parents who emphasized authoritarian rather than more democratic or self-expressive values in the upbringing have lower levels of trust. Similarly, Dinesen (2010) finds a restrictive upbringing leads to lower levels of trust among non-Western immigrants in Denmark. Finally, Stolle and Nishikawa (2011) show that American parents increasingly choose to bring up their children as less trusting in response to increased media portrayals of crime against children.

To summarize, there is evidence for a parental transmission of trust from parents to children as well as the specific ways in which parents shape the trust of their children. However, the transmission varies considerably across time, context, and the population studied. A more systematic approach to studying the transmission comparatively across countries would be fruitful. Moreover, in line with Dohmen et al. (2012), parsing out of the specific transmission mechanisms operating, including whether transmission is primarily social or genetic, would be a very valuable addition to the literature.

Stability of Trust over the Life Course

As a natural extension of studies examining the relative intergenerational stability in trust, a number of studies have also examined the relative stability in trust over the life course.[8] Again, a strong correlation over time indicates a high rank-order consistency in trust but does not say anything about trust levels. Studies based on the aforementioned Niemi-Jennings Youth-Parent Panel Socialization data find a moderate (Stolle & Hooghe, 2004) to fairly strong correlation (Claibourn & Martin, 2000) in trust over the 17-year period from 1965 to 1982 for the youth sample. Similarly, a strong consistency over the same period is found in the parent sample (Claibourn & Martin, 2000). The best evidence on the long-term stability of trust outside of the United States is from a Danish three-wave panel spanning 18 years from 1990 to 2008. Using these data, Sønderskov and Dinesen (2014, 2016) also find a moderately strong correlation over time. Over a shorter time span, with trust measured on three occasions (2002, 2004, and 2006), Bekkers

(2012) finds a strong stability in trust. These findings provide evidence supporting the dispositional perspective, while at the same time not precluding the potential effect of collective experiences influencing everyone in the population equally and hence that trust de- or increases in the aggregate.

The Personality Correlates of Trust

A number of studies have looked at associations between trust and various personality traits. In his influential book, Uslaner (2002) argued and showed empirically that optimism and a sense of control—both typically viewed as stable, partly innate, psychological traits—are strongly positively associated with trust. Similarly, Oskarsson et al. (2012) find personal control to be positively correlated with social trust. Looking at other traits, Couch and Jones (1997) found that shyness, suspicion, and jealousy were negatively associated with trust. Rather than looking at more specific traits, scholars have in recent years focused their attention on the Big Five personality model, which represents human personality by five broad traits, each encompassing six specific facets. Results vary considerably by country context as well as the extensiveness of the Big Five personality measure. In a small American sample using a 10-item personality inventory, Mondak and Halperin (2008) found that only agreeableness is significantly associated (positively) with trust. Conversely, Dinesen, Nørgaard, and Klemmensen (2014) found that all five traits are correlated with trust in a large Danish sample using a 60-item personality inventory. Specifically, they found that agreeableness, openness, and extraversion were positively related to trust, while neuroticism and conscientiousness were negatively related. Similarly, Hirashi et al. (2008) found that all five traits were correlated with trust in a Japanese sample. All correlations were in similar directions as in the Danish sample, except for conscientiousness, which was positively related to trust in Japan. Focusing on a subset of the Big Five traits, Oskarsson et al. (2012) found positive associations for extraversion.

Based on this summary, there is thus considerable evidence that trust is associated with personality traits, including at least a subset of the Big Five traits, most consistently the trait of Agreeableness. A number of questions remain, however. As noted previously, it is unclear to what extent trust is a consequence of these personality traits or in itself a facet under one or more of the traits. This issue is illustrated by "Trust" being one of the six facets under Agreeableness. Interestingly, when removing this facet from the Agreeableness scale, the correlation with trust is considerably reduced (Dinesen et al., 2014; Hirashi et al., 2008). One way of further examining the nature of the relationship between trust and personality traits is to use genetically informed data such as Hirashi et al. (2008) and Oskarsson et al. (2012), who used twin data. Hirashi et al. found that the effects of genetic and environmental factors on trust are to a considerable extent mediated by Agreeableness and Extraversion. Oskarsson et al. found that the relationship between trust and the dispositional traits they examined could be explained by a common genetic factor. Therefore, in conclusion, an important topic for future research—conceptual as well as empirically—is to further clarify whether trust is a part of personal predispositions, specifically personality traits (I), a consequence of these traits (II), or that the relationship between the two is explained by common genetic and/or environmental factors (III).

Intelligence and Trust

Another deeply rooted psychological trait that has been shown to be associated with trust is cognitive ability or intelligence. Across contexts as well as diverse measures of trust and intelligence, five studies find strong overall support for a substantial association between intelligence and trust (Carl & Billari, 2014; Hooghe, Marien, & De Vroome, 2012; Oskarsson et al. 2012; Sturgis, Read, & Allum, 2010; Yamagishi, 2001). This is typically interpreted in line with Yamagishi's theory positing that social intelligence—an ostensible correlate or facet of general intelligence—enables individuals to detect signs of untrustworthiness and thus avoid interactions in which their trust is betrayed. This in turn enables them to develop trust further by engaging in trustful relations with others, as well as refining their ability to detect others' trustworthiness. Conversely, less intelligent individuals will engage in more interactions with untrustworthy others, which will lead them to become less trustful.

Despite the robust support for the association between intelligence and trust, a number of questions remain. In line with the personality-trust nexus discussed previously, an interesting question is whether trust and intelligence share the same underlying genetic factors, or on the contrary, that intelligence, which is highly heritable (and probably more so than trust; see Polderman et al., 2015), mediates the genetic influences on trust. Another highly relevant question lies in disentangling the order of the effects of intelligence and education on trust. Like intelligence, education is also a strong predictor of trust (we discuss this later). Some have suggested that intelligence is a likely mediator of the influence of education on trust based on the assumption that education increases intelligence (Hooghe et al., 2012). However, it is also possible that individuals may sort into the educational system based on their preceding levels of intelligence and thus that the causal order is the other way around. Supporting that intelligence influences trust over and above educational achievement, Sturgis, Read, and Allum (2010) show that intelligence measured at age 10 significantly and rather strongly predicts trust at age 34 and 46. This result even holds up when including subsequent education and a wide range of other variables in the model. At the same time, however, they still find that controlling for intelligence at age 10, higher levels of education is associated with higher levels of trust. From the reported models, it is not possible to discern to which extent the educational effect is confounded by intelligence, although the relatively sparse effects of education compared to results from typical analyses may be taken as an indication of this. In any case, this study provides strong support for a direct effect of intelligence on trust. Further studies attempting to parse out the relative effects of intelligence and education on trust and, not least, the causal sequence of the two in this regard, would be a valuable addition to the literature.

Trust as a Cultural Trait

The final explanation we classify as dispositional is the so-called "cultural perspective", which posits that trust is a feature of the culture of a given society or a group. While cultural transmission more generally has been conceptualized as the result of both parental socialization and subsequent experiences, the cultural perspective within the trust literature has used the concept of cultural transmission in a narrower sense. Specifically, in this approach, trust is assumed to be primarily shaped by parental socialization early in life, which thus resonates with the other dispositional arguments presented earlier (Dinesen, 2012a, 2012b; Uslaner, 2002). Furthermore, the cultural argument holds that culture tends to stick with individuals over the life course and is subsequently passed on to their offspring. In other words, trust is argued to display high rank-order stability over the life course *and* across generations.

The cultural argument as understood in the trust literature has mainly been advanced by studying immigrants, because this in principle allows for an *in toto* examination of whether trust is shaped by culture (i.e., is a socialized persistent trait) or experiences (for a full review of this literature, see Dinesen and Sønderskov, Fortcoming). Specifically, comparing levels of trust of immigrants in a host country to levels of trust among natives who remained in their home country provides an indication of the extent to which the culture of the ancestral country (in terms of the level of trust) persists in the new country. The stronger the correspondence between immigrants present-day trust and trust of the native population in the ancestral country, the stronger the cultural basis of this trait is assumed to be. Conversely, a lack of correspondence between trust of the home country and immigrants' present-day trust is indirectly taken as an indication that experiences *in toto* in the destination country has shaped trust, that is, as evidence for the experiential perspective, which we explore further later.

A number of studies have examined trust of immigrants from various ancestral and destination countries. In their study of individuals in the United States with ancestry in 11 European countries, Rice and Feldman (1997) found a strong correlation between aggregate home country trust and individual-level trust of descendants of immigrants. Similarly, Guiso, Sapienza, and Singales (2008), Algan and Cahuc (2010), and Tabellini (2008) found a strong correlation on a sample of third-generation immigrants in the United States. Uslaner (2008) also found that differences in trust among various groups in the United States covary with the level of trust of the country of their ancestors. The correlation between immigrants' present-day trust and trust of the ancestral country also exists across European countries but only for first-generation immigrants (Dinesen, 2013; Dinesen & Hooghe, 2010). For second-generation immigrants, there is no longer a correlation with trust of the ancestral country (Dinesen & Hooghe, 2010). The fact that the studies from Europe examine trust of immigrants in different destination countries also allow for a straightforward examination of the experiential perspective, namely by examining whether immigrants' present-day trust align with trust of natives in their new country. This is indeed the case, and, generally speaking, the adaptation to the level of trust of natives in the new country is substantially stronger than the persistence of the cultural residues of the ancestral country (Dinesen & Hooghe, 2010; see also Helliwell, Wang, & Xu [2016] for a global analysis). While there have been some attempts to examine the role of experiential factors of shaping trust of immigrants in the United States (Rice & Feldman, 1997; Uslaner, 2008), none have examined these as directly as the noted study from Europe.

More generally, the studies of immigrants suffer from three shortcomings. The first is in the identification of the country of ancestry. This becomes increasingly difficult with individuals having stayed in the destination country for generations, which, *ceteris paribus*, increases the likelihood of having mixed ancestry. A second problem is that accurate measurement of home country trust *at the time of migration* only exists for more recent immigrants. The level of trust in the home country is extrapolated backward in time from more recent studies, under the assumption that trust is relatively stable over time. As evidenced by studies in the United States (Putnam, 2000; Robinson & Jackson, 2001) and Denmark (Sønderskov & Dinesen, 2014)—two countries in which fairly long time series exist—this assumption is very problematic; both countries display very substantial variations in trust over time. A welcome improvement in this literature would thus be more precise measurement of trust at the time of departure of immigrants. With time lapsing and more surveys being conducted, the possibilities for doing this will be improved. A third problem is that the association between aggregate home country trust and immigrants' present-day trust only speaks to the *relative ordering* of trust. If immigrants are influenced in a similar way by the destination-country environment, the *level of trust* of immigrants could in principle have moved away from trust in the ancestral country and toward that of natives in the new country (and vice versa) while still reflecting a cultural residue of the ancestral country. However, this would clearly also indicate an experiential influence on trust. Dinesen (2012a) provides some evidence for this as he shows that trust of first-generation immigrants from Turkey, Italy, and Poland in high-trusting countries in Northern Europe is significantly higher than that of natives in their ancestral country (although still lower than natives in the destination country; see Nannestad, Svendsen, Dinesen, & Sønderskov [2014] for a similar finding). Bagno (2006) provides mixed evidence along the same lines in her study of Jewish immigrants in various countries. Future studies of immigrants should arguably try to incorporate comparisons of both the levels and relative ordering of trust among various immigrant groups to provide further leverage in differentiating cultural and experiential forces shaping trust.

The Experiential Perspective

While the rank-order stability in trust is relatively high, both over the life course and across generations, there is also strong evidence suggesting that trust is malleable. According to the experiential perspective, individuals use experiences—both specifically related to an honoring or a breach of trust, as well as more generally— to mold their social trust. Importantly vis-à-vis the dispositional perspective, the experiential perspective predicts that trust is continuously calibrated throughout life depending on specific experiences.

Beyond the totality of experiences resulting from living in a specific context (as just discussed in relation to studies focusing on immigrants and their adaptation to the level of trust in their contemporary country), there are also a large number of studies examining the role of more specific experiences in shaping trust. The explanations vary in the extent to which the "experience" hypothesized to impact trust is of a more immediate, singular nature (e.g., victimization of crimr) or a more extended kind (e.g., completion of a higher level of education or being active in civic life for years). However, independent of its immediacy and duration, the common logic for the experiential explanations is that exposure to a given experience (compared to absence of this experience) is expected to influence trust. As a larger number of explanations may in principle fall under the "experiential" header, we review only what we consider to be the most prominent ones.

Participation in Civic Life

Participation in civic life, in the form of (active) membership in voluntary associations and other organizations, has been a dominant experiential explanation of trust at least since Putnam's (1993) work on local governance in Italy. Interactions in civic life can provide the basis for trusting others in several ways. Through voluntary associations, citizens get to know specific others, whom they (eventually) learn to trust (McPherson, Popielarz, & Drobnic, 1992). Shared group membership also increases the cost of defection in interactions, including punishment of abuse of trust, and thereby lays the foundation for trust (Coleman, 1994; Putnam, 1993). Crucial for this explanation of trust, the positive interactions with others in associations are expected to spill over to the level of trust in abstract others. Three studies provide support for this premise (Glanville & Andersson, 2013; Glanville & Paxton, 2007; Freitag & Traunmüller, 2009). More generally, a wealth of studies show a positive relationship between participation in voluntary associations and trust, both in single country studies (e.g., Brehm & Rahn, 1997; Paxton, 2007; Siisiäinen & Kankainen, 2014; Wollebaek & Selle, 2002) as well as in cross-country analyses (Anheier & Kendall, 2002; Delhey & Newton, 2003; Stolle, 1998; Sønderskov, 2011a). Using data from the European Values Study 2000 in 21 countries in Europe plus the United States, Anheier and Kendall (2002, p. 344) report "almost a linear relationship between increases in membership and the likelihood of trusting people." However, the evidence for a positive relationship is not unanimous. Controlling for a large number of characteristics at the individual level, Delhey and Newton find that engagement in voluntary associations is significantly related to trust in only three out of seven countries examined, leading them to conclude that "voluntary organizations do not seem to do much, if anything, for generalized trust in most countries." (Delhey and Newton, 2003, p. 112).

Despite the general evidence for a positive relationship between participation in civic life and social trust based on cross-sectional data, this relationship suffers from two potential threats to causal inference: omitted variable bias and reverse causality. It is thus difficult to rule out that the relationship is not driven by some hard-to-observe confounding variables (e.g., various "deep" psychological pre-dispositions) or that trust promotes participation (or that the two reinforce each other; Stolle, 1998; Putnam, 2000; Sønderskov, 2011a). As will become evident, similar methodological challenges—especially regarding confounding by unob-served variables—pertain (to a varying extent) to the other experiences suggested to influence trust.

Longitudinal (panel) data on individuals can to some extent be put to use to address problems of confounding by unobserved variables by means of relating *over-time changes in participation to over-time changes in trust*. In other words, if a person becomes more engaged in associations over time, we would expect his or her level of trust to follow suit if participation in voluntary associations influences trust. The panel data approach takes out time-invariant confounding—for exam-ple, from partly innate psychological traits—of the relationship, but time-invariant confounding still remains an issue (e.g., traumatic personal experiences that influ-ence both trust and associational involvement). Similarly, longitudinal models can to some extent address direction of causality between associational involvement and trust by regressing subsequent levels of one of the variables of interest (e.g., trust measured at time t_1) on prior levels of this variable (trust at time t_0) and the other variable of interest (participation in associations at t_0) plus relevant control variables in so-called cross-lagged or lagged-dependent variable models (and vice versa with engagement in associations as the dependent variable). Longitudinal data can be put to use in a similar fashion for the other experiences we discuss subsequently.

A number of studies have examined the relationship between participation in voluntary associations and trust using longitudinal data. In short, the findings show that to the extent that a relationship exists, it primarily reflects selection, that is, initial trust affecting the likelihood of participation in associations. The effect of trust on participation is supported by findings from the Netherlands (Bekkers, 2012) and the United States (Gross, Aday, & Brewer, 2004) using lon-gitudinal data over relatively short time spans. While not testing it directly, Van Ingen and Bekkers (2015) found indications of the same pattern in Switzerland, the Netherlands, Australia, and the United Kingdom. In a few instances, they found significant effects of participation in voluntary associations on trust, but this increase was only very short lived. Using the Youth-Parent Socialization Panel study (the first three waves in 1965–1973–1982) mentioned earlier, Stolle and Hooghe (2004) also find stronger indications of a positive effect of trust on asso-ciational involvement than the other way around. However, using the same data, Claibourn and Martin (2000) find some support for associational involvement increasing trust but not the reverse relationship.

Two other nonlongitudinal studies deserve mention for their effort to address the causal relationship between engagement in voluntary associations and trust by other means. First, the study by Sønderskov (2011a), which focuses exclu-sively on the effect of trust on organizational membership for those *not active* in organizations. As the purported effect from associational involvement to trust is generally hypothesized to stem from interactions—primarily of the face-to-face type—with others in the associations, this rules out a feedback effect. The analysis concludes that trust stimulates participation in certain types of associations—specifically those associated with provision of public goods. Second, Richey (2007) uses propensity score matching, which under some assumptions can eliminate confounding by observed confounders, to match those participating in various government-induced activities with those who do not. He found that participation in these activities stimulated trust.

Evidence for a correlation between associational involvement and trust exists in abundance, but the *causal* evidence for the relationship is far less convincing. On balance—and in line with Nannestad's (2008) conclusion—to the extent that a relationship exists at all, the methodologically sophisticated studies mostly point to an effect of trust on associational involvement, not the other way around.

Other Types of Social Interactions

Despite the preponderance of studies focusing on participation in civic life as an experiential factor shaping trust, a number of studies have also focused on other social interactions. Upon experiencing such interactions, individuals are expected to adjust their generalized social trust accordingly: trust should increase with positive social interactions and decrease with negative ones.

Among experiences expected to further trust, stronger ties with others—be it relatives, neighbors, or more superficial acquaintances—are expected to breed trust. While Uslaner (2002) finds little evidence for this proposition in the United States, most other studies do support this contention. Although not consistent across all countries in their data, Delhey and Newton (2003) generally find that individuals with more friends, and who interact more frequently with these friends, also display higher levels of trust. Li, Pickles, and Savage (2005) obtain a similar result for social networks more generally, although the effect is markedly reduced when taking prior level of trust into account. Freitag and Traunmüller (2009) find that positive experiences with strangers stimulate trust in Germany, while Glanville and Andersson (2013) find that stronger informal ties with relatives, friends, and neighbors also produce trust in the United States. The latter study is particularly convincing as it employs individual-level panel data and observes that changes in informal ties within individuals are positively associated with changes in trust. Similarly, using advanced structural equation models taking the direction of causality into account, Glanville and Paxton (2007) find that trust in more "localized domains" (particularly trust in neighbors and in store workers)—which is expected to flow from positive interactions with members of these groups—also relate positively to social trust. Similarly, Freitag and Traunmüller (2009) find that trust in particularized others (family, friends, and neighbors) also positively influence generalized social trust using an instrumental variable approach. Overall there is thus considerable causally oriented evidence suggesting that positive social interactions, and the trust in specific others that spring from it, promote trust in the generalized other.

There is also some evidence on the impact of negative social interactions on social trust. Smith (1997) finds that being robbed or burglarized and being hit or shot at/threatened with a gun diminishes trust in the United States. Brehm and Rahn (1997) find a similar result for having experienced burglary the previous year but not robbery. In the UK, Sturgis, Read, and Allum (2010) find that being a victim of theft or violence is associated with a significantly lower level of trust. These studies are based on cross-sectional data and are thus vulnerable to confounding by omitted variables. Illustrating this potential problem, Bauer (2015) finds only negligible effects of various types of victimization on trust using Swiss panel data in which victimized and nonvictimized individuals were balanced on covariates by means of genetic matching. Relatedly, a number of studies look at how experiences and/or perceptions of discrimination in everyday life influence trust. Based on cross-sectional analyses, the picture is inconsistent: Dinesen (2010) finds no effect on young immigrants in Denmark, while Dinesen and Hooghe (2010) find a negative effect on trust in a pooled cross-section of Europeans but not specifically for immigrants. Finally, while not necessarily reflecting personal experiences per se, perceptions of (un)safety in the local area have also been studied as a correlate of social trust. Across a number of countries, studies find cross-sectional evidence for a negative association between feelings of unsafety and trust (Delhey & Newton, 2003; Uslaner, 2002). Taken together, there is thus some—albeit not consistent—evidence for a causal impact of negative personal interactions on trust. Applying causal inference-oriented designs along the line of Bauer (2014) would clearly be worthwhile in this regard.

Sociodemographic Factors: Education, Socioeconomic Standing, and Unemployment

Having focused on social interactions, in civic life and otherwise, we now turn to experiences in a broader sense (i.e., environmental conditioning more generally). This potentially includes a very broad range of factors, which we are unable to cover in total in this chapter. We have therefore narrowed down these explanations to what we perceive to be the most important ones in the literature.

Similar to many other attitudes and indicators of social capital, education is one of the strongest predictors of trust (Helliwell & Putnam, 2004). This has been confirmed in a wealth of cross-sectional analysis, across a large number of contexts (e.g., Alesina & La Ferrara 2002; Borgonovi 2012; Brehm & Rahn 1997; Glaeser, Laibson, Scheinkman, & Soutter, 2000; Helliwell & Putnam 2007; Li et al. 2005; Marschall & Stolle 2004; Paxton 2007; Putnam 2000; Uslaner 2002; Smith 1997; see Huang, Maassen-Van den Brink, and Groot [2009] for a meta-analysis).

Several mechanisms have been suggested to account for the relationship between education and trust, including a better ability to detect trustworthy behavior (Knack & Keefer, 1997) potentially stemming from increased intelligence (Yamagishi, 2001; cf. the previous discussion), more social and economic resources making trusting less risky (Delhey & Newton, 2003; Huang, Maassen-Van den Brink, and Groot, 2011, pp. 291–292), and a socialization of cosmopolitan values correlated with trust (Borgonovi, 2012).

Given the alleged importance of education for trust, it is somewhat surprising that relatively few studies have given explicit consideration to the risk of confounding by omitted variable. As highlighted in a related literature (Kam & Palmer, 2008), education indexes a large number of preadult experiences, which are generally not measured and included in cross-sectional analyses, thereby posing a threat of confounding. As a consequence, the estimates from the cross-sectional analyses are most likely (upward) biased.

While not always the main aim, a number of studies have examined the relationship between education and trust by means of longitudinal data, either in terms of individual-level fixed effects models or cross-lagged models. These studies point toward a positive but limited effect of education in Britain (Li et al., 2005; Sturgis, Patulny, & Allum, 2009, Sturgis, Read, Hatemi, et al., 2010), the United States (Glanville et al., 2013), and Denmark (Sønderskov & Dinesen, 2014, 2016). Other causally oriented designs have also been applied in assessing the education–trust nexus. In an instrumental variable approach, Huang, Maassen van den Brink, and Groot (2011, 2012) find a positive effect of education on trust in the UK using school absence for health reasons as an instrument. Milligan, Moretti, and Oreopoulos (2004) instrument education by compulsory schooling laws and find a positive effect on social trust in the United States. In contrast, Oskarsson, Dinesen, Dawes, Johannesson, and Magnusson (Forthcoming) find no effect of education on trust in Sweden using a co-twin control design in which the relationship between education and trust is assessed within twin pairs to rule out effects of shared genes and common familial environment. This result is consistent with Hooghe and Stolle's (2004) finding that education does not predict present trust when previous levels of trust are included.

Two related points should be highlighted with regard to the impact of education on trust. First, more research—preferably causal inference-oriented—on the relationship is needed. Second, the effect of education on trust should be studied in multiple countries, as it is likely to vary between countries, possibly as a result of the average level of education (Borgonovi, 2012).

Other sociodemographic variables have also been related to social trust. Various indicators of resources—income (own and households'), satisfaction with income, subjective feelings of deprivation, and unemployment—are routinely included as explanations of trust. Since these variables have had the status of control variables in most studies, there has been relatively little theorizing about their effects other than a general notion that being resourceful is likely to lead to better treatment by others, which may ultimately promote trust (Delhey & Newton, 2003; Putnam, 2000). While varying across indicators, and less consistent than for education, cross-sectional evidence suggests a positive relationship between resources and trust (Alesina & LaFerrara, 2002; Brehm & Rahn, 1997; Delhey & Newton, 2003; Putnam, 2000; Smith, 1997; Whiteley, 1999, but see Uslaner [2002] for a differing finding). There is also evidence from panel data supporting this conclusion in Britain (Brandt, Wetherell, & Henry, 2014; Li et al., 2005; Sturgis et al., 2009) and the United States (Brandt et al., 2014) but not in Denmark (Sønderskov & Dinesen, 2014). One of the most interesting findings in this regard is that of Laurence (2015), who shows that job displacement reduces trust. Employing a lagged-dependent variable and change score approach to British panel data of individuals interviewed at age 33 and again at age 50, he finds a "scarring" effect of job displacement. Moreover, the effect of job displacement is concentrated among those with high job centrality, thereby suggesting that psychological mechanisms related to increased mental distress likely account for the effect. Along the lines of this chapter, more theoretically informed studies coupled with rich panel data would clearly be valuable in scrutinizing the understudied role of socioeconomic resources in shaping trust.

Institutional Quality and Institutional Trust

As a final experiential factor, we want to highlight institutional influences. Again, this is an experiential factor in the broader sense; experiencing high- as opposed to low-quality institutions is expected to further social trust. Partly in response to Putnam's (1993) famous claim that trust—as a part of the wider concept of social capital—influences government performance, subsequent work has emphasized how state institutions may themselves shape trust in others. Perhaps most important, state institutions such as the judiciary and the police govern individuals' interactions, and to the extent that these institutions function efficiently and impartially, they can lay the foundations for trust between individuals (Levi, 1996; Rothstein & Stolle, 2008). More generally, state institutions—and especially the public employees that man them—send important signals about the moral stock of the general population. If institutions are represented by corrupt officials (e.g. doctors, teachers and bureaucrats), this send a strong signal (a) about the lack of untrustworthiness of other people (as represented by these public employees) and (b) that corrupt and untrustworthy behavior pays off (Levi, 1996; Rothstein & Stolle, 2008). Both have adverse effects on trust in other people.

States institutions exist in the aggregate, and an extensive number of studies have shown a rather strong empirical association between institutional quality—most often the impartiality component in terms of (freedom from) corruption—of aggregate units (typically countries) and social trust measured either in the aggregate or at the individual level (Dinesen, 2012a, 2013; Freitag & Bühlmann, 2009; Mishler & Rose, 2001; Nannestad et al., 2014; Rothstein & Stolle, 2008; Wang & Gordon, 2011; You, 2012). However, a number of studies have also examined how experiences of institutional (un)fairness channels into (mis)trust (Rothstein & Eek, 2009). Relatedly, a large number of studies examine how perceptions of institutional fairness or trust in institutions—both alleged attitudinal extension of experiences of institutional quality—are associated with social trust. While the result of these studies vary by type of institutions analyzed, as well as the country context, they generally report a positive association between social trust and attitudinal indicators of institutional quality (Alesina & LaFerrara 2002; Brehm & Rahn, 1997; Dinesen, 2012a, 2013; Freitag & Buhlmann 2009; Rothstein & Stolle 2008; Zmerli & Newton 2008). Being based on cross-sectional data, most of these studies are plagued by causal indeterminacy: it cannot be ruled out that perceptions of institutions are themselves shaped by social trust. However, a number of studies have examined the relationship using panel data and other designs better suited for determining causal relations. In an early effort, Brehm and Rahn (1997) found, in a structural equation model, that the path from confidence in institutions to social trust is substantially stronger than the reverse relationship in the United States. Mishler and Rose (2001) use instrumental variables techniques to estimate the relationship between institutional trust and social trust but find no relationship across a number of Eastern European countries. While attention to the direction of causality in these studies has clearly brought the field a step forward, the exogeneity of the alleged exogenous variables can be challenged (Sønderskov & Dinesen, 2016).[9] Two studies have also leveraged panel data to provide more solid causal evidence (Sønderskov & Dinesen, 2014, 2016). Utilizing two different panel data sets from Denmark, Sønderskov and Dinesen (2016) find, by means of cross-lagged models, that causality primarily runs from institutional trust to social trust. Moreover, they find that even when taking unobserved time-invariant confounding into account by means of individual fixed-effect models, institutional trust generally remains a significant predictor of social trust. Presently, this represents the strongest evidence for a causal effect of individual-level attitudinal manifestations of institutional quality (i.e., institutional trust) on social trust. Summing up, there is thus considerable evidence that experiences of institutional quality, and the trust in institutions that ostensibly flows from it, causally influences social trust. Following recent inquiries, and tying in with the experiential perspective, more research on how concrete experiences of institutional quality shape trust would be worthwhile.

■ CONCLUSION

This chapter has reviewed the individual-level causes of social trust. It has addressed explanations falling under the header of two broad classes of explanations: dispositional and experiential explanations. The dispositional perspective takes as its starting point the assumption that trust is a deeply rooted disposition— or a downstream consequence of even "deeper" dispositions—which is stable and only to a limited extent subject to experiential influences after the formative years of adolescence and early adulthood. Conversely, the experiential perspective posits that trust is shaped by contemporary experiences, broadly conceived.

Perhaps unsurprisingly given the vastness of the literature covered and the diverse set of explanations classified as dispositional or experiential, it is not possible to provide any general statements about the relative standing of the two generic explanations. There is considerable evidence for trust being both a dispositional and an experiential trait. At the same time, it is clear that some explanations fare better than others. Perhaps most noteworthy, the previously hailed civil society explanation, focusing on engagement in voluntary associations, has fared quite poorly empirically, and at this point the burden of proof is on those claiming that participation in voluntary associations influences trust. Other explanations— particularly those focusing on alternative social interactions and institutional factors—have received solid empirical backing and now stand as the primary experiential sources of trust.

Finally, the purpose of this review has also been to highlight the varying methodological rigor with which various explanations have been assessed and, not least, pinpoint which unresolved questions exist in the literature. In line with the literature on the causes of social and political attitudes more generally, the research designs used to address various explanations of trust have grown much more sophisticated over the past few years. This is a very welcome addition, which has clearly added to our understanding of the source of trust—perhaps most importantly with regard to which experiences can more robustly be claimed to causally stimulate trust. Further research along these lines will clearly benefit our understanding of the sources of social trust.

■ AUTHORS' NOTE

Peter Thisted Dinesen is the corresponding author. Dinesen wrote the chapter except for the section "Participation in Civic Life," which was drafted by Bekkers with additions by Dinesen.

■ NOTES

1. Similar to the studies focusing on trust as an outcome covered in this review, studies of trust as a cause often employ weak causal identification strategies. While reviewing these studies is beyond the focus of this review, it is arguably fair to say that the causal role of trust is still not fully established and therefore an important empirical matter for future research.

2. An influential early study (Glaeser, Laibson, Scheinkman, & Soutter, 2000) reported a divergence between behavior in trust games and responses to survey questions on trust, but subsequent extensions (Fehr, Fischbacher, von Rosenbladt, Schupp, & Wagner, 2002; Sapienza, Toldra, & Zingales, 2013) have convincingly shown that the two are in fact correlated empirically and therefore appear—at least to some extent—to reflect a common underlying phenomenon.

3. There is some variation in the specific formulation and measurement scale of the items in various surveys. See Revilla and Saris (2013) and Lundmark, Gilljam, and Dahlberg (2016) for a comparison of some of these different formats.

4. Hirashi et al. find a heritability of 31% in Japan. Oskarsson et al. find a heritability of 36% (33% for males and 39% for females) in Sweden. In Australia, Sturgis, Read, Hatemi, et al. (2010) find a heritability of 14% to 36% for four specific items and 66% for a latent trust factor combining these items. Jang, Livesley, Angleitner, Riemann, and Vernon (2002) do not report heritability estimates, but Falconer's formula $h^2 = 2 * (r_{MZ} - r_{DZ})$ yields heritability estimates of 28% in Canada and 44% in Germany. In a previous analysis, Jang, McCrae, Angleitner, Riemann, and Livesley (1998) reported an estimate of 37% in the combined data set. Finally, Van Lange et al. (2014) report a considerably lower heritability estimate of 5% in the Netherlands.

5. Or—to complicate things further—common experiences.

6. The question of absolute differences in trust between parents and children has also been examined, however (see Dinesen 2012b; Stolle & Nishikawa, 2011).

7. Relatedly, Alesina and Giuliano (2011) show that strength of family ties (indicative of "amoral familism") in society is negatively correlated with trust.

8. We refrain from a discussion of age and cohort effects on trust, which are covered in another chapter in this volume.

9. More specifically, the assumption that the instruments employed are only uncorrelated with social trust via institutional trust (conditional on a range of control variables) is problematic.

■ REFERENCES

Alesina, A., & Giuliano, P. (2011). Family ties and political participation. *Journal of the European Economic Association*, *9*(5), 817–839.

Alesina, A., & La Ferrara, E. (2002). Who trusts others? *Journal of Public Economics*, *85*(2), 207–234.

Alghan, Y., & Cahuc, P. (2010). Inherited trust and growth. *American Economic Review*, *100*(5), 2060–2092.

Anheier, A., & Kendall, J. (2002). Interpersonal trust and voluntary associations: Examining three approaches. *British Journal of Sociology*, *53*(3), 343–362.

Bagno, O. (2006, December). The destination does matter. Paper presented at the Graduate Conference, Haifa.

Bauer, P. C. (2015). Negative experiences and trust: A causal analysis of the effects of victimization on generalized trust. *European Sociological Review*, *31*(4), 397–417.

Bekkers, R. (2012). Trust and volunteering: Selection or causation? Evidence from a 4 year panel study. *Political Behavior*, *34*(2), 225–247.

Brehm, J., & Rahn, W. (1997). Individual-level evidence for the causes and consequences of social capital. *American Journal of Political Science*, *41*(3), 999–1023.

Borgonovi, F. (2012). The relationship between education and levels of trust and tolerance in Europe. *British Journal of Sociology*, *63*(1), 146–167.

Brandt, M. J., Wetherell, G., & Henry, P. J. (2014). Changes in income predict change in social trust: a longitudinal analysis. *Political Psychology*, *36*(6), 761–768. doi:10.1111/pops.12228

Carl, N., & Billari, F.C. (2014). Generalized trust and intelligence in the United States. *PLoS One*, *9*(3), e91786.

Claibourn, M. P., & Martin, P. S. (2000). Trusting and joining? An empirical test of the reciprocal nature of social capital. *Political Behavior*, *22*(4), 267–291.

Coleman, J.S. (1994). *Foundations of social theory*. Cambridge, MA: Harvard University Press.

Couch, L. L., & Jones, W. H. (1997). Measuring levels of trust. *Journal of Personality Research*, *31*(3), 319–36.

Dalton, R. J. (1980). Reassessing parental socialization: Indicator unreliability versus generational transfer. *American Political Science Review*, *74*(2), 421–431.

Dawes, R. M., McTavish, J., & Shaklee, H. (1977). Behavior, communication, and assumptions about other people's behavior in a commons dilemma situation. *Journal of Personality and Social Psychology*, *35*(1), 1–11.

Delhey, J., & Newton, K. (2003). Who trusts? The origins of social trust in seven societies. *European Societies*, *5*(2), 93–137.

Delhey, J., & Newton, K. (2005). Predicting cross-national levels of social trust: Global pattern or Nordic excaptionalism? *European Sociological Review*, *21*(4), 311–327.

Dinesen, P. T. (2010). Upbringing, early experiences of discrimination and social identity: Explaining generalised trust among immigrants in Denmark. *Scandinavian Political Studies*, *33*(1), 93–111.

Dinesen, P. T. (2012a). Does generalized (dis)trust travel? Examining the impact of cultural heritage and destination-country environment on trust of immigrants. *Political Psychology, 33*(4), 495–511.

Dinesen, P. T. (2012b). Parental transmission of trust or perceptions of institutional fairness: generalized trust of non-Western immigrants in a high-trust society. *Comparative Politics, 44*(3), 273–289.

Dinesen, P. T. (2013). Where you come from or where you live? Examining the cultural and institutional explanation of generalized trust using migration as a natural experiment. *European Sociological Review, 29*(1), 114–128.

Dinesen, P. T., & Hooghe, M. (2010). When in Rome, do as the Romans do: the acculturation of generalized trust among immigrants in Western Europe. *International Migration Review, 44*(3), 697–727.

Dinesen, P. T., Nørgaard, A. S., & Klemmensen, R. (2014). The civic personality: personality and democratic citizenship. *Political Studies, 62*(Suppl. 1), 134–152.

Dinesen, P. T., & Sønderskov, K. M. (2015). Ethnic diversity and social trust: Evidence from the micro-context. *American Sociological Review, 80*(3), 550–573.

Dinesen, P. T. & Sønderskov, K. M. (Forthcoming). Cultural persistence or experiential adaptation? A review of research examining the roots of social trust based on immigrants. In E. Uslaner (Ed.). *The Oxford Handbook on Social and Political Trust*. Oxford: Oxford University Press.

Dohmen, T., Falk, A., Huffman, D., & Sunde, U. (2012). The intergenerational transmission of risk and trust attitudes. *The Review of Economic Studies, 79*(2), 645–677.

Fehr, E., Fischbacher, U., von Rosenbladt, B., Schupp, J., & Wagner, G. G. (2002). A nationwide laboratory. *Schmollers Jahrbuch, 122*(519), 542.

Freitag, M., & Bühlmann, M. (2009). Crafting trust: The role of political institutions in a comparative perspective. *Comparative Political Studies, 42*(12), 1537–1566.

Freitag, M., & Traunmüller, R. (2009). Spheres of trust: An empirical analysis of the foundations of particularised and generalised trust. *European Journal of Political Research, 48*(6), 782–803.

Glaeser, E. L., Laibson, D., Scheinkman, J. A., & Soutter, C. L. (2000). Measuring trust. *Quarterly Journal of Economics, 115*, 811–846.

Glanville, J. L., & Andersson, M. A. (2013). Do social connections create trust? An examination using new longitudinal data. *Social Forces, 92*(2), 545–562.

Glanville, J. L., & Paxton, P. (2007). How do we learn to trust? A confirmatory tetrad analysis of the sources of generalized trust. *Social Psychology Quarterly, 70*(3), 230–242.

Gross, K., Aday, S. & Brewer, P. R. (2004). A panel study of media effects on political and social trust after September 11, 2001. *The Harvard International Journal of Press/Politics, 9*(4), 49–73.

Guiso, L., Sapienza, P. & Singales, L. (2008). Social capital as good culture. *Journal of the European Economic Association, 6*(2–3), 295–320.

Helliwell, J. F., & Putnam, R. D. (2004). The social context of well-being. *Philosophical Transactions of the Royal Society of London B, 359*, 1435–1446.

Helliwell, J. F., & Putnam, R. D. (2007). Education and social capital. *Eastern Economic Journal, 33*(1), 1–19

Helliwell, J. F., Wang, S. & Xu, J. (2016). How durable are social norms? Immigrant trust and generosity in 132 countries. *Social Indicators Research, 128*, 201–2019.

Hiraishi, K., Yamagata, S., Shikishima, C., & Ando, J. (2008). Maintenance of genetic variation in personality through control of mental mechanisms: A test of trust, extraversion, and agreeableness. *Evolution and Human Behavior, 29*(2), 79–85.

Hooghe, M., Marien S., & De Vroome, T. (2012). The cognitive basis of trust: The relation between education, cognitive ability, and generalized and political trust. *Intelligence, 40*(6), 604–613.

Huang, J., Maassen van den Brink, H., & W. Groot (2009). A meta-analysis of the effect of education on social capital. *Economics of Education Review, 28*(4), 454–464.

Huang, J., Maassen van den Brink, H., & Groot, W. (2011). College education and social trust: an evidence-based study on the causal mechanisms. *Social Indicators Research, 104*(2), 287–310.

Huang, J., Maassen van den Brink, H., & Groot, W. (2012). Does education promote social capital? Evidence from IV analysis and nonparametric-bound analysis. *Empirical Economics, 42*(3), 1011–1034.

Jang, K., Livesley, J., Angleitner, A., Riemann, R., & Vernon, P. (2002). Genetic and environmental influences on the covariance of facets defining the domains of the five factor model of personality. *Personality and Individual Differences, 33*(1), 83–101.

Jang, K., McCrae, R., Angleitner, A., Riemann, R., & Livesley, J. (1998). Heritability of facet-level trait in a cross-cultural twin sample: Support for a hierarchical model of personality. *Journal of Personality and Social Psychology, 74*(6), 1556–1565.

Jennings, M. K., Markus, G. B., & Neimi, R. G. (1991). *Youth-parent socialization panel study, 1965–1982: Three waves combined.* Ann Arbor, MI: Inter-University Consortium for Political and Social Research.

Kam, C. D., & Palmer, C. L. (2008). Reconsidering the effects of education on political participation. *Journal of Politics, 70*(3), 612–631.

Knack, S., & Keefer, P. (1997). Does social capital have an economic payoff? A cross-country investigation. *Quarterly Journal of Economics, 112*(4), 1251–1288.

Knack, S., & Zak, P. (2002). Building trust: Public policy, interpersonal trust, and economic development. *Supreme Court Economic Review, 10*(1), 91–109.

Laurence, J. (2015). (Dis) placing trust: The long-term effects of job displacement on generalised trust over the adult lifecourse. *Social Science Research, 50*(1), 46–59.

Levi, M. (1996). Social and unsocial capital. *Politics and Society, 24*(1), 45–55.

Li, Y., Pickles, A., & Savage, M. (2005). Social capital and social trust in Britain. *European Sociological Review, 21*(2), 109–123.

Lundmark, S., Gilljam, M., & Dahlberg, S. (2016). Measuring generalized trust: An examination of question wording and the number of scale points. *Public Opinion Quarterly, 80*(1), 26–43.

Marschall, M., & Stolle, D. (2004). Race and the city: Neighborhood context and the development of generalized trust. *Political Behavior, 26*(2), 125–153.

McPherson, M., Popielarz, P. A., & Drobnic, S. (1992). Social networks and organizational dynamics. *American Sociological Review, 57*(2), 153–170.

Milligan, K., Moretti, E., & Oreopoulos, P. (2004). Does education improve citizenship? Evidence from the United States and the United Kingdom. *Journal of Public Economics, 88*(9–10), 1667–1695.

Mishler, W., & Rose, R. (2001). What are the origins of political trust? Testing institutional and cultural theories in post-communist societies. *Comparative Political Studies, 34*(1), 30–62.

Mondak, J., & Halperin, K. D. (2008). A framework for the study of personality and political behavior. *British Journal of Political Science, 38*(2), 335-362.

Nannestad, P. (2008). What have we learned about generalized trust, if anything? *Annual Review of Political Science, 11*, 413-436.

Nannestad, P., Svendsen, G. T., Dinesen, P. T. & Sønderskov, K. M. (2014). Do institutions or culture determine the level of social trust? The natural experiment of migration from non-Western to Western countries. *Journal of Ethnic and Migration Studies, 40*(4), 544-565.

Oskarsson, S., Dawes, C., Johannesson, M., & Magnusson, P. (2012). The genetic origins of social trust. *Twin Research and Human Genetics, 15*, 21-33.

Oskarsson, S., Dinesen, P. T., Dawes, C.T., Johannesson, M., Magnusson, P. K. E. (Forthcoming). Education and social trust: Testing a Causal Hypothesis Using the Discordant Twin Design. *Political Psychology.*

Paxton, P. (2007). Associational memberships and generalized trust: A multilevel model across 31 countries. *Social Forces, 86*(1), 47-76.

Polderman, T. J. C., Benyamin, B., De Leeuw, C. A., Sullivan, P. F., Van Bochoven, A., Visscher, P. M., & Posthuma, D. (2015). Meta-analysis of the heritability of human traits based on fifty years of twin studies. *Nature Genetics, 47*, 702-709. doi:10.1038/ng.3285

Portes, A., & Vickstrom, E. (2011). Diversity, social capital, and cohesion. *Annual Review of Sociology, 37*, 461-479.

Putnam, R. D. (1993). *Making democracy work: Civic traditions in modern Italy.* Princeton, NJ: Princeton University Press.

Putnam, R. D. (2000). *Bowling alone: The collapse and revival of American community.* New York: Simon & Schuster.

Putnam, R. D. (2007). E pluribus unum: Diversity and community in the twenty-first century. *Scandinavian Political Studies, 30*(2), 137-174.

Revilla, M. A., & Saris, W. E. (2013). A comparison of the quality of questions in a dace-to-face and a web survey. *International Journal of Public Opinion Research, 25*(2), 242-253.

Rice, T. W., & Feldman, J. L. (1997). Civic culture and democracy: From Europe to America. *Journal of Politics, 59*(4), 1143-1172.

Richey, S. (2007). Manufacturing trust: Community currencies and the creation of social capital. *Political Behavior, 29*(1), 69-88.

Robinson, R. V., & Jackson, E. F. (2001). Is trust in others declining in America? An age-period-cohort analysis. *Social Science Research, 30*(1), 117-145.

Rosenberg, M. (1956). Misanthropy and political ideology. *American Sociological Review, 21*(6), 690-695.

Rothstein B., & Eek, D. (2009). Political corruption and social trust. An experimental approach. *Rationality and Society, 21*(1), 81-112.

Rothstein, B., & Stolle, D. (2008). The state and social capital: an institutional theory of generalized trust. *Comparative Politics, 40*(4), 441-459.

Rotter, J. B. (1967). A new scale for the measurement of interpersonal trust. *Journal of personality, 35*(4), 651-665.

Rotter, J. B. (1971). Generalized expectancies for interpersonal trust. *American psychologist, 26*(5), 443.

Rönnerstrand, B. (2013). Social capital and immunisation against the 2009 A (H1N1) pandemic in Sweden. *Scandinavian Journal of Public Health, 41*(8), 853-859.

Sapienza, P., Toldra, A., & Zingales, L. (2013). Understanding trust. *Economic Journal, 123*(573), 1313-1332.

Schaeffer, M. (2013). *Ethnic diversity, public goods provision and social cohesion: Lessons from an inconclusive literature.* WZB Discussion Paper SP VI 2013-103. Berlin: Wissenschaftszentrum Berlin für Sozialforschung.

Siisiäinen, M., & Kankainen, T. (2014). Trust and participation in voluntary associations of 8th graders in 22 countries. *Voluntas, 26*(2), 1–20.

Smith, T. W. (1997). Factors relating to misanthropy in contemporary American society. *Social Science Research, 26*(2), 170–196.

Sønderskov, K. M. (2011a). Does generalized social trust lead to associational membership? Unravelling a bowl of well-tossed spaghetti. *European Sociological Review, 27*(4), 419–434.

Sønderskov, K. M. (2011b). Explaining large-N cooperation: Generalized social trust and the social exchange heuristic. *Rationality and Society, 23*(1), 51–74.

Sønderskov, K. M., & Dinesen, P. T. (2014). Danish exceptionalism: Explaining the unique increase in social trust over the past 30 years. *European Sociological Review, 30*(6), 782–795.

Sønderskov, K. S., & Dinesen, P. T. (2016). Trusting the state, trusting each other? The effect of institutional trust on social trust. *Political Behavior, 38,* 179–202.

Stolle, D. (1998). Bowling together, bowling alone: The development of generalized trust in voluntary associations. *Political Psychology, 19*(3), 497–525.

Stolle, D., & Hooghe, M. (2004). The roots of social capital: Attitudinal and network mechanisms in the relation between youth and adult indicators of social capital. *Acta Politica, 39*(4), 422–441.

Stolle, D., & Nishikawa, L. (2011). Trusting others—how parents shape the generalized trust of their children. *Comparative Sociology, 10*(2), 281–314.

Sturgis, P., Patulny, R., & Allum, N. (2009). Re-evaluating the individual level causes of trust: A panel data analysis. http://privatewww.essex.ac.uk/~nallum/BJSFINAL.pdf

Sturgis, P., Read, S., & Allum, N. (2010). Does intelligence foster generalized trust? An empirical test using the UK birth cohort studies. *Intelligence, 38*(1), 45–54.

Sturgis, P., Read, S., Hatemi, P., Zhu, G., Trull, T., Wright, M., & Martin, N. (2010). A genetic basis for social trust? *Political Behavior, 32*(2), 205–230.

Tabellini, G. (2008). Presidential address. Institutions and culture. *Journal of the European Economic Association, 6*(2–3), 255–294.

Uslaner, E. (2002). *The moral foundations of trust.* Cambridge, UK: Cambridge University Press.

Uslaner, E. (2008). Where you stand depends upon where your grandparents sat. *Public Opinion Quarterly, 72*(4), 725–740.

Van der Meer, T., & Tolsma, J. (2014). Ethnic diversity and its effects on social cohesion. *Annual Review of Sociology, 40,* 459–478.

Van Ingen, E., & Bekkers, R. (2015). Trust through civic engagement? Evidence from five national panel studies. *Political Psychology, 36*(3), 277–294.

Van Lange, P. A. M. (2015). Generalized trust: Four lessons from genetics and culture. *Current Directions in Psychological Science, 24*(1), 71–76.

Van Lange, P. A., Vinkhuyzen, A. A., & Posthuma, D. (2014). Genetic influences are virtually absent for trust. *PLoS One, 9*(4), e93880.

Wang, L., & Gordon, P. (2011). Trust and institutions: A multilevel analysis. *Journal of Socio-Economics, 40*(5), 583–593.

Whiteley, P. F. (1999). The origins of social capital. In J. W. Van Deth, M. Maraffi, K. Newton, & P. F. Whiteley (Eds.), *Social capital and European democracy* (pp. 25–44). London: Routledge.

Wollebaek, D., & Selle, P. (2002). Does participation in voluntary associations contribute to social capital? The impact of intensity, scope, and type. *Nonprofit and Voluntary Sector Quarterly, 31*(1), 32–61.

Yamagishi, T. (2001). Trust as a form of social intelligence. In K. Cook (Ed.), *Trust in society* (pp. 121–147). London: SAGE.

You, J.-S. (2012). Social trust: Fairness matters more than homogeneity. *Political Psychology, 33*(5), 701–721.

Zmerli, S., & Newton, K. (2008). Social trust and attitudes toward democracy. *Public Opinion Quarterly, 72*(4), 706–724.

6 How Trust in Social Dilemmas Evolves with Age

■ MARTIN G. KOCHER

■ INTRODUCTION

While the importance of trust and trustworthiness in human interaction has been stressed repeatedly in the scholarly literature in the social sciences and in biology, there is still surprisingly little understanding of some of the determinants of trust. How is trust related to experience of trustworthiness? How can trust be repaired after an incidence of breaching trust? To what extent does trust depend on observable characteristics or stereotypes?

In the following, we focus on an aspect of trust that has long been neglected by economists: the relationship between trusting as well as trustworthy behavior in social dilemmas and age.[1] As an observable characteristic, the impact of age on trust and trustworthiness has many real-world implications. For instance, understanding age as a potential determinant of trust among children and adolescents might help develop school curricula and learning environments for children that are conducive to establishing trusting and cooperative relationships among themselves. Comparing trust and trustworthiness of parents and their children in different family situations could be useful in disentangling different intergenerational transmission mechanisms of trust and cooperation. Looking at trust between generations and at a possible drop in trust at old age should provide insights into potential problems associated with an aging society. And finally, understanding the evolution of trust and trustworthiness could be helpful in providing indications on how to repair trust after incidences of trust loss.

Trust and trustworthiness are key determinants of economic success measured both at the micro level and at the macro level. Almost any economic transaction at the micro level requires trust, trustworthiness, and cooperation. Since contracts can never specify all contingencies of an economic exchange—no matter how detailed they are—there is always a required minimum level of trust and trustworthiness to make economic interactions happen, and very often the required level is quite profound, also in high-stakes environments. At the macro level, aggregate trust in a region or a country have shown to be positively correlated with economic outcomes such as gross domestic product (LaPorta, Lopez-de-Silane, Shleifer, & Vishny, 1997), growth (Knack and Keefer, 1997; Zak and Knack, 2001), inflation rates (LaPorta et al., 1997), or, for instance, the volume of trade between countries (Guiso, Sapienza, & Zingales, 2009).

There are several definitions of trust, but recent research in economics usually refers to Coleman (1990), whose characterization of trust is often slightly adapted and relates to a two-person interaction. In the following, we see trust as the voluntary placement of resources or decision-making power in the hands of another party (the trustee) without legal commitment or informal retaliatory options (such as punishment) by a trustor (or investor). To make the setup interesting, trust must potentially bear the expectation to be better off by trusting than by not trusting if the trustee is trustworthy. In other words, the interaction between the trustor and the trustee entails a potential efficiency gain that leaves the trustor better off if the trustee is trustworthy and worse off if not. Trust thus means that the trustor makes him- or herself vulnerable to the decisions of the trustee (Rousseau, Sitkin, Burt, & Camerer, 1998). Given the richness of the definition, it is difficult to directly link trusting and trustworthy behavior to underlying (economic) preferences and beliefs (expectations).

Trust is obviously related to cooperation in social dilemmas (see Gächter, Herrmann, & Thöni, 2004), since cooperation often requires trust in the cooperation of others. Social dilemmas are a more general class of situations. They characterize (potentially multiperson) interactions that entail a trade-off between individual rationality and collective rationality. If everyone cooperates or trusts, everyone is better off than otherwise. However, there is the temptation to unilaterally deviate from trusting or cooperating, which leads to an exploitation of others and an even higher payoff for the deviating individual. If everyone deviates, everyone is worse off.

Trust, trustworthiness, and cooperative inclinations have been measured in many ways in experimental studies and in studies based on field data. The experimental literature started with the famous prisoner's dilemma game (Poundstone, 1992), followed by different versions of the public goods game (Ledyard, 1995). Some decades later the gift-exchange game (Fehr, Kirchsteiger, & Riedl, 1993) and, in particular, the trust (or investment) game (Berg, Dickhaut, & McCabe, 1995) provided experimental workhorses that allowed studying trust and trustworthiness more directly. Concurrently, large-scale international surveys and panels enabled economists and other social scientists to conduct studies on trust and trustworthiness for international comparisons.

The rest of the chapter is organized as follows. The next section starts with a discussion of common methodological challenges when assessing the relationship between trust as well as trustworthiness and age. We then discuss the main empirical findings of nonincentivized survey measures of trust and trustworthiness that take age as a determinant of trust into account. The fourth section looks at survey panels and online studies using partly incentivized methods to study the evolution of trust and trustworthiness with age, and then we survey the experimental literature, mainly focusing on the seminal trust game, including small variations that have been applied in the laboratory or in the field. Next we discuss potential underlying mechanisms that could explain developments of trust and trustworthiness with age. The final section concludes the chapter and lists remaining open puzzles, blind spots in the literature, and avenues for future research.

▨ COMMON CHALLENGES WHEN STUDYING TRUST AND AGE

Eliciting trust and trustworthiness seems straightforward to most researches in the social sciences. The bulk of the literature nowadays uses either a variant of the World Values Survey (WVS) or a variant of the trust game (Berg et al., 1995). In the following, we introduce the two methods very briefly and discuss common methodological challenges when studying trust and trustworthiness in combination with age as an independent variable.

Two Often Applied Methods to Elicit Trust and Trustworthiness

The WVS[2] contains two types of nonincentivized questions related to trust, a binary question and a set of questions on a 4-point scale. The binary question used for more than 30 years reads "Generally speaking, would you say that most people can be trusted or that you need to be very careful in dealing with people?" with answers "Most people can be trusted" and "Need to be very careful." The questions on the 4-point scale are asked in relationship to specific groups: "I'd like to ask you how much you trust people from various groups. Could you tell me for each whether you trust people from this group completely, somewhat, not very much or not at all? Your family [Your neighborhood; People you know personally; People you meet for the first time; People of another religion; People of another nationality]." The answers are rated on the following categories: "Trust completely," Trust somewhat," "Do not trust very much," and "Do not trust at all." These questions exist for three waves of the survey. More questions have been added (e.g., "Now could you tell me whether you agree strongly, agree a little, neither agree nor disagree, disagree a little, or disagree strongly with each of the following statements?: I see myself as someone who is generally trusting."), but they are not consistently used in the waves or exist only since recently. Researchers have used the answers to these and similar questions related to trust and trustworthiness extensively in scientific studies. Interestingly, cooperation in social dilemmas as a general concept has not been researched much based on survey questions, probably because it is more complicated to explain the incentives in a social dilemma within one survey question, and "cooperation" is more difficult to discuss in the abstract, without a specific situation in mind.

When it comes to incentivized elicitation methods of trust and trustworthiness, the trust game introduced by Berg et al. (1995) is the most commonly used paradigm nowadays. It is a two-player, two-stage bargaining game, and it is usually incentivized monetarily. Both the trustor and the trustee have the same initial endowment $X > 0$. The trustor can send a positive amount $x \leq X$ to the trustee. The trustee receives $n * x$ (with $n = 3$, usually) and can return any amount y, with $0 \leq y \leq n * x$. The final payoff for the trustor is $X - x + y$, and for the trustee it is $X + n * x - y$. The decision of the trustor is interpreted as a measure of trust, whereas the decision of the trustee (dependent on the trust level) is interpreted as a measure of trustworthiness or reciprocity. Indeed, as will be discussed in greater detail later, there might be many underlying motives or preferences that would explain the behavior of the two decision-makers without alluding to trust and trustworthiness. Examples are efficiency preferences, specific forms of inequality aversion, or altruism.

In the following, we discuss a set of methodological challenges when measuring trust and trustworthiness across different age groups. Most of these challenges apply to both nonincentivized survey measures and incentivized experiments based on interaction. One important aspect to note in general is that age is, obviously, never an exogenous variable. Even in experiments it is impossible to assign age randomly to experimental participants (although age perception can be influenced by the use of experimental methods to a certain extent; Bargh, Chen, & Burrows, 1996; Doyen, Klein, Pichon, & Cleeremans, 2012). Hence there is no direct causal inference, and differences in behavior across different age groups could potentially stem from other variables that have been omitted or that have not been properly controlled for (e.g., differences in cognitive abilities). As a consequence, methodological aspects and the details of the elicitation procedure become even more important when studying age differences in trust and trustworthiness than they are when assessing concepts that can be exogenously varied.

Sample Selection Issues

Sample selection is a particular concern in studies that compare behavior of different groups. Imagine that one wants to study levels of trust and trustworthiness of children, adolescents, and adults; that is, one aims to characterize trust and trustworthiness over the whole life span, excluding only very young children. Apart from representative samples that are very expensive, it is difficult to balance the sample across different age groups. The problem is particularly severe with younger children, for whom sample selection criteria must be partly based on their parents' or household characteristics. If one conducts experiments in kindergartens and schools, which is often the method of choice for practical reasons, it is obviously important that different kindergarten and school types are comparable and that there is no systematic selection of certain students into certain institutions, for instance, with regard to gender (which, however, can be controlled for) or with regard to the propensity of attending specific school types or pursuing specific educational careers later on. If sample selection is not properly controlled for, age differences in the levels of trust and trustworthiness cannot be ascribed to the variable age; they could also be a consequence of the sample selection.

Procedures of Elicitation

One of the most daunting tasks for the researcher is the choice of proper stimuli and appropriate questions. Obviously, an average eight-year-old has a different level of comprehension and cognitive ability than an adult experimental participant. In a survey-based elicitation, the questions to be asked would potentially have to be age-adjusted, creating possible confounds of age and a change in the elicitation method.

Using incentivized experiments also requires comparable stimuli across different age groups. The description of the trust game has to be as similar as possible across different age groups, without sounding weird or ill-adapted for specific groups. For instance, a description of the trust game suitable for a six-year-old might sound very odd to an 18-year old. A compromise between the two objectives is sometimes difficult. One potential workaround, at least to a certain extent, is the use of comprehension questions after the experimental instructions but before the start of the experiment that give an impression of the level of understanding of the experimental instructions by different age groups and that allow the potential exclusion of participants from the analysis based on comprehension. Again, sample selection could become an issue if the number of excluded observations is larger in certain age groups than in others.

Comparability of Incentives and Reward Media

While nonincentivized questionnaires usually only care for the incentives to participate and to take the survey seriously, incentivized experiments have to be more careful when it comes to the question of how to use incentives and how to make them comparable across different groups.[3] Even though, surprisingly, there is not much hard evidence from the laboratory on differences in behavior in simple games that are fully incentivized and those that are not, most economists think that it is important to incentivize the trust game and not to use it as a hypothetical scenario in order to reduce the influence of social desirability. Potentially, the choice of incentives versus no incentives has differential effects on different age levels, but again, we are not aware of systematic empirical evidence on this question.

The first choice to be taken is the choice of reward medium. For various reasons monetary incentives is the best available choice. There are no serious issues of valuation and comparability. Even young children have a clear understanding of money as a concept and are able to assess monetary amounts, starting at an age of around seven years. For younger children, it is obviously necessary to use alternative reward media, and the best choice here is to use tokens that can be exchanged for a choice from a set of about equally valued small toys. The more tokens one possesses after the interaction, the more toys can be chosen. This basically creates a currency in its own right that is easy to understand for younger children and can be used starting at an age of about four years, as long as absolute numbers involved in the "currency" exchange remain small.

Comparability of stakes across different age groups is supposedly the most difficult problem. Some studies use average weekly allowances of children from their parents as a proxy for different levels of purchasing power, but allowances are usually very hard to compare because they include different required expenses for different age groups in childhood (e.g., older children might be asked to buy lunches from their allowances, whereas younger ones are not). Comparability with wages or income of adults is even harder to achieve.

Interestingly, the exact stake size above a certain minimum does not seem to play an important role in many interactions. While some studies report stake size effects in simple games, usually they are small and do not affect decisions profoundly (see, e.g., Camerer, 2003; Fehr, Tougareva, & Fischbacher, 2014; Kocher, Martinsson, & Visser, 2008). However, most of the empirical results on stake size effects are based on a comparison between standard experimental stakes and higher stakes. There is much less evidence for potential differences in behavior between low stakes versus standard stakes, because experiments in the economics literature usually provide incentives that are at least as high as the opportunity costs of experimental participants.

In Sutter and Kocher (2007), we look at different stake levels for students to be able to exclude that differences in trust and trustworthiness between younger children and students are driven by stake size effects, using also comparatively very small stakes for students in some of the experimental sessions. The results suggest that small stakes go a long way, since we do not observe any significant stake size effects (i.e., we do not observe different choices for different stake levels).

Cross-Section versus Time Series

Ideally, one would like to measure the inclination to trust or to be trustworthy at a certain (young) age level, follow the development of these measures over time at the individual level, and link the measures to real-world decision-making or real-world outcomes that require trust and trustworthiness. To the best of our knowledge, there is no experimental study of trust and trustworthiness that uses a longitudinal dimension of significant duration. Despite how strongly desirable such a large-scale longitudinal study seems to be from a scientific perspective, it requires an enormous effort by researchers with delayed gratification by potential publications. Furthermore, it involves repeated measurement, creating confounding effects of learning or repeated measurement in its own right (e.g., a preference for consistency could suppress certain developments), which makes inference more difficult. If trust and trustworthiness are indeed influenced by individual experience, then it is almost impossible to control for all possible confounding effects.

In practice, the "development" or "evolution" of trust and trustworthiness with age is usually measured using a cross-section of participants of different age levels. While it is very likely that potential differences between the different age groups are driven by age, it is impossible to rule out cultural change or other cohort effects as the source of the differences. One has to bear this interpretation in mind, particularly when a study covers a very wide set of different age groups.

Finally, it seems relevant to emphasize that many of the interesting developments in trust and trustworthiness indeed seem to happen at a young age. Thus it is important to care about confounds and methodological challenges, because they are potentially most relevant in comparison between young and old participants and between differently aged children. Reliable comparisons between differently aged adults are, in general, much easier to achieve.

■ TRUST AND AGE IN SURVEY MEASURES

Despite very large numbers of observations, results on trust and age that are based on nonincentivized survey measures are not fully conclusive. Li and Fung (2013) use data from the 2005 WVS from 38 countries and report a positive relationship between trust and age in adulthood. Fehr (2009) summarizes some evidence for a U-shaped relationship, and Fehr, Fischbacher, von Rosenbladt, Schupp, and Wagner (2003) as well as Naef, Fehr, Fischbacher, Schupp, and Wagner (2008) show a decrease of trust in older age groups for the survey parts of their studies.

More recently, Poulin and Haase (2015) have looked at around 250,000 responses to the binary trust question in the WVS for five waves and 97 societies. At age 20, 23% of the respondents agree that "most people can be trusted." This rate rises to 35% for 80-year-olds. They also analyze data from the General Social Survey Panel in the United States. Based on a sample of more than 1,000 participants, age is again a positive predictor of trust. Interestingly, the authors report a significant increase not only across cohorts but also in terms of the longitudinal dimension. The increase over a four-year horizon is uniform across different age groups, but it is small in absolute terms.

Obviously, large-scale survey studies of trust and trustworthiness do unfortunately not include children and adolescents as respondents.

■ TRUST AND AGE MEASURED WITH LARGE-SCALE SURVEY PANELS OR ONLINE

The beauty of representative survey panels is that they avoid sample selection biases. If they incorporate incentivized experiments, they combine the advantage of representativeness with the advantage of saliently incentivized experiments. However, they usually do not include nonadult participants (i.e., the age span covered is usually confined to adulthood).

Fehr et al. (2003) and Naef et al. (2008) have included a variant of the original trust game into a representative survey of German households in the so-called German Socio-Economic Panel. In particular, they double the transfer x and also the back transfer from the trustee to the trustor. The latter is unusual, but it does not change the basic nature of the game. Thus the final payoff for the trustor is $X - x + 2y$, and for the trustee it is $X + 2x - y$. When looking at the relationship between age and trust as well as trustworthiness, they find that older respondents (in particular those over 65) exhibit lower levels of trust by choosing lower transfers x than respondents in their 30s and 40s.

A somewhat similar finding is provided by Bellemare and Kröger (2007) based on a representative panel of Dutch households and a standard version of the trust game that is also incentivized. They find that the propensity to trust reaches its maximum at 37 years of age, following an inverted-U-shape with age (see further Putnam, 2000; Alesina & La Ferrara, 2002). Interestingly, the results in Bellemare and Kröger seem to suggest that the degree of trustworthiness (i.e., returns y) increases with age, or it follows a U-shaped pattern with age, depending on the particular incentives given. Such a divergence between trust and trustworthiness is difficult to reconcile with rational beliefs, but similar results are provided by incentivized experiments in laboratory settings (see later discussion).

Ermisch, Gambetta, Laurie, Siedler, and Uhrig (2009) use British household members dropping out from the British Household Panel Study as their participants. They apply a binary trust game and find, in contrast to the two studies mentioned previously, an increase in trust with age. However, the sample is comparatively small, and it unclear to what extent all relevant age groups are well-represented in their data.

In general, the magnitudes of the age effects found in the studies mentioned earlier are not very large, however significant at conventional levels. One reason for this could be the fact that there is no (age) information on the interaction partner. Hence, trustors and trustees do not only play against anonymous interaction partners but also against interaction partners whose general characteristics they do not know. Relaxing this uncertainty could have an effect, as some of the papers that are discussed in the next section seem to imply.

Although nowadays an increasing number of experiments are conducted over the Internet and not in the laboratory or in similar environments outside of the laboratory, we are not aware of any incentivized studies that report on the relationship between trust as well as trustworthiness and age over the Internet using Amazon Mechanical Turk (M-turk), similar Web interfaces, or self-developed Web interfaces. Amir, Rand, and Gal (2012) implement a trust game on M-turk with almost 800 participants, but they look at salience effects of different incentives and do not mention age effects in their paper.

■ TRUST AND AGE MEASURED IN INCENTIVIZED LABORATORY OR LAB-IN-THE-FIELD EXPERIMENTS

The set of laboratory and lab-in-the-field experiments that assess the relationship between trust as well as trustworthiness and age, covering a substantial part of the life span, is comparatively small (a comparison of existing experiments is provided in Table 6.1).[4] To the best of our knowledge, Harbaugh, Krause, and Liday (2003) is the first paper that addresses the issue by comparing levels of trust and trustworthiness among children and adolescents with an age range of 8 to 17 years and including an adult participant group. While they do not find any significant correlation between age and trust or trustworthiness, it is possible that their null result is driven by a specific design choice: the use of the strategy vector method. This method asks decision-makers to indicate decisions for different contingencies. More specifically, trustors had to make decisions for five different trustees, each from a different age group out of the set of 8-year-olds, 11-year-olds, 14-year-olds, 17-year-olds, and adults, and trustees were asked to indicate returns for each of the possible transfer levels. Unfortunately, no study exists that assesses the effects of the strategy vector method compared to the direct response method for children, but it is conceivable that any potential bias of the strategy vector

TABLE 6.1. *Laboratory Experiments on the Relationship between Trust, Trustworthiness, and Age*

	Age span	Number of participants	Experimental method	Details of the implemented trust game
Harbaugh, Krause, Liday, & Vesterlund (2003)	8 to 17 years and adult group	153	Partly SVM	*Endowment*: both 4 tokens *Multiplication*: ×3 *Reward*: tokens into presents
Holm and Nystedt (2005)	20 years and 70 years	20-year-olds: 26 70-year-olds: 55	Partly SVM	*Endowment*: both 100 Swedish Kronor *Multiplication*: ×3 *Reward*: money
Sutter and Kocher (2007)	8 to about 80 years	8-year-olds: 90 12-year-olds: 122 16-year-olds: 100 Students: 220 Professionals: 62 Retirees: 68	Direct response	*Endowment*: trustor 10 tokens; trustee zero tokens *Multiplication*: ×3 *Reward*: money (control treatments for different stake sizes)
Evans et al. (2013)	4 to 5 years and 9 to 10 years	4/5-year-olds: 81 9/10-year-olds: 91	Direct response; no trustees (deception)	*Endowment*: 1 bag *Multiplication*: ×4 *Reward*: bags with toys

Note. SVM = strategy vector method.

method (either an experimenter demand effect or possible confusion mitigating treatment effects) is stronger with children than with adult participants.

Sutter and Kocher (2007) apply the direct response method and cover an even larger age span from eight-year-olds to a group of retired participants. However, they focus on the interactions between trustors and trustees on the same age level, including common knowledge of this. In other words, 8-year-old trustors know that they interact with an anonymous 8-year-old trustee; 12-year-old trustors know that they interact with an anonymous 12-year-old trustee; and so on. The results in Sutter and Kocher, based on a slightly modified version of the standard trust game with no initial endowment for the trustee, indicate an almost linear increase in trust levels in childhood and adolescence and a stable pattern for adults, with the exception of their retired participants whose trust level is significantly lower than those of their working professional group and their student group. More specifically, 8-year-olds transfer only an average of 20% of their endowment to trustees, 12-year-olds transfer 36%, 16-year-olds transfer 55%, and the adult groups (excluding the group of retirees—with 54%) transfer more than 65%.

Low levels of trust among the young participants in this study are rationalized by even lower levels of trustworthiness. The youngest age group, the 8-year-olds, returns only 10% of whatever they have received. This rate increases to 15% for 12-year-olds and to more than 30% for 16-year-olds. It seems that the level of trustworthiness is quite stable from an age of around 15 to 16 years on, with return rates between 30% and 40% for all age groups aged 16 and older, with the notable exception of the group of retired participants who exhibit a spectacular return rate of 57%.

To summarize the main findings in Sutter and Kocher (2007) in a nutshell, we highlight three aspects. First, trust seems to increase with age in childhood and adolescence and to stay constant in adulthood. Second, trustworthiness or reciprocity seems to reach a certain average level (of around one-third, which is notably exactly the threshold for making trust profitable for the trustor, on average, if the transfer is tripled) already at a younger age and then stays rather constant. Third, retired decision-makers constitute an interesting exception with a lower level of trust than younger adults and a much higher level of trustworthiness, respectively reciprocity. Interestingly, the latter results seem in line with the evidence from panel surveys (see the previous section).[5]

Holm and Nystedt (2005) combine aspects of the experiment of Harbaugh, Krause, Liday, and Vesterlund (2003) and Sutter and Kocher (2007). They implement a mail-based trust game involving two groups of participants: 20-year-old young adults and 70-year-old retirees. The mail-based implementation requires the use of the strategy vector method for the return of the trustee. One interesting feature of the experiment is the option to provide a ranking of the preferred interaction partner for the game based on age and gender. More precisely, each trustor had to indicate a ranking of the four categories (women aged 20, men aged 20, women aged 70, and men aged 70) in terms of what category they wanted the trustee to come from. Matching was implemented in a way that ensured consideration of the ranking, and participants knew that.

In line with Sutter and Kocher (2007), younger participants trusted more, on average, than older participants in the study of Holm and Nystedt (2005). The difference is, however, not significant at conventional levels, which is probably a consequence of a comparatively small sample size. With regard to the preference over different interaction partners, the data show a clear in-group bias. Old decision-makers tend to prefer old decision-makers, and young decision-makers prefer young decision-makers as interaction partners. Both have a preference for female trustees. The comparison of young and old trustees in terms of levels of trustworthiness is less conclusive. The slope of the strategy vector of return transfers of the group of old decision-makers seems to be steeper than the slope of the 20-year-olds (i.e., they are more sensitive to the transfer levels chosen by trustors).

Evans, Athenstaedt, and Krueger (2013) extend the research to younger children, with all the problems associated with explaining a trust game to a four-year-old. They implement three games, of which one is a binary variant of the trust game. In particular, the experimenter shows the participant in the role of the trustor a "surprise bag" containing toys such as pencils, key rings, stickers, or balloons. Toys are wrapped and cannot be identified. The child can decide to keep the bag or send it to another child (in the role of the trustee) who would then receive four bags. The trustee can return two bags or none. Two other versions of the game (termed "altruism game" and "temptation game") are implemented to disentangle potential motives at different age levels. Participants were kindergarten children (age 4 to 5 years) and primary school kids (age 9 to 10 years).

The main result of the study is that primary school children are much more trusting (79%) than kindergarten children (27%), even if the proper control for altruism (a "trust" game without the second stage; i.e., the trustee could not return any of the four bags that he or she might have received depending on the decision of the trustor) is applied at the individual level in a logistic regression.

Unfortunately, the experiment did not involve "real" trustees. The experimenters would come back to the children after a few days with two surprise bags and tell all children who had trusted that the trustee had returned two bags. Therefore, no decisions regarding trustworthiness could be recorded. Moreover, the time delay that was known to the children already when deciding could have had a stronger effect on kindergarten children than on primary school children.

In a second experiment children were "interacting" with the other age group (i.e., kindergarteners also interacted with primary school children and vice versa), and the delay for the feedback was removed. The original results were replicated, and, not very surprisingly, a greater sensitivity of older children with regard to the age of the interaction partner was observed.

■ MECHANISMS THAT "EXPLAIN" TRUST AND TRUSTWORTHINESS

Can we "explain" the differences in trust and trustworthiness in different age groups? Since the most important developments seem to happen at young age, here we mainly focus on evidence for children.

Trust and trustworthiness are complicated social concepts, potentially relating to many motives or underlying preferences (e.g., Cox, 2004; Fehr, 2009). First and foremost, trust is a risky decision—thus the alternative name "investment game" for the trust game (Eckel & Wilson, 2004). The risk is not a natural risk but a social risk. While it is well-known that people might differ in their inclination to take natural risks on the one hand and social risks on the other (Bohnet & Zeckhauser, 2004), there are not enough studies that assess this difference, often termed "betrayal aversion" (capturing the observation that people seem to be more willing to take natural than social risks). In particular, there is no study that looks at the degree of betrayal aversion for different age levels in childhood and adolescence. Thus we are left to consider natural risk attitudes when we want to address the risk component in trusting behavior for differently aged children. Sutter, Kocher, Glätzle-Rützler, and Trautmann (2013) do not find any significant change of natural risk attitudes, comparing 10-year-olds and 16- to 17-year-olds. A similar result holds for ambiguity attitudes that might be closer in nature to social risk because they imply unknown probabilities. Harbaugh, Krause, and Vesterlund (2002) find evidence for a stronger degree of risk-seeking behavior or less risk-averse behavior among children than among adults. If relevant for the trust game, such behavior would imply more trust among kids than among adolescents, as opposed to the observed lower levels of trust. As a consequence, it is safe to rule out that potential changes in risk attitudes with age can explain the change in trusting behavior with age in childhood and adolescence.

A much more promising line of explanation for the age differences in trust and trustworthiness is a potential change in prosocial attitudes when growing up. Psychologists have long been interested in studying the development of prosocial behavior in childhood and adolescence (e.g., Eisenberg, Boehnke, Schuhler, & Silbereisen, 1985; Eisenberg & Fabes, 1998; Eisenberg & Mussen, 1989). Unfortunately, most of these studies do not distinguish between different motives behind prosocial behavior and are thus not directly applicable to economic game situations or fall short of "explaining" particular changes. However, there is a growing literature in economics assessing certain kinds of prosocial motives among children and adolescents, trying to disentangle their influence.

The common finding of almost all studies on social behavior among children is that prosociality becomes more prevalent the older children become. While the early results on bargaining behavior of children in versions of the ultimatum game in Murnighan and Saxon (1998) and the public goods game in Harbaugh and Krause (2002) are not fully conclusive when it comes to prosocial behavior and age, later papers mostly provide clear patterns. Harbaugh, Krause, and Liday (2003) show that offers and transfers in ultimatum and dictator games increase with age, and Benenson, Pascoe, and Radmore (2007) report similar developments for a dictator game and for children at a younger age—a finding in line with Gummerum, Hanoch, Keller, Parsons, and Hummel (2010), using stickers in a dictator game (for a survey of bargaining experiments with children and adolescents, see Van Damme et al., 2014).

Angerer, Glätzle-Rützler, Lergetporer, and Sutter (2015) provide evidence for a very large sample (more than 1,000 children, ages 7 to 11 years) that also exhibits an increasing inclination with age to donate money to a real charity. Looking at different motivations, Fehr, Bernhard, and Rockenbach (2008) show that, at an age of three to four years, children are mostly selfish, but when they grow older (seven to eight years), they become more inequity averse (for theoretical models of inequity aversion, see Bolton and Ockenfels, 2000; Fehr and Schmidt, 1999). Fehr, Glätzle-Rützler, and Sutter (2013) extend this result to older children. Almas, Cappelen, Sorensen, and Tungodden (2010) show that equity rather than equality norms are more important for older children. Martinsson, Nordblom, Rützler, and Sutter (2011) and Sutter et al. (2015) highlight the importance of social welfare concerns (i.e., efficiency concerns) that seem to constitute a more relevant aspect for social decision-making the older children are (for a theoretical model of efficiency concerns, see Charness & Rabin, 2002).[6] Interestingly, many studies find gender differences in development and preferences (e.g., Cárdenas, Dreber, von Essen, & Ranehill, 2014; Sutter et al., 2015). In the interest of space, we do not go into details here.

Taking the evidence on a development of different forms of prosocial behavior in childhood and adolescence together, a change in prosociality seems to be a good candidate as explanation for the change in levels of trust and trustworthiness of children when growing older. It is beyond the scope of this chapter to go into the details of the (ultimate) causes of such a development of prosociality and trust as well as trustworthiness with age. Obviously, emotional regulation (Crone, Will, Overgaauw, & Güroğlu, 2014) and cognitive abilities change with age. It is not surprising that the trust game has been used extensively to study emotions, in particular guilt and a potential aversion of humans toward guilt (Charness & Dufwenberg, 2006; Ellingsen, Johannesson, Tjøtta, & Torsvik, 2010). Genetic predispositions, neurological processes, and hormone correlates of behavior are all fascinating aspects when it comes to understanding the determinants of trust and their development with age. For the social scientist, trust experience at young age seems to be a relevant and much understudied determinant of individual differences in trusting behavior and trustworthiness at older age.

▪ CONCLUSION

After all, we do not know nearly enough about the relationship between trust, trustworthiness, and cooperation on the one hand and age on the other hand. The development of trust and trustworthiness and cooperation in children is well-documented and well-understood, but how can it be explained? How can individual heterogeneity in trust and trustworthiness at the same age level be understood? The relative influence of genetic predispositions, proximate mechanisms such as emotions, and trust experience has not been researched a lot, and white spots in the literature are vast.

The development of trust and trustworthiness at old age is even more of a puzzle. The results from incentivized experiments and representative survey experiments, on the one hand, and questionnaire answers without marginal incentives, on the other hand, diverge, and no conclusive take-home message can be provided. Sociologists have been arguing that levels of trust are correlated with the number of interactions of an individual. This would imply that experience is shaping trusting behavior, but unfortunately, no study so far has been able to convincingly show whether this relationship is causal. Finding a good instrument seems to be a very valuable endeavor. However, even if we knew that there is a causal relationship between experience (and hence, indirectly, age) and trust, we still have a long way to go to understand how exactly good and bad experience with (trust) relationships might shape the specifics of trusting and trustworthy behavior. For cooperation, Van Lange, Otten, De Bruin, and Joireman (1997) provide results based on the elicitation of social value orientation. They show that childhood experience and patterns of social interaction shape cooperative attitudes of adults.

There is also a lack of methodological contributions. The literature has focused on comparing incentivized and nonincentivized measures of trust (i.e., game interaction and questionnaires) to address the issue of consistency (e.g., Gächter et al., 2004; Glaeser, Laibson, Scheinkman, & Soutter, 2000; Thöni, Tyran, & Wengström, 2012). However, such studies have not been conducted on children, to the best of our knowledge. Incentives may work very differently for children, adolescents, and adults. Large-scale validations of methods to elicit trust and trustworthiness are very scarce, again in particular for children and adolescents. While intercultural studies on trust based on survey questionnaires are abundant, there is much less intercultural evidence for the incentivized trust game and almost no cross-cultural evidence for children and adolescents. Knowledge of cultural differences in the development of trust and trustworthiness may help us gain a better grip on issues related to the potentially causal relationship between experience and trust. A related interest is on the effects of institutions (such as schools or the social environment) on trust and trustworthiness of individuals (e.g., Kocher, Martinsson, & Visser, 2012; Van Lange et al., 1997), and again there is little conclusive evidence.

More work is needed to assess trust and trustworthiness in the direct interaction between different groups (e.g., Falk & Zehnder, 2013), in particular between different age groups. With children, the difference between trust within the family or the circle of close friends compared to trust toward strangers seems of special scholarly interest. The two levels appear to develop very differently, and pathological developments could potentially explain the existence of out-group hate or other severe problems in social interactions. Finally, trust within networks and the spread of trust in networks (i.e., peer effects of trust and trustworthiness) have barely been assessed.

Given the relevance of trust for understanding economic activity, but also for understanding dysfunctional aspects of societies such as discrimination or stereotypes (see, e.g., Fershtman & Gneezy, 2001), it is surprising how little we still know about its development, its roots, and its determinants. While social psychologists and developmental psychologists naturally have a vested interest in the research questions associated with the development of trust and trustworthiness, there are also many links to economic models and many aspects relevant to economists. Understanding the development of trust and trustworthiness together with understanding their determinants ultimately means understanding growth, trade, and investment—concepts at the core of traditional economics.

■ AUTHOR'S NOTE

I am indebted to Lisa Spantig and Paul van Lange for very helpful comments and suggestions.

■ NOTES

1. For an early literature overview in psychology see Bernath and Feshbach (1995).
2. http://www.worldvaluessurvey.org
3. An obvious example in the literature for the relevance of comparability of incentives is the comparison of trust and trustworthiness in students and CEOs (Fehr and List, 2004).
4. Unfortunately, Johnson and Mislin (2011), who provide a meta-study of trust game results, do not look at age as a determinant of trust, but the reason for the omission seems to be the small number of studies reporting age as an independent variable.
5. Very similar results are provided by van den Bos, Westenberg, van Dijk, and Crone (2010), however, based on another variant of the trust game.
6. Dahlman, Ljungqvist, and Johannesson (2007) look at children aged three to eight years and analyze the extent of their reciprocal behavior (for theoretical models of reciprocity, see Dufwenberg and Kirchsteiger, 2004; Falk and Fischbacher, 2006). Results are

consistent with what has been said so far. For evidence for even younger children, see for instance Warneken and Tomasello (2013).

■ REFERENCES

Alesina, A., & La Ferrara, E. (2002). Who trusts others? *Journal of Public Economics, 85*, 207–234.

Almas, I., Cappelen, A. W., Sorensen, E. O., & Tungodden, B. (2010). Fairness and the development of inequality acceptance. *Science, 328*, 1176–1178.

Amir, O., Rand, D. G., & Gal, Y. K. (2012). Economic games on the Internet: The effect of $1 stakes. *PLoS One, 7*, e31461.

Angerer, S., Glätzle-Rützler, D., Lergetporer, P., & Sutter, M. (2015). Donations, risk attitudes and time preferences: A study on altruism in primary school children. *Journal of Economic Behavior and Organization, 115*, 67–74.

Bargh, J. A., Chen, M., & Burrows, L. (1996). Automaticity of social behavior: Direct effects of trait construct and stereotype-activation on action. *Journal of Personality and Social Psychology, 71*, 230–244.

Bellemare, C., & Kröger, S. (2007). On representative social capital. *European Economic Review, 51*, 183–202.

Benenson, J. F., Pascoe, J., & Radmore, N. (2007). Children's altruistic behavior in the dictator game. *Evolution and Human Behavior, 28*, 168–175.

Berg, J., Dickhaut, J., & McCabe, K. (1995). Trust, reciprocity, and social history. *Games and Economic Behavior, 10*, 121–142.

Bernath, M. S., & Feshbach, N. D. (1995). Children's trust: Theory, assessment, development, and research directions. *Applied and Preventive Psychology, 4*, 1–19.

Bohnet, I., & Zeckhauser, R. (2004). Trust, risk and betrayal. *Journal of Economic Behavior and Organization, 55*, 467–484.

Bolton, G. E., & Ockenfels, A. (2000). ERC—A theory of equity, reciprocity and competition. *American Economic Review, 90*, 166–193.

Camerer, C. F. (2003). *Behavioral game theory. Experiments in strategic interaction.* Princeton, NJ: Princeton University Press.

Cárdenas, J.-C., Dreber, A., von Essen, E., & Ranehill, E. (2014). Gender and cooperation in children: Experiments in Colombia and Sweden. *PLoS One, 9*, e90923.

Charness, G., & Dufwenberg, M. (2006). Promises and partnership. *Econometrica, 74*, 1579–1601.

Charness, G., & Rabin, M. (2002). Understanding social preferences with simple tests. *Quarterly Journal of Economics, 117*, 817–869.

Coleman, J. (1990). *Foundations of social theory.* Cambridge, MA: Belknap Press of Harvard University Press.

Cox, J. C. (2004). How to identify trust and reciprocity. *Games and Economic Behavior, 46*, 260–281.

Crone, E. A., Will, G.-J., Overgaauw, S., & Güroğlu, B. (2014). Social decision-making in childhood and adolescence. In P. A. M. van Lange, B. Rockenbach, & T. Yamagishi (Eds.), *Reward and punishment in social dilemmas* (pp. 161–181). New York: Oxford University Press.

Dahlman, S., Ljungqvist, P., & Johannesson, M. (2007). Reciprocity in young children. Working Paper, Stockholm School of Economics.

Doyen, S., Klein, O., Pichon, C.-L., & Cleeremans, A. (2012). Behavioral priming: It's all in the mind, but whose mind? *PLoS One, 7*, e29081.

Dufwenberg, M., & Kirchsteiger, G. (2004). A theory of sequential reciprocity. *Games and Economic Behavior, 46*, 268–298.

Eckel, C. C., & Wilson, R. K. (2004). Is trust a risky decision? *Journal of Economic Behavior and Organization, 55*, 447–465.

Eisenberg, N., Boehnke, K., Schuhler, P., & Silbereisen, R. K. (1985). The development of prosocial behavior and cognitions in German children. *Journal of Cross-Cultural Psychology, 16*, 69–82.

Eisenberg, N., & Fabes, R. A. (1998). Prosocial development. In W. Damon (Ed.), *Handbook of child psychology*. New York: Wiley.

Eisenberg, N., & Mussen, P. (1989). *The roots of prosocial behavior in children*. Cambridge, UK: Cambridge University Press.

Ellingsen, T., Johannesson, M., Tjøtta, S., & Torsvik, G. (2010). Testing guilt aversion. *Games and Economic Behavior, 68*, 95–107.

Ermisch, J., Gambetta, D., Laurie, H., Siedler, T., & Uhrig, N. S. C. (2009). Measuring people's trust. *Journal of the Royal Statistical Society: Series A, Statistics in Society, 172*, 749–769.

Evans, A. M, Athenstaedt, U., & Krueger, J. I. (2013). The development of trust and altruism during childhood. *Journal of Economic Psychology, 36*, 82–95.

Falk, A., & Fischbacher, U. (2006). A theory of reciprocity. *Games and Economic Behavior, 54*, 293–315.

Falk, A., & Zehnder, C. (2013). A city-wide experiment on trust discrimination. *Journal of Public Economics, 100*, 15–27.

Fehr, E. (2009). On the economics and biology of trust. *Journal of the European Economic Association, 7*, 235–266.

Fehr, E., Bernhard, H., & Rockenbach, B. (2008). Egalitarianism in young children. *Nature, 454*, 1079–1083.

Fehr, E., Fischbacher, U., von Rosenbladt, B., Schupp, J., & Wagner, G. G. (2003). A nation-wide laboratory: Examining trust and trustworthiness by integrating behavioral experiments into representative surveys. Working Paper 141. Institute for Empirical Research in Economics, University of Zurich.

Fehr, E., Glätzle-Rützler, D., & Sutter, M. (2013). The development of egalitarianism, altruism, spite and parochialism in childhood and adolescence. *European Economic Review, 64*, 369–383.

Fehr, E., Kirchsteiger, G., & Riedl, A. (1993). Does fairness prevent market clearing? An experimental investigation. *Quarterly Journal of Economics, 108*, 437–460.

Fehr, E., & List, J. A. (2004). The hidden costs and returns of incentives—Trust and trustworthiness among CEOs. *Journal of the European Economic Association, 2*, 743–771.

Fehr, E., & Schmidt, K. (1999). A theory of fairness, competition, and cooperation. *Quarterly Journal of Economics, 114*, 817–868.

Fehr, E., Tougareva, E., & Fischbacher, U. (2014). Do high stakes and competition undermine fair behaviour? Evidence from Russia. *Journal of Economic Behavior and Organization, 108*, 354–363.

Fershtman, C., & Gneezy, U. (2001). Discrimination in a segmented society: An experimental approach. *Quarterly Journal of Economics, 116*, 351–377.

Gächter, S., Herrmann, B., & Thöni, C. (2004). Trust, voluntary cooperation, and socio-economic background: Survey and experimental evidence. *Journal of Economic Behavior and Organization, 55*, 505–531.

Glaeser, E. L., Laibson, D., Scheinkman, J. A., & Soutter, C. L. (2000). Measuring trust. *Quarterly Journal of Economics, 115*, 811–846.

Guiso, L., Sapienza, P., & Zingales, L. (2009). Cultural biases in economic exchange? *Quarterly Journal of Economics, 124*, 1095–1131.

Gummerum, M., Hanoch, Y., Keller, M., Parsons, K., & Hummel, A. (2010). Preschoolers' allocations in the dictator game: The role of moral emotions. *Journal of Economic Psychology, 31*, 25–34.

Harbaugh, W. T., Krause, K., & Liday, S. G. Jr. (2003). Bargaining by children. Working Paper, University of Oregon.

Harbaugh, W. T., Krause, K., Liday, S. G. Jr., & Vesterlund, L. (2003). Trust in children. In E. Ostrom & J. Walker (Eds.), *Trust, reciprocity and gains from association: Interdisciplinary lessons from experimental research*. New York: Russell Sage Foundation.

Harbaugh, W. T., Krause, K., & Vesterlund, L. (2002). Risk attitudes of children and adults: Choices over small and large probability gains and losses. *Experimental Economics, 5*, 53–84.

Holm, H., & Nystedt, P. (2005). Intra-generational trust—A semi-experimental study of trust among different generations. *Journal of Economic Behavior and Organization, 58*, 403–419.

Johnson, N. D., & Mislin, A. A. (2011). Trust games: A meta-analysis. *Journal of Economic Psychology, 32*, 865–889.

Knack, S., & Keefer, P. (1997). Does social capital have an economic payoff? *Quarterly Journal of Economics, 112*, 1251–1273.

Kocher, M. G., Martinsson, P., & Visser, M. (2008). Does stake size matter for cooperation and punishment? *Economics Letters, 99*, 508–511.

Kocher, M. G., Martinsson, P., & Visser, M. (2012). Social environment, cooperative behavior and norm-enforcement. *Journal of Economic Behavior and Organization, 81*, 341–354.

LaPorta, R., Lopez-de-Silane, F., Shleifer, A., Vishny, R. W. (1997). Trust in large organizations. *American Economic Review, 87*, 333–338.

Ledyard, J. (1995). Public goods. A survey of experimental research. In A. Roth & J. Kagel (Eds.), *Handbook of experimental economics* (pp. 111–193). Princeton, NJ: Princeton University Press.

Li, T., & Fung, H. H. (2013). Age differences in trust: An investigation across 38 countries. *Journals of Gerontology Series B: Psychological Sciences and Social Sciences, 68*, 347–355.

Martinsson, P., Nordblom, K., Rützler, D., & Sutter, M. (2011). Social preferences during childhood and the role of gender and age—An experiment in Austria and Sweden. *Economics Letters, 110*, 248–251.

Murnighan, J. K., & Saxon, M. S. (1998). Ultimatum bargaining by children and adults. *Journal of Economic Psychology, 19*, 415–445.

Naef, M., Fehr, E., Fischbacher, U., Schupp, J., & Wagner, G. (2008). Decomposing trust: Explaining national and ethnic trust differences. Working Paper, Institute for Empirical Research in Economics, University of Zurich.

Poulin, M. J., & Haase, C. M. (2015). Growing to trust: Evidence that trust increases and sustains well-being across the life span. *Social Psychological and Personality Science, 6*, 614–621.

Poundstone, W. (1992). *Prisoner's dilemma*. New York: Doubleday.

Putnam, R. (2000). *Bowling alone: The collapse and revival of the American community*. New York: Simon & Schuster.

Rousseau, D. M., Sitkin, S. B., Burt, R. S., & Camerer, C. (1998). Not so different after all: A cross-discipline view of trust. *Academy of Management Review, 23*, 393–404.

Sutter, M., Feri, F., Glätzle-Rützler, D., Kocher, M. G., Martinsson, P., & Nordblom, K. (2015). Social preferences in childhood and adolescence. A large-scale experiment. Working Paper, University of Innsbruck.

Sutter, M., & Kocher, M. G. (2007). Trust and trustworthiness across different age groups. *Games and Economic Behavior, 59*, 364–382.

Sutter, M., Kocher, M. G., Glätzle-Rützler, D., & Trautmann, S. T. (2013). Impatience and uncertainty: Experimental decisions predict adolescents' field behavior. *American Economic Review, 103*, 510–531.

Thöni, C., Tyran, J.-R., & Wengström, E. (2012). Microfoundations of social capital. *Journal of Public Economics, 96*, 635–643.

Van Damme, E., Binmore, K., Roth, A., Samuelson, L., Winter, E., Bolton, G. E., . . . Azar, O. H. (2014). How Werner Güth's ultimatum game shaped our understanding of social behavior. *Journal of Economic Behavior and Organization, 108*, 292–318.

van den Bos, W., Westenberg, M., van Dijk, E., & Crone, E. A. (2010). Development of trust and reciprocity in adolescence. *Cognitive Development, 25*, 90–102.

Van Lange, P. A. M, Otten, W., De Bruin, E. M. N., & Joireman, J. A. (1997). Development of prosocial, individualistic, and competitive orientations. Theory and preliminary evidence. *Journal of Personality and Social Psychology, 73*, 733–746.

Warneken, F., & Tomasello, M. (2013). The emergence of contingent reciprocity in young children. *Journal of Experimental Child Psychology, 116*, 338–350.

Zak, P. J., & Knack, S. (2001). Trust and growth. *Economic Journal, 111*, 295–321.

PART II
Trust in Dyads, Groups, and Organizations

7 Let Me Help You Help Me

Trust Between Profit and Prosociality

■ JOACHIM I. KRUEGER,
ANTHONY M. EVANS,
AND PATRICK R. HECK

> For each individual, the ideal community would be one in which
> everybody else is honest and alone is a thief. It follows that a social
> institution is necessary if the interest of the individual is to be recon-
> ciled with that of the community.
> — BERTRAND RUSSELL (1957, p. 195)

Trust and trustworthiness are among the personal, noninstitutional answers to Russell's dilemma. Trust creates wealth. Its causal effect of trust has been observed across countries and across generations (Algan & Cahuc, 2010). In the laboratory, the design of experimental trust and investment games ensures the positive effect of trust on wealth. One participant (the trustor) receives money or symbolic monetary units (MU) with the permission to share any amount with another player (the trustee). The experimenter triples the transferred amount. Total wealth therefore increases unless the trustor sits on her stash. The more she sends, the more there is to be shared. Whether the trustee reciprocates is immaterial to total wealth but critical to its distribution. A fully trustworthy trustee splits the received sum so that both players finish with the same amount—unless she also received a participation fee (Johnson & Mislin, 2011). A miserly trustee reimburses the trustor the invested amount, and a selfish one keeps all the money. These and other patterns of reciprocity have been observed in the laboratory (Berg, Dickhaut, & McCabe, 1995).

Traditional game theory sees the trustee playing a dictator game (Forsythe, Horowitz, Savin, & Sefton, 1994). She has resources to distribute and need not account for her decision. Assuming only self-interest and rationality, the trustee is expected to return nothing to the trustor. If self-interest and rationality are common knowledge, the trustor will send no money in the first place. Refuting this Spartan view of rationality, research shows that positive exchanges do happen, which has been taken to mean that the trustee's proposed final distribution reflects a mix of individual and social preferences or values. A preference for benefitting the other (benevolence) or a preference for equality (fairness) suggest an even split. Self-interest, by contrast, demands a tight fist. A preference to maximize collective wealth gets no play; whatever the trustee does, the combined wealth of the two players remains the same. The trustee may, however, be sensitive to the social norm of reciprocity (Gouldner, 1960; Trivers, 1971). When fully internalized, this norm may *feel* like a preference (Bicchieri, 2006). "I prefer to give back to those who have trusted me."

The trustor may also be seen as a dictator but a vulnerable one (Krueger & Evans, 2013). She determines the initial division of the purse into savings and investment, and by saving some money she can assure herself of a positive final outcome. By transferring funds she puts her material well-being at the mercy of the trustee's social preferences and respect for the norm of reciprocity. How does the trustor decide what to send and how much to save? Suppose a trustor is so benevolent that she values the other person's wealth half as much as she values her own. This trustor would prefer the trustee having 30MU and herself having nothing to having 10MU and the trustee having nothing. Cox (2004) tested the benevolence hypothesis by barring the trustees from reciprocating. Not able to expect reciprocation, most trustors behaved like selfish dictators: they transferred very little (see also Evans, Athenstaedt, & Krueger [2013] for similar findings with children). A preference for fairness is not a strong motivator of trust either because, at least temporarily, a fully trusting person creates a state of maximum inequality. In theory, trust is consistent with a desire to maximize collective wealth, but again, the findings from games without the possibility of reciprocation suggest that this desire is easily quashed.

Might trust, like trustworthiness, be norm-driven? The norm of reciprocity is universal and powerful. It is grounded in sociocultural (Gouldner, 1960), biological (Trivers, 1971), and game-theoretic (Rabin, 1993) foundations. To not reciprocate a favor—particularly one that was costly to its initiator and that made her vulnerable—is universally regarded as a moral offense. There is, however, no corresponding social norm that demands trust (Bicchieri, Xiao, & Muldoon, 2011; see Dunning, Anderson, Schlösser, Ehlebracht, & Fetchenhauer [2014] for a dissenting view). Mothers do not teach their children to trust indiscriminately. Reciprocation is an obligation, but trust is a question of permission.

If social preferences and respect for social norms are essential to prosociality, then trust is not a prototypically prosocial phenomenon. Perhaps trustors are rational decision-makers who weigh what they might gain from taking the risk of trusting against the possibility of betrayal and loss. Under this model, the trustor's task is not just to act in accordance with her own social values but to accurately assess the trustee's social values in order to arrive at a rational choice. Trustors, in other words, have a rational interest in calibrating their decisions to the characteristics of trustees.

In this chapter, we describe a model of the trustor as a boundedly rational decision-maker (Evans & Krueger, 2011, 2014). The critical boundary to full rationality is the difficulty of paying full attention to the incentives available to the trustee. For the trustor, an egocentric focus on her own potential payoffs is a convenient heuristic, but it compromises judgments of the probability of reciprocation. An additional boundary to full rationality is the difficulty of using probabilistic information optimally even when the probabilities themselves have been estimated accurately. Even those trustors who judge the probability of reciprocation well may have trouble using it properly when estimating the expected value of trust.

Understanding trustors as boundedly rational decision-makers clashes with the perception of trustors as moral agents. When judging the character of trustors or trustees who had either transferred nothing, a middling amount, or the maximum amount, research participants strongly associated larger transfers with greater moral goodness regardless of the person's role in the exchange (Krueger, Massey, & DiDonato, 2008). In contrast, ratings of the person's competence or rationality were close to the middle of the scale regardless of the size of the transfer. This finding suggests a strong association between the specific phenomenon of trust and the general theme of prosociality—at least in the eyes of those who themselves are currently not faced with the decision dilemma of trust. Perhaps in their role of observers, people simply focus on the act of giving, even when there is no risk (in the case of the trustee), when there is no increase in the collective good (the trustee), or when there is the possibility of personal gain (the trustor). Again, however, the perceived association between trust and prosociality does not take a normative turn. Those who do not trust are not punished, whereas those who do not reciprocate trust are (Bicchieri et al., 2011).

■ TYPES OF GAMES

Before we describe the expected-value model of bounded rationality, we review variants of prosociality we encounter in different social contexts. Three major categories of social situation (or game) are the following: unilateral, bilateral, and sequential. The dictator game is the prototype of a unilateral (i.e., nonstrategic) situation, in which one person (the distributor or dictator) has all the power and the other person has none. The prisoner's dilemma, the assurance game, and the game of chicken are intensively studied bilateral games (Kollock, 1998). In the simplest version of these games, two players, who do not know each other and who cannot communicate, choose between a cooperative strategy and a defecting strategy. These games are social dilemmas because the outcome of mutual cooperation is better than the outcome of mutual defection. Yet each game offers an incentive to defect (Dawes, 1980). Though perfectly interdependent, players need not act strategically. As they act at the same time, their choices cannot affect what the other will do. The trust game, along with the ultimatum game, belongs to a class of sequential games with a separation of roles. Whereas the first player faces a judgment under uncertainty, the second player is merely invited to act out preferences. Hence, only the first player can don the cap of the strategist.

The Dictator Game

Suppose we give Joey 10 peanuts and tell him he can give as many to Jimmy as he likes. Joey is the dictator; Jimmy is the subject. Often, the dictator game serves as a measure of the effectiveness of experimental interventions. For instance, Joey will likely share more peanuts with Jimmy if a prosocial norm is primed (Shariff & Norenzayan, 2007), or if Joey finds himself in a good mood (Tan & Forgas, 2010). The other, more common use of the game is to use its outcomes as measures of trait-like social preferences. There are, however, no straightforward inferences to be drawn from an isolated dictator game. Someone who splits the purse evenly may do so because of benevolence, a taste for fairness, or both. Therefore, efforts to extract scale values for these social preferences require several decomposed games, in which the various strategies are pitted against one another (Murphy, Ackermann, & Handgraaf, 2011; Tajfel, Billig, Bundy, & Flament, 1971).

The scale values obtained with sets of games predict prosocial behavior in other games and in the field (Fiedler, Glöckner, Nicklisch, & Dickert, 2013; Kanagaretnam, Mestelman, Nainar, & Shehata, 2009; Peysakhovich, Nowak, & Rand, 2014; but see Yamagishi et al., 2013). Compared with selfish dictators, benevolent dictators are also more likely to cooperate in simultaneous games and to trust in sequential games. This correlational evidence is consistent with the idea that social preferences cause prosocial behavior. However, the scale values of social preferences fail to predict an important feature of the data obtained with the dictator game: they cannot explain why a dictator would neither keep all nor be perfectly fair.

Consider three value functions (van Lange, 1999). The first function combines self-interest with benevolence but ignores fairness. Let the payoff for the self, S, range from .5 to 1 and the payoff for the other be its complement, $1 - S$. Let the weight, w, attached to S range from .5 to 1 and the weight given to the other's payoff be its complement, $1 - w$. The value of a distributive choice is $V = wS + (1 - w)(1 - S)$. For any $w > .5$, V is maximized at $S = 1$. If $w = .5$, any distribution yields the same V, thus providing no guidance to the decision-maker (see Krueger et al. [2008] for derivations). Even a person who is not indifferent to the material well-being of others has no incentive to share. The result of this analysis can be checked against intuition. One might think that a person who assigns a weight of .7 to her own payoff and a weight of .3 to the other person's payoff will propose a 7:3 split. She might propose it, but it would not be rational for her to do it. Given her preferences, $V = .7 * .7 + .3 * .3 = .58$. If she kept all, however, $V = .7 * 1 + .3 * 0 = .7$, and $.7 > .58$.

The second value function combines self-interest with a taste for fairness and ignores benevolence. If we construe unfairness as the absolute difference between S and $S - 1$, weigh it by the complement of the weight of self-interest, and subtract it from weighted self-interest, we have $V = wS - (1 - w)(|2S-1|)$. V is maximized at $S = 1$ for weights close to 1, and it is maximized at $S = .5$ for weights close to .5. A self-interested person who also values fairness will either keep it all or split it evenly. She might split the money unevenly, perhaps to strike a compromise between self-interest and fairness, but a rational consideration of her own preference demands that she not.

The third value function combines self-interest with both benevolence and fairness so that $V = wS + (1-w)(1 - S) - (1 - w)(|2S-1|)$. The results are similar to the model including only self-interest and fairness. In these examples, the weights placed on own and other's payoffs are complementary. One may ask what happens when self-interest is always weighted at 1 while the weight placed on benevolence and fairness varies. With this arrangement, the rational decision-maker never shares.

The positive correlations found between measures of social preference and prosocial behavior may mimic or obscure the operation of other psychological processes enabling sharing, cooperation, and trust. The dictator game in particular is not a suitable context for the study of the causal role of social preferences because there *should* be a positive correlation between measures of social preference and sharing simply because the measures of social preference are derived from the very type of dictator games whose outcomes they serve to predict.

Some social preference models assume that values transmute into concave psychological utility functions (e.g., Fehr & Schmidt, 1999). Under such a model, a dictator may feel that the difference between 8 and 10MU is less significant than is the difference between 0 and 2 for the subject. Combining weighted utilities, instead of values, intermediate sharing may be modeled mathematically. Further complications arise, however, because the dictator may perceive her cooperative sharing either as a loss to the self or simply as less of a gain. If she perceives the initial endowment as personal property, she is likely loss averse. She would be more cooperative if she framed her 8MU as a gain against the baseline of receiving nothing (Kahneman & Tversky, 1984; see also Crockett, Kurth-Nelson, Siegel, Dayan, & Dolan, 2014).[1]

One-shot games are parsimonious and aesthetically appealing. Yet, there is a reason for why one-shot dictator games may underestimate the true prevalence of prosocial sharing, and there is a different reason for why they may overestimate it. Alas, there is no reason to believe that these two reasons cancel each other out so that the net error is nil. Consider underestimation. It is well known that prosociality is anchored on the self and steeply graded. The greater the social distance between a person and a potential beneficiary, the less prosociality there is. Hamilton (1964) built a theory of inclusive fitness on this idea, and others have supported it empirically (Burnstein, Crandall, & Kitayama, 1996; Jones & Rachlin, 2006; Krueger, Ullrich, & Chen, 2016; Locey, Safin, & Rachlin, 2013). As a perfect stranger lies far down on the scale of social distance, we may expect people to be more prosocial when interacting with those whom they know and like (Bohnet & Frey, 1999). Merely referring to the receiving player as a "partner" instead of an "opponent" is enough to soften a dictator's selfishness—although this labeling involves more than a difference in social distance (Burnham, McCabe, & Smith, 2000; but see Messick & McClintock's [1968] classic study, which failed to find a labeling effect).

The idea that the dictator game may overestimate prosocial behavior requires a look at the social context surrounding the game. When Joey receives 10 peanuts for distribution and Jimmy receives none, Joey may wonder why this is. He finds himself in a situation he rarely encounters outside the lab. There are no clues to explain the experimenter's dictatorial decision, and Joey must fish for suitable mental models. Naïve Joey might think that the experimenter considers him worthier than Jimmy. This would explain the uneven split, and it would suggest that the split be maintained (Babcock & Loewenstein, 1997). A more sophisticated

Joey might be familiar with the method of random assignment to role. From this perspective, Joey may see his task as rectifying a random error committed by the experimenter and the flipped coin. When participants are not told that they have been "provisionally allocated $10" and that their task is to "divide" it, they share less (Hoffman, McCabe, & Smith, 1996). Participants in the dictator game face a situation that, as social situations do, is underspecified. In societies, in which most individuals sustain themselves by selling their labor, unexplained windfalls are rare. People can account for most of their assets; they know how they earned them, and they are rarely invited to share them with random strangers (who did not ask them to do so), and they rarely do.[2]

To see how the dictator game transforms a property-based economy, consider a pair of players who inhabit both roles simultaneously and who play repeatedly. Assume that their preferred distribution of wealth is stable like a personality trait. If Joey has all the money at the outset, and if both he and Jimmy prefer a 7:3 split favoring themselves once they have anything, it takes only four rounds to attain a distribution of wealth within the 51:49 window. If the preferred split is 9:1, it takes nine rounds; if it is 6:1, it takes only three. If people were as generous as they appear in the one-shot laboratory game, we would already be living in an equalitarian society. When we assume that both Joey and Jimmy think that Joe ought to be favored 7:3, the final distribution departs from their preferences. After a few rounds, Joey has either 8.8 or 6.2MU in this pocket with little change but alternation thereafter. His average wealth (7.5) is greater than both he and Jimmy prefer, and Jimmy's is less.

As these examples show, the distributional preferences held by individuals need not predict the distribution of wealth in a society. To see if there is a more general dissociation, we ran four computer simulations, each consisting of 100 stylized individuals and 100 rounds of play between random pairs. Half of the simulated individuals were endowed with 10MU, while the other half had nothing. In the first simulation, the preferences of giving away 0%, 10%, . . ., 50% were uniformly distributed and randomly reassigned to each player for each successive round. Figure 7.1A shows the final distribution of wealth. Although no one had nothing, median wealth was below the average of 5MU. The rich were distinctive. In the second simulation, the individual distributional preferences were treated as stable person properties. Now we see radical inequality (Figure 7.1B). Most individuals had nothing, while a few had a lot, although differences among the rich remained. For the third simulation, we assumed that 99 individuals were highly individualistic (sharing a mere 10%), while one individual was perfectly selfish. These preferences were reshuffled for each round of play. Though not leading to perfect equality, the final distribution was tightly packed around the mean (Figure 7.1C). The final simulation again assumed stable preferences. Here, the one strict egoist ended up with the entire wealth (Figure 7.1D). These simulations show that the distribution of wealth will not reflect individuals' distributional preferences and that stark inequality will emerge when preferences are stable within individuals.

As a research tool, the one-shot dictator game precludes redistribution. Only with this assumption of no redistribution can resource transfers be taken as

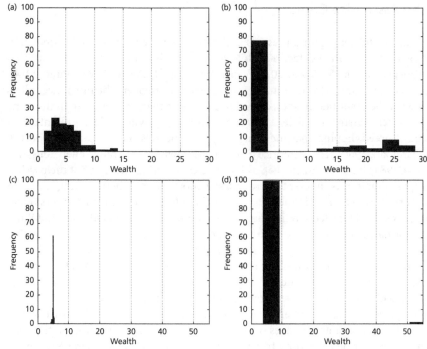

Figure 7.1. Distribution of wealth after 100 rounds of a bilateral dictator game.

expressions of social preferences. The subjects are defined into a position of perfect selfishness; they must keep everything they receive from the dictator. Even the
benevolent dictator would be expected to be selfish if the roles were exchanged. In
other words, social preferences can be demonstrated in the dictator game only if
none exist.[3] Yet, one-shot games among strangers are taken to reveal pure trait-like
preferences. "Preference" is a shortcut for "attitude," and in the Allportian tradition, an attitude is as much a characteristic of a person as is a personality trait.
Being trait-like, a preference is expected to be faithfully expressed across different
social contexts.

    An alternative view is that dictators' decisions tell us more about how they con-
strue the situation (Halevy & Katz, 2013) and about the intuitions they bring to
the task (List, 2007). Equal splits, for example, may as easily arise from a heuristic
about how to divide *anything* in a highly uncertain situation as from principled
preferences (Almy & Krueger, 2013; Gigerenzer, 2008). Nonetheless, a careful
analysis of the dictator game is essential for an understanding of interpersonal
trust, where the trustee is essentially a dictator. As already noted, a trustee-dictator
does not face the uncertainties of the ahistorical dictator in the unilateral game.
The trustee knows that receiving money reflects an act of trust (Rabin, 1993).
However, she still does not know why the experimenter cast her in this role and
not the other, but this is no longer critical.

The Assurance Game

A class of bilateral games presents social dilemmas because mutual cooperation is better than mutual defection, while cooperation is not the dominating strategy (Krueger, Smith, & Wang, 2015; Van Lange, Balliet, Parks, & Van Vugt, 2014). Indeed, defection is the dominating strategy in the prisoner's dilemma. Regardless of what the other player does, defection pays more than cooperation. In the game of chicken, where mutual defection is catastrophic, individual players might defect out of greed, hoping that the other player cooperates out of fear (Rapoport & Chammah, 1966). The assurance game (also known as "stag hunt" after Rousseau, 1754/1984) is similar to chicken as it lacks a dominating strategy, but the psychological situation is different. Here, mutual cooperation is best, leaving no room for greed. However, individual players might defect if they fear that others might (Skyrms, 2001). Defection in the assurance game can thus be oddly self-fulfilling.

Formally, the assurance game can be described by the inequalities of $R > T = P > S$, where R refers to the "Reward" payoff for mutual cooperation, T to the "Temptation" payoff for unilateral defection, P to the "Penalty" payoff for mutual defection, and S to the "Sucker" payoff for unilateral cooperation.[4] As a bilateral game with simultaneous decisions, assurance is a two-sided trust game, but as each player is also the other's trustee, the game conflates trust with trustworthiness. If Joe cooperates, he does so trusting that Jim will cooperate too. At the same time, Joe may be said to be trustworthy if he cooperates with someone who is presumably placing his trust in him.

Game theory predicts that a rational player cooperates with a probability derived from the payoffs. The mixed-strategy equilibrium probability $p = (S - P)/(S + T - R - P)$ guards against exploitation. There is no strategy, or set of strategies, another player can deploy to get the better of an equilibrium player. A game theorist who observes an act of cooperation or defection in a one-shot assurance game will not speculate about the psychological preferences or processes beneath these choices. However, real people caught in a one-shot assurance game may curse game theory because it does not tell them how to cooperate with a probability of, say, .3. The savvy player, who has figured out the equilibrium probability, might de-psychologize the process and throw a die.

Most social scientists and the people they study seem to agree that individuals faced with an assurance dilemma make a definitive choice in the sense that they think that either cooperation or defection is the right path. In their minds, either strategy may have come to dominate (Thomas, DeScioli, Haque, & Pinker, 2014). Social preference models predict that benevolence will make cooperation more likely. Suppose the payoffs are $R = 4$, $T = P = 3$, and $S = 1$. Here, the equilibrium probability is 2/3. Now, if players value each others' payoffs as much as their own (i.e., $R = 4 + 4 = 8$; $T = 3 + 1 = 4$; $P = 3 + 3 = 6$; $S = 1 + 3 = 4$), the equilibrium probability *drops* to 1/3. In other words, a pair of caring individuals will cooperate *less* than a pair of selfish individuals, if they are otherwise rational. For argument's sake, assume the benevolent players care 100 times as much about the others' outcomes than about their own; the equilibrium probability of cooperation falls to

.0066. No matter how benevolent they are, cooperation will never be the dominating strategy; if $P = T > S$, then $S + wT < P + wP$. Even self-sacrificial saints must rely on positive expectations and trust that others will cooperate.[5]

The present analysis has assumed that both players are either benevolent or not. When only one player is benevolent, and the other player knows it, the other will cooperate less—if she is game-theoretically rational (Tsebelis, 1989). This is an unsettling conclusion. Benevolent social values are exploitable even without assuming that they increase the probability of cooperation.

A prosocial alternative to benevolence is the desire to attain the best outcome for the collective (i.e., maximize the sum of the payoffs). In the assurance game, the collective best also happens to be the best for each individual. The concept of "team reasoning" has been proposed as one relevant psychological process (Colman, Pulford, & Lawrence, 2014). Team reasoners identify the combination of choices yielding the largest sum of payoffs and then ask what they can do to bring this combination about. When, as in the assurance game, mutual cooperation yields the greatest return, team reasoners cooperate, knowing that their own cooperation is necessary, though not sufficient, for the desired outcome. Eye-tracking data show that, indeed, many players focus on the maximum joint payoffs when studying the game (Halevy & Chou, 2014; see also Kiyonari, Tanida, & Yamagishi, 2000).[6] The question remains, however, how liking the most efficient outcome translates into making a choice that accepts the risk of being suckered.

A third possibility is that people consider cooperating and that they project this choice to others. They then estimate the expected value of cooperation based on the assumption that others will be more likely to make the same choice than the opposite choice. They also consider defecting and estimate its expected value based on the expectation that others are more likely to come to the same than to a different decision. If the expected value of cooperation is greater than the expected value of defection, a player will cooperate (Krueger, 2013; Krueger, DiDonato, & Freestone, 2012). To appreciate the role of projection, imagine a world without it. One's own behavior would be mysterious because one could never attribute it to any stimulus or context, which affects many people in the same way.

The projection hypothesis can explain why there is more cooperation in easy games (where there is not much to lose from unilateral cooperation) than in difficult games, and it can explain why people are more cooperative with in-group members (Balliet, Wu, & De Dreu, 2014) or other similar others than with outgroup member or dissimilar others (see also Fischer, 2012). A more significant implication of the projection hypothesis in the present context is that it undercuts the great "fundamental assumption: that decisions in cooperation games reflect a domain-general tendency towards prosociality" (Peysakhovich et al., 2014, p. 2). With projection, a social good is achieved without any prosocial motive or goal. A projecting participant in a social dilemma may be entirely self-regarding and egocentric. When the assumption of self-other similarity leads to cooperation (and to mutual cooperation if there are many projectors), the collective good is maximized without any individual necessarily being motivated to achieve this outcome.

The Trust Game

In sequential games, the second player knows what the first one did, and she can apply the so-called "strategy method." She only needs to articulate her best response given her self-interest, social preferences, respect for social norms, and reputational concerns, if applicable. In the trust game, the second player is the trustee, and game theory says that her best response—given her presumed self-interest and rationality—is to keep the transfer and its added value. However, a trustee who looks beyond the low game-theoretic horizon realizes that a trustor who expects her to be rational in this limited sense will not transfer anything. In the world outside of the anonymous one-shot paradigm, trustees must be strategic and signal their trustworthiness. These signals must be credible, but they might be deceptive (DeSteno, 2014; Miller, 1997). The players' interdependence makes the trustee's task more difficult than the task of the unilaterally acting dictator. The trustor's task is harder still. She must attempt to predict how the trustee solves *her* strategic dilemma, and then decide accordingly. Strategic signaling is not the trustor's primary concern; mind reading is.

Mind reading is "the human capacity to read another person's thoughts or intentions by placing themselves in the position and information state of the other person" (McCabe, Smith, & LePore, 2000, p. 4404). How might trustors go about reading trustees' minds? One possibility is to use the heuristic of social projection, which is so useful in many bilateral games. In a sequential game, however, role differentiation places a barrier between the trustor and her accurate prediction of the trustee's intention. As McCabe et al. note, the trustor cannot simply assume that her own act of trust is a valid predictor of another person's trustworthiness; she needs to ask first what she herself would do if she were in the trustee's role. Predicting one's own behavior in a different role is not error-free. Often, people fail to understand how context will affect them, and they rely too much on their general intentions and wishes (Epley & Dunning, 2000). Then, the trustor must predict the trustee's trustworthiness from her own predicted trustworthiness in that role (Van Boven & Loewenstein, 2005). A projective prediction achieved as the combination of two fallible predictions is unlikely to be precise, and thus far, there is no good evidence for the idea that people engage in this sequence of prediction when estimating trustworthiness.

There is, however, evidence to suggest that decisions to trust (or not) are egocentric even when important information is available that is diagnostic of the trustee's likely strategy. In a series of studies, we found that trustors are biased in how they select and attend to outcome information. Using an experimental design, in which participants could explore the various payoffs of the game, most trustors began by gathering information about how much they stood to gain or lose by trusting and how much they would get to keep if they did not trust (Evans & Krueger, 2014). These self-relevant payoffs combine into an overall index of risk, that is, (distrust—betrayal)/(rewarded trust—betrayal), and risk (inversely) predicts trust. Trustors attended to the trustee's payoffs only later, and they did not spend much time looking at them, if they searched for them at all. Yet, a fully rational person would carefully consider the trustee's payoffs (what the trustee would gain from choosing betrayal instead of reciprocation) because these payoffs are valid cues to the trustee's temptation to betray trust (Becker, 1976). Empirically, however, the trustee's temptation is more strongly related to her actual choice than to the trustee's choice as predicted by the trustor. In other words, trustors are not sensitive enough to how the game presents itself to the trustee. Still, given their own subjective beliefs about the trustee's behavior, trustors are biased in assessing the expected value of trust. They focus on their own risk and neglect the trustee's temptation to betray them (see also Evans & Krueger, 2011).

Many believe that people should trust more (Van Lange, 2015), whereas some scholars (e.g., Dunning et al., 2014) think that people trust too much. It is not hard to see that the question of overall bias is ill posed. On the one hand, it may seem that people do not trust enough. Trust, after all, creates wealth, whether or not the trustor suffers. Arrow (1974) famously remarked that trust is the lubricant that makes the economy (and much else) go round. With more trust, there will be greater wealth, and the economy will grow faster (Algan & Cahuc, 2010). On the other hand, it has been clear since the earliest studies (Berg et al., 1995) that most trustors barely break even and that only a few profit. Most of the efficiency gains go to the trustees. It is thus necessary to do careful analyses at the level of the individual, assessing their decisions in light of the subjective expected values of their options. When this is done, it becomes clear that the main effect of over- versus undertrusting is not the most informative result. Instead, the central error is that trustors neglect probabilities in their decisions. They overtrust when the probability of reciprocation is low (because of high temptation), which trustors, due to their egocentric biases, fail to see. Conversely, individuals undertrust when the probability of reciprocation is high. In short, there are two kinds of error—trusting too much and trusting too little—and both can be reduced by steering trustors away from a limited egocentric approach to the available information.

Egocentrism is not limited to the trustor. Trustees were also primarily interested in their own payoffs. Arguably, trustees should care about the trustor's risk so that they might reward a trustor according to the extent of that person's vulnerability. Again, players in the game do take each other's perspective but only modestly so.[7] Yet, when trustees are told that the trustor was given no choice but to transfer money, they send less money back (Cox, 2004). The decision to reciprocate in a regular trust game is largely a matter of rewarding intentional acts of trust instead of a simple application of social preferences.

The studies reported in Evans and Krueger (2014) yielded further, yet unpublished, results that shed light on how social preferences affect decisions in trust dilemmas. Prosocials, as identified by the triple-dominance method (Van Lange, 1999), were more trusting than proselfs (i.e., individualists), as one might expect, but they were also more sensitive to the trustee's level of temptation. This finding is consistent with the idea that social preferences are sensitive to context. Most prosocials, although they care about others and about fairness, are not strict altruists. Instead, they cooperate if they know or expect others to do the same (e.g., Bogaert, Boone, & Declerck, 2008; Fehr, Fischbacher, & Kosfeld, 2005). In our studies, prosocials also inspected their own potential payoffs more carefully than proselfs did. Together, these findings suggest that the prosocial approach to interpersonal behavior involves more than acting on a set of preferences. Prosocials appear to bring a richer understanding to the task. They engage in perspective-taking in order to comprehend how their own decisions will affect outcomes in conjunction with the decisions of others, and they remain mindful of their own material interests. By contrast, many individualists fail to think strategically; rather, they content themselves with a heuristic assessment of their own prospects.[8]

What can one expect when the trust game is repeated many times among many pairs of individuals? In the case of the dictator game, we saw that distributions of social preferences do not translate neatly into corresponding distributions of wealth. The main result of our simulations was that stable individual differences in social values produce stark inequalities in wealth. To see how wealth is created and distributed in a society in which each person is both a trustor and a trustee, we ran another four simulations. Again, there were 100 virtual individuals in each simulation, and in each round a given individual assumed either the role of the trustor or the role of the trustee. Initial trustors were endowed with 10MU, while the trustees had nothing. Because wealth accretes fast in the standard trust game, the games ended after 15 rounds.

The first simulation assumed a uniform distribution of the proportion transferred. Trustors transferred from 0% to 100% of their wealth on any given round, and trustees returned from 0% to 50%. Pairs were randomly reshuffled after each round. The resulting distribution was left-skewed, with many individuals having little and few having much. The overall wealth of the society was 290,10MU (Figure 7.2A). When the proportion of wealth transferred was stable within individuals and consistent in both roles, the final distribution looked similar (Figure 7.2B), but overall wealth was cut in half (134,450MU). In this second simulation, a person's final wealth was negatively correlated ($r = -.5$) with willingness to transfer. Those who trusted the least and reciprocated the least accumulated the most wealth. The third and fourth simulation assumed a preponderance of selfish individuals. One person did not trust or reciprocate at all, whereas the other 99 transferred 20% of their capital as trustors and gave back 10% as trustees. The final distributions of wealth looked similar. Neither when pairs were randomly shuffled after each round (Figure 7.2C) nor when preferences were stable (Figure 7.2D) was there much skew. Final total wealth was low and virtually identical (~2,240MU).

These simulations reveal the dilemmatic nature of trust. The more people trust, the more efficient (i.e., wealthy) they become collectively, while those who trust the most benefit the least. Along with the previous simulations of the dictator game, the results also show that the distribution of social preferences in a group or a society of interacting individuals is a poor predictor of the distribution of wealth. Few individuals end up with what they prefer, and few see their society in a state that they would like. The distribution of wealth in a society is an emergent

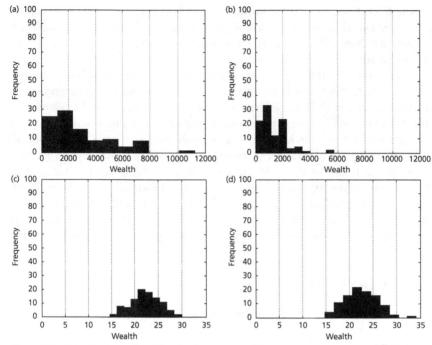

Figure 7.2. Distribution of wealth after 15 rounds of the trust game.

property of the interactions among many interdependent agents and thus difficult to predict. It does seem, though, that with a few reasonable assumptions regarding the input parameters, it is more likely to observe a negative skew than a positive skew in the final distribution. This general outcome is common in the real world. There are more societies comprising a few rich against the background of poor or middling masses than vice versa (Stieglitz, 2013).

■ CONCLUSION

This short ramble through the psychology and behavioral economics of trust has shown that, indeed, trust is suspended between profit and prosociality. As the "Let me help you" slogan[9] says, trust comprises an offer of help to others with an invitation to help in return. If profit were merely incidental, little social or economic exchanges would take place. The incentive for personal gain is part of the fabric of trust. Hence, the psychology of trust comprises self-regarding preferences and egocentric biases in decision-making. Yet, trust is also suffused with prosociality. Trustors must rely on trustees' prosocial willingness to sacrifice and share some of the gains that come from interpersonal exchange. Trustors perfectly locked into an egocentric frame of mind would not be able to do this. They must, at minimum, be able to mentally simulate the trustees' prosocial considerations. As we assumed in our simulations, virtually everyone plays the role of the trustor and the trustee in the course of their social and economic lives. These are two closely related social roles and frames of mind. It is unlikely that prosocial values and preferences are only activated when a person is in the role of the trustee.

Trust is the most basic social dilemma (Krueger & Evans, 2013). In this chapter, we have put trust in the context of social games to document the progression of psychological complexity and challenge. The dictator game is not a dilemma at all. A dictator might experience a conflict between selfishness and prosociality but has no strategic worries. Participants in an assurance game (or a prisoner's dilemma or a game of chicken) are called upon to integrate their values with their expectations regarding the choices or others who are doing the same at the same time. It is left to the trustor, however, to face the challenge of greatest vulnerability. The trustor's considerations are manifold, and research has begun to reveal how ordinary people deal with this challenge. Broad claims that people should either trust more or less overall are not be particularly helpful as they dismiss the depth of the dilemma.

■ AUTHORS' NOTE

We thank Philipp Gerlach for helpful comments on a draft of this chapter.

■ NOTES

1. When own losses weigh less than others' gains, the dictator game may serve as a model for helping in general and the bystander situation in particular (Darley & Latané, 1968; Fischer et al., 2011).

2. When game is rare and fleet, successful hunters share their kill, knowing that tomorrow they may depend on the kindness of others (Hill, 2002). Their repeated exchanges reveal reciprocal altruism, not dictatorship (Kropotkin, 1902).

3. Hoffman et al. (1996) speculated that some dictators share value in one-shot games because they have found this strategy to be beneficial in the repeated reciprocal encounters outside the laboratory. They support this idea with an example from a hunter-gatherer culture, in which success in hunting is rare and probabilistic (see note 1). In a property-driven society, however, most generosity is a response to a direct plea or demand.

4. Some assurance games provide T > P.

5. In contrast, benevolence turns cooperation into the dominating strategy in the prisoners dilemma if $W > \dfrac{T-R}{R-S} \cap W > \dfrac{P-S}{T-P}$.

6. Halevy and Chou's (2013) data are most consistent with a two-step process in which players first focus on symmetrical outcomes (mutual cooperation and mutual defection in the assurance game) and then choose the strategy associated with the better personal payoff.

7. We applied a stopping rule in our analysis of the trustor's attempts to read the trustee's mind. When gauging the strength of the trustee's temptation to betray, we thought trustors only consider the trustee's payoffs, ignoring the possibility that trustees reward those trustors more cheerfully who accepted a large as opposed to a small risk.

8. This analysis may seem to contradict the recent claim that cooperation is the intuitive choice, whereas defection the thoughtful one (Rand et al., 2014). Note, however, that our argument is about a difference between attitudinal types, not between their eventual decisions.

9. Which we found emblazoned on a T-shirt at a department store.

■ **REFERENCES**

Algan, Y., & Cahuc, P. (2010). Inherited trust and growth. *The American Economic Review*, *100*, 2060–2092.

Almy, B. K., & Krueger, J. I. (2013). Game interrupted: The rationality of considering the future. *Judgment & Decision Making*, *8*, 521–526.

Arrow, K. (1974). *The limits of organization*. New York: Norton.

Babcock, L., & Loewenstein, G. (1997). Explaining bargaining impasse: The role of self-serving biases. *The Journal of Economic Perspectives*, *11*, 109–126.

Balliet, D., Wu, J., & De Dreu, C. K. W. (2014). Ingroup favoritism in cooperation: A meta-analysis. *Psychological Bulletin, 140*, 1556–1581.

Becker, G. S. (1976). *The economic approach to human behavior*. Chicago: University of Chicago Press.

Berg, J., Dickhaut, J., & McCabe, K. (1995). Trust, reciprocity, and social-history. *Games and Economic Behavior, 10*, 122–142.

Bicchieri, C. (2006). *The grammar of society*. New York: Cambridge University Press.

Bicchieri, C., Xiao, E., & Muldoon, R. (2011). Trustworthiness is a social norm, but trusting is not. *Politics, Philosophy & Economics, 10*, 170–187.

Bogaert, S., Boone, C., & Declerck, C. (2008). Social value orientation and cooperation in social dilemmas: A review and conceptual model. *British Journal of Social Psychology, 47*, 453–480.

Bohnet, I., & Frey, B. S. (1999). Social distance and other-regarding behavior in dictator games: comment. *American Economic Review, 89*, 335–339.

Burnham, T., McCabe, K., & Smith, V. L. (2000). Friend-or-foe intentionality priming in an extensive-form trust game. *Journal of Economic Behavior & Organization, 43*, 57–73.

Burnstein, E., Crandall, C., & Kitayama, S. (1996). Some neo-Darwinian decision rules for altruism: Weighing cues for inclusive fitness as a function of the biological importance of the decision. *Journal of Personality and Social Psychology, 67*, 773–789.

Colman, A. M., Pulford, B. D., & Lawrence, C. L. (2014). Explaining strategic coordination: Cognitive hierarchy theory, strong Stackelberg reasoning, and team reasoning. *Decision, 1*, 35–58.

Cox, J. C. (2004). How to identify trust and reciprocity. *Games and Economic Behavior, 46*, 260–281.

Crockett, M. J., Kurth-Nelson, Z., Siegel, J. Z., Dayan, P., & Dolan, R. J. (2014). Harm to others outweighs harm to self in moral decision making. *Proceedings of the National Academy of Sciences, 111*, 17320–17325. pnas.org/cgi/doi/10.1073/pnas.1408988111

Darley, J. M., & Latané, B. (1968). Bystander intervention in emergencies: Diffusion of responsibility. *Journal of Personality and Social Psychology, 8*, 377–383.

Dawes, R. M. (1980). Social dilemmas. *Annual Review of Psychology, 31*, 169–193.

DeSteno, D. (2014). *The truth about trust*. New York: Penguin.

Dunning, D., Anderson, J. E., Schlösser, T., Ehlebracht, D., & Fetchenhauer, D. (2014). Trust at zero acquaintance: More a matter of respect than expectation of reward. *Journal of Personality and Social Psychology*, *107*, 122–141.

Epley, N., & Dunning, D. (2000). Feeling "holier than thou": Are self-serving assessments produced by errors in self- or social prediction? *Journal of Personality and Social Psychology*, *79*, 861–875.

Evans, A. M., Athenstaedt, U., & Krueger, J. I. (2013). The development of trust and altruism during childhood. *Journal of Economic Psychology*, *36*, 82–95.

Evans, A. M., & Krueger, J. I. (2011). Elements of trust: Risk taking and expectation of reciprocity. *Journal of Experimental Social Psychology*, *47*, 171–177.

Evans, A. M., & Krueger, J. I. (2014). Outcomes and expectations in dilemmas of trust. *Judgment & Decision Making*, *9*, 90–103.

Fehr, E., Fischbacher, U., & Kosfeld, M. (2005). Neuroeconomic foundations of trust and social preferences: Initial evidence. *The American Economic Review*, *95*, 346–351.

Fehr, E., & Schmidt, K. M. (1999). A theory of fairness, competition, and cooperation. *The Quarterly Journal of Economics*, *114*, 817–868.

Fiedler, S., Glöckner, A., Nicklisch, A., & Dickert, S. (2013). Social value orientation and information search in social dilemmas: An eye-tracking analysis. *Organizational Behavior and Human Decision Processes*, *120*, 272–284.

Fischer I. (2012). Similarity or reciprocity? On the determinants of cooperation in similarity-sensitive games. *Psychological Inquiry*, *23*, 48–54.

Fischer, P., Krueger, J. I., Greitemeyer, T., Vogrinic, C., Kastenmüler, A., Frey, D., Wicher, M., & Kainbacher, M. (2011). The bystander effect: A meta-analytic review on bystander intervention in dangerous and non-dangerous emergencies. *Psychological Bulletin*, *137*, 517–537.

Forsythe, R., Horowitz, J. L., Savin, N. E., & Sefton, M. (1994). Fairness in simple bargaining experiments. *Games and Economic Behavior*, *6*, 347–369.

Gigerenzer, G. 2008). Why heuristics work. *Perspectives on Psychological Science*, *3*, 20–29.

Gouldner, A. W. (1960). The norm of reciprocity: A preliminary statement. *American Sociological Review*, *25*, 161–179.

Halevy, N., & Chou, E. Y. (2014). How decisions happen: Focal points and blind spots in interdependent decision making. *Journal of Personality and Social Psychology*, *106*, 398–417.

Halevy, N., & Katz, J. J. (2013). Conflict templates: Thinking through interdependence. *Current Directions in Psychological Science*, *22*, 217–222.

Hamilton, W. D. (1964). The genetical evolution of social behaviour. I and II. *Journal of Theoretical Biology*, *7*, 1–52.

Hill, K. (2002). Altruistic cooperation during foraging by the Ache, and the evolved human predisposition to cooperate. *Human Nature*, *13*, 105–128.

Hoffman, E., & McCabe, K., & Smith, V. L. (1996). Social distance and other-regarding behavior in dictator games. *The American Economic Review*, *86*, 653–660.

Johnson, N. D., & Mislin, A. A. (2011). Trust games: A meta-analysis. *Journal of Economic Psychology*, *32*, 865–889.

Jones, B. A., Rachlin H. (2006). Social discounting. *Psychological Science*, *17*, 283–286.

Kahneman, D., & Tversky, A. (1984). Choices, values, and frames. *American Psychologist*, *39*, 341–350.

Kanagaretnam, K., Mestelman, S., Nainar, K., & Shehata, M. (2009). The impact of social value orientation and risk attitudes on trust and reciprocity. *Journal of Economic Psychology, 30*, 368–380.

Kiyonari, T., Tanida, S., & Yamagishi, T. (2000). Social exchange and reciprocity: confusion or heuristic? *Evolution and Human Behavior, 21*, 411–427.

Kollock, P. (1998). Social dilemmas: The anatomy of human cooperation. *Annual Review of Sociology, 24*, 183–214.

Kropotkin, P. A. (1902). *Mutual aid: a factor of evolution*. New York: McClure, Philips & Co.

Krueger, J. I. (2013). Social projection as a source of cooperation. *Current Directions in Psychological Science, 22*, 289–294.

Krueger, J. I., DiDonato, T. E., & Freestone, D. (2012). Social projection can solve social dilemmas. *Psychological Inquiry, 23*, 1–27.

Krueger, J. I., & Evans, A. M. (2013). Fiducia: Il dilemma sociale essenziale/Trust: The essential social dilemma. *In-Mind: Italy, 5*, 13–18.

Krueger, J. I., Massey, A. L., & DiDonato, T. E. (2008). A matter of trust: From social preferences to the strategic adherence to social norms. *Negotiation & Conflict Management Research, 1*, 31–52.

Krueger, J. I., Smith, A. T., & Wang, Y. E. (2015). Victory of tragedy. Review of "Social dilemmas" by Van Lange et al. *American Journal of Psychology, 127*, 540–543.

Krueger, J. I., Ullrich, J., & Chen, L. J. (2016). Expectations and decisions in the volunteer's dilemma: effects of social distance and social projection. *Frontiers in Psychology: Cognition, 7*, article 1909. doi: 10.3389/fpsyg.2016.01909

List, J. A. (2007). On the interpretation of giving in dictator games. *Journal of Political Economy, 115*, 482–493.

Locey, M. L., Safin, V., & Rachlin, H. (2013). Social discounting and the prisoner's dilemma game. *Journal of the Experimental Analysis of Behavior, 99*, 85–97.

McCabe, K. A., Smith, V. L., & LePore, M. (2000). Intentionality detection and "mindreading": Why does game form matter? *Proceedings of the National Academy of Sciences, 97*, 4404–4409.

Messick, D. M., & McClintock, C. G. (1968). Motivational bases of choice in experimental games. *Journal of Experimental Social Psychology, 4*, 1–25.

Miller, G. F. (1997). Protean primates: The evolution of adaptive unpredictability in competition and courtship. In A. Whiten & R. W. Byrne (Eds.), *Machiavellian intelligence II: Extensions and applications* (pp. 312–340). New York: Cambridge University Press.

Murphy, R. O., Ackermann, K. A., & Handgraaf, M. J. J. (2011). Measuring social value orientation. *Judgment and Decision Making, 6*, 771–781.

Peysakhovich, A., Nowak, M. A., & Rand, D. G. (2014). Humans display a 'cooperative phenotype' that is domain general and temporally stable. https://papers.ssrn.com/sol3/papers.cfm?abstract_id=2426473

Rabin, M. (1993). Incorporating fairness into game theory and economics. *The American Economic Review, 83*, 1281–1302.

Rand, D. G., Peysakhovich, A., Kraft-Todd, G. T., Newman, G. E., Wurzbacher, O., Nowak, M. A., & Greene, J. D. (2014). Social heuristics shape intuitive cooperation. *Nature Communications, 5*, art. no. 3677.

Rapoport, A., & Chammah, A. L. (1966). The game of chicken. *The American Behavioral Scientist, 10*, 10–28.

Rousseau, J.-J. (1984). A discourse on inequality. Translated by M. Cranston. New York: Penguin. (Original work published 1754)

Russell, B. (1957). *Why I am not a Christian.* London: Allen & Unwin.

Shariff, A. F., & Norenzayan, A. (2007). God is watching you: Priming God concepts increases prosocial behavior in an anonymous economic game. *Psychological Science, 18,* 803–809.

Skyrms, B. (2001) The stag hunt. *Proceedings and Addresses of the American Philosophical Association, 75,* 31–41.

Stieglitz, J. E. (2013). *The price of inequality: How today's divided society endangers our future.* New York: Norton.

Tajfel, H., Billig, M. G., Bundy, R. P., & Flament, C. (1971). Social categorization and intergroup behavior. *European Journal of Social Psychology, 1,* 149–178.

Tan, H. B., & Forgas, J. P. (2010). When happiness makes us selfish, but sadness makes us fair: Affective influences on interpersonal strategies in the dictator game. *Journal of Experimental Social Psychology, 46,* 571–576.

Thomas, K. A., DeScioli, P., Haque, O. S., & Pinker, S. (2014). The psychology of coordination and common knowledge. *Journal of Personality and Social Psychology, 107,* 657–676.

Trivers, R. L. (1971). The evolution of reciprocal altruism. *The Quarterly Review of Biology, 46,* 35–47.

Tsebelis, G. (1989). The abuse of probability in political analysis: The Robinson Crusoe fallacy. *American Political Science Review, 83,* 77–91.

Van Boven, L., & Loewenstein, G. (2005). Cross-situational projection. In M. D. Alicke, D. Dunning, & J. I. Krueger (Eds.), *The self in social judgment* (pp. 43–64). New York: Psychology Press.

Van Lange, P. A. M. (1999). The pursuit of joint outcomes and equality in outcomes: An integrative model of social value orientation. *Journal of Personality and Social Psychology, 77,* 337–349.

Van Lange, P. A. M. (2015). Generalized trust: Four lessons from genetics and culture. *Current Directions in Psychological Science, 24,* 71–76.

Van Lange, P. A. M., Balliet, D., Parks, C. D., & Van Vugt, M. (2014). *Social dilemmas: The psychology of human cooperation.* New York: Oxford University Press.

Yamagishi, T., Mifune, N., Li, Y., Shinadad, M., Hashimotod, H., Horitae, Y., . . . Simunovic, D. (2013). Is behavioral pro-sociality game-specific? Pro-social preference and expectations of pro-sociality. *Organizational Behavior and Human Decision Processes, 120,* 260–271.

8 The Mysteries of Trust

Trusting Too Little and Too Much at the Same Time

■ DETLEF FETCHENHAUER, DAVID
DUNNING, AND THOMAS SCHLÖSSER

Over the past two decades, the intrapsychic and interpersonal dynamics underlying trust have become a major topic in the behavioral and social sciences, with scholars from anthropology, biology, economics, political science, psychology, and sociology all opening research accounts about what prompts people to trust versus distrust one another (e.g., Johnson & Mislin, 2011; Kosfeld, Heinrichs, Zak, Fischbacher, & Fehr, 2005; Snijders & Keren, 2001; Van Lange, 2015; Wilson & Eckel, 2011).

The reason for this burgeoning interest is completely understandable. Trust represents several mysteries of critical importance. Here is just one: Trust is essential for any social arrangement to thrive, whether it is between two individuals, within an organization, or even in a nation or society (Fukuyama, 1995; Kramer, 1998; Simpson, 2007). Without trust, it is difficult, even impossible, to imagine people engaging in stable, efficient, and mutually rewarding social relations. That said, a strict "rational actor" perspective on social behavior suggests that trust is risky and unwise, in that intelligent people focused exclusively on their own material self-interest will be sorely tempted to exploit any trust offered to them rather than reward it (Berg, Dickhaut, & McCabe, 1995; Bolle, 1998). Thus how does one maintain the essential behavior of trust among people when it is demonstrably an irrational choice?

Although many of the scholars delving into the mysteries of trust differ in the exact meaning they imbue in the word, most of them, explicitly or implicitly, follow a definition similar to the one proposed by Rousseau, Sitkin, Burt, and Camerer (1998) that: "Trust is a psychological state comprising the intention to accept vulnerability based upon positive expectations of the intentions or behavior of another" (p. 395). Consistent with this definition, Rotter's (1967) famous scale of interpersonal trust focuses on whether people have positive or negative expectations about the intentions of others (e.g., *Parents usually can be relied on to keep their promises.*). So, too, does the World Value Survey, which in its questions about trust focuses squarely on beliefs about whether other people are trustworthy (Johnson & Mislin, 2012).

Thus, in much scholarship, trust is defined as tantamount to one's expectations about the trustworthiness of others. One will trust if optimistic that others are trustworthy but forgo trust if and when one is more cynical. The definition of trust as anticipated trustworthiness implies a strong connection between behavior and cognition: Humans trust each other on the behavioral level exactly *because* they expect that their trust will be rewarded at the cognitive level. For example: I will lend you my car because I expect you to bring it back in good shape. If I do not, I will either not lend you my car at all or I insist on a formal contract legally obliging you to fix any potential damage.

This is where our research comes in. As we summarize in this chapter, our data compels us to question the assumption that trust at the cognitive level is tantamount to trust as behavior. Trust is much more multifaceted than that. Often, we find that people trust each other in a behavioral level (i.e., they "accept vulnerability" to potential exploitation by the other) even though they fail to have sufficient cognitive trust to support it. That is, they make themselves vulnerable to exploitation by another despite having little or no "positive expectations about the intentions or behavior" of the other person.

Thus this chapter makes two central points. The first is that trust at the cognitive level is not identical to trust at the behavioral level. The two are dissociated, and that can lead to patterns of thought and behavior suggesting, somewhat paradoxically, that people trust both too little and too much at the same time, depending on the level of trust one is focusing on.

Second, because trust is much more than behavior based on rational expectation concerning the trustworthiness of others, additional factors can importantly influence when and if people trust. Indeed, we find that the actual meaning of trust behavior itself—what the choice to trust signifies—matters a great deal, sometimes more than the possible outcomes that follow from that behavior (Dunning & Fetchenhauer, 2010, 2013; Dunning, Fetchenhauer, & Schlösser, 2012). Among its many facets, trust involves a complex association of behavior with beliefs, norms, and emotions. Our work has confronted us with this complexity for many years, and although we have not uncovered all of its nuances, we do want to describe what we have found on our way about what influences trust beyond expectations about the trustworthiness of others.

■ THE TRUST GAME AS A METHOD TO MEASURE TRUST

Before the advent of game theoretical tools in both economics and psychology, trust was usually measured by simply asking participants to self-report about their trustfulness (e.g., Rotter, 1967). Unfortunately, such verbal reports do not necessarily tell much about human behavior when people are called upon to act in vivo. Thus many economists and psychologists turned, as have we, to a laboratory exercise called the "trust game" or "investment game" (Berg et al., 1995) to assess trust.

In this game, people playing the role of Person A are given an amount of money. Person A can keep it all, which means that the game is over. Or, they give some proportion of that money to a Person B. If they give a portion to Person B, that portion is multiplied by a certain factor. For example, in some games, if Person A hands over €5, Person B receives a total of €15 (the multiplication factor would be 3). In a second step, Person B must then decide whether to keep all the money received or to give some part of it back to Person A. As such, this game constitutes a behavioral measure of trust as defined earlier. When Persons A hands over (some or all of his) money they make themselves vulnerable, in that the financial fate of his "investment" is totally dependent on whether Person B rewards or exploits that vulnerability.

In the original version of the game, Persons A could freely decide the percentage of their money, from 0% to 100%, they wanted to give Person B, and Persons B could freely decide the percentage of the total money they received, from 0% to 100%, they could give back (Berg et al., 1995). In a newer version of the game, Persons A face a binary choice (e.g., Fetchenhauer & Dunning, 2009). They can either keep all their money or they give it all to Persons B. In return, Persons B also face a binary choice; they can keep everything for themselves or split the money evenly between themselves and Person A.

The binary version of the trust game is less often used than the investment game, but we think that from a psychological perspective it has a number of advantages—and thus it is the game we typically use in our trust work. First, it forces both Persons A and B to make an unequivocal decision. Persons A either trust or they do not; there is no half measure. In response, Persons B prove to be trustworthy or they are not. Therefore, both persons' behavior can be more clearly interpreted than in the original form of the game. Consider a Person A with an endowment of €10 giving €6 to Person B and keeping €4 for herself. Should that be considered more a signal of trust or one of distrust? And is that person being rational? Mostly rational? Irrational?

In our work, we opt for a binary game because it is also clearer to us whether the behavior of Person A is rational, according to economic principles, at least when the game is played anonymously and in a one-shot paradigm: Persons B have no material incentive to give anything back to Person A and, thus, will keep all the money for themselves. Persons A should rationally anticipate this behavior (based on the so-called "common knowledge assumption") and, thus, keep all their money for themselves. Of course, both players will go home with much less money than would have been possible. This is not due to their foolishness but rather to their intelligence. Regrettably, this analysis suggests that individual rationality will make greater collective benefit impossible.

■ TRUST AT THE COGNITIVE LEVEL

However, we know from our work, and most of our participants suspect, that some people as Persons B give money back, hence showing some trustworthiness in behavior. Thus we have operationalized trust at the cognitive level as the expectation of others' trustworthiness (Fetchenhauer & Dunning, 2009). We ask participants to estimate the percentage of Persons B who will split the money evenly. Individual participants vary quite a bit in their expectations, with some assuming that 100% would share the money evenly ("I can't imagine someone to be that selfish"), and some assuming the exact opposite ("I can't imagine someone not to understand this golden opportunity").

But summing across individuals, we tend to get a clear collective answer about the presumed trustworthiness of others, with the average estimate converging around a value a little less than 50% (Dunning, Anderson, Schlösser, Ehlebracht, & Fetchenhauer, 2014; Fetchenhauer & Dunning, 2009). Thus, on average, participants expect that slightly more than one out of every two Persons B would keep the whole amount of money for themselves and that their peers are slightly more prone to exploit rather than honor trust. Thus, if we were to characterize the level of trust we see at the cognitive level, we would describe it as moderate, at most.

However, from our experiments, we can characterize this rate of trust at the cognitive level more specifically: It is much too cynical, given the real rates of trustworthiness that Persons B display. Thus, at the cognitive level, people trust much too little. In all of the approximately 70 to 80 occasions in which we have conducted trust games with different participants, a vast majority of Persons B turn out to be trustworthy, with the exact percentage on average hovering between 75% and 90%—much higher than the roughly 40% to 50% estimate provided on average by Persons A. Interestingly, we have found this pattern of undue wariness on the part of Persons A and commonplace generosity on the part of Persons B in the United States, Germany, and the Netherlands; in studies with students and managers; with 8- to 10-year-old children; and with pensioners (Dunning et al., 2014; Fetchenhauer & Dunning, 2009, 2010, 2012). This result is extremely stable.

Given these results, one task we have naturally taken on is explaining why people are so mistaken in their estimates of trustworthiness—underestimating the likelihood that Persons B will reward trust by some 30 to 40 percentage points. Why the error? There are many candidate explanations.

First, one might argue that such a misperception of other's trustworthiness is just another example of the *illusory superiority* (Alicke & Govorun, 2005). Time and again it has been shown that people think of themselves as morally superior to others, which might prompt them to overestimate their own moral character or underestimate the moral character of others (Allison, Messick, & Goethals, 1989; Van Lange & Sedikides, 1998). This tendency has often been attributed to humans' need to bolster their "moral self-esteem" (i.e., to perceive themselves as moral and ethical). Second, a more economical explanation would be that participants are just not sufficiently motivated to produce a valid estimate of human trustworthiness. This might explain that the average estimate of trustworthy Persons B lies around 50% (which might be the easiest guess of all) as well as the fact that so many estimates are rather extreme. We hear this critique mainly from economists who often argue that judgments or estimates of participants are only "cheap talk" if there are not linked to a monetary incentive.

But what if their estimates were not cheap talk? In one of our studies, participants watched 56 videos of stimulus-persons and estimated which decision each had made in a trust game played right after the video was recorded. We informed our participants that they would earn an extra €0.50 for each valid estimate but would lose €0.50 for each wrong guess. Thus participants played for a possible total of €28. However, their estimates were no more accurate than those we gathered in a control condition without any financial incentives (Fetchenhauer & Dunning, 2010).

In another study, we explained the logic of the trust game to participants and asked them to come up with a valid estimate of Persons' B decisions. In a classroom experiment, half of all participants were just told to do their very best; the other half of the participants were told that the best "judge of character" would earn €100. It turned out that the averages did not differ between conditions. However, there was indirect evidence that participants in the incentive condition tried harder to come up with valid estimates than participants in the control condition. Participants in the control conditions provided mostly rather rough estimates (e.g., "60%"), whereas participants in the incentive condition often came up with rather sophisticated estimates (e.g., "61.45%") (Fetchenhauer & Schlösser, 2015).

We would argue that these incentive results rule out both the hypothesis described earlier, that people either want to boost their moral superiority or do not care enough to come up with valid estimates. Monetary incentives should counteract participants' desire to boost their moral self-esteem and should lead them to seek more valid estimates, respectively. Yet, this is not what we observed.

Another explanation of why people tend to underestimate others' trustworthiness stems from a functional perspective on trust decisions. When deciding whether to trust another person, people can make two different kinds of mistakes. They can either distrust another person who is actually trustworthy or they can trust a person who has untrustworthy intentions. Which mistake is the more severe? One could argue that unwarranted distrust merely results in a missed chance of cooperation but that unwarranted trust may result in severe and more permanent consequences.

Thus, from an evolutionary perspective, the underestimation of others' trustworthiness would just be another example of "error management" (Haselton & Buss, 2000). Error management theory posits that humans' perception has not evolved to maximize accuracy but rather to avoid costly mistakes. The theory has been applied to explain to a vast number of phenomena, such as why men overestimate their own chance of romantic success with an attractive woman or why humans tend to assume evil even if an outcome is the consequence of pure chance (e.g., the illness of a loved one). Outside the field of evolutionary psychology this concept is also known as the "smoke detector principle": a smoke detector must not remain silent when a fire is actually there, but it is not a big issue when sometimes an alarm goes off without any fire at hand.

However, there is one last explanation suggestion that the bias toward cynicism arises naturally from the lessons people learn from their life experience. Regrettably, that life experience is compromised and, thus, hides just how trustworthy other people tend to be. Consider the following: When we decide to trust another person and that person turns out not to be trustworthy, life will usually inform us about such a mistake. The money is not repaid, our personal secret is told, or our car is returned—if at all—in much worse shape. However, what if we make the opposite mistake: Withholding trust from a person would actually honor it. In this instance, we will likely never be informed about our mistake. Withholding trust prevents us the other person from disabusing us of our mistaken pessimism. No evidence emerges to erase our cynical error. It is as Hemingway once said: "The best way to find out if you can trust somebody is to trust them." Not trusting another person leads to censored feedback; we will never know whether our hesitation to trust was warranted or not.

We argue that people are not aware of such a bias in the feedback they receive in their trust behavior. Thus, when being asked to estimate others' trustworthiness, their estimates will show the impact of "false positives" (i.e., cases in which they trusted and their trust was betrayed) but not "false negatives" (i.e., cases in which they did not trust although trust would have been warranted). To test this hypothesis, we showed participants again those short videos of 56 stimulus-persons (Fetchenhauer & Dunning, 2010). In each video the participants saw a person sitting behind a desk talking into the camera. These videos were rather short (10 seconds) and mute. From an earlier study, we knew that 80% of the stimulus-people had split the money evenly; about 20% had kept all the money for themselves. Participants observing the videos were given €7.50 for their participation and asked, for each stimulus-person, whether they would risk that participation fee in a binary trust game. They were told that they could either keep their endowment of €7.50 for sure or that they could hand it over to the stimulus-person. If they handed over their money and the stimulus-person had acted trustworthy, they would receive a total of €15. If that stimulus-person had not acted trustworthy, participants would go home empty-handed. Participants were told that their decisions were not hypothetical but that they would play one of the 56 trust games for real.

To test our hypothesis about compromised feedback, we tested the effects of three feedback conditions. In the *no feedback condition* participants never received any feedback about the actual decision of any of the 56 stimulus-persons. In the *real life feedback condition,* participants were only informed about the behavior of their specific interaction partner if they decided to trust that interaction partner— but not if they decided to withhold trust. In the *unconditional feedback condition* participants received feedback irrespective of their own decisions to trust or not. Thus, in this final condition, participants received feedback that we argued real life deprived them of.

The results very much confirmed out hypothesis that the type of feedback mattered. When we asked participants before they saw the videos to estimate the number of trustworthy Persons B, their estimates hovered around the usual 50%, with no differences between conditions. When we asked them the same question afterward in the no feedback condition, we found no significant change in those estimates. We found the same lack of a difference in the *real life condition.* That is, although they discovered that roughly 80% of the stimulus-persons they trusted turned out to be trustworthy, they did not learn that those they decided not to trust would reciprocate trust at roughly the same rate. However, supplying that feedback in the *unconditional feedback* condition caused their biased estimates to vanish. In this last condition, estimates grew to become close to the actual trustworthiness rate of the stimulus-persons (Fetchenhauer & Dunning, 2010).

■ TRUST AT THE BEHAVIORAL LEVEL

But what about behavior? If people are somewhat pessimistic about the trustworthiness of others, and thus trust too little, does behavior show the same pessimistic pattern? Up to now we have only been talking about trust at the cognitive level, that is, estimates of Persons' B trustworthiness. In this section we discuss how participants in our studies actually decide when they are in the role of Person A.

From a strict rational choice model, behavior in trust or investment games should follow a straightforward decision rule: (a) estimate the likelihood of being coupled with a trustworthy or untrustworthy Person B (b) and ask whether the likelihood of return and expected monetary outcome is rich enough to be acceptable given one's tolerance for risk. For example, if the estimated chance of receiving $10 back in the trust game is 60% and one would gladly gamble $5 on a lottery to win $10 if the likelihood of success was over 55%, then one should risk in the trust game. In essence, the reasoning of trustors should follow the same rules as when making a nonsocial financial decision (e.g., gambling in a lottery): Does the likelihood and the size of that reward outweigh any aversion the person might have for risk?

Prospect theory tells us (Kahneman & Tversky, 1979), and many studies have confirmed with data (Wu, Zhang, & Gonzalez, 2004), that most people are risk-averse in gambles such as coin flips. They would likely forgo a chance to double their money if the odds of winning were only 50/50. To induce them to gamble, either the payoffs or the chance of winning have to be much larger. In our own data, we typically see that people demand, on average, a 75% chance of winning to entice them to gamble their $5 on the prospect of winning $10 (Fetchenhauer & Dunning, 2009)—thus displaying conspicuous levels of risk aversion. Thus, applying the same logic to the trust game, most Persons A should then hand their money to Person B only if they estimate the proportion of trustworthy Persons B to be much higher than 50%.

Thus, across several studies, we have allowed participants to play the trust game, asking them additional questions to determine if their behavior follows a rational actor model. First, to determine their risk tolerance, we ask them to indicate the minimum likelihood of winning they would demand to induce them to risk $5 on a lottery in which they could win $10. Second, to gauge expectations that their trust will be rewarded, we ask participants to indicate the percentage of people as Persons B they believe would return $10 back in a trust game. If participants approached the trust game as rational actors, they should trust the other person only when their expectations of their trust being rewarded equals or exceeds the chance they demanded to win on the lottery.

According to our calculations, in our typical study, only 25% to 35% of participants should trust if they were acting purely as a rational actor, in that rather cynical views of peers, as seen earlier, equal or exceed their tolerance for risk for only a minority of our participants. However, in virtually all our studies, it is a *majority* of participants, not a minority, who decide to hand over the $5 (Dunning et al., 2014; Fetchenhauer & Dunning, 2009, 2010, 2012)—with rates of trust reaching as high as 75%. If, at the cognitive level, people are trusting too low; at the behavioral level, given their cynicism and aversion to risk, they are trusting way too much.

In another study, we directly compared trust decisions to decisions made in a lottery to see if people treat both the same, as a rational actor model would presume (Fetchenhauer & Dunning, 2012). We gave participants $5 and asked them whether they would bet that money in a lottery to possibly win $10 as well as asked them if they would hand over the money to a Person B in order to possibly gain the same amount. Of key importance, half of the participants were told that their chance of winning in both the lottery and the trust-game was 80%. For the other half, the chance of gaining money for both lottery and the trust game was a mere 46%. Order of decisions was counterbalanced across participants, and no deception was used in any decision. We had already run the Persons B involved in this study and arranged them into groups who returned $10 at a rate of either 80% or 46%. For lottery decisions, choices aligned well with the rational actor model. Risk-taking was largely dependent on the chance of winning. However, in the trust game, this was not the case. The chance of receiving $10 had no significant effect on trust decisions. Indeed, in the 46% chance of winning condition, the rate of those handing their money to Person B was nearly twice as high as the rate gambling in the lottery, 54% versus 29%, respectively.

What produces these high rates of trust in the face of undue cynicism and pervasive risk aversion? Let us first review a number of plausible explanations that have been ruled out via data. Then we elaborate along which lines we see an actual explanation.

First, when we ask our participants in debriefing sessions why they hand over their money to Person B, by far the most common response we receive is "It's only five bucks." That is, people may trust only because the stakes are quite small. This might be a valid point, but when playing lotteries for the same amounts of money, participants precisely follow their preferences for risk aversion—with the $5 suddenly too big to risk on a lottery.

Second, one could argue that our specific version of the trust game might drive Persons A's behavior via inequality aversion (Fehr & Schmidt, 1999). Trusting Person B is the only way to insure both Persons A and B receive an equal amount of money, assuming Person B returns the $10. However, data fail to affirm this account of trust. In a number of studies (Fetchenhauer & Dunning, 2007; Götmann, 2014) we played versions in which both Person A and Person B started out with an identical endowment, but this did not significantly change the behavior of Person A. In addition, a reanalysis of data from Bolton and Ockenfels (2010; described in Fetchenhauer & Dunning, 2012) found no effect of inequality aversion in the choices participants made between monetary allocations between two people.

Third, perhaps we are observing a "house money" effect (Thaler & Johnson, 1990). Our participants are asked to gamble with money we have furnished them rather than funds they bring on their own. Thus, Persons' A largesse toward Persons B might simply arise because they are being generous with someone else's money. However, in one of our studies, participants had to work one hour for a payment of €7.50, which they then could use in a trust game. It was their money, earned via their participation in the experiment. However, as it turned out, participants in that situation proved to trust more, not less, than those in a control condition (Fetchenhauer & Dunning, 2009, Study 2). In another set of studies we let participants bring their own €5 to the lab that they could then use as Person A in a trust game. Once again, no difference could be observed compared with our usual studies (Schlösser, Mensching, Dunning, & Fetchenhauer, 2016).

Fourth, perhaps Persons A are not solely focused on their own outcomes but instead work to maximize their joint outcome with Person B. To an economist, this is the efficiency hypothesis; people wish to create as much wealth as possible, enlarging the pie, and do not ultimately care about how it is divided. We tested this idea in a study by asking participants to consider three different types of gambles in which they were given €5 and they could either keep it or risk in order to win €10. The first gamble was an ordinary coin-flip in which they had a 50% chance to win €10 and an equal chance to lose their €5. The second gamble was an ordinary trust game (in which participants roughly gauged the chance that their trust would be rewarded to be no different from 50%). The third gamble, the key one, was an "extended coin-flip" that involved payoffs to another person as well as the self. If participants won the coin flip, they would receive $10, as would another random person participating in the experiment. But if they lost, they would lose their $5, but another random person would receive $20. In short, the outcomes described for the extended coin-flip presented participants with outcomes that exactly matched the payoff structure of a two-person trust game.

If the decisions of Persons A in our trust game were driven by the motivation to enlarge the pie for all, then participants should have been equally likely to gamble on the extended coin-flip as they were in the trust game and significantly more than they would in the ordinary coin-flip condition. But this is not what we found. Across two studies, the percentage of risky choices was virtually identical in both coin-flip conditions, with decisions to take a risk significantly higher only in the trust game (Schlösser et al., 2016).

■ NORMS AND EMOTION IN BEHAVIORAL TRUST

Across our studies, only one explanation has been ruled in by data to explain why so many people trust at the behavioral level despite their cynicism and aversion to risk. People appear to follow an injunctive norm that impels them to trust the character of Person B. That is, people feel they *should* trust Person B, and they show the emotional hallmarks of trusting out of a social duty or obligation.

In short, participants are not "giving" when they decide to trust Person B as much as they are "giving in" (Cain, Dana, & Newman, 2014) to some directive that trust is the behavior they ought to choose. In particular, they appear to trust because they must honor the potential good character and good will of Person B. To be sure, they may not be optimistic that Person B is a benevolent person, but their behavior must honor that presumption that he or she is. Their choice must send a social signal that Person B is an honorable individual who is respected. To do otherwise, to distrust, would be impolite and would represent a violation of "positive face" (Brown & Levinson, 1987; Goffman, 1958).

Across a broad range of studies, we have found evidence for this injunctive norm impelling trust well beyond the rate anticipated by economic variables. When asked, people overwhelmingly say they *should* trust Person B, and ratings of what they "should" do significantly predict trust decisions. This is in stark contrast to what people "want" to do. Over several studies, people appear to have a slight lean toward wanting to keep the money (Dunning et al., 2014).

The emotions that surround the trust decision also suggest a psychology of norms. Namely, emotions of social anxiety surround and predict the decision to trust much more than other emotions, and theories of norms suggest that the thought of violating a norm causes people to feel tense, nervous, and guilty (Higgins 1987, 1989). Consistent with that logic, we find that participants feeling the highest social anxiety about keeping the money, relative to giving it, are the ones most likely to trust. And, again, most participants feel more anxious about keeping the money than giving it, suggesting an overall push toward trust. Other emotions, such as those associated with the "warm glow of altruism" (i.e., happiness, contentment) are much less tied to the decision to trust (Dunning et al., 2014).

Finally, when we remove the specific norm we believe is at play—that people must respect the character of the other individual—we find that trust rates collapse. In one study, we compared our trust game to a version in which Persons' B decision was not their own. Instead, Persons B were instructed to flip a coin to determine whether to give $10 back to Person A. This change in procedure, essentially taking Person B's character out of the equation, prompted Persons A's trust rates to collapse from 67% in the usual game to 44% in this coin-driven version—even though participants thought they had a greater chance of receiving $10 when a coin flip was involved. In a follow-up study, we gave participants three options in a trust study: to keep the $5, give it to Person B as before, or to give it to Person B but force him or her to flip a coin to decide about returning money back. A significantly higher percentage of people (54%) opted to give Person B a free choice about whether to return the $10 then to force the coin flip (22%), even though participants thought the odds that they would receive any money back was greater if Person B was compelled to flip the coin (Dunning et al., 2014).

Other work suggests that behavioral trust involves politeness norms distinguish it from other decisions. In most recent work, we have compared trust decisions to other choices like simple gambles, such as flipping a coin. We find that people are also responsive to what they say they "should" do when they decide whether to flip a coin, even one with extended consequences for other people. When faced with such gamble, people think they should avoid gambling (even though most "want" to risk it), and this belief strongly predicts whether they will choose to gamble or stand pat.

What is interesting, however, is what people mean by "should" in this circumstance. We asked participants to describe the meaning they place on the word. When considering a simple gamble, "should" refers to what the smart, logical, and objective decision would be. For simple gambles, people think it is smart to refuse to gamble. In decisions to trust, those same themes arise when people describe what they "should" do, but they also add a social dimension to the word, stating that "should" also refers to what the socially appropriate, respectful, and polite action would be. The addition of this social dimension prompts people to think they should take a risk on the other person (Schlösser et al., 2015).

■ OPEN QUESTIONS

In sum, our work suggests two central conclusions, although they must remain tentative pending additional work. The first conclusion is that trust at the cognitive level is not tantamount to trust at the behavioral level. The decision to trust does not directly indicate that people have optimistic views about the trustworthiness of others, and it would be a mistake to think that cognitive and behavioral trust are mutually identical to each other. People can hold quite cynical beliefs about their peers yet go ahead and make themselves vulnerable to strangers via their actions. As such, trust as a cognitive phenomenon must be distinguished from trust as a behavioral event.

Second, trust at the behavioral level is not only responsive to economic, or rather *consequentialist* variables, such as the perceived likelihood of reward as well as the size of that reward. In particular, trust at the behavioral level is responsive to injunctive norms that promote it (Dunning & Fetchenhauer, 2013). People choose to trust, even when they expect that trust is likely to be exploited, out of a norm of respect for the character of another individual. In that, trust decisions can also be considered *expressive*, in that people trust not because of what they think about the outcomes but because they are concerned about what the behavior that they choose signifies. It is the behavior itself, and not its downstream consequences, that people are concerned about.

We consider the work tentative because of two questions we feel must be pursued in future research. When we conducted our first trust game many years ago, our intuition told us that the trust game would follow a very different psychology. More specifically, we expected participants to be much more reluctant about taking a risk on another person in a trust game than taking one on a lottery. Losing a coin-flip is just bad luck. However, having one's trust violated is a betrayal by another human being—which is a harsher outcome, bringing with it feelings of outrage and humiliation. Because of these added emotional penalties, we presumed people would chose to avoid trust.

Indeed, if one looks at the economic literature, one finds evidence for such *betrayal aversion* in trust games. For example, Bohnet and Zeckhauser (2004) played a trust game in which participants were given $10 that they could either keep or hand over to Person B. If they indeed handed over their money, Persons B got a total of $30 and could either give $15 or $8 to Person B (keeping $15 or $22 for themselves, respectively). From here, the structure of the game differed from the one we used. Instead of asking for a choice, Bohnet and Zeckhauser asked Persons A to indicate the minimum probability that Person B would reward their trust (from 0% to 100%), that would make them to trust Person B behaviorally. In another condition, participants had to provide the minimum chance of winning in a lottery they would require to induce them to gamble, in a game that presented the same payoff structure as described earlier to Persons A and B.

Thus participants considered one of two situations, each involving payoffs to the self and the other person. However, Persons' A ultimate payoffs depended in the first situation on the choice of Person B, who could possibly then betray the trust of Person A. The second situation allowed no such choice. What Persons A or B won was dependent solely on a lottery; thus there was no chance at betrayal. In line with the notion of betrayal aversion, participants accepted significantly more risk in the lottery than they did in the trust game, citing that a much lower probability would induce them to gamble.

More recently, Aimone and Houser (2012) have replicated and extended this effect. In their paradigm, participants in a control condition played a binary trust game in which they could either keep their $5 endowment to themselves or hand it over to Person B. If that happened, Persons B received $30 and could either give $15 or $2 back to Person A. In another condition, Persons A were told that their chance of winning would be derived from a pool of participants who had to indicate their decision as Persons B. Thus in the first condition losing one's money meant being exploited (i.e., betrayed) by one specific other person whereas in the second participants played a lottery based on the average trustworthiness of Persons B in the experiment. The results showed that participants were much more risk-taking in the second condition relative to the first.

What are we to make of these contradictory results? In both our laboratories, participants prefer taking a risk on Person B's conscious choice than one on a lottery. Yet, economic experiments on betrayal aversion show the opposite. We believe future work will be necessary to resolve the contradiction, and we believe we can suspect what that resolution will be. First, in studies demonstrating betrayal aversion, we have noticed that researchers tend to present participants with very attractive gambles that induce high rates of risk-taking. We wonder if betrayal aversion would survive if more unattractive gambles were used. After all, we have found that trust decisions are rather unresponsive to the appeal of the gamble offered and that people are more likely to trust than to gamble on a lottery when those terms are lackluster, such as there being only a 46% chance of winning (Fetchenhauer & Dunning, 2012). Thus less attractive gambles may reveal that people are not necessarily focused on betrayal in decisions to trust.

Second, we have begun to extend our analysis of the trust game to other forms of social dilemmas. Does that same dissociation in responses between cognitive and behavioral levels arise in other interpersonal transactions, like the prisoner's dilemma game? Our initial work suggests that games that look quite similar to each other can provoke very different reactions in people. In one recent study, we asked participants to play a trust game and also a prisoner's dilemma game that offered the same exact payoffs as the trust game for the mutual decisions of Persons A and B. We found that the same participants reacted to the two games quite differently, even though the games presented the exact same economic terms; 59% of participants trusted yet only 30% cooperated in the prisoner's dilemma (Dunning, Anderson, Fetchenhauer, & Schlösser, 2015).

Moreover, participants were more likely to state they "should" trust than they were to claim they should cooperate, and they felt more socially anxious about distrusting than they did about defecting in the prisoner's dilemma. In short, the two games differed in terms of how much they evoked an injunctive norm to take a risk on another person—and that difference explained why participants acted in a more prosocial manner in the trust game than in the prisoner's dilemma (Dunning et al., 2015). Now the question remains as to why the trust game arouses an injunctive norm that an economically identical prisoner's dilemma game leaves dormant.

■ CONCLUSION

It would be difficult if not impossible to overemphasize the importance of trust to human interaction. What this chapter suggests, in addition, is that the study of trust is somewhat of an Alice through the looking glass experience, filled with complications, contradictions, and nuances that can both excite and frustrate the researcher. Trust at the cognitive level does not produce the same conclusions as trust at the behavioral level. And trust at the behavioral level is responsive to situational features not anticipated by a traditional analysis from economics.

We believe our conceptual journey about trust has just begun, and we hope that other researchers feel the same. There is much to learn about this most essential of social behavior. We trust the road ahead will contain a few surprises but also many lessons well worth learning.

■ REFERENCES

Aimone, J. A., & Houser, D. (2012). What you don't now won't hurt you: A laboratory analysis of betrayal aversion. *Experimental Economics, 15*, 571–588.

Alicke, M. D., & Govorun, O. (2005). The better-than-average effect. In M. D. Alicke, D. Dunning, & J. Kruger (Eds.), *The self in social judgment* (pp. 85–106). New York: Psychology Press.

Allison, S. T., Messick, D. M., & Goethals, G. R. (1989). On being better but not smarter than others: The Muhammad Ali effect. *Social Cognition, 7*, 275–296.

Anderson, J. E., & Dunning, D. (2014). Behavioral norms: Variants and their identification. *Personality and Social Psychology Compass, 8*, 721–738.

Berg, J., Dickhaut, J., & McCabe, K. (1995). Trust, reciprocity, and social history. *Games and Economic Behavior, 10*, 122–142.

Bohnet, I., & Zeckhauser, R. (2004). Trust, risk and betrayal. *Journal of Economic Behavior & Organization, 55*, 467–484.

Bolle, F. (1998). Rewarding trust: An experimental study. *Theory and Decision, 45*, 83–98.

Bolton, G. E., & Ockenfels, A. (2010). Betrayal aversion: Evidence from Brazil, China, Oman, Switzerland, Turkey, and the United States: Comment. *American Economic Review, 100*, 628–633.

Brown, P., & Levinson, S. C. (1987). *Politeness: Some universals in language usage.* Cambridge, UK: Cambridge University Press.

Cain, D. M., Dana, J., & Newman, G. E. (2014). Giving versus giving in. *The Academy of Management Annals, 8*, 505–533.

Dunning, D., Anderson, J. E., Fetchenhauer, D., & Schlösser, T. (2015). *Comparing two experimental paradigms aimed at understanding human prosocial behavior: On trust and cooperation.* Unpublished manuscript, Cornell University.

Dunning, D., Anderson, J. E., Schlösser, T., Ehlebracht, D., & Fetchenhauer, D. (2014). Trust at zero acquaintance: More a matter of respect than expectation of reward. *Journal of Personality and Social Psychology*, *107*, 122–141.

Dunning, D., & Fetchenhauer, D. (2010). Trust as an expressive rather than an instrumental act. In S. Thye & E. Lawler (Eds.), *Advances in group processes* (Vol. 27, pp. 97–127). New York: Emerald.

Dunning, D., & Fetchenhauer, D. (2013). Behavioral influences in the present tense: On expressive versus instrumental action. *Perspectives on Psychological Science*, *8*, 142–145.

Dunning, D., Fetchenhauer, D., & Schlösser, T. (2012). Trust as a social and emotional act: Noneconomic considerations in trust behavior. *Journal of Economic Psychology*, *33*, 686–694.

Fehr, E., & Schmidt, K. M. (1999). A theory of fairness, competition, and cooperation. *Quarterly Journal of Economics*, *114*,817–868.

Fetchenhauer, D., & Dunning, D. (2009). Do people trust too much or too little? *Journal of Economic Psychology*, *30*, 263–276.

Fetchenhauer, D., & Dunning, D. (2010). Why so cynical? Asymmetric feedback underlies misguided skepticism in the trustworthiness of others. *Psychological Science*, *21*, 189–193.

Fetchenhauer, D., & Dunning, D. (2012). Betrayal aversion versus principled trustfulness: How to explain risk avoidance and risky choices in trust games. *Journal of Economic Behavior and Organization*, *81*, 534–541.

Fetchenhauer, D., & Schlösser, T. (2015) [Effects of incentives on estimates of trustworthiness]. Unpublished data, University of Cologne.

Fukuyama, F. (1995). *Trust: The social virtues and the creation of prosperity.* New York: Free Press.

Goffman, E. (1958). *The presentation of self in everyday life.* New York: Random House.

Haselton, M., & Buss, D. (2000). Error management theory: A new perspective on biases in cross-sex mind reading. *Journal of Personality and Social Psychology*, *78*, 81–91.

Higgins, E. T. (1987). Self-discrepancy: A theory relating self and affect. *Psychological Review*, *94*, 319–340.

Higgins, E. T. (1989). Continuities and discontinuities in self-regulatory and self-evaluative processes: A developmental theory relating self and affect. *Journal of Personality*, *57*, 407–445.

Johnson, N. D., & Mislin, A. A. (2011). Trust games: A meta-analysis. *Journal of Economic Psychology*, *32*, 865–889.

Johnson, N. D., & Mislin, A. (2012). How much should we trust the World Values Survey trust question? *Economic Letters*, *116*, 210–212.

Kahneman, D., & Tversky, A. (1979). Prospect theory: An analysis of decision under risk. *Econometrica*, *47*, 263–292.

Kosfeld, M., Heinrichs, M., Zak, P. J. Fischbacher, U. & Fehr, E. (2005). Oxytocin increases trust in humans. *Nature*, *435*, 673–676.

Kramer, R. M. (1998). Paranoid cognition in social systems: Thinking and acting in the shadow of doubt. *Personality and Social Psychology Review*, *2*, 251–275.

Rotter, J. B. (1967). A new scale for the measurement of interpersonal trust. *Journal of Personality*, *35*, 651–665.

Rousseau, D. M., Sitkin, S. B., Burt, R., & Camerer, C. (1998). Not so different after all: A cross-discipline view of trust. *Academy of Management Review*, *23*, 393–404.

Schlösser, T., Mensching, O., Dunning, D., & Fetchenhauer, D. (2016). Trust and rationality: Shifting normative analyses in risks involving other people versus nature. *Social Cognition, 33*, 459–482.

Simpson, J. A. (2007). Foundations of interpersonal trust. In A. W. Kruglanski & E. T. Higgins (Eds.), *Social psychology: Handbook of basic principles* (2nd ed., pp. 587–607). New York: Guilford.

Snijders, C., & Keren, G. (2001). Do you trust? Whom do you trust? When do you trust? *Advances in Group Processes, 18*, 129–160.

Thaler, R. H., & Johnson, E. J. (1990). Gambling with the house money and trying to break even: The effects of prior outcomes on risky choice. *Management Science, 36*, 643–660.

Van Lange, P. (2015). Generalized trust: Four lessons from genetics and culture. *Current Directions in Psychological Science, 24*, 71–76.

Van Lange, P. A. M., & Sedikides, C. (1998). Being more honest but not necessarily more intelligent than other: Generality and explanations for the Muhammad Ali effect. *European Journal of Social Psychology, 28*, 675–680.

Wilson, R., & Eckel, C. C. (2011). Trust and social exchange. In J. N. Druckman, D. P. Green, J. H. Kuklinski, & A. Lupia (Eds.), *The handbook of experimental political science* (pp. 243–257). New York: Cambridge University Press.

Wu, G., Zhang, J., & Gonzalez, R. (2004). Decision under risk. In D. J. Koehler & N. Harvey (Eds.), *Blackwell handbook of judgment & decision making* (pp. 399–423). Malden, MA: Blackwell.

9 Trust and Cooperation

Survey Evidence and Behavioral Experiments

■ CHRISTIAN THÖNI

■ INTRODUCTION

Most if not all human interactions are sufficiently rich in potential outcomes such that it is difficult and costly to account for all the contingencies in a formal contract. If full contracting was the only option, many gains from interaction would be left unexploited. Fortunately, writing a complete contract is usually not necessary, because many humans display a willingness to forgo short-run gains in favor of costly cooperative actions, acts that are often referred to as *trust* and *trustworthiness*. Numerous authors argue that trust is a key ingredient for societies to thrive (see, e.g., Coleman, 1990; Fukuyama, 1996). These ideas spurred an empirical literature showing that survey-measured trust can contribute to explaining differences in economic prosperity across countries (see, e.g., Knack and Keefer, 1997; Algan and Cahuc, 2010). While this empirical literature suggests a link on the macro level, the link would not be entirely convincing if it was not possible to provide evidence on the micro level. In this chapter I discuss a number of studies focusing on providing micro-foundations for the relation between trust, as measured by large-scale opinion poll surveys, and trust as measured by behavioral experiments.

The canonical behavioral game to measure trust is the game introduced by Berg, Dickhaut, and McCabe (1995). In this game, the *trust game*, a first mover can transfer money to a second mover, the money transferred is tripled by the experimenter, after which the second mover can send back any amount to the first mover. Efficiency gains (tripling of money) can only be achieved if the first mover is willing to make an investment. Assuming that the transfer of the first mover is not purely motivated by altruism, the action can be interpreted as trust.

The central element of the trust decision—exposing oneself to the risk of being "exploited" by others in favor of more efficient outcomes—is present in many other games. Most prominent among them is the prisoner's dilemma. The focus of this chapter lies on the public goods game, which is basically a generalization of the prisoner's dilemma game to a strategic situation with more than two players and a richer strategy set. While the trust game models an asymmetric strategic interaction where a trustee has to interact with a trustor, the public goods game models a situation in which all players are in the same situation and must act as trustee and trustor at the same time. The trust game is a model for asymmetric interactions, like, for example, buying a credence good, whereas the public goods game models symmetric social dilemmas such as working in a team.

The link between trust and cooperation is not entirely straightforward. In accordance with Yamagishi (1986, p. 111), who argued that "mutual trust is the key to actual cooperation," I start with a theoretical argument about why behavior in public goods games is related to trust. The remainder of this chapter is organized as follows: The second section describes the game and the theoretical argument. The third section discusses the literature on conditional cooperation, which is one of the prerequisites for the public goods game to measure trust. In the fourth section I discuss evidence on the link between survey items on trust and behavior in the experiment. The discussion focuses on a small number of articles. For a much more encompassing survey of the literature, see Balliet and Van Lange (2013). The fifth section explores the link between survey and behavioral measures in a cross-cultural data set, and the last section concludes.

■ DOES THE PUBLIC GOODS GAME MEASURE TRUST?

The public goods game models a symmetric social dilemma, in which a group of people simultaneously decide upon their contribution to a common pool, from which all players profit equally. The simplest version of this class of games is the linear public goods game. In this game a group of $n \geq 2$—typically three to five—players are endowed with $e > 0$ monetary units. They simultaneously decide how much of their endowment to contribute to the "public good"; that is, they choose $g_i \in [0,e], i = 1,\ldots,n$. Monetary payoffs of the game are

$$x_i(g_i, g_{-i}) = e - g_i + \gamma \sum_{j=1}^{n} g_j,$$

where γ is the marginal per capita return of the public good with $\frac{1}{n} < \gamma < 1$. Solving this game with the tools of game theory requires assumptions about the players' utility functions. A standard solution is to postulate selfish preferences, meaning that each player cares only about his or her own monetary payoff, formally: $u_i = u_i(x_i)$. Under this assumption, the game has a unique Nash equilibrium in which all players contribute zero and earn a monetary payoff of e. The game constitutes a social dilemma, because the joint payoff is maximized when all players contribute e, which would result in a profit of γne, which is larger than e due to the lower bound for γ. However, contributing positive amounts cannot be part of a Nash equilibrium because, independent of the contributions of the other players, the marginal benefit of contributing is γ and thus lower than the marginal cost of one.

Explaining positive contributions in the public goods game requires a richer utility function. A simple extension would be to postulate altruistic preferences, in the simplest case assume that a player seeks to maximize joint payoff ($u_i(\sum x_j)$). Marginal benefit of contributing would then be equal to γn. Since this is by assumption larger than the marginal cost of one, the player contributes e independent of what others do.

For selfish as well as altruistic players, trust in other players—understood as belief about their strategies—does not matter. Beliefs do matter, however, if we assume that players care for equality. Fehr and Schmidt (1999) postulate a utility function $u_i(x_i, x_{-i})$, which incorporates inequality aversion; that is, player i cares about the payoffs of the other players (x_{-i}), but prefers these payoffs to be equal to his or her own payoff. If the players are sufficiently concerned about inequality, then there exist equilibria in which the players contribute $g_i = g$, where $g \in [0, e]$.[1] A player's best-response function is $g_i = R(g_{-i}) = \min\{g_j\}$; that is, it is optimal for him or her to match the lowest of all other contributions. Assuming inequality averse preferences changes the nature of the game. The public goods game is then no longer dominance solvable, and beliefs about other players' contributions become important. Even if a player believes that the others are sufficiently inequality averse, there is still a multitude of equilibria to pick from. While inequality averse players are willing to contribute if others do so, they dislike being the sucker even more than selfish players.[2] This renders the contribution decision into a genuine trust situation: Maximum contributions by all players is the utility maximizing solution, and it is a Nash equilibrium. However, contributing fully entails a considerable risk for any player to end up as a sucker.[3]

The theoretical discussion so far has shown that contributions in public goods games are a measure for trust if we assume preferences that produce positively sloped best-response functions. While the notion of inequality aversion can rationalize these best-response functions, it is by no means the only way to get there. Positively sloped reaction functions also follow from other flavors of social preferences, such as, for example, reciprocity, conformity, or aversion to norm-breaking.[4] For the purpose of this chapter it is, however, not important which flavor of social preferences best matches human motives. It is sufficient to show that the reaction function is positively sloped, a behavioral pattern that is better known under the term *conditional cooperation*.

■ CONDITIONAL COOPERATION

Conditional cooperation means that a player is willing to contribute to the public good if others do so as well. If players move simultaneously, then the behavior of others is only observable ex-post, which means that a player has to rely on his or her beliefs about other players' contributions. Using a sample of roughly 1,500 subjects from all walks of life in Denmark, Thöni, Tyran, and Wengström (2012) ran an Internet experiment with a one-shot public goods game and elicited both contributions and beliefs. The parameters of their public goods game were $n = 4$, $e = 50$, $\gamma = .5$. The left panel of Figure 9.1 shows a bubble chart relating a subject's belief about the average contribution of others to her own contribution. The thin line shows the 45-degree line. Observations along this line stem from subjects contributing exactly the same amount as they believe others to contribute. The bold line shows the results of a simple linear regression. The results confirm a

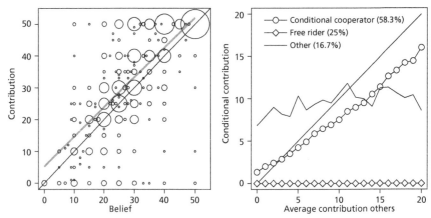

Figure 9.1 Left panel: Bubble chart of beliefs and contributions in a one-shot public goods game. The thin line shows the 45-degree line, the bold line shows the OLS regression line; data source: Thöni, Tyran, and Wengström (2012). Right panel: Average conditional contribution schemes, separated by types; data source: Volk, Thöni, and Ruigrok (2012).

well-documented fact in the literature on public goods (Ledyard, 1997): There is a very strong positive relation between beliefs and contributions. While this observation clearly fits the notion of conditional cooperation, the pattern is also compatible with other contribution behaviors. It might still be that individual contributions are independent of the others' contributions, and, when asked about their belief, subjects do just naively assume that the others will contribute the same amount as themselves.

Unambiguous evidence on conditional cooperation comes from an experimental design that allows subjects to condition their contributions on the contributions of the other subjects. A design introduced by Fischbacher, Gächter, and Fehr (2001) applies a variant of the strategy method to the one-shot public goods game ($n = 4$, $e = 20$, $\gamma = .4$). All subjects enter two contributions, an unconditional and a conditional contribution. The unconditional contribution is a number between zero and e. For the conditional contribution subjects are presented with a "contribution table," which allows them to indicate a preferred contribution for each average contribution of the other subjects in the group (usually rounded to integer). To make both entries incentive compatible, a random draw determines one of the subjects as the conditional cooperator and the other subjects as unconditional cooperators. The latter contribute their unconditional contribution. The average of these contributions is calculated, and the conditional contributor's decision is taken from the corresponding entry of his or her contribution table. Fischbacher et al. use this conditional contribution table to identify individual types. A subject is classified as *conditional cooperator* if his or her contribution is systematically increasing when the average contribution of the other subjects increases. An obvious second category are *free riders*, who contribute zero irrespective of what others do. A third category of subjects, whose conditional contribution is an increasing function of the others' contributions up to a point and decreasing thereafter, is called *triangle contributors*. A fourth category comprises all the remaining cases. Interestingly, subjects entering a constant but nonzero amount in the whole contribution table are virtually nonexistent in these data; that is, the pure benevolent altruist is a very rare species. Fischbacher et al. find 50% of their subjects to fall into the category of *conditional cooperators*, while about 30% are *free riders*.[5]

This experimental design was replicated numerous times with various subject pools. For example, Herrmann and Thöni (2009) report results from four subject pools in Russia and find 55.6% conditional cooperators but only 6.3% free riders. Kocher, Cherry, Kroll, Netzer, and Sutter (2008) replicated the experiment in Austria, Japan, and the United States. They find a very high percentage of conditional cooperators in the United States, while in Japan and Austria the percentage is somewhat below 50%. More recently, Volk, Thöni, and Ruigrok (2012) report results from a replication using a subject pool in St. Gallen. The right panel of Figure 9.1 shows the distribution of types and the average conditional contribution pattern. Similar to Fischbacher et al. (2001), the largest share of the population (58.3%) can be categorized as conditional cooperators, while 25% are free riders. The category of triangle contributors is omitted, because only very few observations show that pattern. While the pattern of the free riders is at zero by definition, the average pattern of conditional cooperators reveals an interesting regularity observed in most replications of the Fischbacher et al. design. The slope of the pattern is somewhat flatter than the 45-degree line (indicating the locus where the conditional contribution exactly matches the average contribution of the other subject). Thus, while subjects are willing to contribute if others do so as well, they tend to opt for a somewhat lower contribution than the others' average contribution. This pattern is often referred to as conditional cooperation with a self-serving bias.[6]

To conclude, as I argued earlier, it depends on peoples' preferences whether contribution in the public goods game is a measure of trust. If we assume selfish or strongly altruistic preferences, then we cannot learn much about trust when observing contributions in the public goods game. While the research presented in this section does not allow us to infer the exact nature of social preferences, it does provide compelling evidence for conditional cooperation to be the predominant behavioral pattern for contributions in experimental public goods games. Thus, for a large percentage of the subjects, contributing in a public goods game is very much a matter of beliefs about other subjects' strategies and thus a genuine trust situation.

■ EVALUATING SURVEY ITEMS
WITH EXPERIMENTAL DATA

If the contribution decision in public goods games is a behavioral measure for trust, we can use it to explore the relation to other measures of trust. In this section I discuss evidence on the correlation between standard survey items for trust and cooperative behavior in public goods games. Gächter, Herrmann, and Thöni (2004) report results from one-shot public goods games ($n = 3$, $e = 20$, $y = .5$). After the public goods game, subjects are asked to fill in a questionnaire containing

TABLE 9.1. *Questions for* TRUST *and* FAIR *as Elicited in the Postexperimental Questionnaire*

Variable	Description
TRUST	"Generally speaking, would you say that most people can be trusted or that you can't be too careful in dealing with people?" – 0: "Can't be too careful" – 1: "Most people can be trusted"
FAIR	"Do you think most people would try to take advantage of you if they got a chance, or would they try to be fair?" – 0: "Would take advantage" – 1: "Would try to be fair"

standard survey items used by large-scale surveys such as the World Values Survey or the General Social Survey. Table 9.1 shows two questions asking for subjects' trust and—which turned out relevant for explaining contributions—their expectations about others' fairness. This data allows us to relate survey-measured trust to contributions in the public goods game on an individual level.

Gächter et al. (2004) observe contributions from a sample of about 300 subjects in Russia and Belarus. Participants are both students and nonstudents. The authors find a positive relation between both survey measures and cooperation. The effect is small and insignificant for TRUST; in the case of FAIR it is more pronounced and highly significant. The left panel of Figure 9.2 shows standard error bars of the contributions for both survey items and the corresponding p values of Wilcoxon rank-sum tests. Subjects who state that "most people would take advantage" contribute on average 3.4 units less than subjects who say that most people "would try to be fair." This is quite a strong effect; in particular, it is stronger than the effects of age, gender, or socioeconomic status typically observed in the literature on public goods games.

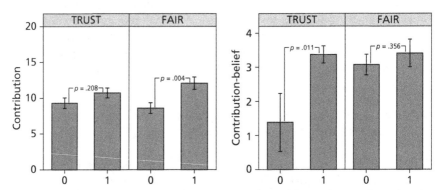

Figure 9.2 Left panel: Average contributions in one-shot public goods game dependent on questionnaire items TRUST and FAIR; data source: Gächter, Herrmann, and Thöni (2004). Right panel: Difference between contribution and belief and measures for TRUST and FAIR; data source: Thöni, Tyran, and Wengström (2012).

Merely observing contributions in one-shot public goods games does not allow us to discern the influence of beliefs and preferences on cooperation. To explore this, we can look again at the data reported in Thöni et al. (2012). As we have already seen, the data contains elicitation of beliefs and contributions. In addition, all subjects answered the TRUST and FAIR question. Individuals indicating trust contribute on average 35.4 units (out of 50), whereas nontrusting individuals contribute 30.9 units ($p < .001$, Wilcoxon rank-sum test). A closer analysis reveals that both TRUST and FAIR significantly predict contributions in the public goods game, however, through different channels. Regression models explaining beliefs about other participants' contributions show that participants with a high score in FAIR have significantly higher beliefs, whereas TRUST does not have a systematic impact on beliefs when estimated jointly with FAIR.[7] In estimates explaining contributions and controlling for beliefs, the opposite is true: Participants indicating TRUST are willing to contribute significantly more given their belief than nontrusting participants. The right panel of Figure 9.2 illustrates this effect. The vertical axis shows the difference between contribution and belief. On average, contributions are systematically higher than beliefs.[8] The difference is, however, clearly affected by TRUST, which is not the case for FAIR. Apart from the one-shot public goods games discussed earlier, Thöni et al. do also report data from experiments using the Fischbacher et al. (2001) design. They find a very high share of conditional cooperators (69%) and a relatively low share of free riders (15%). The data allow us to double-check the results on TRUST and FAIR influencing contributions via different channels. Recall that the Fischbacher et al. design measures cooperativeness controlled for beliefs. If the FAIR mostly influences beliefs, then it should not be important with respect to a participant's type in the Fischbacher et al. experiment. When estimating the probability of being a conditional cooperator, Thöni et al. find indeed that FAIR is unrelated while TRUST is significantly positive.

Taken together, results from various subject pools suggest that survey measures of trust and expected fairness are informative with regard to the cooperativeness of individuals. The prominent and widely used TRUST question seems to be a measure for *preferences* for cooperative behavior, that is, the willingness to take a leap of faith when entering a social dilemma.[9] FAIR, on the other hand, refers directly to beliefs about others' behavior. In the end, both ingredients, preferences and beliefs, are key to cooperative behavior. A central tenet to economic theory is the assumption that preferences are relatively stable, while beliefs may quickly adapt to new environments. If that is correct we could hypothesize that TRUST scores measured by large-scale survey should be more stable over time (e.g., less affected by macro-economic events like the business cycles) than FAIR scores.

■ CROSS-CULTURAL RESEARCH AND THE RADIUS OF TRUST

While the studies discussed in the previous section explored the connection between survey measures and experimental measures in a given country, it remains an open question whether the results are specific to the particular setting or reflect a general pattern. There are a number of reasons the connection might be restricted to particular settings. For example, even if there is a positive relation between trust and cooperation among the individuals in a given country, it does not directly follow that country-level differences in the trust measure explain differences in cooperation across countries. Furthermore, the elicitation of data in various countries is complicated by the fact that the material has to be adapted to the local context, in particular to the language. Adequate translation that ensures the equivalence of the data elicitation has long been recognized as one of the great challenges in cross-cultural empirical research (Brislin, 1970; Roth, Prasnikar, Okuno-Fujiwara, & Zamir, 1991). Conducting behavioral experiments also relies to some extent on language, as the procedures are usually explained in natural language. However, there is a distinct advantage of having a well-defined game in the background. While there is certainly a degree of ambiguity when it comes to translating the instructions of the public goods game to different languages, all the formally defined elements of the game are held constant: the number of players, the strategy space of each player, the sequence of actions, the monetary payoff function, and the information feedback during game play.

This argument is discussed in Kistler, Thöni, and Welzel (forthcoming), who designed and conducted an online public goods game that made extensive use of graphical elements instead of language to explain the game to the participants ($n = 2$, $e = 100$, $\gamma = .75$). The instructions include an interactive exploratory stage, where participants can shift around resources on the screen to calculate the payoff consequences of hypothetical outcomes of the game. The subjects of this experiment are the respondents of the sixth wave of the World Values Survey in Germany, who were invited to participate in the online study. Unlike the studies discussed before, the survey measures for TRUST were not elicited in a post-experimental questionnaire (and thus potentially influenced by what happened during the experiment). Instead, the measures were taken from the face-to-face interview conducted for the World Values Survey before the online experiment. In the sample of roughly 250 participants from the set of respondents of the World Values Survey, Kistler et al. find a significant relation between TRUST and contributions in the public goods game. Trusting participants contribute about five (out of 100) units more than nontrusting participants. While these results are for the moment confined to the population of Germany, Kistler et al. designed their online experiment so that it is very easy to adapt it to other languages, in order to run the study in other countries.

To investigate the relation between TRUST and FAIR in a cross-cultural context, I use the data from Herrmann, Thöni, and Gächter (2008), who conducted public goods games in 16 cities around the globe ($n = 4$, $e = 20$, $\gamma = .4$).[10] The experimental design used in this study differs in an important dimension from the studies discussed so far. Participants play a repeated game; that is, they play 10 rounds of a public goods game in stable groups, and they receive information about the contributions of the other subjects at the end of every round. This feature introduces additional strategic incentives to cooperate, and it also allows subjects to learn about the cooperativeness of their group and to update their beliefs.[11] It is likely that beliefs become more accurate over time in the repeated public goods games. Consequently, other factors that influence beliefs (like trust) presumably become less important in later rounds. In the following analysis, I therefore focus on the first period of the repeated public goods game. On the other hand, from a game-theoretic perspective the final period of a repeated game is in principle much more akin to a one-shot game than the first period. Because there is no future interaction, players can decide free from strategic considerations regarding other players' reactions to their behavior. For this reason, I also consider the final round of the repeated public goods game.

Figure 9.3 shows the 16 cities in which the data was collected. In all cities participants were university students. Though not necessarily representative of the whole population of the country, they represent in all places a similarly selected sample. Table 9.2 shows summary statistics of the variables of interest for all the locations, sorted by the contribution in the first round (g_1). On average the experiment was conducted with roughly 60 participants in each city so that the total number of subjects used for the analysis is 920.[12] Average contributions in the first period of the repeated public goods game range from 7.96 in Riyadh to 14.1 in Copenhagen, that is, from 40% to 70% of the endowment. In accordance with countless previous experiments on repeated public goods games, contributions decline over the course of the 10 rounds in all participant pools. Still, there remain substantial differences across participant pools in the final round, ranging from average contributions of 1.30 in Melbourne up to 8.68 in Dnipropetrovsk.[13]

In a next step I use the combined data from the two most recent waves of the World Values Survey and the most recent wave of the European Values Study to explore the connection between survey-measured trust in a population (identified by country) and behavior as observed in the laboratory.[14] While TRUST is always measured using the same question as shown in Table 9.1, the format of the FAIR

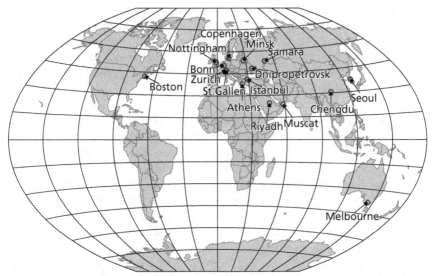

Figure 9.3 Location of the subject pools in the data from Herrmann, Thöni, and Gächter (2008).

TABLE 9.2. *Experimental and Survey Measures for Each Participant Pool*

Participant pool	n	g_1	g_{10}	TRUST	FAIR	TRUST INGROUP	TRUST OUTGROUP
Copenhagen (Denmark)	68	14.10	5.29	0.76	8.00		
Boston (USA)	56	12.96	2.95	0.37	5.69	0.74	0.52
Zurich (Switzerland)	48	12.06	4.33	0.55	6.81	0.79	0.55
St. Gallen (Switzerland)	48	11.88	2.73	0.55	6.81	0.79	0.55
Minsk (Belarus)	32	11.00	8.47	0.40	5.53	0.74	0.39
Dnipropetrovsk (Ukraine)	44	10.95	8.68	0.27	5.64	0.75	0.42
Nottingham (UK)	56	10.93	2.39	0.36	6.04	0.81	0.58
Bonn (Germany)	60	10.85	4.00	0.41	5.75	0.75	0.44
Samara (Russia)	80	10.84	5.80	0.28	5.83	0.75	0.37
Chengdu (China)	96	10.09	2.97	0.58	7.10	0.77	0.30
Muscat (Oman)	52	9.54	7.52				
Istanbul (Turkey)	64	8.94	1.36	0.10	4.73	0.78	0.34
Seoul (South Korea)	84	8.25	3.81	0.27	6.62	0.73	0.37
Melbourne (Australia)	40	8.23	1.30	0.49	6.32	0.78	0.53
Athens (Greece)	44	8.14	5.36	0.22	4.14		
Riyadh (Saudi Arabia)	48	7.96	5.88				

Notes. Number of observations (n), contributions in the first (g_1) and final period (g_{10}); observations sorted by g_1; data source: Herrmann, Thöni, and Gächter (2008). Average scores for trust and fairness questions; data sources: World Values Survey and European Values Study.

changed to a 10-point scale. In the sample of about 100 countries for which the measures are available, there is a huge variety. On average 26% (SD: 15.8 percentage points) of respondents indicate trust. In the countries with the lowest trust levels (e.g. Brazil, the Philippines), less than 10% of the respondents answer the trust question affirmatively, while at the other end of the scale (northern Europe) 75% of the population indicate trust in other people. The locations in the sample of Herrmann et al. (2008) cover almost the entire range of trust scores with Turkey (9.9%), and Denmark (76%). Similarly, for FAIR the worldwide scores range from 3.57 to 8.00, while in the sample the scores range from 4.14 (Greece) to the highest ranking country worldwide (Denmark). The two measures are strongly correlated.[15]

Table 9.3 shows the results of ordinary least squares regressions explaining the individual contributions in the first or the final round of the repeated public goods game. In parentheses are the robust standard errors, estimated with clustering on the level of participant pool. All survey measures are standardized using the data from all available countries. The first model uses simply a country's TRUST score as the independent variable. This model shows a highly significant positive effect of about one, indicating that in a country scoring one standard deviation higher on trust than the average we should expect an increase in the contribution of about one unit (out of 20). Given the R^2 of 3%, it is evident that a large part of the contribution decision remains unexplained. In the second column of Table 9.3 I add a number of individual control variables to the model, such as gender, age, family background, and social integration. None of the control variables is significantly linked to the contributions in the first round, and the overall fit of the model does

TABLE 9.3. *Trust and Contribution*

	Dependent variable			
	g_1	g_1	g_{10}	g_{10}
TRUST	0.980***	0.821*	0.004	0.085
	(0.325)	(0.428)	(0.481)	(0.512)
Constant	9.764***	11.528***	4.063***	2.798*
	(0.434)	(0.703)	(0.787)	(1.373)
Controls	No	Yes	No	Yes
F test	9.1	33.9	0.0	17.5
Prob > F	0.010	0.000	0.993	0.000
R^2	0.027	0.034	0.000	0.046
N	820	739	820	739

Notes. Ordinary least squares estimates. Dependent variable is contribution in the first round (first two models) or the final round (last two models). Independent variable is the normalized measures for TRUST from the World Values Survey. Controls are age, gender, and a number of socioeconomic variables. Robust standard errors, clustered on participant pool, in parentheses.
*$p < 0.1$, ** $p < 0.05$, ***$p < 0.01$.

hardly improve.[16] Including the controls reduces the coefficient of TRUST and makes the estimate less precise. Repeating the same estimates using FAIR instead of TRUST reveals similar but weaker effects (not shown in Table 9.3). Without controls the coefficient for FAIR is weakly significant ($\beta = 0.780$; $SE = 0.379$); with controls the coefficient is insignificant.

The remaining two models in Table 9.3 show the estimates explaining contributions in the final round. The substantial differences in contributions observed in the experiment seem unrelated to TRUST, and the same holds true for the corresponding estimates with FAIR. The former is somewhat surprising, given that the results from the one-shot experiments suggested that TRUST is related to preferences for trusting acts. The results here suggest that the final round of a repeated public goods game is behaviorally very different from a true one-shot game.

A reason for a weaker connection between the widely used trust question and behavior might be that the question is very unspecific. In particular, respondents do not receive an indication of whom to think of when they indicate their trust. The question might be perceived differently in different languages and cultures, when for example some people think about their relatives, while others think about complete strangers. Delhey, Newton, and Welzel (2011) refer to this problem as the "radius of trust" and show that indeed there is evidence that respondents vary systematically with respect to whom they think of when they answer the trust question. To improve on the measurement of trust, the two most recent waves of the World Values Survey include six additional questions for which a particular social sphere is specified. Table 9.4 shows the six questions. They can be grouped into two categories, providing us with a measure for OUTGROUPTRUST (strangers, unrelated), and a measure for INGROUPTRUST (family and friends).[17] For both categories the score is equal to the average of the three questions. To date

TABLE 9.4. *Questions for In- and Out-Group Trust*

Question	Answers
I'd like to ask you how much you trust people from various groups. Could you tell me for each whether you trust people from this group	– 1: completely – .67: somewhat – .33: not very much – 0: not at all

Variable	Group
INGROUPTRUST	1. Your family 2. Your neighborhood 3. People you know personally
OUTGROUPTRUST	4. People you meet for the first time 5. People of another religion 6. People of another nationality

Note. Six additional trust question used in wave 5 and 6 of the World Values Survey (Welzel, 2010).

the two new trust scores are available for 77 countries. Interestingly, the correlation with TRUST is almost identical for the two new measures ($\rho = .479$; $p = .000$ for OUTGROUPTRUST, and $\rho = .464$; $p = .000$ for INGROUPTRUST). Among the countries with experimental data the connection is weaker and insignificant. Table 9.2 shows the scores for the locations of the experiments.

How should these two measures of trust relate to cooperation as observed in the experiment? The experiments were run in sessions with 20 to 28 participants. The recruiting is typically done by individual mail contact, and subjects are randomly drawn from a large subject pool. This means that participants are usually unfamiliar with the other participants. In addition, when matched to groups of four, participants never learn the identity of the three other participants in their group. Thus presumably the situation is perceived by most participants as an out-group situation, at least in reference to how the trust questions were asked.[18] If that is the case, then we should expect OUTGROUPTRUST to be positively related to contributions, whereas the influence of INGROUPTRUST is unclear.

Table 9.5 shows the results of estimates similar to those reported in Table 9.3 for the new trust measures. In the first column I use only the two trust variables to explain initial cooperation. The effect of OUTGROUPTRUST is marginally significant, and the regression model as a whole is insignificant.[19] Unlike in the case of TRUST, controlling for individual characteristics does lead to stronger results, with both the coefficient becoming larger and significant at 5%. The effect size is also similar; that is, a standard deviation increase in OUTGROUPTRUST is associated with an average increase in the contributions of one unit. INGROUPTRUST, on the other hand, does not seem to contribute to explaining cooperation in the first round of the public goods game. These results are basically the same in estimates using only one of the trust measures at a time.

For the final round of the public goods game the results are surprising (see the last two models in Table 9.5). Similar to TRUST there is no evidence for an effect of OUTGROUPTRUST. There is, however, a very strong and significant negative effect of INGROUPTRUST on contributions. The size of the coefficient is substantial: An

TABLE 9.5. *In-Group and Out-Group Trust Explaining Contribution*

	Dependent variable			
	g_1	g_1	g_{10}	g_{10}
OUTGROUPTRUST	0.831*	1.062**	0.222	0.355
	(0.418)	(0.394)	(0.494)	(0.420)
INGROUPTRUST	−0.443	−0.505	−2.724*	−2.934**
	(1.137)	(0.977)	(1.339)	(1.049)
Constant	10.277***	12.080***	4.629***	3.299**
	(0.580)	(0.706)	(0.714)	(1.161)
Controls	No	Yes	No	Yes
F test	2.2	18.0	2.9	13.1
Prob $> F$	0.154	0.000	0.098	0.000
R^2	0.012	0.032	0.027	0.082
N	708	655	708	655

Notes. Ordinary least squares estimates. Dependent variable is contribution in the first round (first two models) or the final round (last two models). Independent variables are normalized measures for in-group and out-group trust from the World Values Survey. Controls are age, gender, and a number of socioeconomic variables. Robust standard errors, clustered on participant pool, in parentheses.
$^*p < 0.1$, $^{**}p < 0.05$, $^{***}p < 0.01$

increase in INGROUPTRUST of one standard deviation reduces average contributions by about three units. This strong effect comes at a surprise, and—given its ex-post nature—should be handled with care. One could argue that over the course of the 10 rounds the social distance toward the other participants decreases and the situation shifts from out-group towards in-group. There is evidence that reducing the social distance by letting the subjects familiarize themselves with each other prior to experimental play increases contributions (see, e.g., Yamagishi & Sato, 1986; Gächter & Fehr, 1999). Surprisingly, the results reported here point in the opposite direction: Participants from societies with high INGROUPTRUST seem especially concerned not to be the sucker in the final round of the game.

■ **CONCLUSION**

A large body of evidence shows that cooperative behavior identified in behavioral experiments does relate to trust as expressed in surveys. This holds both on an individual level and for societies as a whole. The result that FAIR identifies beliefs while TRUST identifies preferences, established in a large sample in Denmark, needs further replication. In particular, it remains an open question whether the relation can also be found in surveys conducted in other languages or surveys conducted among respondents with different cultural backgrounds. If it holds, it might be interesting to explore whether there is evidence for preferences to be more stable than beliefs. For example, one could expect TRUST to be less variable than FAIR with respect to economic downturns or changes in political stability.

From a policy perspective one might then focus the attention on "belief management," that is, use public communication to focus the attention on the prevalence of fair behavior in the society, as opposed to biasing the communication toward antisocial elements. The results on cross-cultural cooperation suggests that TRUST is a valid proxy for cooperative behavior in situations where people are unfamiliar with their group members. In particular, OUTGROUPTRUST seems to capture an important element of the contribution decision at the beginning of a repeated public goods game. Interestingly, toward the end of the repeated public good games, INGROUPTRUST becomes a strong predictor of contributions. Whether this is just spurious correlation or an indication of a systematic effect will only be answered by future research.

■ AUTHOR'S NOTE

I thank and the editors of this volume, the reviewers, and Deborah Kistler for their helpful comments and suggestions.

■ NOTES

1. See Fehr and Schmidt (1999, proposition 4) for a characterization of these equilibria.

2. The highest contributor in the group is not only unhappy due to the low payoff he gets. In addition, he also suffers from the fact that others have a higher payoff than himself.

3. The strategic situation is akin to the minimum-effort game (Van Huyck, Battalio, & Beil, 1990), which has a large number of Pareto-ranked equilibria.

4. See, e.g., Thöni and Gächter (2015) for a recent overview of the models of social preferences.

5. These percentages are surprisingly similar to the distribution of types found in simple, nonstrategic tasks on social value orientation. For example, Van Lange (1999) classifies respondents from a large Dutch sample into prosocials (53%), individualists (22%), and competitors (8%). In the public goods games the latter two categories would both correspond to free riders, resulting in the same estimated prevalence of 30%.

6. For intermediate levels of average others' contributions this pattern could be explained by inequality aversion. As shown previously, an inequality averse player typically seeks to match the lowest of all other contributions. As the contributions in this experiment can only be conditioned on the *average*, subjects might draw inference about the minimum contribution in the group and try to match the minimum.

7. See Table 1 in Thöni et al. (2012) for details. Unlike the previously discussed studies, the measure for FAIR is not measured on a binary scale but as a score from 1 to 10.

8. This observation is somewhat inconsistent with the self-serving bias in conditional cooperation discussed earlier. It might be due to the fact that beliefs were elicited after the choices.

9. There is a literature investigating whether trusting behavior can be explained by risk preferences. Typically one does not find a strong relation between risk preferences (elicited in individual lottery decisions) and strategic games such as the trust game. Thus risk from

natural events (random draws) seems to be different from risk from social interactions; see, e.g., Eckel and Wilson (2004), Houser, Schunk, and Winter (2010).

10. This study primarily focuses on the results of public goods games with punishment, conducted after the public goods game I consider here. The analysis by Gächter, Herrmann, and Thöni (2010) suggests that cultural differences are much stronger in the public goods game with punishment than in the public goods game.

11. Gächter and Thöni (2005) show that subjects strongly update their beliefs when learning about the contributions of others in their group. They show that when subjects with similar initial contributions are grouped together, then they continue to contribute similarly in later periods. In particular, cooperative subjects manage to maintain high contributions.

12. The number of observations in Herrmann et al. (2008) is higher because they also report results from experiments where participants played a public goods game with punishment prior to the public goods game. For the analysis here I do not use this data.

13. A Kruskal-Wallis test allows us to reject the null hypothesis that the contributions across subject pools stem from the same distributions at $p < .001$, both for the first and the final round. The test was calculated using the independent group averages as observations.

14. www.worldvaluessurvey.org, wave 5 (2005–2009), wave 6 (2010–2014); www.europeanvaluesstudy.eu, wave 4 (2008–2010).

15. Correlation coefficients: World sample $n = 100$, $\rho = .596$, $p = .000$, Countries with experimental data $n = 13$, $\rho = .857$, $p = .002$.

16. The controls are the same as used in Herrmann et al. (2008), see their Table S2 for details. This is in accordance with the studies on one-shot public goods games discussed earlier, which also find hardly any substantial correlates when trying to explain contributions in public goods games with individual characteristics. One of the few things that seem to correlate to some degree are the Big Five personality traits; see, e.g., Volk, Thöni, and Ruigrok (2011). This is in stark contrast to risk preferences, where one regularly finds pronounced gender differences; see. e.g. von Gaudecker, van Soest, and Wengström (2011).

17. The measure of out-group trust can be seen as a proxy for "generalized trust"; see, e.g., Van Lange (2015).

18. In principle the notion of in- and out-group is relative. Typically all participants are students from the same university, so relative to the broad population they might perceive their co-students as in-group. On the other hand, relative to their family and close friends, their fellow students are most likely out-group.

19. This is likely due to the fact that we lose two countries relative to the regression analysis for TRUST. For example, there is no data for Denmark, which probably would score high on OUTGROUPTRUST. Imputing a high value for OUTGROUPTRUST for Denmark is sufficient to render the estimates for this coefficient significant at 5%.

■ REFERENCES

Algan, Y., & Cahuc, P. (2010). Inherited trust and growth. *American Economic Review*, *100*(5), 2060–2092. doi:10.1257/aer.100.5.2060

Balliet, D., & Van Lange, P. A. M. (2013). Trust, conflict, and cooperation: A meta-analysis. *Psychological Bulletin*, *139*(5), 1090–1112. doi:10.1037/ a0030939

Berg, J., Dickhaut, J., & McCabe, K. (1995). Trust, reciprocity, and social history. *Games and Economic Behavior*, *10*(1), 122–142. doi:10.1006/ game.1995.1027

Brislin, R. W. (1970). Back-translation for cross-cultural research. *Journal of Cross-Cultural Psychology, 1*(3), 185–216. doi:10.1177/135910457000100301

Coleman, J. S. (1990). *Foundations of social theory.* Cambridge, MA: Harvard University Press.

Delhey, J., Newton, K., & Welzel, C. (2011). How general is trust in "most people"? Solving the radius of trust problem. *American Sociological Review, 76*(5), 786–807. doi:10.1177/0003122411420817

Eckel, C. C., & Wilson, R. K. (2004). Is trust a risky decision? *Journal of Economic Behavior & Organization, 55*(4), 447–465. doi:10.1016/j. jebo.2003.11.003

Fehr, E., & Schmidt, K. M. (1999). A theory of fairness, competition, and cooperation. *Quarterly Journal of Economics, 114*(3), 817–868. doi:10.1162/003355399556151

Fischbacher, U., Gächter, S., & Fehr, E. (2001). Are people conditionally cooperative? Evidence from a public goods experiment. *Economics Letters, 71*(3), 397–404. doi:10.1016/S0165-1765(01)00394-9

Fukuyama, F. (1996). *Trust: The social virtues and the creation of prosperity.* New York: Free Press.

Gächter, S., & Fehr, E. (1999). Collective action as a social exchange. *Journal of Economic Behavior & Organization, 39*(4), 341–369. doi:10.1016/ S0167-2681(99)00045-1

Gächter, S., Herrmann, B., & Thöni, C. (2004). Trust, voluntary cooperation, and socio-economic background: Survey and experimental evidence. *Journal of Economic Behavior & Organization, 55*(4), 505–531. doi:10.1016/j.jebo.2003.11.006

Gächter, S., Herrmann, B., & Thöni, C. (2010). Culture and cooperation. *Philosophical Transactions of the Royal Society B: Biological Sciences, 365,* 2651–2661. doi:10.1098/rstb.2010.0135

Gächter, S., & Thöni, C. (2005). Social learning and voluntary cooperation among like-minded people. *Journal of the European Economic Association, 3*(2–3), 303–314. doi:10.1162/jeea.2005.3.2-3.303

Herrmann, B., & Thöni, C. (2009). Measuring conditional cooperation: A replication study in Russia. *Experimental Economics, 12*(1), 87–92. doi:10.1007/s10683-008-9197-1

Herrmann, B., Thöni, C., & Gächter, S. (2008). Antisocial punishment across societies. *Science, 319*(5868), 1362–1367. doi:10.1126/science.1153808

Houser, D., Schunk, D., & Winter, J. (2010). Distinguishing trust from risk: An anatomy of the investment game. *Journal of Economic Behavior & Organization, 74*(1–2), 72–81. doi:10.1016/j.jebo.2010.01.002

Kistler, D., Thöni, C., & Welzel, C. (forthcoming). Survey Response and Observed Behavior: Emancipative and secular values predict pro-social behaviors. *Journal of Cross-Cultural Psychology.*

Knack, S. & Keefer, P. (1997). Does social capital have an economic payoff? A cross-country investigation. *Quarterly Journal of Economics, 112*(4), 1251–1288. doi:10.1162/003355300555475

Kocher, M. G., Cherry, T. L., Kroll, S., Netzer, R. J., & Sutter, M. (2008). Conditional cooperation on three continents. *Economics Letters, 101*(3), 175–178. doi:10.1016/j.econlet.2008.07.015

Ledyard, J. O. (1997). Public goods: A survey of experimental research. In J. H. Kagel & A. E. Roth (Eds.), *The handbook of experimental economics* (pp. 111–194). Princeton, NJ: Princeton University Press.

Roth, A. E., Prasnikar, V., Okuno-Fujiwara, M., & Zamir, S. (1991). Bargaining and market behavior in Jerusalem, Ljubljana, Pittsburgh, and Tokyo: An experimental study. *American Economic Review, 81*(5), 1068–1095.

Thöni, C., & Gächter, S. (2015). Peer effects and social preferences in voluntary cooperation. *Journal of Economic Psychology, 48*, 1–47. doi:10. 1016/j.joep.2015.03.001

Thöni, C., Tyran, J.-R., & Wengström, E. (2012). Microfoundations of social capital. *Journal of Public Economics, 96*(7–8), 635–643. doi:10.1016/ j.jpubeco.2012.04.003

Van Huyck, J. B., Battalio, R. C., & Beil, R. O. (1990). Tacit coordination games, strategic uncertainty, and coordination failure. *American Economic Review, 80*(1), 234–248.

Van Lange, P. A. M. (1999). The pursuit of joint outcomes and equality in outcomes: An integrative model of social value orientation. *Journal of Personality and Social Psychology, 77*(2), 337–349. doi:10.1037/0022-3514.77.2.337

Van Lange, P. A. M. (2015). Generalized trust: Four lessons from genetics and culture. *Current Directions in Psychological Science, 24*(1), 71–76. doi:10.1177/ 0963721414552473

Volk, S., Thöni, C., & Ruigrok, W. (2011). Personality, personal values and cooperation preferences in public goods games: A longitudinal study. *Personality and Individual Differences, 50*(6), 810–815. doi:10.1016/j. paid.2011.01.001

Volk, S., Thöni, C., & Ruigrok, W. (2012). Temporal stability and psychological foundations of cooperation preferences. *Journal of Economic Behavior & Organization, 81*(2), 664–676. doi:10.1016/j.jebo.2011.10.006

von Gaudecker, H.-M., van Soest, A., & Wengström, E. (2011). Heterogeneity in risky choice behavior in a broad population. *American Economic Review, 101*(2), 664–694. doi:10.1257/aer.101.2.664

Welzel, C. (2010). How selfish are self-expression values? A civicness test. *Journal of Cross-Cultural Psychology, 41*(2), 152–174. doi:10.1177/ 0022022109354378

Yamagishi, T. (1986). The provision of a sanctioning system as a public good. *Journal of Personality and Social Psychology, 51*(1), 110–116. doi:10.1037/0022-3514.51.1.110

Yamagishi, T. & Sato, K. (1986). Motivational bases of the public goods problem. *Journal of Personality and Social Psychology, 50*(1), 67–73. doi:10.1037//0022-3514.50.1.67

10 The Future of Organizational Trust Research

*A Content-Analytic Synthesis of Scholarly
Recommendations and Review of Recent
Developments*

■ BART A. DE JONG, DAVID P. KROON,
AND OLIVER SCHILKE

■ INTRODUCTION

> "I am not interested in the past, I am interested in the future, for that
> is where I expect to spend the rest of my life."
> —CHARLES F. KETTERING (1876–1958)

In organizational contexts, actors often face a social dilemma in that they need to choose whether or not to cooperate with others, recognizing that doing so could be mutually beneficial but could also put them at risk (Kong, Dirks, & Ferrin, 2014). In such social dilemma situations, trust serves as a key mechanism that helps organizational actors suspend these risks and vulnerabilities and proceed in a cooperative manner. As such, it is not surprising that trust is one of the most frequently studied concepts in management research today and considered essential to the performance of individual employees (Colquitt, Scott, & LePine, 2007), teams (De Jong, Dirks, & Gillespie, 2016), and organizations (Cao & Lumineau, 2015). Organizational trust continues to be an enduring and vibrant area of research that spans scholarly disciplines (Rousseau, Sitkin, Burt, & Camerer, 1998), levels of analysis (Fulmer & Gelfand, 2012), theoretical lenses (Möllering, 2006), and methodological approaches (Lyon, Möllering, & Saunders, 2012). Scholarly interest in the topic is overwhelming and has produced a wealth of insights, in which organizational trust has been conceptualized and operationalized in a variety of ways (McEvily, 2011; McEvily & Tortoriello, 2011), studied in numerous contexts (Saunders, Skinner, Dietz, Gillespie, & Lewicki, 2011), and linked to a multitude of antecedents and consequences (Fulmer & Gelfand, 2012).

While this immense scholarly interest is encouraging, the field suffers from fragmentation and a lack of cumulative research. One of the reasons for this is the diversity in approaches to organizational trust research (Lewicki & Brinsfield, 2012). Differences between disciplinary backgrounds, research traditions, and levels of analysis tend to generate self-constructed silos of trust scholars (DeNisi, 2010) that evolve and coexist in a disconnected manner. This issue is further compounded by the fact that management scholars often include trust as part of their investigations without treating it as a core variable of interest (De Jong et al., 2016). As a result, insights and future research suggestions provided by these studies may largely go unnoticed and fail to converge. Due to these two factors, a common research agenda is currently lacking, and it remains unclear how the field of organizational trust research should move forward.

The current chapter aims to address this issue by examining scholarly recommendations for future research on organizational trust as well as reviewing the latest developments in the field. First, we offer bottom-up insights into what the field as a whole believes future research on organizational trust should look like by synthesizing scholarly recommendations for future research regarding (a) the nature of trust itself, (b) its dynamics and relationships with antecedents and consequences, (c) the underlying causal mechanisms through which it operates, and (d) the contextual and level-of-analysis assumptions that bound the generalizability of these relationships. Hence, rather than providing research directions based on our personal opinion about what we think is the way forward, our review is data-driven and inductively derived based on recommendations provided by the (organizational) trust field. Second, building on this synthesis, we review the latest developments in organizational trust research, providing insights into (a) issues that were recommended and are currently receiving considerable scholarly attention, (b) issues that were recommended but have not been (fully) addressed by scholars, and (c) new topics that were not anticipated by earlier scholarly recommendations. We conclude this chapter with reflections on how individual researchers and the trust community as a whole can build on our findings.

▪ SCHOLARLY RECOMMENDATIONS FOR FUTURE RESEARCH

In order to synthesize the field's recommendations for future research, we performed a content analysis of suggestions made by scholars in journal articles on trust and complemented these secondary data with a survey we administered to active trust scholars. In the following we first describe our research design and the content-analytic procedures we followed to code the scholarly recommendations. We then discuss the substantive themes that emerged from our analysis as well as the extent to which these themes were commonly recognized by scholars.

▪ METHODS

Sample and Data Collection

In identifying scholarly recommendations for future research on organizational trust, we relied on two complementary data sources. The first source comprised journal articles on trust that were published or in press between 2007 and 2011. We selected 2007 as the starting publication year since both an influential synthesis of prior research and a summary of future research directions on trust were published in that year (Colquitt et al., 2007; Schoorman, Mayer, & Davis,

2007). We chose 2011 as the final year to allow us to assess to what extent recent research has, in fact, followed up on these research directions (see the second part of this chapter). To identify relevant articles, we performed an online search using the ABI/INFORM and ProQuest search engines for papers containing the word "trust" in their titles and/or abstracts. Given our focus on organizational trust, we made sure to search through the major journals in management (e.g., *Academy of Management Journal*), but we also considered high-impact[1] journals in related fields—including (social) psychology (e.g., *Annual Review of Psychology*), sociology (e.g., *American Sociological Review*), economics (e.g., *American Economic Review*), and information systems (e.g., *MIS Quarterly*)—to expand the breadth of recommendations. This procedure yielded 347 articles published across 58 scholarly journals, including 28 management journals and 30 journals from related fields.

To counterbalance potential selective reporting of recommendations in articles (e.g., due to editor and reviewer influences) and increase the scope and variety of the recommendations, we also obtained primary survey data from active organizational trust scholars. Our survey was administered in 2011 to scholars who either (co-)authored one of the aforementioned articles, were involved in Academy of Management annual meeting sessions on trust between 2007 and 2011, or attended the 2010 EIASM Workshop on Trust Within and Between Organizations. The survey asked scholars to provide at least three substantive recommendations for future research on trust. We received useable responses from 162 scholars.

Data Analysis

We started our analysis by reading the articles' discussion and limitations sections as well as the responses to the survey in order to identify recommendations for trust research. We identified a statement as a future research recommendation only when it explicitly focused on trust (rather than on something else) and when the recommendation was substantive (rather than methodological) in nature. We then created a coding scheme that helped us to identify specific recommendations related to how the scholarly community viewed the ways to move trust research forward. Throughout our qualitative data analysis, we followed an iterative approach, moving back and forth between our data and existing theoretical frameworks (Duriau, Reger, & Pfaffer, 2007; Strauss & Corbin, 1990).

Following the tenets of the "Gioia methodology" (Gioia, Corley, & Hamilton, 2013), we began by identifying first-order codes illustrated with simple descriptive phrases or quotes. As multiple codes began to capture the views of multiple article recommendations/respondents on the same topic, we collapsed several codes into first-order concepts that represented the foundation of our emerging understanding of the recommendations for future organizational trust research. In classifying scholarly recommendations, we relied on existing frameworks from the organizational trust literature and the broader management literature whenever possible. Specifically, in coding recommendations about examining specific trustors and trustees, we applied Currall and Inkpen's

(2006) framework, which identifies nine trustor–trustee relationships based on the respective level of analysis of the trustor and the trustee (i.e., individual, group, organizational level). In coding recommendations about antecedents and consequences of trust, we used Fulmer and Gelfand's (2012) framework, which (a) organizes antecedents of trust into individual-level characteristics of the trustor and trustee, shared characteristics, organizational characteristics, and extra-organizational characteristics and (b) organizes consequences into attitudes and preferences, knowledge sharing and organizational learning, communication, cooperation, and conflicts, viability (commitment and turnover), and performance. In coding recommendations about studying trust dynamics, we drew on Rousseau et al.'s (1998) distinction between trust building, stability/maintenance, and dissolution/violation. Finally, in coding recommendations about boundary conditions, we used Whetten, Felin, and King's (2009) distinction between contextual and level-of-analysis boundary assumptions. Regarding contextual boundary assumptions, we drew on Whetten's (1989) notions of "who," "where," and "when" to distinguish between assumptions about generalizability across parties, locations, and temporal phases.

After the initial first-order coding was complete, we searched for relationships between these concepts and began assembling related concepts into higher order themes. For instance, the statement "future research could allow the dimensions of trust and distrust to vary within a construct" yielded two first-order codes: "definition of trust" and "multiple dimensions: general." Later, these two categories were subsumed under the second-order theme "nature and dimensions." We also allowed recommendations to generate codes for different themes when appropriate. For example, the statement "there are many unexplored research avenues in areas regarding the formation of trust, the appropriate aggregation of trust, and a deeper insight into the causal nexus through which trust acts" yielded the code "trust-level dynamics" as well as the codes "levels and referents" and "mediating mechanisms."

After several iterations of this thematic organizing, we were able to collapse the second-order themes into overarching dimensions that captured classes of recommendations at a more aggregate level. In this process, the fundamental building blocks of a theory summarized by Whetten (1989) formed an important basis for our integrative framework; our analyses revealed what, how, why, and who/where/when as the main dimensions along which the second-order recommendations could be classified. "What" recommendations pertain to the nature and properties of the core construct under investigation—in our case, organizational trust. "How" recommendations pertain to the pattern, sequence, and form of the relationships between trust and other dependent and independent variables of interest (e.g., consequences and antecedents). "Why" recommendations pertain to assumptions about the underlying causal mechanisms that explain why trust is related to other variables. These assumptions and explanations are typically articulated in and supplied by foundational theories. Finally, "who/where/when" recommendations pertain to the articulation of the boundary conditions under which the predicted relationships are most and least likely to hold. These conditions limit the generalizability of the proposed relationships between trust and other variables.

Figure 10.1 and Table 10.1 present a comprehensive overview of the coding process as well as illustrative examples of emergent themes. We subsequently generated count data—that is, we quantified qualitative data based on the number of times a recommendation within a higher order theme was made—to assess the extent to which themes were commonly recognized among scholars.

■ RESULTS

Emerging Themes across "What" Recommendations

Our findings clearly suggest that scholars agree that more work needs to be done to improve construct clarity regarding trust. At the same time, scholars seem to disagree about how trust should be conceptualized; while some recommend conceptualizing trust as a (rational) decision or behavioral choice, others recommend conceptualizing it as an attitude or psychological state. Thus our data suggest that the scholarly debate about the definition of trust is still ongoing and should be continued in the future. Indeed, the issue remains especially salient in the field of interorganizational trust, where scholars debate about whether organizations are entities that are capable of experiencing trust psychologically or whether they can only choose to trust in a behavioral sense.

In addition to the need to clarify the overall trust construct, our findings suggest that scholars agree on the need to distinguish between different types and dimensions of trust. At the same time, we also observe scholarly disagreement about which dimensions need to be studied and how. First, scholarly recommendations differ regarding the dimensions or types of trust that need to be studied; some point toward focusing on cognitive versus affective dimensions of trust, while others suggest a focus on competence versus goodwill trust or institutional versus process-based trust. Second, while some scholarly recommendations suggest that dimensions or types of trust should be studied as discrete manifestations, others suggest that they should be studied in combination and/or as hybrid forms of trust.

A third theme that emerged from our data is the need for bilateral and multilateral approaches to studying trust that take multiple parties into account. This need manifests in recommendations to study a variety of conceptual extensions of trust. For instance, scholars recommend investigations into "being trusted" and "felt trust," pointing toward the need to assess trust not only from the trustor's but also from the trustee's perspective. Furthermore, recommendations to examine third-party trust and trust asymmetry imply the need to account for trust levels between two or more parties, thus shifting the focus toward bilateral and multilateral approaches. Finally, recommendations to study "trust (in)accuracy" suggest the need to simultaneously consider both the trustor's perceptions about the trustee's trustworthiness and the trustee's actual trustworthiness. All of these recommendations consistently point to the need to move beyond the dominant unilateral approach in which trust is studied exclusively from the perspective of a single trustor.

Finally, organizing scholarly recommendations using Currall and Inkpen's (2006) level-of-analysis framework reveals important trends regarding the nature

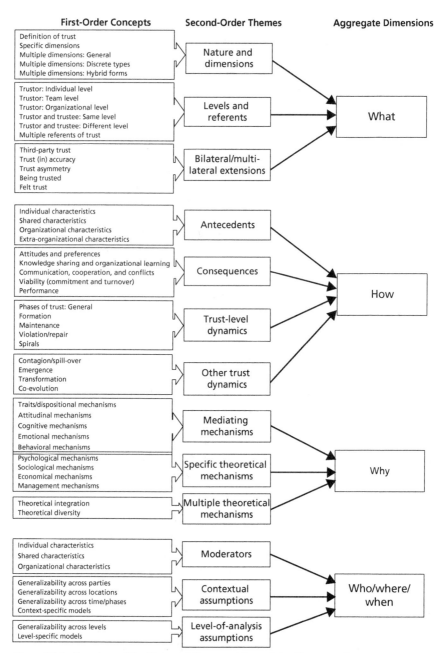

First-Order Concepts	Second-Order Themes	Aggregate Dimensions
Definition of trust Specific dimensions Multiple dimensions: General Multiple dimensions: Discrete types Multiple dimensions: Hybrid forms	Nature and dimensions	
Trustor: Individual level Trustor: Team level Trustor: Organizational level Trustor and trustee: Same level Trustor and trustee: Different level Multiple referents of trust	Levels and referents	What
Third-party trust Trust (in) accuracy Trust asymmetry Being trusted Felt trust	Bilateral/multi-lateral extensions	
Individual characteristics Shared characteristics Organizational characteristics Extra-organizational characteristics	Antecedents	
Attitudes and preferences Knowledge sharing and organizational learning Communication, cooperation, and conflicts Viability (commitment and turnover) Performance	Consequences	How
Phases of trust: General Formation Maintenance Violation/repair Spirals	Trust-level dynamics	
Contagion/spill-over Emergence Transformation Co-evolution	Other trust dynamics	
Traits/dispositional mechanisms Attitudinal mechanisms Cognitive mechanisms Emotional mechanisms Behavioral mechanisms	Mediating mechanisms	
Psychological mechanisms Sociological mechanisms Economical mechanisms Management mechanisms	Specific theoretical mechanisms	Why
Theoretical integration Theoretical diversity	Multiple theoretical mechanisms	
Individual characteristics Shared characteristics Organizational characteristics	Moderators	
Generalizability across parties Generalizability across locations Generalizability across time/phases Context-specific models	Contextual assumptions	Who/where/when
Generalizability across levels Level-specific models	Level-of-analysis assumptions	

Figure 10.1. Structure of the Data and Emergent Organizing Framework

TABLE 10.1. *Illustrative Evidence*

Second-Order Concepts	Illustrative Statements	Number of Recommendations
	"What"	
Nature and dimensions	"We think that by understanding this common 'architectural structure' of the trust construct a better dialogue could be developed between researchers." (Castaldo et al., 2010, p. 666) [*definition of trust*]	99
	"Future research should also capitalize on our current set of findings to further explore how the two types of trust relate to other organizational variables." (Chua et al., 2008, p. 448) [*specific dimensions*]	
Levels and referents	"Further research should also examine other ways of fostering the development of managerial trust. Certain management practices or reward systems may enhance the development of managerial trust in an NPD team." (Dayan et al., 2009, p. 33) [*trustor and trustee: different level*]	337
	"Future studies of the mediating role of trust in PJ-outcome relationships should consider multiple justice foci as well as multiple trust foci within a single study." (Yang et al., 2009, p. 152) [*multiple referents*]	
Bilateral/ multilateral extensions	"Of course, this line of inquiry itself may raise new issues in terms of the degree to which each negotiator trusts the third party (and how much the third party trusts each negotiator, and so on)." (Tomlinson et al., 2009, p. 182) [*third-party trust*]	26
	"Clearly, additional empirical research is needed to fully understand how being trusted by management influences customer service." (Salamon & Robinson, 2008, p. 599) [*being trusted*]	
	"How"	
Antecedents	"Given the robust findings for leadership style on trust, future research would also benefit from continuing this line of inquiry and exploring other managerial characteristics. One can imagine that a particularly agreeable or extraverted manager may be especially adept at fostering trust among subordinates." (Holtz & Harold, 2008, p. 797) [*individual characteristics*]	42
	"Future research could investigate whether and how national stereotypes impact on institutional trust." (Maguire & Phillips, 2008, p. 395) [*extra-organizational characteristics*]	
Consequences	"Future research should extend this line of inquiry by examining other work-related outcomes, such as turnover intentions." (Yang & Mossholder, 2010, p. 60) [*viability (commitment and turnover)*]	72
	"How the level of organizational trust impacts performance is a very interesting path for future research." (Mach et al., 2010, p. 789) [*performance*]	

(continued)

TABLE 10.1. *Continued*

Second-Order Concepts	Illustrative Statements	Number of Recommendations
Trust-level dynamics	"A theme that warrants further attention is the impact of intra-organizational conflicts and inter-organizational coalitions on the establishment and maintenance of inter-organizational trust." (MacDuffie, 2011, p. 38) [*maintenance*]	87
	"Finally, another interesting avenue for future research on restoration processes in exchange relations is to investigate what level of overcompensation is most effective in restoring trust." (Desmet et al., 2011, p. 85) [*violation/repair*]	
Other trust dynamics	"It has been argued that a trust relationship at early stages may be more cognitively-based, whereas at latter stages it may become more affectively-based. Questions such as how it evolves from a cognitive to an affective base have not as yet been examined. Therefore, research addressing this issue would prove to be fruitful." (Yang & Mossholder, 2010, p. 60) [*transformation*]	13
	"A key research area is the co-evolution of trust and alliances." (Nielsen, 2011, p. 171) [*coevolution*]	

"Why"

Second-Order Concepts	Illustrative Statements	Number of Recommendations
Mediating mechanisms	"In this manner, it is expected that joint-behavioral outcomes will mediate the relationship between trust congruence and actual joint gain." (Tomlinson et al., 2009, p. 182) [*behavioral mechanisms*]	40
	"For example, it may be the case that collective felt trust affects customer service through affective variables, such as positive mood. Clearly, additional empirical research is needed to fully understand how being trusted by management influences customer service." (Salamon & Robinson, 2008, p. 599) [*emotional mechanisms*]	
Specific theoretical mechanisms	"These clearly merit future research and further theoretical development through Social Identity Theory." (Lowry et al., 2010, p. 311) [*psychological mechanisms*]	22
	"Future research may serve to enhance the literature on coworker trust by using team member exchange (TMX) theory." (Lau & Liden, 2008, p. 1136) [*sociological mechanisms*]	
Multiple theoretical mechanisms	"We note that while different theoretical perspectives have been brought to bear on various referents at this level, there are opportunities for cross-fertilization." (Fulmer & Gelfand, 2012: 1203) [*theoretical integration*]	8
	"Our review revealed great theoretical diversity across levels, which can be considered a strength that contributes to our understanding of trust in organizations and should continue to be leveraged in future research." (Fulmer & Gelfand, 2012, p. 1206) [*theoretical diversity*]	

TABLE 10.1. *Continued*

Second-Order Concepts	Illustrative Statements	Number of Recommendations
	"Who/Where/When"	
Moderators	"It is interesting that informational justice of the band director had no effect on trustworthiness perceptions while informational justice as it pertained to the section leaders did influence trustworthiness perceptions, which we discuss next. Future research could address this issue by examining the extent to which organizational hierarchy may influence this relationship." (Frazier et al., 2010, p. 65) [*organizational characteristics*]	55
	"Another interesting research direction is to examine whether task interdependency moderates the shared work values-trust-effectiveness relationship. As task interdependency increases, shared work values might have stronger effects on trust and team member effectiveness." (Chou et al., 2008, p. 1733) [*shared characteristics*]	
Contextual assumptions	"Future research might attempt to test the ideas developed in this study across different settings." (Madjar & Ortiz-Walters, 2008, p. 962) [*generalizability across locations*]	117
	"Future research could investigate whether and how national stereotypes impact on institutional trust in cross-border mergers." (Maguire & Phillips, 2008, p. 395) [*context-specific models*]	
Level of analysis assumptions	"Another intriguing avenue for future research is to examine our assertion that the assumptions and recommendations for interpersonal trust repair are not readily transferable to other levels." (Gillespie & Dietz, 2009, p. 142) [*generalizability across levels*]	16
	"More research is needed to confirm these quasi-isomorphic patterns, as few studies have examined the role of networks in trust processes at the team level and within an organization at the organizational level." (Fulmer & Gelfand, 2012, p. 1207) [*level-specific models*]	

of the trustors and trustees that should be studied in the future. Although researchers suggest that more work is needed at all levels of analysis, they place a clear emphasis on moving beyond the individual level of analysis and studying trust at aggregate levels, such as the team and organizational level. Second, scholars recommend that future studies should continue focusing on trustors and trustees at similar levels of analysis (i.e., interpersonal trust, inter-/intragroup and interorganizational trust), as has been the dominant focus in the literature. Finally, relative to scholarly recommendations about trust in a single referent, only some scholars recognize the need to study trust in multiple referents at the same time.

Emerging Themes across "How" Recommendations

Our findings reveal a clear push toward examining the nomological network of trust—that is, the antecedents and consequences associated with trust. One trend we observe is a strong emphasis on examining consequences over antecedents of trust. Thus it seems that scholars feel that more work is needed to demonstrate that trust matters to organizations (i.e., consequences) before turning to the question of how trust can be built and "managed" (i.e., antecedents). Two other themes that emerged from our analyses pertain to the content of the variables involved. First, of all the types of antecedents distinguished in Fulmer and Gelfand's (2012) literature review, individual-level characteristics of trustors and trustees (e.g., attitudes, behaviors, emotions, and predispositions) are most often recommended for examination by scholars, with an emphasis on trustor attitudes and trustee behaviors. Although recommendations were made about examining other types of antecedents (e.g., shared characteristics, communication processes, structural characteristics, and organizational characteristics), these were substantially fewer in number. Second, among the consequences distinguished by Fulmer and Gelfand, scholars overwhelmingly agree on performance as the most critical consequence that should be examined in relation to trust in the future. Indeed, this is not surprising, since research on the performance implications of trust continues to suffer from mixed findings, and there is thus a pressing need to resolve this issue. While our count data also indicated reasonable scholarly recognition of the need for studying communication, cooperation, and conflict behaviors, they show considerably less recognition for studying the other types of consequences identified by Fulmer and Gelfand, namely, attitudes and preferences, knowledge sharing and organizational learning, and viability.

Besides the two clear trends of studying individual-level characteristics as antecedents and performance (both at the individual and the aggregate level) as a consequence of trust, we observe a remarkable breadth in the variables recommended by scholars in relation to trust. Taken together, these recommendations collectively suggest that many scholars expect trust to be relevant in relation to a wealth of organizational antecedents and consequences and that more research is needed to further explore and expand the nomological network of trust.

Our findings further highlight the need for more research into the dynamics of trust. For example, our analysis shows scholarly recognition for the need to study specific phases of trust, including trust building, trust stability/maintenance, and trust recovery after a violation (Rousseau et al., 1998). In addition to dynamics in the *degree* of trust, other (albeit considerably fewer) recommendations indicate the need to examine the dynamic *diffusion* of trust across parties, including the phenomenon of trust "trickling down" from higher to lower organizational levels, social contagion of trust among parties, and the emergence of shared perceptions of trust among members of an organizational group. In addition, a few recommendations were made to study other trust dynamics, such as how the substantive meaning of trust changes over time and how trust coevolves at different levels of analysis. Together, these recommendations clearly indicate the need to move beyond static approaches to trust and to conduct more research into the dynamics of organizational trust.

Emerging Themes across "Why" and "Who/Where/When" Recommendations

The overwhelming scholarly recognition of the need to understand the nature of trust and its relationships with antecedents and consequences stands in stark contrast to scholarly acknowledgment of the need to understand the causal mechanisms through which trust operates and is affected (i.e., why) and boundary assumptions underlying these relationships (i.e., who/where/when). The count data show that most of the recommendations made about mediating mechanisms focused on mechanisms operating at the individual level, with an emphasis on attitudinal and behavioral as opposed to cognitive or affective mechanisms. While the majority of scholars recommend a single theoretical base for understanding how trust operates and is impacted by other variables, scholars seem to disagree about what theoretical base should be used. This is reflected by the fact that scholars recommend as many as 21 different theories (e.g., social identity theory, power dependence theory, social exchange theory). On the one hand, this variety demonstrates the theoretical richness of the field; on the other hand, it shows that little theoretical pruning or integration has taken place so far (Leavitt, Mitchell, & Peterson, 2010; Okhuysen & Bonardi, 2011). Indeed, our count data indicate that few scholars advocate integrating theories as a way to enhance our understanding of trust.

Our findings further show that scholars commonly agree that more research is needed that analyzes the generalizability (or, conversely, the context-specificity) of current insights on trust. Classifying these recommendations using Whetten et al.'s (2009) framework reveals an emphasis on examining contextual boundaries over examining level-of-analysis boundaries. Within the recommendations about contextual boundaries, there is a clear emphasis on the need to assess the generalizability across parties and locations (i.e., who and where) over the generalizability across temporal phases (i.e., when; Whetten, 1989). Besides assessing the generalizability of *current* insights on trust post hoc, a small portion of scholars also advocate incorporating boundary assumptions a priori into *future* theories by building context- and level-specific models of trust. Together, the why and who/where/when recommendations point toward an emerging scholarly recognition for the need for a more fine-grained understanding of the relationships between trust and its antecedents and consequences.

■ THE LATEST DEVELOPMENTS IN THE FIELD

Having examined scholarly recommendations up until 2011 allowed us to assess how organizational trust research has developed since then. We address this issue by reviewing recent findings in 111 recent articles published in 31 top-tier management journals (e.g., *Journal of Management, Academy of Management Journal,*

Strategic Management Journal, Organization Science, Journal of Applied Psychology)
that were either published or in press between 2012 and the time of writing this
chapter (i.e., March 2015). Overall, it is clear that many calls for future research
have been vigorously followed up on; however, we also identify a number of issues
that were suggested by earlier studies but that have not yet been fully addressed,
as well as various new topics that were not entirely anticipated by earlier research
suggestions. We discuss these developments in more detail later, organizing them
along the aggregate dimensions that emerged from our content analysis of scholarly recommendations (see Figure 10.1).

"What" Developments

Based on our review of the recent literature, there appears to be an increasing
consensus on the nature and conceptualization of trust. Recent work has almost
exclusively built on either Mayer et al.'s (1995) or Rousseau et al.'s (1998) definition of trust. While scholarly agreement on the general definition is encouraging,
we observe an growing disagreement about the central underlying dimensions
of trust, with some studies distinguishing between ability-, benevolence-, and
integrity-based trust (Zapata, Olsen, & Martins, 2013) and others differentiating between dispositional, categorization-, and rule-based trust (Muethel &
Bond, 2013); between calculative and relational trust (Poppo, Zhou, & Li, 2015);
or between rule-, role-, and identification-based trust (van der Werff & Buckley,
2014).While these research efforts have added nuance and richness to the understanding of trust dimensions, little progress has been made in exploring how different typologies may map onto each other or how some of the dimensions may be
complements or substitutes for one another.

A related discussion that has received much attention (probably more than
anticipated by most scholars) regards the relationship between trust and distrust.
An increasing number of studies have treated distrust as a separate construct
(Bijlsma-Frankema, Sitkin, & Weibel, 2015) and theorized on its role above and
beyond that of trust (Connelly, Miller, & Devers, 2012; Lumineau, 2014).

With respect to levels and referents of trust (Fulmer & Gelfand, 2012), significant contributions to our understanding of trust continue to be made at the
individual, team, and organizational level, and there is an increasing accumulation of insights at each respective level (Cao & Lumineau, 2015; De Jong et al.,
2016; Zhong, Su, Peng, & Yang, 2014). In contrast, however, very little progress is
being made in terms of cross-level research on trust. One exception is the study by
Braun, Peus, Weisweiler, and Frey (2013), who examined the impact of intrateam
trust on both team- and individual-level performance. The continued lack of
scholarly attention to cross-level effects is surprising, given that trust itself is a
multilevel phenomenon (Currall & Inkpen, 2002) and that we know that antecedents and consequences exist across different levels of analysis (Fulmer & Gelfand,
2012). We believe cross-level investigations have great potential to advance our
understanding of organizational trust, and we therefore look forward to more
research in this area.

We have further witnessed a burgeoning interest in bilateral/multilateral extensions of trust, mostly in micro-level investigations. Korsgaard, Brower, and Lester (2015), for instance, provide a review of dyadic-level extensions of trust, distinguishing between mutual, reciprocal, and asymmetric trust. Among the different extensions of trust, trust asymmetry and felt trust have probably received the most attention in recent studies (Carter & Mossholder, 2015; De Jong & Dirks, 2012; Lau, Lam, & Wen, 2014). Unfortunately, these developments have not yet diffused to macro-level studies of trust, which continue to focus exclusively on the trust experienced by only one of the parties in the relationship and to implicitly assume that trust is mutual and symmetric.

One extension that has frequently been suggested but has received little recent attention is third-party trust—that is, the issue of whether trust is transferred from a better known third party to a closely associated, but less well-known, entity. Given the prevalence of situations in which a trustor has had no prior interactions with a trustee but is familiar with certain other actors in that trustee's immediate network, the factors promoting and hindering third-party trust transfer clearly deserve greater attention. Another extension that has seen several calls for more research but has not been followed up on recently is trust (in)accuracy. While an exact match between a trustor's trust and a trustee's trustworthiness is rare, we know very little about the antecedents and consequences of mismatches—that is, over- and under-trust (Priem & Nystrom, 2014). We therefore recommend further research into how trust accuracy emerges and operates in organizational settings.

"How" Developments

While earlier "how" recommendations primarily emphasized studying consequences of trust, recent studies have given essentially equal attention to studying antecedents to trust. Recognizing that trust can stem from a variety of factors, researchers have started to integrate and juxtapose different types of antecedents, comparing their relative effects and joint impact on trust (Schilke & Cook, 2015; Zhong et al., 2014). Among the types of antecedents studied, extraorganizational characteristics have received increased attention (Ribbink & Grimm, 2014; Roy, 2012). In addition, we have seen an exploding number of studies looking at contractual governance as an antecedent to trust (Cao & Lumineau, 2015; Connelly et al., 2012). Moreover, researchers have identified a variety of previously largely unexplored antecedents, such as status (Lount & Pettit, 2012), cultural metacognition (Chua, Morris, & Mor, 2012), language barriers (Tenzer, Pudelko, & Harzing, 2014), social comparison (Dunn, Ruedy, & Schweitzer, 2012), organizational transparency (Schnackenberg & Tomlinson, 2016), and organizational culture (Schilke & Cook, 2015), among others. Together, these developments have contributed to further expanding the nomological network surrounding trust as well as to a more balanced examination of antecedents and consequences.

Among the consequences suggested by scholars, performance has by far received the most attention recently (De Jong, Bijlsma-Frankema, & Cardinal, 2014; Kong et al., 2014), in line with prior recommendations. While this growing interest in the bottom-line consequences of trust is laudable, recent studies have reported mixed results regarding the trust–performance relationship, with some studies showing trust to be positively associated with performance (Drescher, Korsgaard, Welpe, Picot, & Wigand, 2014; Ferguson & Peterson, 2015) but others reporting a nonsignificant relationship between the two (Braun et al., 2013; Chung & Jackson, 2013). Clearly, a systematic integration of these inconsistent findings regarding the performance consequences of trust is warranted (De Jong et al., 2016). After all, the assumption of trust leading to beneficial individual and collective outcomes is at the core of much organizational trust research, making additional empirical insight into this issue a priority.

Although there has been a proliferation of research focusing on the functional outcomes of trust, a modest but growing recognition of the dark side of trust has developed as well (Bammens & Collewaert, 2014). Lumineau (2014), for instance, provides a comprehensive overview of some of the dysfunctional consequences of trust and develops propositions regarding how contractual provisions may enhance or diminish such negative trust outcomes. Other studies have started to elucidate the mechanisms responsible for negative effects of trust (Baer et al., 2015; Kong et al., 2014). As research focusing on the limits and liabilities of trust is still in its infancy, there is great potential for meaningful contributions in this area.

We furthermore see significant advancements being made in exploring trust-level dynamics. Recent research has started to examine how initial trust affects trust at subsequent stages of a relationship (Ferguson & Peterson, 2015; Schilke, Reimann, & Cook, 2013) and to differentiate between antecedents to trust that are relevant at different developmental stages (Lander & Kooning, 2013; van der Werff & Buckley, 2014). In line with scholarly recommendations, the developmental stage that has received the most attention recently is trust recovery following a breach of trust. Recent studies have, for instance, explored the types of breach, how transgressors address a breach (Harmon, Kim, & Mayer, 2015), the impact of whether the betrayed party is an individual or a group (Kim, Cooper, Dirks, & Ferrin, 2013), and how trustors cognitively process a breach (Schilke et al., 2013). A developmental phase that has recently sparked an unanticipated amount of attention is initial or "swift" trust. This research is particularly focused on the question of how one can explain trust perceptions without prior interactions and how such initial perceptions can have long-lasting effects on the relationship (Holtz, 2015; Wildman et al., 2012).

Relative to research into trust *level* dynamics, we have seen relatively little progress in understanding other trust dynamics, such as how the *nature and meaning* of trust may change over time. A notable exception is a study by Schilke and Cook (2013), who develop a multistage, cross-level process theory of trust development in which the meaning of trust changes as it transforms from interpersonal to interorganizational trust. Future research may use other approaches to conceptualizing qualitative changes in the meaning of trust that might occur over time (e.g., by employing one of the trust dimension typologies discussed earlier).

"Why" Developments

Compared to the limited number of scholarly recommendations on the "why" dimension, the number of studies considering mediating mechanisms has exploded in recent years. Scholars have examined a wide range of attitudinal (Lount & Pettit, 2012), cognitive (Colquitt, LePine, Piccolo, Zaphata, & Rich, 2012), emotional (Dunn et al., 2012), and behavioral mechanisms (De Jong et al., 2014). In addition to an increased interest in examining mediating mechanisms in a general sense, we also witness more and more efforts to purposefully use a single theoretical base as the foundation for developing an integrative model of trust and explicitly testing the multiple mediating mechanisms specified by these theories. Kong et al. (2014), for instance, use social exchange theory to develop and test an integrative model of how trust affects negotiation outcomes, while Baer et al. (2015) draw on conservation of resources theory to test an integrative model of how felt trust affects individual performance. This trend signals an increasing sophistication and theoretical precision in the scholarly understanding of how trust operates in relation to antecedents and consequences.

Another indicator of theoretical progress in recent research is a trend of combining and integrating multiple theories. Most notably, many investigations have combined social exchange theory with complementary theoretical approaches, including attribution theory (De Jong & Dirks, 2012), self-determination theory (Aryee, Walumbwa, Mondejar, & Chu, 2015), social identity theory (Schaubroeck, Peng, & Hannah, 2013), and social resources theory (Reiche, 2012). Additionally, we have witnessed an increasing number of cross-disciplinary investigations that combine social-psychological and economic approaches to understand how antecedent factors affect trust (Schilke & Cook, 2015; Zhong et al., 2014). Together, these studies signal a growing scholarly recognition of the value of integrating and reconciling diverse theories regarding trust.

"Who/Where/When" Developments

Along with the surge of interest in mediating mechanisms, researchers have become increasingly interested in contingency factors. Among the contingencies studied are various individual characteristics (Brown, Crossley, & Robinson, 2014), shared characteristics (Ertug, Cuypers, Noorderhaven, & Bensaou, 2013), and organizational characteristics (Crossley, Cooper, & Wernsing, 2013). Other studies have picked up on scholarly recommendations to develop more context-specific models of trust by examining trust among particular parties (Schnackenberg & Tomlinson, 2016), at particular locations (Chen, Eberly, Chiang, & Cheng, 2014), and in particular types of relationships (Mortensen & Neeley, 2012). While research in specific organizational contexts can provide deep insight into the way trust operates within particular contexts, it does not address the issue of whether and how insights on trust generalize across level of analyses (Whetten et al., 2009). This is an important issue that future research should address.

■ DISCUSSION

Where Do We Go from Here?

In this chapter, we first synthesized scholarly recommendations for future research across social science disciplines, resulting in an emergent framework that organizes these research directions into a parsimonious set of theoretical building blocks (i.e., *what, how, why, who/where/when*). Applying this framework to more recent management research on trust revealed insights into current trends in the field as well as understudied directions, such as the integration of trust typologies, conceptual extensions at the macro level, trust and performance, cross-level examinations, and generalizability across contexts and levels of analysis. Our ambition with this synthesis and review has been to build a common research agenda by capturing the trust community's beliefs about how to move forward, which we view as much more critical for advancing the field than personal opinions, including our own. We therefore resist the temptation of providing our opinions on *which* directions to pursue but instead offer our suggestions on *how* scholars can build on the recommendations and developments we identified to move the field forward. In doing so, we differentiate between the role of individual researchers and the organizational trust community as a whole.

Just as the recommendations and developments we analyzed oftentimes comprised of multiple categories, so can individual researchers use the substantive categories (i.e., theoretical building blocks, second-order themes) we identified to think more systematically about the contribution of their envisioned study. While we framed these categories as discrete, some are interrelated such that one naturally implies the other. Consequently, one possibility for researchers is to pursue a substantive research direction that allows them to contribute to multiple theoretical building blocks at the same time, thereby enhancing the scope of their contribution. For instance, examining the temporal generalizability of insights on trust (i.e., *when*) implies the need to conduct longitudinal research into trust dynamics (i.e., *how*). The same principle applies at the level of the second-order themes in our framework. For example, bilateral and multilateral extensions of trust require trust to be conceptualized and operationalized at aggregate levels of analysis. On the other hand, some of the categories that comprise our framework coexist independently of one another. As such, a fruitful strategy for increasing the scope and novelty of one's potential contribution is to combine categories in (meaningful) ways that have not been attempted before. For instance, examining mediating mechanisms of conceptual extensions of trust at the macro level allows scholars to contribute insights into the *why*'s of understudied manifestations of trust (i.e., *what*). Likewise, studying hybrid forms of trust at transition points during changes in the meaning of trust over time enables them to contribute novel insights into the understudied topic of trust dynamics and contribute to both the aggregate dimensions of *what* and *how*.

We also see two roles for the trust community as a whole in moving the field forward, based on the two sources of fragmentation we identified in our introduction. The first source is organizational research that includes trust but does not treat it as a core variable of interest. This research is likely to yield incremental insights on trust at best while also contributing to increased fragmentation and divergence of the field. We believe therefore it is critical for the trust community to counterbalance these trends by keeping track of knowledge accumulation and integration across primary studies (e.g., through narrative and meta-analytic syntheses) and by tackling substantive issues surrounding trust that are characterized by a lack of integration (e.g., the persistence of multiple trust typologies, a lack of research into the generalizability of insights across contexts and levels of analysis). The second source we identified was the existence and persistence of subcommunities of trust scholars (e.g., the interorganizational and intraorganizational trust communities, the qualitative and quantitative trust community). We therefore believe it is critical for scholars from these different subcommunities to more actively exchange ideas, learn from each other, and test whether theories and insights from one domain can be meaningfully transferred to another. These efforts would not only potentially increase knowledge transfer across subcommunities but also facilitate the development of common terminology, concepts, and theoretical frameworks, which would no doubt benefit the field as a whole.

■ CONCLUSION

By synthesizing scholarly recommendations and reviewing recent developments, this chapter offers systematic insight into the future of organizational trust research. In doing so, we hope not only to guide individual researchers in finding an interesting topic for their future projects but also to help the field of organizational trust research to develop in a more coherent and cumulative manner. Given that trust is linked to such a plethora of organizationally relevant variables and issues, we are convinced that by advancing the understanding of organizational trust, researchers are able to make important and meaningful contributions to the broader organization science literature. This potential, we believe, can only be realized through working together as a community. We hope this chapter will inspire trust researchers to do so.

■ AUTHORS' NOTE

This study was partially funded by the Netherlands Organisation for Scientific Research (NWO), grant number 016.145.243, awarded to the first author.

■ NOTE

1. Journals with an ISI impact factor greater than 1 were considered "high-impact." A comprehensive list of all the included journals and articles can be obtained from the first author.

◼ REFERENCES

Aryee, S., Walumbwa, F. O., Mondejar, R., & Chu, C. W. L. (2015). Accounting for the influence of overall justice on job performance: Integrating self-determination and social exchange theories. *Journal of Management Studies, 52*(2), 231–252.

Baer, M., Dhensa-Kahlon, R., Colquitt, J., Rodell, J. B., Outlaw, R., & Long, D. (2015). Uneasy lies the head that bears the trust: the effects of feeling trusted on emotional exhaustion. *Academy of Management Journal, 58*(6), 1637–1657.

Bammens, Y., & Collewaert, V. (2014). Trust between entrepreneurs and angel investors: Exploring positive and negative implications for venture performance assessments. *Journal of Management, 40*(7), 1980–2008.

Bijlsma-Frankema, K. M., Sitkin, S. B., & Weibel, A. (2015). Distrust in the balance: The emergence and development of intergroup distrust in a court of law. *Organization Science, 26*(4), 1018–1039.

Braun, S., Peus, C., Weisweiler, S., & Frey, D. (2013). Transformational leadership, job satisfaction, and team performance: A multilevel mediation model of trust. *Leadership Quarterly, 24*, 270–283.

Brown, G., Crossley, C., & Robinson, S. L. (2014). Psychological ownership, territorial behavior, and being perceived as a team contributor: The critical role of trust in the work environment. *Personnel Psychology, 67*(2), 463–485.

Cao, Z., & Lumineau, F. (2015). Revisiting the interplay between contractual and relational governance: A qualitative and meta-analytic investigation. *Journal of Operations Management, 33–34*, 15–42.

Carter, M. Z., & Mossholder, K. W. (2015). Are we on the same page? The performance effects of congruence between supervisor and group trust. *Journal of Applied Psychology, 100*(5), 1349–1363.

Chen, X.-P., Eberly, M. B., Chiang, T.-J. F., J.-L., & Cheng, B.-S. (2014). Affective trust in Chinese leaders: Linking paternalistic leadership to employee performance. *Journal of Management, 40*(3), 796–819.

Chua, R. Y. J., Ingram, P., & Morris, M. (2008). From the head and the heart: Locating cognition- and affect-based trust in managers' professional networks. *Academy of Management Journal, 51*(3), 436–452.

Chua, R. Y. J., Morris, M. W., & Mor, S. (2012). Collaborating across cultures: Cultural metacognition and affect-based trust in creative collaboration. *Journal of Organizational Behavior, 118*(2), 116–131.

Chung, Y., & Jackson, S. E. (2013). The internal and external networks of knowledge-intensive teams: The role of task routineness. *Journal of Management, 39*(2), 442–468.

Colquitt, J. A., LePine, J. A., Piccolo, R. F., Zaphata, C. P., & Rich, B. L. (2012). Explaining the justice-performance relationship: Trust as exchange deepener or trust as uncertainty reducer? *Journal of Applied Psychology, 97*, 1–15.

Colquitt, J. A., Scott, B. A., & LePine, J. A. (2007). Trust, trustworthiness, and trust propensity: A meta-analytic test of their unique relationships with risk taking and job performance. *Journal of Applied Psychology, 92*(4), 909–927.

Connelly, B. L., Miller, T., & Devers, C. E. (2012). Under a cloud of suspicion: Trust, distrust, and their interactive effect in interorganizational contracting. *Strategic Management Journal, 33*(7), 820–833.

Castaldo, S., Premazzi, K., & Zerbini, F. (2010). The meaning (s) of trust. A content analysis on the diverse conceptualizations of trust in scholarly research on business relationships. *Journal of Business Ethics, 96*(4), 657–668.

Crossley, C. D., Cooper, C. D., & Wernsing, T. S. (2013). Making things happen through challenging goals: Leader proactivity, trust, and business-unit performance. *Journal of Applied Psychology, 98*(3), 540–549.

Currall, S. C., & Inkpen, A. C. (2002). A multilevel approach to trust in joint ventures. *Journal of International Business Studies, 33*(3), 479–495.

Currall, S. C., & Inkpen, A. C. (2006). On the complexity of organizational trust: A multilevel co-evolutionary perspective and guidelines for future research. In R. Bachmann & A. Zaheer (Eds.), *Handbook of trust research* (pp. 235–263). Cheltenham, UK: Edward Elgar.

Dayan, M., Di Benedetto, C. A., & Colak, M. (2009). Managerial trust in new product development projects: its antecedents and consequences. *R&D Management, 39*, 21–37.

De Jong, B. A., Bijlsma-Frankema, K. M., & Cardinal, L. B. (2014). Stronger than the sum of its parts? The performance implications of peer control combinations in teams. *Organization Science, 25*(6), 1703–1721.

De Jong, B. A., & Dirks, K. T. (2012). Beyond shared perceptions of trust and monitoring in teams: Implications of asymmetry and dissensus. *Journal of Applied Psychology, 97*(2), 391–406.

De Jong, B. A., Dirks, K. T., & Gillespie, N. (2016). Trust and team performance: A meta-analysis of main effects, moderators, and Covariates. *Journal of Applied Psychology, 101*(8), 1134–1150.

DeNisi, A. S. (2010). Presidential address—Challenges and opportunities for the academy in the next decade. *Academy of Management Review, 35*, 190–201.

Desmet, P. T. M., De Cremer, D., & Dijk, E. van. (2011). In money we trust? The use of financial compensations to repair trust in the aftermath of distributive harm. *Organizational Behavior and Human Decision Processes, 114*, 75–86.

Deutsch Salamon, S., & Robinson, S. L. (2008). Trust that binds: The impact of collective felt trust on organizational performance. *Journal of Applied Psychology, 93*(3), 593–601.

Drescher, M. A., Korsgaard, M. A., Welpe, I. M., Picot, A., & Wigand, R. T. (2014). The dynamics of shared leadership: Building trust and enhancing performance. *Journal of Applied Psychology, 99*(5), 771–783.

Dunn, J., Ruedy, N. E., & Schweitzer, M. E. (2012). It hurts both ways: How social comparisons harm affective and cognitive trust. *Organizational Behavior and Human Decision Processes, 117*(1), 2–14.

Duriau, V. J., Reger, R. K., & Pfaffer, M. D. (2007). A content analysis of the content analysis literature in organization studies: Research themes, data sources, and methodological refinements. *Organizational Research Methods, 10*(1), 5–34.

Ertug, G., Cuypers, I. R. P., Noorderhaven, N. G., & Bensaou, B. M. (2013). Trust between international joint venture partners: Effects of home countries. *Journal of International Business Studies, 44*, 263–282.

Ferguson, A. J., & Peterson, R. S. (2015). Sinking slowly: diversity in propensity to trust predicts downward trust spirals in small groups. *Journal of Applied Psychology, 100*(4), 1012–1024.

Fulmer, C. A., & Gelfand, M. J. (2012). At what level (and in whom) we trust: Trust across multiple organizational levels. *Journal of Management, 38*(4), 1167–1230.

Gillespie, N., & Dietz, G. (2009). Trust repair after an organization-level failure. *Academy of Management Review, 34*(1), 127–145.

Gioia, D. A., Corley, K. G., & Hamilton, A. L. (2013). Seeking qualitative rigor in inductive research: Notes on the Gioia methodology. *Organizational Research Methods, 16*(1), 15–31.

Harmon, D. J., Kim, P. H., & Mayer, K. J. (2015). Breaking the letter vs. spirit of the law: How the interpretation of contract violations affects trust and the management of relationships. *Strategic Management Journal, 36*(4), 497–517.

Holtz, B. C. (2015). From first impression to fairness perception: Investigating the impact of initial trustworthiness beliefs. *Personnel Psychology, 68*(3), 499–546.

Holtz, B. C., & Harold, C. M. (2008). When your boss says no! The effects of leadership style and trust on employee reactions to managerial explanations. *Journal of Occupational and Organizational Psychology, 81*, 777–802.

Kim, P. H., Cooper, C. D., Dirks, K. T., & Ferrin, D. L. (2013). Repairing trust with individuals versus groups. *Organizational Behavior and Human Decision Processes, 120*(1), 1–14.

Kong, D. T., Dirks, K. T., & Ferrin, D. L. (2014). Interpersonal trust within negotiations: Meta-analytic evidence, critical contingencies, and directions for future research. *Academy of Management Journal, 57*(5), 1235–1255.

Korsgaard, M. A., Brower, H. H., & Lester, S. W. (2015). It isn't always mutual: A critical review of dyadic trust. *Journal of Management, 41*(1), 47–70.

Lander, M. W., & Kooning, L. (2013). Boarding the aircraft: Trust development amongst negotiators of a complex merger. *Journal of Management Studies, 50*(1), 1–30.

Lau, D. C., & Liden, R. C. (2008). Antecedents of coworker trust: Leaders' blessings. *Journal of Applied Psychology, 93*, 1130–1138.

Lau, D. C., Lam, L. W., & Wen, S. S. (2014). Examining the effects of feeling trusted by supervisors in the workplace: A self-evaluative perspective. *Journal of Organizational Behavior, 35*, 112–127.

Leavitt, K., Mitchell, T. R., & Peterson, J. (2010). Theory pruning: Strategies to reduce our dense theoretical landscape. *Organizational Research Methods, 13*, 644–667.

Lewicki, R. J., & Brinsfield, C. (2012). Measuring trust beliefs and behaviors. In F. Lyon, G. Möllering & M. N. K. Saunders (Eds.), *Handbook of research methods on trust* (pp. 46–64). Cheltenham, UK: Edward Elgar.

Lount, R. B., & Pettit, N. C. (2012). The social context of trust: The role of status. *Organizational Behavior and Human Decision Processes, 117*(1), 15–23.

Lowry, P. B., Zhang, D., Zhou, L., & Fu, X. (2010). Effects of culture, social presence, and group composition on trust in technology-supported decision-making groups. *Information Systems Journal, 20*, 297–315.

Lumineau, F. (2014). How contracts influence trust and distrust. *Journal of Management.* Advance online publication. doi:10.1177/0149206314556656

Lyon, F., Möllering, G., & Saunders, M. N. K. (Eds.). (2012). *Handbook of research methods on trust.* Cheltenham, UK: Edward Elgar.

MacDuffie, J. J. (2011). Inter-organizational trust and the dynamics of distrust. *Journal of International Business Studies, 42*(1), 35–47.

Mach, M., Dolan, S., & Tzafrir, S. (2010). The differential effect of team members' trust on team performance: The mediation role of team cohesion. *Journal of Occupational and Organizational Psychology, 83*, 771–794.

Madjar, N., & Ortiz-Walters, R. (2008). Customers as contributors and reliable evaluators of creativity in the service industry. *Journal of Organizational Behavior, 29*, 949–966.

Maguire, S., & Phillips, N. (2008). 'Citibankers' at Citigroup: A study of the loss of institutional trust after a merger. *Journal of Management Studies, 45*(2), 372–401.

Mayer, R. C., Davis, J. H., & Schoorman, F. D. (1995). An integrative model of organizational trust. *Academy of Management Review, 20*(3), 709–734.

McEvily, B. (2011). Reorganizing the boundaries of trust: From discrete alternatives to hybrid forms. *Organization Science, 22*(5), 1266–1276.

McEvily, B., & Tortoriello, M. (2011). Measuring trust in organisational research: Review and recommendations. *Journal of Trust Research, 1*(1), 23–63.

Möllering, G. (2006). *Trust: Reason, routine, reflexivity.* New York: Elsevier.

Mortensen, M., & Neeley, T. B. (2012). Reflected knowledge and trust in global collaboration. *Management Science, 58*(12), 2207–2224.

Muethel, M., & Bond, M. H. (2013). National context and individual employees' trust of the out-group: The role of societal trust. *Journal of International Business Studies, 44*(4), 312–333.

Nielsen, B. B. (2011). Trust in strategic alliances: Toward a co-evolutionary research model. *Journal of Trust Research, 1*(2), 159–176.

Okhuysen, G., & Bonardi, J. P. (2011). The challenges of building theory by combining lenses. *Academy of Management Review, 36*(1), 6–11.

Poppo, L., Zhou, K. Z., & Li, J. J. (2015). When can you trust "trust"? Calculative trust, relational trust, and supplier performance. *Strategic Management Journal, 37*(4), 724–741.

Priem, R. L., & Nystrom, P. C. (2014). Exploring the dynamics of workgroup fracture: Common ground, trust-with-trepidation, and warranted distrust. *Journal of Management, 40*(3), 764–795.

Reiche, B. S. (2012). Knowledge benefits of social capital upon repatriation: A longitudinal study of international assignees. *Journal of Management Studies, 49*(6), 1052–1077.

Ribbink, D., & Grimm, C. M. (2014). The impact of cultural differences on buyer-supplier negotiations: An experimental study. *Journal of Operations Management, 32*(3), 114–126.

Rousseau, D. M., Sitkin, S. B., Burt, R. S., & Camerer, C. (1998). Not so different after all: A cross-discipline view of trust. *Academy of Management Review, 23*(3), 393–404.

Roy, J. P. (2012). IJV partner trustworthy behaviour: The role of host country governance and partner selection criteria. *Journal of Management Studies, 49*(2), 332–355.

Saunders, M., Skinner, D., Dietz, G., Gillespie, N., & Lewicki, R. J. (2011). *Trust across cultures: Theory and practice.* Cambridge, UK: Cambridge University Press.

Schaubroeck, J. M., Peng, A. C., & Hannah, S. T. (2013). Developing trust with peers and leaders: Impacts on organizational identification and performance during entry. *Academy of Management Journal, 56*(4), 1148–1168.

Schilke, O., & Cook, K. S. (2015). Sources of alliance partner trustworthiness: Integrating calculative and relational perspectives. *Strategic Management Journal, 36*(2), 276–297.

Schilke, O., Reimann, M., & Cook, K. S. (2013). Effect of relationship experience on trust recovery following a breach. *Proceedings of the National Academy of Sciences, 110*(38), 15236–15241.

Schnackenberg, A. K., & Tomlinson, E. C. (2016). Organizational transparency: A new perspective on managing trust in organization-stakeholder relationships. *Journal of Management, 42*(7), 1784–1810.

Schoorman, F. D., Mayer, R. C., & Davis, J. H. (2007). An integrative model of organizational trust: Past, present, and future. *Academy of Management Review, 32*(2), 344–354.

Strauss, A., & Corbin, J. (1990). *Basics of qualitative research: Grounded theory procedures and techniques.* Newbury Park, CA: SAGE.

Tenzer, H., Pudelko, M., & Harzing, A. W. (2014). The impact of language barriers on trust formation in multinational teams. *Journal of International Business Studies, 45*, 508–535.

Tomlinson, E. C., Dineen, B. R., Lewicki, R. J. (2009). Trust congruence among integrative negotiators as a predictor of joint-behavioral outcomes. *International Journal of Conflict Management, 20*(2), 173–187.

van der Werff, L., & Buckley, F. (2014). Getting to know you: A longitudinal examination of trust cues and trust development during socialization. *Journal of Management.* Advance online publication. doi:10.1177/0149206314543475

Whetten, D. A. (1989). What constitutes a theoretical contribution? *Academy of Management Review, 14*(4), 490–495.

Whetten, D. A., Felin, T., & King, B. G. (2009). The practice of theory borrowing in organizational studies: Current issues and future directions. *Journal of Management, 35*(3), 537–563.

Wildman, J. L., Shuffler, M. L., Lazzara, E. H., Fiore, S. M., Burke, C. S., Salas, E., & Garven, S. (2012). Trust development in swift starting action teams: A multilevel framework. *Group & Organization Management, 37*(2), 138–170.

Yang, J., Mossholder, K. W., & Peng T. K. (2009). Supervisory procedural justice effects: The mediating roles of cognitive and affective trust. *Leadership Quarterly, 20*(2), 143–154.

Zapata, C. P., Olsen, J. E., & Martins, L. L. (2013). Social exchange from the supervisor's perspective: Employee trustworthiness as a predictor of interpersonal and informational justice. *Organizational Behavior and Human Decision Processes, 121*(1), 1–12.

Zhong, W., Su, C., Peng, J., & Yang, Z. (2014). Trust in interorganizational relationships: A meta-analytic integration. *Journal of Management.* Advance online publication. doi:10.1177/0149206314546373

PART III
Trust in Different Cultures

11 Individualism-Collectivism, the Rule of Law, and General Trust

■ TOSHIO YAMAGISHI

▦ INDIVIDUALISM PROMOTES GENERAL TRUST AT THE NATIONAL LEVEL

I began my book on trust (Yamagishi, 1998; the English edition was published in 2011) with this statement: "This book is written around the central message that the collectivist society produces security but destroys trust" (p. 1). This assertion was partly based on a comparison of the levels of general trust in the United States and Japan, which showed that, across several studies, *general trust was higher among culturally individualistic American samples than in collectivist Japanese samples.* I can now show that this statement is broader and not limited to the comparison of American and Japanese samples.

Figure 11.1 shows a powerful, positive link between national averages of individualism-collectivism, taken from the Hofstede Center's website (http://geert-hofstede.com/) and countrywide levels of general trust reported on the website of the World Values Survey (WVS) (http://www.worldvaluessurvey.org/wvs.jsp; the 2005–2008 wave and the 2010–2014 wave). In this graph, I used the national means of the responses to the WVS question "I'd like to ask you about how much you trust people from various groups. Could you tell me for each whether you trust people from this group completely, somewhat, not very much or not at all? People you meet for the first time."[1] Figure 11.1 shows the proportion of the first two responses ("trust completely" or "trust somewhat") that indicate the extent of general trust nationwide. Data from 56 countries and regions were available on individualism-collectivism and general trust.

The graph shows that the national level of general trust rises along with the national level of individualism-collectivism. The correlation between individualism-collectivism and general trust is $r = .63$ ($p < .0001$).[2] The positive link between individualism and general trust might be a spurious one caused by the effect of the countries' economic prosperity on these two, as suggested by the fact that per capita gross domestic product[3] (GDP) is related to both individualism-collectivism ($r = .46, p < .0001$) and general trust ($r = .51, p < .0001$). However, the positive correlation between them remains highly significant, even after controlling for per capita GDP ($r = .54, p < .0001$; see a later section for more detailed analysis).[4]

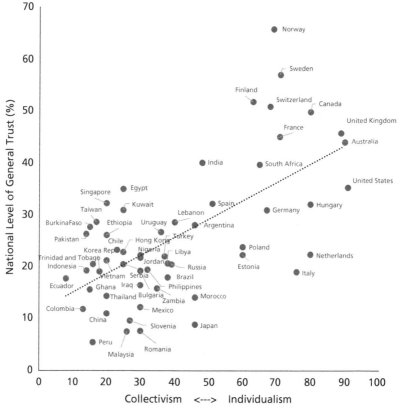

Figure 11.1. The relationship between the countrywide level of individualism-collectivism (http://geert-hofstede.com/) and the national level of general trust (percentage of the positive responses ["trust completely" and "somewhat"] to a question in the World Values Survey Waves 5 and 6 asking about the respondent's level of trust in "people you meet for the first time").

The pattern shown in Figure 11.1 might surprise those who have a naïve view of individualism and collectivism, seeing the difference between them as similar to the distinction between proself and prosocial value orientations, which are used in social dilemmas research (Van Lange, Otten, Bruin, & Joireman, 1997). According to this naïve view of individualism-collectivism, individualists care about their personal well-being without much concern for the welfare of others, whereas collectivists care equally or more about others in the same group. According to this caricature view of individualism-collectivism, people living in countries with a high degree of individualism disregard the welfare of others; thus they are not likely to be trustworthy. Conversely, people living in countries with a high degree of collectivism care about others and are more likely to be trustworthy. Then why do residents of individualist countries have a high amount of general trust (i.e., they trust strangers whom they meet for the first time), while citizens in collectivist countries have low levels of general trust?

André van Hoorn (2015) suggests an answer by showing that the trust radius (i.e., the social distance among people who trust each other at a given level) is larger in individualistic societies than in collectivist ones. Specifically, he showed that among collectivists, general trust (GSS$_{trust}$, see later discussion) is more strongly linked with in-group trust versus out-group trust. For collectivists, trust in "most people" closely relates to their trust in those whom they know personally.

Among individualists, general trust is more strongly connected to out-group trust, where trusting "most people" means trusting those with whom they do not have personal relationships. These findings by van Hoorn (2014) are consistent with the idea that collectivists' trust is limited to closely related people and that individualists' trust expands beyond closely related persons. Robert Putnam (2000) suggested a similar notion using the distinction between *bridging (inclusive) social capital* and *bonding (exclusive) social capital*, as did Granovetter (1973), who used the contrast between weak and strong ties. People without sufficient resources to survive hardship often join strong-tie networks, such as ethnic fraternal organizations, in which people exchange mutual help to overcome suffering. According to Putnam (2000), "[d]ense networks in ethnic enclaves, for example, provide crucial social and psychological support for less fortunate members of the community" (p. 22). Bonding social capital, comprised of a tight-knit circle, offers security for people connected by strong ties. Those who depend on this social capital will come to feel that they can count on in-group members but think that "anyone else [who are not in-group members] is a thief" (a Japanese saying).

Bridging social capital consists of networks of weak ties through which people mostly exchange information rather than mutual help. Bridging social capital offers opportunities to leave closed circles and "get ahead" (Putnam, 2000) by expanding interactions with diverse potential partners. This implies that people with a high level of bridging social capital are willing to give the benefit of the doubt to those they might interact with, even when they are not connected via secure, personal relationships.[5] In other words, they have a high level of general trust (in contrast with personal trust).

The findings by van Hoorn (2015) suggest that bonding social capital prevails in collectivist societies, where individuals depend on each other to survive because they cannot do so alone. Individualist societies are characterized by bridging social capital, where people seek interaction partners beyond the small circle of those they are linked to via strong ties. In this chapter, I propose that *the distinction between individualistic and collectivist societies reflects the different ways that social order is produced and maintained.* However, before presenting my argument, let me draw the reader's attention to the relationship between general trust and individualism-collectivism at the individual level.

■ COLLECTIVISM IS POSITIVELY RELATED TO GENERAL TRUST AT THE INDIVIDUAL LEVEL

Given the powerful link between individualism and general trust (as shown in Figure 11.1), it is natural to expect that people with individualistic values and beliefs tend to have higher levels of general trust than those with collectivist values

TABLE 11.1. *Correlation Coefficients between Measures of General Trust at the Individual Level*

	GSS$_{trust}$	T$_{first}$	T$_{personal}$	IGTS	IGTS$_{belif}$	IGTS$_{pref}$
GSS$_{trust}$	0.57	558	558	454	484	466
T$_{first}$	.33""	2.01	562	457	487	469
T$_{personal}$	.23""	.18""	3.30	457	487	469
IGTS	.52""	.30""	.34""	4.34	458	458
IGTS$_{belif}$	.50""	.29""	.32""	.88""	4.46	458
IGTS$_{pref}$	.33""	.21""	.24""	.79""	.39""	4.18

Note: The diagonal entries represent means. The upper triangle shows the numbers used to calculate the correlations (Model III).
"" $p < .0001$.

and beliefs. However, the positive correlation between individualism and general trust on a macro (countrywide) scale does not exist at the individual level. Rather, the link between general trust and individualism (vis-à-vis collectivism) at the individual level is more in line with the naïve view of individualism-collectivism mentioned earlier (individualists care about their own well-being without much concern for the welfare of others, whereas collectivists care equally or more about others in the same group).

Table 11.1 shows the relationships between several measures of general trust and individualism-collectivism in this study, which was conducted in Japan.[6] Initially, 564 nonstudent residents living in a relatively wealthy Tokyo suburb participated. The project lasted 3.5 years and took place in six waves, during which various economic games were conducted and a series of psychological tests were performed. In the following analysis, we used participants' responses to the general trust measures listed in Table 11.1.

GSS$_{trust}$ is the standard question on trust used in GSS and WVS, which asks: "Generally speaking, would you say that most people can be trusted or that you can't be too careful in dealing with people?" The participants were asked to choose between "can be trusted" and "can't be too careful." In the analysis, "can be trusted" was indicated by 1 and "can't be too careful" by zero. T$_{first}$ asked about the level of trust that respondents had in a person whom they met for the first time (the same question as used in Figure 11.1, although responses were provided on a 7-point scale, rather than the four categories used in WVS). T$_{personal}$ asked about the level of trust they had in someone they knew personally.[7]

The Inclusive General Trust scale (IGTS) consists of two subscales. The first, the IGTS$_{belief}$, measures respondents' beliefs about the trustworthiness of other people (Yamagishi et al., 2013; Yamagishi & Yamagishi, 1994) is combined with the newly constructed scale, the aim being to gauge respondents' preference for behaving in a trustful way (IGTS$_{pref}$; Yamagishi et al., 2015). The diagonal entries in Table 11.1 show the mean of each measure. The upper triangle reveals the pairwise number of participants, which was used to calculate the correlation coefficient, and the lower triangle displays the correlation coefficient. The relationships shown in Table 11.1 are mostly positive and significant.

TABLE 11.2. *Correlation Coefficients
between Measures of Individualism and Collectivism
at the Individual Level*

	vCol	hCol	vInd	hInd
vCol	5.38	470	470	470
hCol	.43****	6.44	470	470
vInd	.09	−.09*	5.04	470
hInd	−.02	.17***	.28****	4.34

Note: The diagonal entries represent means. The upper triangle shows
the numbers used to calculate the correlations (Model III).
$^*p < .001$, $^{**}p < .001$, $^{***}p < .001$, $^{****}p < .0001$.

Table 11.2 displays the measures of individualism and collectivism used in this study. The four scales of individualism/collectivism (vInd, vCol, hInd, and hCol)—developed by Singelis, Triandis, Bhawuk, and Gelfand (1995)—were assessed in Wave 5 and represent individualism and collectivism on vertical and horizontal axes; these four scales each consist of eight items. The entries in Table 11.2 have the same meaning as in Table 11.1. All three measures of collectivism are positively correlated, as are the two measures of individualism.

In addition to the measures of general trust and individualism-collectivism, we analyzed participants' prosocial preference via the distribution of resources using three versions of social value orientation (SVO). The triple-dominance method (Van Lange et al., 1997) was used in Wave 3, followed by the slider method (Murphy, Ackermann, & Handgraaf, 2011) in Wave 5 and the ring measure (Liebrand, 1984) in Wave 6. To evaluate overall SVO, we used the proportion of measures in which the participant was classified as prosocial (e.g., a participant deemed prosocial during all three methods received a score of 1) as the overall measure of SVO.

Table 11.3 displays the individual-level correlations between general trust and individualism-collectivism and the correlations of SVO prosociality with general trust and individualism-collectivism. In this analysis, we constructed vertical and horizontal IndCol by subtracting collectivism score from the respective individualism score. The individual-level results are very different from the national-level results shown in Figure 11.1. The overall pattern of correlations show that

TABLE 11.3. *Individual-Level Correlation Coefficients between and
Correlations of SVO Prosociality to Measures of General Trust,
Individualism-Collectivism*

	GSS_{trust}	T_{first}	$T_{personal}$	IGTS	$IGTS_{belif}$	$IGTS_{pref}$	SVO
vIndCol	−.15**	−.10*	−.16***	−.27****[4]	−.27****	−.17***	−.20***
hIndCol	−.22****	−.12**	−.23****	−.39****	−.35****	−.32****	−.21***
SVO	.22****	.06	.12**	.36****	.26****	.33****	−

Note. SOV = social value orientation.
$^*p < .001$, $^{**}p < .001$, $^{***}p < .001$, $^{****}p < .0001$.

TABLE 11.4. *Individual-Level Partial Correlation Coefficients between Measures of General Trust and Vertical and Horizontal Individualism-Collectivism, after controlling for SVO, Agreeableness, and Machiavellian Personality*

	GSS_{trust}	T_{first}	$T_{personal}$	IGTS	$IGTS_{belif}$	$IGTS_{pref}$
vIndCol	.04	−.02	−.02	−.04	−.05	−.00
hIndCol	.01	.00	−.07	−.16**	−.07	−.18***

Note. SOV = social value orientation.
** $p < .001$, *** $p < .0001$.

collectivism is positively associated with general trust (especially the IGTS measure of general trust).

A similar pattern was found between individualism-collectivism and trust in those the respondents knew personally ($T_{personal}$), and the correlations were stronger. As expected, measures of general trust, particularly IGTS, are positively correlated with SVO prosociality. Collectivism measures are positively correlated with SVO prosociality, although the correlations are weak, and individualism measures are negatively linked with SVO prosociality. The overall pattern in Table 11.3 shows that *collectivist beliefs and values are associated with prosocial dispositions and promote general trust, whereas individualistic beliefs and values, especially those associated with vertical individualism, reduce general trust and prosocial dispositions.* These findings are consistent with the naïve view of cultural individualism and collectivism mentioned earlier, equating collectivism with concerns for other people's welfare and individualism with lack of such concerns, at least at the individual difference level. In fact, SVO prosociality was negatively correlated both with vIndCol and with hIndCol.

We further analyzed personality traits included in our data set and found that the Big 5 Agreeableness trait was positively correlated and the Machiavellian Personality Scale was negatively correlated with both individualism-collectivism and general trust. When these trait variables were controlled, most of the correlations between individualism-collectivism and general trust were reduced to nonsignificant levels (see Table 11.4.). The within-country correlations (in Japan) seem to reflect more general personality traits such as agreeableness and manipulative tendency.

■ ECOLOGICAL CORRELATIONS

The inconsistency we found between individualism and general trust at the individual and macro levels is not unique to this particular example. Since the 1950s, scholars have known about a similar incongruity between the individual and macro levels, referred to as the *ecological correlation problem* (Robinson, 1950). The most well-known example is the relationship between the rate of illiteracy (not being able to read or write in English or any other language) and the percentage of immigrants at the macro level (such as the 50 states of the United States). A strong negative correlation ($r = -.53$)[8] existed in 1930 (per the US National

Census, for the population 10 years old and above) between the state illiteracy rate and the proportion of immigrants (people born outside the United States) in each respective state. This negative correlation indicates that the illiteracy rate was lower in states with more immigrants than in states with fewer immigrants.

However, this does not mean that immigrants were more literate than natives. In fact, at the individual level, the correlation between being illiterate and being born outside the United States was positive ($r = .12$); that is, immigrants were more likely to be illiterate than natives. Despite this positive relationship at the individual level, the pattern was reversed at the macro level; this means that the traits of the state that attracted immigrants caused the correlation at the state level, not the aggregation of the relationship between illiteracy and place of birth at the individual level. For example, immigrants might have been attracted to prosperous states where the general public was more educated.

The lack of cross-level correspondence between general trust and individualism-collectivism (mentioned earlier in this chapter) is another example of an ecological correlation, whereby the correlation's direction changes at the individual and macro levels, as in the example of immigration and illiteracy. In order to understand the meaning of the positive correlation in Figure 11.1, we now face the challenge of identifying the macro factor, which leads to positive links between individualism-collectivism and general trust at the macro level.

■ THE GENUINE MACRO FACTOR: AN EXAMPLE OF THE IMPACT OF TEACHING EFFECTIVENESS

The critical factor that produces an ecological correlation varies across macro units, such as the state or the country, and remains constant between individuals within each unit. To illustrate how a macro factor generates a macro-level correlation without producing the same link at the individual level, I use a hypothetical example of three elementary school teachers who vary in their teaching effectiveness. In Japan, one teacher is responsible for teaching a class of most required subjects such as language, mathematics, and science. Suppose that three instructors (A, B, and C) teach their respective classes on language, mathematics, and science. Instructor A is highly experienced and successfully teaches all three subjects. Teacher C lacks experience and has difficulty teaching any subjects. Teacher B is between A and C in her teaching effectiveness.

Suppose that all the children have taken the same aptitude tests on the three topics. The average scores will vary between the classes; the scores will be highest in Class A, intermediate in Class B, and lowest in Class C. As a result, positive correlations will emerge among the mean scores of the three subjects at the macro (class) level. The instructor's effectiveness is a genuine macro factor that differs only between classes (instructors) and remains constant across children in each class who are taught by the same instructor.

Because teaching effectiveness is a trait of the macro unit (i.e., the classroom/instructor), it cannot cause correlations among individual children in each class who have the same teacher. Although there might be correlations at the individual level, reflecting the children's family backgrounds and their overall learning abilities, the elements that lead to the individual-level correlation are independent of the instructor's ability. The genuine macro factor—such as the instructor's characteristics, which only vary at the macro level (between instructors)—is not an aggregation of individuals' traits, which are responsible for individual-level correlations (such as children's family backgrounds). There is no reason to expect consistency between the macro-level correlations that reflect differences in the instructors' qualities and the individual-level correlations that reflect unique differences in each child's abilities and family background.

■ SOCIAL INSTITUTIONS AS A GENUINE MACRO FACTOR

In this chapter, I focus on the social institution that produces and maintains social order in each society as a possible macro factor responsible for the correlation between individualism-collectivism and general trust at the national (but not the individual) level. By "institution," I mean a "self-sustaining system of shared beliefs about how the game is played" (rather than specific organizations such a police agencies or courts of law); this is how Masahiko Aoki, a renowned comparative institutional economist, uses the term (Aoki, 2001, p. 185).

In the context of this chapter, a social institution is *a situation where a group of people share beliefs about how to respond to specific actions by an individual,* such that the individual can expect which action would yield an outcome that favors him or her. An institution in this sense exists when individual actions that enhance expected outcomes for the actor collectively constitute a pattern of behavior consistent with the group's belief about the outcomes of actions. In short, individuals behave in a way that collectively makes the belief a reality—that is, the pattern of behavior taken by most members of the society; then the belief becomes self-sustaining.

Consider, for example, the use of bribery in some societies. People believe that a police officer will harass an innocent person for minor violations unless that person pays the officer a bribe. Thus individuals pay the bribe and expect a desirable outcome (e.g., escaping harassment). Most people who expect this result will pay the bribe. Such consequences make the belief a reality, which convinces people of the belief's validity.

In this chapter, I discuss two types of social institutions: one collectivist and the other individualist. When I use "individualism-collectivism," I am defining both parts of the term as features of macro social institutions, rather than the values and preferences of individuals. Macro social institutions create and maintain social order and vary across countries, but they affect the citizens of each nation in more or less similar ways (such as the instructor's teaching effectiveness in the example mentioned earlier).

In modern societies, social order is maintained through the legal system, which is enforced by various authoritative entities, such as the police and courts of law. The legal system protects all citizens against criminal victimization. In the absence of a functional, lawful framework supported by an impartial enforcement agency, citizens must find their own way to protect themselves against victimization (as assumed in Thomas Hobbes's famous phase in *Leviathan*, "the war of all against all").

To seek protection, people often form coalitions among like-minded individuals in which members help each other. I use the term *collectivist institution* to describe a situation in which individuals linked by closed relationships expect help and protection from their peers. In this sense, a collectivist institution provides social order within the bounds of a caring group setting (Greif, 1994). The world outside is a jungle where individuals must defend themselves against social predators.

The legal system protects those who do not live within collectivist institutions and makes it possible to seek opportunities outside them. The legal system thus encourages actions such as trade, which benefit opportunity-seeking activities across groups (as in the case of Roman laws that facilitated trading in the Roman Empire). Through encouraging the opportunity-seeking activities outside strong-tie networks, the rule of law nurtures psychological and behavioral traits that help people successfully explore opportunities (Yamagishi, 1998/2011).

I use "individualistic social institution" to describe a situation where the legal system provides social order and allows people to act independently of the constraints posed by networks of strong ties. In societies where the rule of law is not fully established, the need for group protection is much higher, causing people to forego outside opportunities.

■ BEHAVIORAL AND PSYCHOLOGICAL ADAPTATIONS TO MACRO INSTITUTIONS

The differences in macro institutions generate societal distinctions in psychological and behavioral traits, including general trust. These qualities fall under the rubric of individualism-collectivism at the macro level but do not necessarily create associations between traits within each society.[9] In order to adapt to individualistic social institutions, people must acquire certain psychological and behavioral characteristics that are subsumed under the rubric of independent self-construal, which are largely different from the characteristics that are summarized as the interdependent self-construal needed to adapt to a collectivist social institution.

Those who aspire to succeed in individualistic social institutions face the challenge of exploring opportunities while minimizing the potential risk that prevails outside networks. They deal with prospective interaction partners whose behavior is not restricted by the mutual monitoring and sanctioning of strong ties. While the legal system regulates possible risks to a certain extent, people must cope with remaining risks on their own.

One way to cope with these risks is to develop a specific type of social intelligence to select the right people to interact with and to acquire the ability to discern internal traits—such as honesty and trustworthiness—of potential interaction partners. In addition, a person must be honest about his or her own traits and communicate to prospective partners that he or she shares similar qualities. If a potential partner knows the other person has similar traits, the partner's desire to interact increases.

North Americans and western Europeans tend to focus attention on a focal figure (Masuda & Nisbett, 2001, 2006) and seek causes of an interaction partner's behavior inside that person (this process is known as *internal attribution*; Masuda & Kitayama, 2004; Miyamoto & Kitayama, 2002). North Americans and western Europeans practice internal attribution more often than East Asians, because it is part of the general strategy of adapting to individualistic institutions.

In addition to acquiring competency to discern the internal traits of potential interaction partners such as trustworthiness, those living in the individualistic institutions must successfully signal to prospective interaction partners that they too have similar internal traits as a desirable interaction partner such as honesty and trustworthiness. That is, adapting to an individualistic social order requires a person to have the social intelligence to figure out others' internal traits and the willingness and skills to make his or her future behavior predictable to others.

People can make their behavior predictable by acting in a consistent way that others can anticipate (see the discussion of the commitment problem in economics, e.g., Frank, 1988). The human disposition toward cognitive consistency is more strongly observed in North America and western Europe than East Asia (e.g., Heine & Lehman, 1997); this finding of cultural psychology can be seen as a part of the adaptive strategy under the individualistic institution.

Another way to make oneself predictable is to express one's private thoughts, values, and intentions—a tendency that is more widespread in North America and western Europe than East Asia. Thus the core of adapting to individualistic social orders is comprised of focusing on others' character traits, making oneself predictable by adhering to consistent behavioral principles, and expressing one's thoughts. We call this type of adaptive strategy[10] an individualistic one, because the goal is to promote interacting with those who are not connected by strong ties (Granovetter, 1973).

In a collectivist social institution created by a system of strong ties, another type of adaptive strategy—namely, a collectivist strategy—will prevail. Recent theoretical studies in mathematical biology (e.g., Nowak & Sigmund, 2005) explain the evolution of cooperation through indirect reciprocity. Indirect reciprocity is a strategy (a behavioral principle) of acting altruistically toward people who have a reputation of being nice and who likewise behave kindly. In a group where the majority behaves in an indirect, reciprocal manner, having a positive reputation promotes one's welfare, because it encourages others to help that individual and provide him or her with resources. In order to build a good reputation, an individual must act selflessly toward people who also behave altruistically. Thus those who aim to create positive reputations in a system of indirect reciprocity voluntarily cooperate and behave altruistically toward others who have good reputations. Mathematical models indicate that the behavioral principle of indirect reciprocity and the resulting state of group cooperation can emerge under some conditions (Nowak & Sigmund, 2005; Ohtsuki, Hauert, Lieberman, & Nowak, 2006).

The logic of indirect reciprocity lies at the core of the collectivist institution. Being nice to people allows one to receive kind treatment from others in the system. Under the collectivist social order, individuals must acquire the necessary resources only from others in the network. Only those who maintain a positive reputation in the network can successfully acquire the necessary resources. Thus sensitivity and a willingness to accommodate others' needs lie at the core of the collectivist strategy for survival in the collectivist institution. People living in collectivist institutions protect each other, help each other, and acquire indispensable resources from those within their network; they cannot survive once they lose the protection and help the network provides.

Naturally, they will develop a shared belief that humans cannot be independent from others, and they will understand the need to value strong ties (which is called *interdependent self-construal* in cultural psychology; Markus & Kitayama, 1991). Collectivist social orders thus foster collectivist beliefs, though individuals in the same collectivist institution will have differences, reflecting their need to depend on strong ties for survival.

■ THE RULE OF LAW PROMOTES INDIVIDUALISM AND GENERAL TRUST AT THE SOCIETAL LEVEL

The rule of law allows individuals to pursue their personal goals outside closed relationships. Willingness to have general trust or give someone the benefit of the doubt encourages people to venture into the social sphere, where protections from strong ties are absent. Figure 11.2 provides a support to this argument about the macro factor, which is responsible for the macro-level correlation between individualism-collectivism and general trust. Figure 11.2 displays the relationships between the following factors:

1. *The rule of law index* composed by the World Bank (the Worldwide Governance Indicators; http://www.worldbank.ord/) (horizontal axis). According to the Worldwide Governance Indicators[11] prepared by the World Bank, the rule of law index "captures perceptions of the extent to which agents have confidence in and abide by the rules of society, and in particular the quality of contract enforcement, property rights, the police, and the courts, as well as the likelihood of crime and violence."
2. *The mean level of individualism-collectivism* (left vertical axis).
3. *General trust* (trust in the person whom the respondent meets for the first time; right vertical axis).

The rule of law index has a positive linear effect ($\beta = .64$, $p < .0001$, Adj$R^2 = .40$) on individualism-collectivism when the rule of law index was used as the sole independent variable. When the quadratic effect (from the rule of law index) is added, the linear effect stays significant ($\beta = .48$, $p = .003$), and the quadratic effect is not significant ($\beta = .22$, $p = .174$; Adj$R^2 = .41$). The linear effect of the rule of law index on general trust is significant ($\beta = .60$, $p < .0001$, Adj$R^2 = .40$). When the quadratic effect is added, the linear effect becomes statistically marginal ($\beta = .26$, $p = .097$), whereas the quadratic effect emerges as significant ($\beta = .47$, $p < .003$; Adj$R^2 = .41$). As shown in Figure 11.2, an increase in the rule of law affects the level of individualism-collectivism across its whole range. The positive effect of the rule

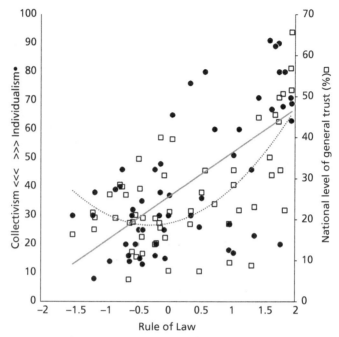

Figure 11.2. The rule of law index (the Worldwide Governance Indicators, the World Bank; http://www.worldbank.ord/) as it relates to individualism-collectivism (left vertical axis, country indicated with black dots) and the percentage of positive responses (see Figure 11.1) to a question about the level of trust in "people you meet for the first time" (right vertical axis with white squares).

of law index on general trust starts later; the rule of law has a weak, negative effect on general trust until it reaches around zero or the global mean level.

Figure 11.2 shows that individualism and general trust are positively linked to the rule of law (at least once it reaches mid-level). However, other factors, such as national prosperity reflected in per capita GDP, could be responsible for a spurious relationship between the rule of law and individualism; thus per capita GDP was controlled in order to test for this possibility. Table 11.5 displays the results of a series of regression analyses, which examined how controlling for per capita GDP affects the relationships between the rule of law and the two variables. First, Table 11.5 reveals that per capita GDP strongly impacts the country's levels of general trust and individualism-collectivism (Model I). However, controlling for per capita GDP does not greatly influence the rule of law's effect on general trust or individualism-collectivism (Model III), and the effects of the rule of law and its quadratic term stayed at about the same level as those observed when per capita GDP was not controlled (Model II). These results show that the rule of law's effect on general trust and individualism-collectivism is not a spurious one caused by national economic prosperity.

TABLE 11.5. *The Effect of Per Capita GDP on General Trust and Individualism-Collectivism*

dv = General Trust	I	II	III
Per-capita GDP	.51••••		.06
Rule of Law		.22	.21
Rule of Law²		.48••••	.46••••
R² (adjusted)	.24	.42	.41
dv = Ind-Col			
Per-capita GDP	.46•••		−.02
Rule of Law		.63••••	.68••••
R² (adjusted)	.20	.38	.41

Note. GDP = gross domestic product.
•• $p < .01$, ••• $p < .001$, •••• $p < .0001$.

Figures 11.3 and 11.4 further support the view that social order based on the rule of law fosters individualism and general trust. The horizontal axis of these two figures is another index created by the World Bank to measure political stability and the absence of violence and terrorism. This second index "captures perceptions of the likelihood that the government will be destabilised or overthrown by unconstitutional or violent means, including politically-motivated violence and terrorism." These numbers suggest that a high level of individualism and general

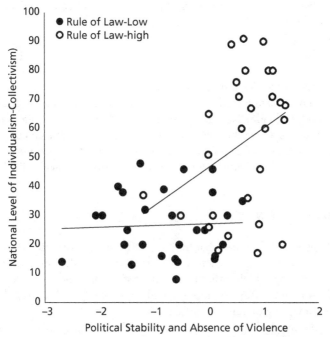

Figure 11.3. Political stability and the absence of violence index, provided by the World Bank (the Worldwide Governance Indicators, http://www.worldbank.ord/), and the national level of individualism vis-à-vis collectivism.

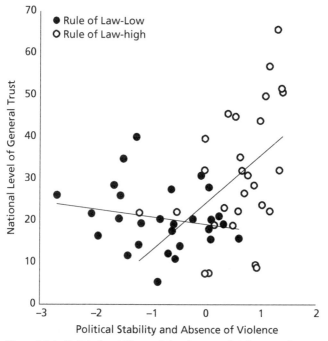

Figure 11.4. Political stability and the absence of violence index, provided by the World Bank (Worldwide Governance Indicators, http://www.worldbank.ord/), and the national level of general trust.

trust requires a stable form of governance via the rule of law. In countries where the rule of law is firmly established (white circles), improving political stability increases both individualism and general trust, whereas improving political stability in countries where the rule of law is weak does not have an effect on these elements. This suggests that political stability maintained by means other than the rule of law (e.g., via dictatorial governance) does not enhance individualism or general trust.

■ CONCLUSION

In this chapter, I have argued that individualistic social institutions based on the rule of law promote a set of beliefs, which are normally called the culture of "individualism." Having a high level of general trust—that is, not limiting the radius of trust (van Hoorn, 2015) to those bonded via strong ties—is part of the general strategy for adapting to individualistic institutions.

These adaptive strategies free people from depending on networks of strong ties and influence them to pursue their personal goals at their own risk (which lessens when the legal system provides protection). General trust encourages individuals to seek relationships with new prospective partners and pursue actions that bring them out of their secure but narrow circle of security; general distrust and the belief that "everyone is a thief" discourages people from doing so.

In the absence of legal protection, those who depend on a network would be better off staying under the security of a strong-tie network than leaving it in search of better opportunities. Leaving the circle of secure connections could be maladaptive in the absence of legal protection, because the outside world seems too dangerous. When giving the benefit of the doubt to an unknown person is too risky, individuals should not have a high level of general trust; rather, they should only trust those with whom they are connected by strong ties.

The individualistic social institution provides a macro-level foundation where general trust plays an adaptive role, encouraging people to pursue opportunities at their own risk. This results in a national-level correlation between individualism and general trust. However, this positive correlation (caused by institutional differences) on the national scale has no counterpart at the individual level. Citizens in each country face the same institutional arrangements that foster or suppress general trust for most residents. As illustrated in the earlier example of classroom teaching, the factors that produce within-group correlations (such as students' family backgrounds) can be independent of the factors that produce between-group correlations (such as teachers' effectiveness). Psychological dispositions, such as agreeableness and manipulative tendencies, could produce a connection between collectivism and general trust at the individual level. However, such individual level mechanisms for generating the collectivism-general trust correlation functions independent of the effect of the macro, institutional factors.

Cross-level comparisons of the relationship between individualism-collectivism and general trust provide fertile ground for understanding how macro factors function. Such understanding often escapes the attention of researchers who investigate social dilemmas from a psychological perspective. Since many real-life solutions to social dilemmas are only possible when certain macro factors are present, it is especially important to focus on cross-level comparisons when studying these dilemmas. For example, punishing people who violate social norms works well in societies where the rule of law prevails but not in societies where the rule of law is weak (Herman, Thöni, & Gächter, 2008). There is much room to improve social dilemmas research by focusing on macro institutional factors.

■ NOTES

1. This question has been included in the list of questions in the WVS since the 2005–2008 wave. In countries where this question was asked in both waves, I reported the responses in the 2010–2014 wave. I used responses to this question, rather than responses to the more widely used one: "Generally speaking, would you say that most people can be trusted, or that you can't be too careful in dealing with people?" This latter question is a double-barreled one; the first choice—that people can be trusted—is clearly about trust. The second choice—that one cannot be too careful in dealing with people—is about prudence. Yamagishi (1998/2011; Yamagishi & Yamagishi, 1994; Yamagishi, Cook, & Watabe, 1998) argues that being careful in social situations does not indicate a lack of general trust. Trustful people might realize the need to be wary in certain contexts. The need to be

prudent reflects the nature of the social environment, rather than the individual's levels of general trust in the society.

2. A slightly stronger correlation ($r = -.67$, $p < .0001$) is seen between the same measure of general trust and the level of in-group collectivism used in the GLOBE study of 62 countries (House, Hanges, Javidan, Dorfman, & Gupta, 2004). The link between Hofstede's individualism-collectivism and House et al.'s in-group collectivism is strong ($r = -.76$, $p < .0001$). This chapter uses that measure of individualism-collectivism, rather than the GLOBE measure of in-group collectivism, because using the former increased the number of countries included in the analysis.

3. The World Bank Database (http://www.worldbank.org/data/home.aspx) for 2012. The per capita GDP reported here is expressed in the international dollar equivalent for the purchasing power of the US dollar in the United States.

4. The partial correlation is $r = -.59$, $p < .0001$, when House et al.'s (2004) in-group collectivism is used.

5. See Yamagishi (1998/2011) for the claim that general trust is the willingness to give someone the benefit of the doubt (to assume a person is trustworthy until proven otherwise), rather than unconditionally expecting that all people are trustworthy.

6. A part of this study has been reported in Yamagishi, Li, Takagishi, Matsumoto, and Kiyonari (2014).

7. Personal trust is conceptually distinct from general trust; personal trust is included in the table to see if it reveals a different pattern of correlation with individualism-collectivism at the individual level.

8. Grotenhuis, Eisinga, and Subramanian (2011) point out some problems with Robinson's original method of calculating correlations, but for the purpose of this chapter, their revised ones are not much different.

9. When different sectors of a country, such as social classes, are under the influence of their own institutions, a within-country correlation can be generated as a between-segment correlation.

10. The term *strategy* is used here as it is used in evolutionary and behavioral biology, not as a conscious, rational choice.

11. "These aggregate indicators combine the views of a large number of enterprise, citizen and expert survey respondents in industrial and developing countries. They are based on 32 individual data sources produced by a variety of survey institutes, think tanks, nongovernmental organizations, international organizations, and private sector firms" (http://info.worldbank.org/governance/wgi/index.aspx#home).

■ REFERENCES

Aoki, M. (2001). *Toward a comparative institutional analysis.* Cambridge, MA: MIT Press.

Frank, R. H. (1988). *Passions within reason: The strategic role of emotions.* New York: W. W. Norton.

Granovetter, M. S. (1973). The strength of weak ties. *American Journal of Sociology, 78*(6), 1360–1380.

Greif, A. (1994). Cultural beliefs and the organization of society: A historical and theoretical reflection on collectivist and individualist societies. *Journal of Political Economy, 102,* 912–950.

Grotenhuis, M. T., Eisinga, R., & Surramanian, S. (2011). Robinson's *Ecological Correlations and the Behavior of Individuals*; methodological corrections. *International Journal of Epidemiology, 40*, 1123-1125.

Heine, S. J., & Lehman, D. R. (1997). Culture, dissonance, and self-affirmation. *Personality and Social Psychology Bulletin, 23*, 389-400.

House, R. J., Hanges, P. J., Javidan, M., Dorfman, P. W., & Gupta, V. (2004). *Culture, leadership, and organizations: The GLOBE study of 62 societies.* Thousand Oaks, CA: SAGE.

Liebrand, W. B. G. (1984). The effect of social motives, communication and group size on behavior in an N-person multi-stage mixed-motive game. *European Journal of Social Psychology, 14*, 239-264.

Markus, H., & Kitayama, S. (1991). Culture and the self: Implications for cognition, emotion, and motivation. *Psychological Bulletin, 98*, 224-253.

Masuda, T., & Kitayama, S. (2004). Perceived-induced constraint and attitude attribution in Japan and in the US: A case for cultural dependence of the correspondence bias. *Journal of Experimental Social Psychology, 40*, 409-416.

Masuda, T., & Nisbett, R. (2001). Attending holistically vs. analytically: Comparing context sensitivity of Japanese and Americans. *Journal of Personality and Social Psychology, 81*, 922-934.

Masuda, T., & Nisbett, R. (2006). Culture and change blindness. *Cognitive Science, 30*, 381-399.

Miyamoto, Y., & Kitayama, S. (2002). Cultural variation in correspondence bias: The critical role of attitude diagnosticity of socially constrained behavior. *Journal of Personality and Social Psychology, 83*, 1239-1248.

Murphy, R. O., Ackermann, K. A., & Handgraaf, M. J. (2011). Measuring social value orientation. *Judgment and Decision Making, 6*, 771-781.

Nowak, M. A, & Sigmund, K (2005). Evolution of indirect reciprocity by image scoring. *Nature, 393*, 573-577.

Ohtsuki, H., Hauert, C., Lieberman, E., & Nowak, M. A. (2006). A simple rule for the evolution of cooperation on graphs. *Nature, 441*, 502-505.

Putnam, R. D. (2000). *Bowling alone: The collapse and revival of American community.* New York: Simon & Schuster.

Robinson, W. S. (1950). Ecological correlations and the behavior of individuals. *American Sociological Review, 15*, 351-357.

Singelis, T. M., Triandis, H. C., Bhawuk, D. P., & Gelfand, M. J. (1995). Horizontal and vertical dimensions of individualism and collectivism: A theoretical and measurement refinement. *Cross-Cultural Research, 29*, 240-275.

Van Hoorn, A. (2015). Individualist–collectivist culture and trust radius: A multilevel approach. *Journal of Cross-Cultural Psychology, 46*, 269-276.

Van Lange, P. A. M., Otten, W., De Bruin, E. M. N., & Joireman, J. A. (1997). Development of prosocial, individualistic, and competitive orientations: Theory and preliminary evidence. *Journal of Personality and Social Psychology, 73*, 733-746.

Yamagishi, T. (1998). *Shinrai no kozo: Kokoroto shakaino shinnka geemu.* Tokyo: Tokyo University Press. [*Trust: The evolutionary game of mind and society*]. (English edition: New York: Springer, 2011)

Yamagishi, T. (2011). Micro-macro dynamics of the cultural construction of reality: A niche construction approach to culture. *Advances in Culture and Psychology, 1*, 251-308.

Yamagishi, T., Akutsu, S., Cho, K., Inoue, Y., Li, Y., & Matsumoto, Y. (2015). Two component models of general trust: Predicting behavioral trust from attitudinal trust. *Social Cognition, 33*(5), 436–458.

Yamagishi, T., Cook, K. S., & Watabe, M. (1998). Uncertainty, trust and commitment formation in the United States and Japan. *American Journal of Sociology, 104*, 165–194.

Yamagishi, T., Li, Y., Takagishi, H., Matsumoto, Y., & Kiyonari, T. (2014). In search of Homo economicus. *Psychological Science, 25*, 1699–1711.

Yamagishi, T., Mifune, N., Li, Y., Shinada, M., Hashimoto, H., Horita, Y., . . . Simunovic, D. (2013). Is behavioral pro-sociality game-specific? Pro-social preference and expectations of pro-sociality. *Organizational Behavior and Human Decision Processes, 120*, 260–271.

Yamagishi, T., & Yamagishi, M. (1994). Trust and commitment in the United States and Japan. *Motivation and Emotion, 18*, 129–166.

12 The Influence of Globalization and Ethnic Fractionalization on Cooperation and Trust in Kenya

■ NANCY R. BUCHAN AND ROBERT ROLFE

■ INTRODUCTION

The commodities boom in the past decade has helped spark the greatest surge of economic growth Sub-Saharan Africa has experienced since the 1960s (Leke, Lund, Roxburgh, & van Wamelen, 2010). In the past decade, Sub-Saharan African countries have democratized their governments and liberalized their economies (Radelet, 2010), becoming more integrated with the global economy. They have opened their borders to foreign investors and have attracted investments in natural resources projects and agricultural ventures.

While freer economies and political systems have brought accolades from the governments of the United States and European Union, these reforms may actually create more instability by exacerbating existing tensions. The degree of ethnic fractionalization present in many African countries and its effect on economic growth and political stability has long been debated. Traditionally, researchers believed that Africa's high level of ethnic fractionalization, especially when combined with exploitable natural resources, such as minerals or oil, has led to political instability, ethnic conflict, and low economic growth (Easterly & Levine, 1997). Free markets and increasing globalization tend to concentrate spectacular wealth in the hands of a resented business-controlling ethnic minority; in contrast, the majority populations in these countries feel comparatively few of the positive effects of globalization (Chau, 2002).

Conversely, others suggest that ethnic fractionalization can have positive effects by weakening tribal or local identities. Lentz (1995) states that there is a "detribalization" occurring as rural populations in Africa migrate to the cities, flooding urban areas with hosts of immigrants, essentially fragmenting the racial population and reducing the relevance of parochial identities. These weakened local identities may have positive effects for trust among the population and national-level cooperation.

This chapter explores the impact of ethnic fractionalization and globalization on generalized trust and national cooperation in Kenya. Like most countries in Africa, Kenya has a very heterogeneous population with more than 40 different ethnic groups speaking almost 70 different languages (Kenya National Bureau of Statistics, 2010), with each ethnic group tending to form ethnically based enclaves wherever they reside in the country. This diversity has complicated the development of a national identity, and even though the country has been independent for 50 years, many Kenyans still identify themselves primarily with their own ethnic groups and not the nation as a whole (Bratton & Kimenyi, 2008).

We focus on how ethnic fractionalization and globalization affect the levels of trust and cooperation individual Kenyans extend to one another in an experimental public goods game in which players contribute to, and benefit from, a national account. Participants were literate Kenyan male and female adults, ages 18 to 60, from two of Kenya's largest ethnic groups: the Kikuyu and the Luo. We conducted the experiments in Nairobi, the very ethnically fragmented capital, and in two ethnically homogeneous rural areas. Individual levels of trust and globalization were measured via questionnaire following the experiment.

In the next sections we review previous studies examining ethnic fractionalization, globalization, and cooperation. A brief overview of ethnicity and globalization in Kenya is discussed in order to provide a context for this study's hypotheses. This is followed by a description of the experiment methodology. An analysis of the results and discussion of their implications then follow.

■ ETHNIC FRACTIONALIZATION, TRUST, AND COOPERATION

Research in economics and political science suggests that high levels of ethnic fractionalization may impede national-level cooperation; ethnic divisions increase the difficulty of establishing links across groups, negatively affecting the development of trust and cooperation. For example, Putnam (2007) asserts that ethnic diversity tends to reduce trust and cooperation because members of ethnic groups "hunker down" in their own communities and emphasize parochial interests over those of a wider collective. Similarly, Alesina and La Ferrara (2005) concluded that a neighborhood's ethnic diversity negatively affected participation in social activities in the United States. Lancee and Dronkers (2008) found this also to be valid for ethnically diverse neighborhoods in the Netherlands, while Reilly and Phillpot (2002) suggest that higher ethnic fractionalization impeded the development of social capital in Papua New Guinea. They concluded that a high level of ethnic fractionalization can hinder the development of social capital and national cooperation, threatening political stability and the attractiveness of the business environment. Furthermore, when people living in an ethnically diverse community believe that public goods will benefit other groups or the mix of those goods is different from what they would have preferred, they may decide to lower their compliance with tax laws and other forms of cooperation (Lassen, 2007); large informal sectors are likely to result.

These conclusions may also be valid for Africa. In an analysis of eight African countries, Zerfu et al. (2008) established that residents in large African cities (which are typically highly ethnically fragmented) were less trusting of other groups. Similarly, Collier (1998) demonstrated empirically that high ethnic diversity lowers the level of trust in Sub-Saharan Africa. Living in a large, diverse urban area may actually strengthen ethnic allegiances. Eifert et al. (2010) found strong evidence that Africans in the modern sector of the economy are more likely to identify in ethnic terms than those in the more traditional or informal sectors. The identity politics employed by politicians reminds citizens of their differences. Less social capital is built, which fosters less cooperation between ethnic groups nationally (Collier, 1998).

Nairobi, like many capital cities in Africa, is very ethnically diverse. Virtually all of Kenya's ethnic groups are represented in the city of 4 million people with the Kikuyu (30%), Kamba (19%), Luhya (16%), and Luo (14%) forming the largest groups (Kenya Bureau of Statistics, 2010). Over 70% of the people live in more than 100 slums surrounding the central business district. In contrast, scattered throughout the countryside are the traditional homelands of various ethnic groups, resulting in geographic areas that are much more homogeneous. Research demonstrating that trust and cooperation are lower in ethnically fractionalized areas suggests that participants in this research, who are living in ethnically fragmented Nairobi, will be less cooperative on a national level than those living in homogeneous countryside locations.

H1a: Participants from the highly ethnically fragmented city of Nairobi will be less trusting and cooperative with others from their country than will be participants from the ethnically homogeneous countryside locations.

In contrast, other researchers have concluded that urbanization can actually weaken ethnic divisions by reducing the relevance of ethnicity. Increased interethnic exposure may lead to reduction in interethnic conflict (Pettigrew & Tropp, 2006) and high-quality personal contact with people of other ethnicities can lead to higher generalized trust (Stolle et al., 2008). The theory of "detribalization" from anthropology suggests that immigration in African countries from rural areas to the cities yields urban areas that are highly fragmented ethnically but with a noticeable weakening of parochial tribal identities (Lentz, 1995).

These studies suggest that research participants in ethnically fragmented Nairobi would be more generally trusting and cooperative with others nationally than participants in more ethnically homogeneous areas in the countryside.

H1b: Participants from the highly ethnically fragmented city of Nairobi will be more cooperative with others from their country than will be participants from the ethnically homogeneous countryside locations.

■ GLOBALIZATION, TRUST, AND COOPERATION

Theories regarding the influence of globalization on trust and cooperation tend to fall into two camps. The first suggests that increases in the frequency and intensity of global economic, cultural, and social exchanges are often accompanied by increases in general trust toward unknown others. Access to new economic, cultural, and social resources afforded by globalization—as well as the diffusion of international non governmental organizations, which provide a "global framework through which trustworthy behavior can be interpreted" (Polillo, 2012, p. 48)—may prompt people to be more accepting toward others out of a moral obligation toward global values such as universalism or tolerance (Polillo,2012).

This argument is compatible with those who suggest that rather than reinforcing parochialism, globalization (which includes indicators such as immigration and increased exposure to ethnic groups other than one's own) weakens the relevance of ethnicity or locality as sources of identity such that individuals overcome the in-group/out-group tension of parochialism (Beck, 2006; Hannerz, 1992) and experience a sense of common belonging merely by virtue of inhabiting the same planet; humankind becomes a "we" where there are no "others" (Giddens, 1990).

Supporting this theory, Buchan et al. (2009) demonstrated in a multicountry cooperation experiment that as country and individual levels of globalization increase, individual cooperation at the global level vis-à-vis the local level also increases. In essence, "globalized" individuals draw broader group boundaries than others, eschewing parochial motivations in favor of cosmopolitan ones. Cooperation with the distal other becomes more likely as people come to identify with others beyond their local group (Buchan et al. 2011) be they national or global.

This would lead us to hypothesize that individual-level globalization is positively related to generalized trust and national cooperation.

H2a: Participants in this study with higher individual levels of globalization will demonstrate higher levels of general trust and cooperation with other Kenyans than will participants with lower individual levels of globalization.

Yet there is recognition that globalization is an uneven process and that the positive impacts of globalization may be offset by tensions arising between those who benefit from globalization and those who do not. In the Global South, globalization is not only associated with increases in foreign direct investment but also with increases in income inequality (Kentor, 2001). In his analysis of trust determinants in 100 countries, Bjørnskov (2008) demonstrated that economic inequality and political disparity, not ethnic diversity, have a significant negative impact on trust. Furthermore, Alesina et.al. (2012) demonstrate that fractionalization by itself does not negatively impact a country's economic performance. Using micro-data in 17 African countries, they showed that it is the combination of fractionalization with ethnic inequality that strongly negatively impacts per capita income. Controlling for various individual characteristics, including ethnicity, participants had lower education levels and inferior public goods when they lived in areas with high ethnic inequality. In sum, these theories suggest that globalization influences social trust in two ways, first by increasing income inequality and also by undermining the sense of a shared fate within society (Polillo 2012; Uslander 2002).

Majority populations in countries such as Kenya feel little of the positive effects of globalization when comparing themselves to the rich ethnic minority (Ayenagbo et al., 2012). In this research we contrast participants from the Luo ethnic group living in Kendu Bay, a rural part of Nyanza Province[1] and a particularly marginalized area of Kenya, with participants living in Nairobi and in Central Province, the two wealthiest parts of Kenya. Central Province is the homeland of the Kikuyu, Kenya's largest ethnic group (21% of the population). They are also the largest ethnic group in Nairobi. The Kikuyu group is perceived by many Kenyans as having done very well after independence (Chua, 2002). Three of Kenya's four presidents have been Kikuyu, and the tribe has a reputation for its competitive business skills. Nyanza Province is the homeland of the Luo group, traditional rivals of the Kikuyu (Branch, 2011). They are the fourth largest group in the country (12%) and the fourth largest in Nairobi (14%). Luo tradition in Nyanza Province maintains they were once elite but were forced into abject poverty because of a jealous Kikuyu enemy (Hornsby, 2013; Morrison, 2006). The differences in social well-being between Nyanza Province, Nairobi, and Central Province, the homeland of the Kikuyu, are striking. The poverty rate in Nyanza Province, at 70%, is twice that of Central Province and more than 50% higher than that in Nairobi. This disparity extends to infrastructure: 31.6% of the people in Nyanza Province have access to water within 15 minutes compared to 71% of the people in Central Province and 96% in Nairobi. Access to electricity is almost four times higher in Central Province (19.2%) and 14 times higher in Nairobi than it is in Nyanza Province (5.1%). Health measures are just as skewed, with infant mortality three times higher in Nyanza Province than in Central Province and twice as high as in Nairobi. The HIV rate in Nyanza Province is the highest in the country, and only 38% of the children in Nyanza have received all of their recommended vaccinations compared to 79% in Central Province and 63% in Nairobi (Society for International Development, 2004).

Kenyans perceive most of the benefits from Kenya's economic boom going to the capital and small segments of the population such as Kenyans of Asian ancestry and to the Kikuyu, the president's own ethnic group (Barkan, 2011). The Luo in Nyanza Province particularly feel marginalized. Nyanza Province's large cotton industry collapsed with globalization while its fishing industry suffered from climate change and erratic international markets (Ohito, 2005). In contrast, Nairobi and the Kikuyu's Central Province prospered with the development of new horticultural markets in Europe, major infrastructure projects, and increased tourism (Muuru, 2009).

Based on the studies emphasizing the importance of ethnic inequality and the negative influence of globalization, we would anticipate that the Luo living in Kendu Bay in Nyanza Province, the most economically marginalized group in the study, will be less trusting and cooperative nationally than the other groups participating in this study.

H2a: We expect trust and national-level cooperation among the Luo participants from Kendu Bay to be lower than the cooperation exhibited by participants from Central Province and Nairobi.

■ METHOD

In this research, participants make a series of decisions regarding public goods. Public goods represent a large-scale social dilemma; everyone collectively is better off if all contribute to the good, but any single individual can maximize his or her own wealth by free riding on others' contributions (Dawes, 1980). Examples of public goods include collective efforts to ration water in times/locations of scarcity, providing safe public parks, or preventing the spread of infectious diseases. We studied people's level of cooperation when these public goods decisions involved groups of people from their own community locally, other people within Kenya, and other people from around the world. For purposes of this particular research, we focus only on the national cooperation, that is, contributions to the Kenyan public good.

We sampled Kikuyu and Luo participants from relatively more rural locations and from Nairobi, settings that differ in levels of ethnic fractionalization. Nairobi is highly ethnically fragmented with all 14 of Kenya's tribes represented plus many people of other nationalities due to immigration. Karatina in the Central Province is populated by nearly 100% Kikuyu individuals, and Kendu Bay in the Nyanza Province comprises nearly 100% Luo individuals. Notably, the research participants were not college students, as is traditional for experimental research, but instead were drawn from the general population. Eligible participants were required to be members of the particular ethnic group, ages 18 to 60, male or female, with at least a fourth-grade education level. The "real citizens" nature of our research population provides greater external validity to the research and to any policy implications that result.

Recruitment was done in places where it was determined a random sample of the population gathers, such as a community center or bus station. Participants were paid the purchasing power equivalent of US$8 as a show-up fee. Participants randomly chose an identification number to identify themselves throughout the experiment; never were participants' names or other personally identifying information provided to the researchers or to other participants. To the extent possible, participants were isolated from one another so that privacy was maintained throughout the experiment. A minimum of four participants participated in each session. Average total take-home earnings from the experiment were the purchasing power equivalent of US$30.

Experimental Paradigm

Individual propensities to cooperate with national others were assessed in a multilevel sequential contribution (MSC) experiment. The MSC protocol resembles that of a standard multilevel public goods experiment (Blackwell &

McKee, 2003; Wit & Kerr, 2002). The full experiment consisted of three contribution decisions—the local, national, and global public goods. In the current research we focus only on the national decision data.[2] For each decision participants were given 10 tokens. One token was worth the purchasing power equivalent of US$0.50.

At each session's start, participants were told that they would be making decisions with other people, some of whom were from their local community (but perhaps not currently in the room), some from elsewhere in the same country, and some from other countries. Furthermore, they were informed that some participants may have already made their decisions; the participant's choices and the choices of others would be matched by computer and payoffs in real money would be determined. Participants received payoffs at the end of the experiment, thus no feedback was provided regarding decisions during the session.

In the Local Decision, participants faced the same incentives as in a standard public goods game. This two-choice decision familiarized participants with the experimental task and established baseline levels of cooperation. In the Local Decision, participants decided how to allocate tokens between their "personal" and "local" accounts. Each token put into the personal account was saved and worth a single token. Each token put into the local account was doubled by the experimenter and shared equally between the participant and three other (anonymous) participants from the same local area. Likewise, the participant received an equal share from the tokens that the other three local participants put into their local accounts. Therefore, the return to each individual for each token allocated to the local account—the marginal per capita return (MPCR)—was 0.5. In contrast, the return to the group—the marginal social return (MSR)—equaled 2. Selfish individuals would allocate all their tokens to their personal account because of its larger return relative to the collective account. If all individuals are selfish, each participant would keep his or her initial 10 tokens. In contrast, if all individuals of a group chose to allocate their endowment to their local accounts, each group member would receive a 20-token payoff.

After the instructions were read, participants worked several example decisions to make sure they understood the nature of the task and the effects of their own and others' choices on their outcomes. Finally, participants made their actual allocations by putting red tokens into envelopes labeled "Personal" and "Local." An experiment assistant collected the envelopes and took them into the control room where the tokens were recorded in the algorithm and payoffs calculated.

In the National Decision participants chose how much to allocate among their personal account, their local account, and their "Kenya" account. The structure of incentives of the personal and local accounts was identical to that of the Local Decision. Tokens placed in the Kenya account were instead *tripled* by the experimenter and split equally among a "Kenya" group of 12 people. The Kenya group was made up of the participant, a new group of three (anonymous) local people benefitting from the local account, plus two groups of four people from different areas in Kenya. Participants were not told which specific areas these other participants were from but were informed that these areas were from any of the three areas where the research was being conducted. Each participant received a one-twelfth share of the allocations that all 12 people made to their Kenya accounts.

The MPCR from allocations to the Kenya account equals .25; less than the MPCR from the local account, .50. In contrast, the MSR of contributions to the Kenya account equals 3.0, larger than the MSR of the local account, 2.0. Consequently, if all individuals allocated their endowment to their Kenya account in the Kenya Decision, this would result in a larger payoff (30 tokens) to each participant than if all allocated their endowment to their local accounts (20 tokens). This structure of incentives characterizes a multilevel public goods dilemma. A contribution to a higher order public good typically benefits a larger number of people but at a smaller rate of return than a contribution to a lower order public good.

Again, participants completed several example decisions to be certain they understood the nature of the nested global public good. Participants then made their allocations by putting yellow tokens into envelopes labeled "Personal," "Local," and "Kenya," and the envelopes were collected. The global public good was conducted next and was structured analogously to the Kenyan public good.

Figure 12.1 illustrates how the national public good works. Assume a participant put all 10 tokens in the "Personal" envelope. Others put a total of 10 blue tokens in their "Luo community in Nairobi" envelopes. Finally, 12 blue tokens are put in the "Kenya" envelopes. Those "Kenya" envelope tokens are tripled, and the participant receives an equal share. The participant would receive 10 tokens from the "Personal" envelope. Second, he or she would receive 5 tokens from the "Luo community in Nairobi" share (the 10 tokens would be doubled and his or her share is 5). Finally, the participant would receive 3 tokens from the Kenya share (the 12 tokens would be tripled to 36 and divided by 12, so the participant receives 3). The participant's total is 18 blue tokens, and for that he or she would receive a payout of KSh 360.

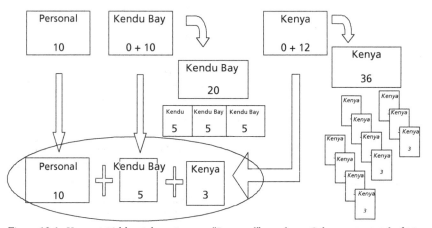

Figure 12.1. You put 10 blue tokens in your "Personal" envelope. Others put a total of 10 blue tokens in their "Kendu Bay" envelopes. Finally, 12 blue tokens are put in the "Kenya" envelopes.

We regard contributions to "Local" as reflecting parochial interests and contributions to "Kenya" as reflecting more cosmopolitan national interests. The design of this game maps onto the nature of local–national relations in that globalization does not exclude cooperation or interaction with the local constituency but expands inclusion to both local and nonlocal actors.

Because the experiment was conducted among participants whose education was varied, all instructions were given orally and participants were presented with visual representations of the design.

After participants completed the three decisions, there was a waiting period while their outcomes (earnings paid in real cash) were determined. Outcomes were calculated using an algorithm that matched participants' decisions with decisions made by other people in their locality and country and by others around the world. Starting data for these decisions was provided by pilot tests, which occurred in each locality prior to the experiment. Data in the algorithm was updated as the experiments ensued. A participant then was matched with other participants and their joint actions determined the participant's payoff. The instructions explicitly pointed out that other people's decisions (coupled with their own decisions) would determine their payment. As well, the participant's own choices would determine the payments to others—depending on the group into which the participant was mixed.

Experiment Questionnaire

While payoffs were being calculated, participants completed a questionnaire containing demographic information as well as our measures of interest.

Individual-Level Globalization Index

The Individual-Level Globalization Index (IGI) is analogous to the Country-Level Globalization Index published the Center for the Study of Globalization and Regionalization at the University of Warwick and measures the degree to which an individual participates in the network of global economic, social, political, and cultural relations. A typical question asks the frequency with which the individual utilizes a certain medium of global connection. For example, a question regarding cultural interaction is, "How often do you watch a television program or movie from a different country?" A typical question may also regard the scope with which the individual utilizes the global connection. For example, a social interaction question asks, "If you use a mobile phone, do you use it to contact people living in other parts of your country, or people living in other countries?" Finally, questions may simply query whether the individual is involved in an interaction that is global in character. For example, a question regarding economic interactions is, "Do you work for a multinational or foreign-owned company?" The resulting index assigns higher scores to individuals who are frequently connected in worldwide interactions and lower scores to individuals who are rarely connected and do so on a more limited territorial scope. At the lowest end of the scale are those individuals lacking connectivity all together.[3]

Social Identity

A three-item measure assessed social identification at the levels of the local community, the nation, and the world. For example, in Kenya these items read: "How strongly do you feel attachment to your community in Kendu Bay?" "How strongly do you feel attachment to your community in Kenya?" "How strongly do you feel attachment to the world as a whole?" "How strongly do you define yourself as a member of your community in Kendu Bay?" "In Kenya," ". . . of the world as a whole?" "How close do you feel to other members of your community in Kendu Bay?" ". . . in Kenya?" ". . . to the world as a whole?" Each item was Likert-scaled from 1 to 4 where 4 = *very much* and 1 = *not at all*.

The Cronbach alpha of the three social identity items was .78 at the local level, .69 at the national level, and .78 at the world level. The social identification scale at each level (Local Social Identity [LSI], National Social Identity [NSI], and Global Social Identity, [GSI]) was summated with all three items equally weighted, resulting in possible scores ranging from 3 to 12.

Generalized Trust

The well-known generalized trust question from the World Value Survey served as our measure of trust: "Generally speaking, would you say that most people can be trusted or that you can't be too careful in dealing with people?" Responses to the question are dichotomous: 0 = *Can be trusted*, 1 = *Can't be too careful*. For purposes of logical consistency, responses were reverse-scored for the analysis.

Experiment Controls

The international and experimental character of this research warrants that we control for country and culture-specific variables that could influence results. Specifically, we address the following as suggested by Roth et al. (1991) and modified by Buchan et al. (2009).

1. *Controlling for participant pool equivalency.* To ensure as similar a participant pool as possible, we limited our sample to members of the particular ethnic group, ages 18 to 60, male or female, with at least a fourth-grade education level in each location studied. Second, we included a number of demographic questions on the questionnaire; answers to these questions were entered as covariates in the final analysis of results.
2. *Controlling for understanding.* Several different understanding checks were administered throughout the experimental task. Where it was apparent that participants did not understand the task, their data was omitted from the analysis.
3. *Controlling for experimenter effects.* To control for any face-saving or impression management behaviors specifically due to the presence of foreign

researcher, only the local researcher and assistants interacted with research participants during the experiment.

4. *Controlling for construct equivalence/local adaptation.* The local collaborators were consulted as to what elements in the experimental method and in the questionnaire needed local adaptation. For example, local collaborators advised as to the most appropriate method of participant recruitment.

■ RESULTS

Two hundred seventy participants successfully completed all comprehension quizzes, and their data were used in the analysis: 71 Luo participants in Nairobi, 67 Kikuyu participants in Nairobi, 67 Luo participants in Kendu Bay in Nyanza Province, and 70 Kikuyu participants in Karatina in Central Province. The number of participants who were dropped from the research due to lack of comprehension varied between four and six participants in each location; there was not a significant difference in rates of failure across locations. Among these 270 individuals, missing questionnaire data (single items that may have been overlooked, etc.) occurred randomly across people and locations. To address this we used PROC MI, a multiple imputation procedure in SAS, to represent a random sample of the missing values (Rubin, 1996). Table 12.1 provides basic descriptive statistics from our sample across populations and locations in Kenya on the key measures of interest.

Tests of Hypotheses

The objective of this research is to gain a deeper understanding of the influence of ethnic fractionalization and globalization on generalized trust and national-level cooperation. Existing research on the influence of ethnic fractionalization leads to conflicting hypotheses. On one hand theories originating from economics and political science suggest that higher levels of ethnic fractionalization may be related to lower trust and propensities to cooperate with others nationally (H1a); on the other, the theory of detribalization from anthropology suggests the reverse (H1b). We test these hypotheses by comparing mean rates of cooperation among Luo and Kikuyu populations in Nairobi, a highly ethnically fragmented location, with those of Luo and Kikuyu populations in ethnically homogeneous areas in the countryside. As shown in Table 12.1, levels of generalized trust do not differ among locations, thus ethnic fractionalization does not seem to be significantly related to generalized trust. Contributions among populations in the countryside are somewhat higher than average contributions in Nairobi, prompting a weakly significant locational difference in cooperation ($p < .06$). Thus there is weak support for theories suggesting that increased ethnic fractionalization is associated with lower levels of cooperation with the national collective (H1a). However, what is more interesting regarding the National Contribution results is the highly significant Location × Tribe interaction ($p < .001$). This suggests a more complex

TABLE 12.1. *Descriptive Statistics*

| | Urban (Nairobi) | | Rural | | F-test results | | |
| | Luo | Kikuyu | Luo | Kikuyu | Location | Tribe | L × T |
	(N = 71)	(N = 62)	(N = 67)	(N = 70)			
Gender (% male)	51	44	52	58	ns	ns	ns
Age (birth year)	78.26 (8.94)	75 (20.04)	76.24 (15.07)	77.95 (12.35)	ns	ns	ns
Education[a]	2.53 (1.04)	2.95 (0.82)	2.26 (0.59)	2.22 (0.68)	ns	ns	ns
Employment informal (1) or informal sector	1.78 (0.41)	1.81 (0.39)	1.79 (0.41)	1.77 (0.42)	ns	ns	ns
IGI	0.4276 (0.09)	0.3915 (0.10)	0.3872 (0.10)	0.3946 (0.09)	0.07	ns	0.07
LSI	10.18 (2.5)	10.54 (2.36)	10.8 (2.09)	11.45 (1.36)	0.002	0.03	ns
NSI	9.97 (2.5)	10.93 (1.71)	10.97 (2.09)	10.65 (1.70)	0.07	ns	0.01
GSI	8.91 (3.44)	9.41 (2.76)	9.61 (2.76)	10.51 (2.3)	0.008	0.03	ns
National Contribution	4.7 (2.89)	3.8 (3.56)	3.8 (3.02)	6.0 (3.4)	0.06	0.07	0.001
General Trust	0.422 (.487)	0.387 (.491)	0.403 (.494)	0.371 (.486)	ns	ns	ns

Note. IGI = Individual-Level Globalization Index; LSI = Local Social Identity; NSI = National Social Identity; GSI = Global Social Identity.
[a] 1 = grade school, 2 = high school, 3 = technical school, 4 = bachelor's, 5 = master's, 6 = PhD.

relationship between National Contributions and ethnic fractionalization, which is captured solely by location as a proxy for fractionalization.

Our analyses now turn to understanding the relationship between individual levels of globalization (IGI), trust, and contributions to the national account, controlling for demographic variables, baseline cooperation (local contributions), and local, national, and global identity. Overall correlations among the variable are shown in Table 12.2. We see that national contributions are weakly correlated with location and tribe and highly correlated with local and global contributions. Though beyond the scope of this chapter, the finding of positive correlations between contributions at various levels is consistent with that demonstrated in prior research (Buchan et al., 2009; Buchan et al., 2011). That is, cooperation at the local level does not necessarily exclude cooperation at the national and global levels. Rather, the propensity toward positive interaction with the local constituency is compatible with cooperation with members of the broader, more distal group.

The results of regression analyses on National Contribution are shown in Table 12.3; these analyses will help us tease out H2a and H2b. Understanding that there is a strong relationship between trust and cooperative behaviors (e.g., Dawes, 1980; Rothstein, 2005), we add generalized trust to the regression on national contributions to better understand the role of trust on cooperation in the contexts of this particular experiment.

H2a draws on prior research showing a link between individual levels of globalization generalized trust and cooperation with global others and suggests that higher levels of IGI will be associated with higher trust and propensities to cooperate nationally. The overall correlations shown in Table 12.2 do not bear this relationship with globalization out for either trust or national contributions; the correlations between IGI and trust ($r = .04$, ns) and IGI and cooperation ($r = -0.07$, ns) are both nonsignificant. Furthermore, in the overall regression incorporating data from all 270 participants, we see that IGI alone is not a significant predictor of contributions to the national public good ($p > .10$, ns). Thus, on its face, H2a is not supported. However, there exists a highly significant interaction of IGI and location on national contributions ($p < .02$), prompting us to look more closely at the regressions within each location to fully understand the influence of individual globalization on cooperation at the national level. We note that NSI has a highly significant positive effect on contributions ($p < .05$); this is in line with prior research demonstrating a link between identification with a collective and cooperation with it (e.g., Brewer & Kramer, 1986; Wit & Kerr, 2002). Finally, we observe that in our overall data, national-level cooperation is not accompanied by generalized trust ($p > .10$, ns).

The next regression using data only from participants in Nairobi ($N = 133$), reveals that LSI ($p < .001$) and NSI ($p < .01$) are significant predictors of contributions to the national account after controlling for baseline cooperation (Local1). Among participants living in Nairobi, generalized trust was weakly linked to cooperation at the national level ($p < .10$). Interestingly, the regression using data only from participants in the Countryside ($N = 137$), reveals a highly significant negative effect of IGI ($p < .002$) and a highly significant interaction of IGI ×

TABLE 12.2. Overall Correlations

Column 1	IGI	Gender	Year	Education	Employment	Location	Tribe	Local	National	World	Trust	GSI	NSI
IGI	1												
Gender	-0.1017* 0.0954	1											
Year	0.13686** 0.0245	-0.15259 0.0121	1										
Education	0.2542*** <0001	-0.10291* 0.0915	0.10784* 0769	1									
Employment	-0.15706*** 0.0097	-0.08073 0.186	0.12658** 0.0376	-0.11965** 0.0495	1								
Location	-0.10201* 0.0944	-0.04503 0.4612	0.03974 0.5156	-0.15945*** 0.0087	-0.01956 0.7489	1							
Tribe	-0.07666 0.2092	0.02307 0.7059	0.07698 0.2073	-0.00283 0.9631	-0.00242 0.9684	0.04479 0.4636	1						
Local Contribution	0.05002 0.413	0.14644*** 0.016	-0.1212** 0.0466	-0.08526 0.1624	-0.10226* 0.0936	0.1658*** 0.0063	0.03888 0.5247	1					
National Contribution	-0.07561 0.2156	0.04819 0.4303	-0.08925 0.1436	-0.04978 0.4153	-0.08914 0.1441	0.10566* 0.0831	0.10847* 0.0752	0.54463*** <.001	1				
World Contribution	0.01393 0.8197	0.04823 0.43	-0.1269** 0.0372	-0.06714 0.2714	-0.115561** 0.0579	0.05299 0.3858	0.03939 0.5192	0.52485*** <.0001	0.71982*** <.0001	1			
Generalized Trust	0.04527 0.4583	0.08363 0.1706	-0.07179 0.2397	-0.08191 0.1796	-0.02618 0.6684	-0.01958 0.7488	-0.03501 0.5668	0.04792 0.433	-0.05377 0.3788	-0.00643 0.9162	1		
GSI	0.01216 0.8423	-0.11997** 0.0489	-0.09582 0.1162	-0.07652 0.2101	0.03784 0.5358	0.16042*** 0.0083	-0.04447 0.4669	0.01845 0.7629	0.05407 0.3762	0.18207*** 0.0027	0.11321* 0.0632	1	
NSI	-0.06632 0.2775	-0.11006* 0.071	-0.00595 0.9225	-0.0128 0.8342	0.13952** 0.0218	0.09002 0.1401	0.06452 0.2908	-0.04326 0.4791	0.06762 0.2682	0.11997** 0.0489	-0.072 0.2384	0.60706*** <.0001	1
LSI	-0.14881*** 0.0144	-0.0341 0.577	0.04478 0.4637	-0.15605*** 0.0102	0.14812*** 0.0148	0.15584*** 0.0103	-0.0824 0.177	0.02114 0.7295	0.01476 0.8092	0.02822 0.6444	-0.02934 0.6313	0.33659*** <.0001	0.52134*** <.0001

Notes. IGI = Individual-Level Globalization Index; GSI = Global Social Identity; NSI = National Social Identity; LSI = Local Social Identity. *P* value of the correlation reported under the Spearman ρ. Pearson correlation coefficients, $N = 270$, Prob > |r| under H0: Rho = 0.

$* p = <0.1$, $** p = <0.05$, $*** p = <0.01$.

TABLE 12.3. *Regression Analyses*

Contributions to the National Account

Standardized Estimates and Significance Levels

	Overall	Nairobi	Countryside	Kikuyu Countryside	Luo Countryside	Kendu Bay vs Non Kendu Bay	Non-Kendu Bay
Gender	-0.03813 (.4705)	-0.01454 (.8515)	-0.06447 (.3745)	-0.02611 (.8371)	-0.14447 (.113)	-0.03832 (.4632)	-0.02716 (.6703)
Age	0.00462 (.9317)	-0.02917 (.7132)	0.08801 (.2393)	-0.01008 (.9376)	0.1722 (.0674)	0.01201 (.8205)	-0.035 (.589)
Education	-0.00886 (.8707)	0.00884 (.9085)	-0.0373 (.6116)	0.00242 (.9853)	-0.12416 (.188)	-0.01175 (.827)	0.00683 (.916)
Employment	-0.06793 (0.2008)	-0.18844** (0.0129)	0.02473 (.7390)	0.06885 (.6082)	-0.01726 (.8477)	-0.06955 (.1867)	-0.09144 (.1541)
Local 1	0.51452*** (.0001)	0.55611*** (.0001)	0.4270** (.0001)	0.30417** (.02)	0.50653*** (.0001)	0.52861*** (.0001)	0.52138*** (.0001)
Location	1.39287** (.0465)						
Kendu Bay						0.5933*** (.0063)	
Kendu Bay=1							
Tribe	0.63413 (.3652)	0.01992 (.9489)	-0.52493* (.0882)				
IGI	0.76149 (.1399)	-0.01692 (.9413)	-0.7226** (.0023)	-0.02761 (.8383)	-0.44305*** (.001)	0.34911** (.0294)	-0.0329 (.6108)
Location × Tribe	-1.32808 (.1717)						
IGI × Location	-1.8648** (.0217)						

(continued)

TABLE 12.3. *Continued*

| | | Contributions to the National Account | | | | | |
| | | Standardized Estimates and Significance Levels | | | | | |
	Overall	Nairobi	Countryside	Kikuyu Countryside	Luo Countryside	Kendu Bay vs Non Kendu Bay	Non-Kendu Bay
IGI × Tribe	-0.85 919	-0.01628	.89111**				
	(.2907)	(.9621)	(.0215)				
IGI × Kendu						-0.79591***	
						(.0019)	
Allway	1.73494*						
	(.0979)						
GSI	-0.0084	-0.03694	0.01685	0.04393	-0.08401	-0.00647	-0.00218
	(.8984)ʳ	(.6847)ʳ	(.8531)ʳ	(.7643)	(.5276)ʳ	(.9209)ʳ	(.9768)
NSI	0.13991*	0.31918***	-0.07123	-0.11029	-0.00534	.14591**	0.18561*
	(.0529)ʳ	(.0018)ʳ	(.4884)ʳ	(.5135)ʳ	(.9706)ʳ	(.0416)	(.0272)
LSI	-0.05363	-0.20106**	0.15355*	0.17514	0.15336	-0.05803	-0.08461
	(.3862)	(.0160)	(.0944)	(.2734)	(.1642)	(.3439)	(.2401)
Generalized Trust	1.3	1.84*	0.33	0.83	1.98**	1.39	0.91
	(0.196)	(0.0681)	(0.7417)	(0.4084)	(0.0521)	(0.1646)	-0.3648
Observations	270	133	137	70	67	270	203
R²	0.3561	0.4124	0.3826	0.1327	0.57	0.352	0.3074

Note. IGI = Individual-Level Globalization Index; GSI = Global Social Identity; NSI = National Social Identity; LSI = Local Social Identity.

Tribe ($p < .02$). No relation between generalized trust and cooperation was found ($p > .10$, ns). This suggests once again that we need to delve more deeply to discern the true influence of globalization on cooperation at the national level—this time by examining each tribe within the countryside locations.

The regression focusing on Kikuyu participants residing in the countryside location of Karatina in Central Province yields only a significant effect of baseline cooperation (Local1) ($p < .02$). However, the regression focusing on Luo participants in the countryside location of Kendu Bay in Nyanza Province yields not only a highly significant effect of baseline cooperation (Local1) ($p < .0001$) but also a highly significant negative effect of IGI ($p < .0001$). At last, this result helps us get to the bottom of the spiraling interactions involving globalization seen in these analyses. In essence, what seems to be driving the significant interactions is a highly significant negative effect of individual-level of globalization on national cooperation among the Luo population in Kendu Bay and the lack of significant effect of IGI among the Kikuyu population in Karatina or among the population as a whole in Nairobi. Therefore, H2a is not supported; higher individual levels of participation in globalization are not associated with greater cooperativeness at the national level. On the contrary, when IGI does have a significant effect in this data, the effect on cooperation is negative. We do note, however, that it is only among the Luo population in Kendu Bay that generalized trust and national cooperation are highly significantly related ($p < .05$).

H2b is motivated by research suggesting that those who have suffered negatively from the effects of globalization and who are on the losing end of ethnic inequality will be less inclined to cooperate at a national level than those on the prosperous end of such inequality. To test this hypothesis we compare analyses involving the Luo population from Kendu Bay versus the other three populations in this research (Kikuyus from Karatina and Luos and Kikuyus in Nairobi). As shown in Table 12.4, of key importance is the fact that the "Kendu Bay vs. Non-Kendu Bay" regression

TABLE 12.4. *Regression of National Contributions on Components of IGI*

	Contributions to the National Account
	Kendu Bay Luos
Economic IGI	−6.56** (0.04)
Political IGI	−.583 (0.854)
Social IGI	−4.47 (0.182)
Cultural IGI	−4.423 (0.102)
Observation	67
R^2	0.26

Note. IGI = Individual-Level Globalization Index.

analysis exposes a highly significant effect for the Kendu Bay variable ($p < .006$). This suggests that, compared to Kendu Bay, the Non-Kendu Bay locations demonstrate higher contributions to the national account, lending support for H2a. Yet, again, there is a highly significant IGI × Kendu Bay interaction yielding a negative estimate ($p < .0019$). When we compare the regression analysis of Kendu Bay only with that for the Non-Kendu Bay locations, we see again that it is the significant negative effect of globalization in Kendu Bay that is driving the interaction ($p < .0001$).

■ DISCUSSION

The goal of this research was to gain a greater understanding of the role of globalization and ethnic fractionalization in helping or hindering generalized trust and national cooperation among ethnic groups in Kenya. Our results indicate that high ethnic fractionalization does not by itself affect trust or cooperation. There were no differences in levels of trust across ethnically homogeneous or fractionalized locations. But the Luo in the ethnically homogeneous region of Kendu Bay did exhibit significantly less national cooperation than did their fellow Kenyans in ethnically fractured Nairobi and in ethnically homogeneous Central Province. These results are consistent with the arguments that it is not ethnic fractionalization, per se, that is associated with lower social capital but increased ethnic inequality (Alesina et al., 2012; Bjornskov, 2008).

Follow-up analyses on the IGI in Kendu Bay, as shown in Table 12.5, provide additional support that a negative experience with economic globalization may be the impetus for the lower rates of cooperation among the Kendu Bay Luos.

TABLE 12.5. *Regression of National Contributions on Components of Economic IGI*

	Contributions to the National Account
	Kendu Bay Luos
Credit/Fax	1.20 (0.13)
Work MNC	−1.42 (0.119)
Investments	−1.04 (0.184)
Own Foreign Car	−.857 (0.205)
Foreign Food/Clothing/ Restaurants	−.994*** (.0001)
Observations	67
R^2	0.29

Note. MNC = Multinational Corporation.
*** $p = < 0.01$.

Specifically, the IGI is composed of four components: the cultural index, the political index, the social index, and the economic index. A regression analysis on national contributions using the four IGI components as independent variables demonstrates that it is the economic index that seems to be wholly responsible for the negative effect of individual level globalization ($p < .04$).

Furthermore, if we break the economic index down into its constituent parts, we see that it is the extent of interaction Kendu Bay Luos have with foreign food, clothing, and restaurants that is motivating the negative association of globalization with national cooperation. To be clear, it is not that Kendu Bay Luos lack experience with globalization; rather, these results suggest that the Luos in Kendu Bay are participating in globalization by consuming foreign food and clothing (perhaps not out of choice but necessity), and they are reacting against it.

A few decades ago, before the recent wave of globalization, the Kendu Bay region was relatively prosperous with a thriving cotton industry. The dock on Lake Victoria was a major transportation hub with ships coming from as far away as Uganda and Tanzania. Now the cotton industry is gone and the port is stagnant. The unemployment rate has skyrocketed, and many people have gone back to subsistence farming. In the meantime, economically dominant elites in Nairobi and Central Provinces have become wealthier. These citizens of Kendu Bay are exhibiting a classic reactance to globalization (Buchan & Grimalda, 2011), whereby the losers from globalization are choosing to opt out or, at least, let others carry more of the collective burden (Lassen, 2007).

■ CONCLUSION

The literatures concerning the influence of ethnic fractionalization and globalization on generalized trust and cooperation have tended to be mixed and inconclusive. If there is to be a concluding remark from the current research to contribute to these literatures, it would be a resounding, "it's complicated." As pointed out by Dinesen and Sonderskov (2012), studies at the aggregate country level have demonstrated that ethnic fractionalization is associated with lower generalized trust in Anglo-Saxon countries but that evidence from cross-European studies has shown positive or no influence. The current study in three municipalities in Kenya—one extremely ethnically fractionalized and the other two extremely ethnically homogeneous—demonstrates no differences across populations in levels of generalized trust. It is possible, as suggested by Kokkonen, Esiasson, and Gilljam (2014) that the quality and nature of the contact between individuals matters more than whether they live or do not live side by side. Their study of 30,000 individuals in workplaces in 22 countries demonstrates a positive effect of ethnic diversity on trust when intergroup contacts are difficult to avoid and supported by supervisors. Thus it may be that as long as the nearly 40 different ethnic groups living together in Nairobi remain separate from one another within their ethnically based enclaves, the benefits of ethnic diversity will go unfulfilled.

One final note is that it was only among the Luo population in Kendu Bay that generalized trust had a strongly significant positive relationship with national contributions. Granted, contributions among the Kendu Bay Luos were quite low (mean = 3.8 vs. mean = 4.7 for Luos in Nairobi and mean =4.6 overall), but it is interesting to see the positive relationship. Follow-up analyses show that the correlation among Kendu Bay Luos between generalized trust and the IGI was not significant; thus while a reactance against globalization seems to have prompted lower national-level cooperation, trust was not affected.

The meta-analysis by Steblay (1987) of helping behaviors in rural versus urban environments may be instructive here. She concludes that, in general, helping is more likely to occur in a nonurban than urban contexts but that the difference appears to be a function of situational variables that are "not completely defined but clearly includes both environmental and social characteristics" (p. 354). In this research we do find a weakly significant effect of urban versus rural location, but the real puzzle of cooperative and trusting behavior in Kenya seems to be entwined in the processes of ethnic fractionalization and globalization and the implications of these processes on the local environment. In both Western and non-Western societies, when ethnic fractionalization exacerbates income inequality—often prompted by globalization—enmities and tensions among ethnicities is increased and cooperation is lessened (Chua, 2002). Yet the positive correlations among local, national, and global contributions in the current research in Kenya and in a former study in multiple countries (Buchan et al. 2009) seem to indicate that cooperation with one's local ingroup does not crowd out cooperation with distal others. Instead, this positive relationship among levels of contributions suggests that "situational variables" may depress cooperation with everyone—be they local, national, and global—or serve to increase it overall.

■ NOTES

1. The historic provinces of Kenya were abolished in 2013 and replaced under the country's new constitution with 47 counties. As the experiment was conducted before the new constitution came into effect, the historic names are used to describe the experimental locations.

2. We note that the correlation between contributions to the national account and contributions to the global account was .70.

3. For more detail on the content of the IGI and scale formation, please consult Buchan et al. (2009) and Buchan and Grimalda (2011).

■ REFERENCES

Alesina, A., & La Ferrara, E. (2005). Ethnic diversity and economic performance. *Journal of Economic Literature*, 43(2), 762–800.

Alesina, A., Michalopoulos, S., & Papaioannou, E. (2012). *Ethnic inequality*. NBER Working Paper 18512, CEPR Discussion Paper 9225. Cambridge, MA: National Bureau of Economic Research.

Ayenagbo, K, Rongcheng, W., Wengjing, W., Nguhi, S., Kimatu, J., & Patrick, J. (2012). The impact of globalization on African countries' economic development. *African Journal of Business Management*, 6(44), 11057–11076.

Barkan, J. (2011). *Kenya: Assessing risks to stability*. Washington, DC: Center for Strategic International Studies.

Beck, U. (2006). *The cosmopolitan vision*. Cambridge, UK: Polity Press.

Bjørnskov, C. (2008). Social trust and fractionalization: A possible reinterpretation. *European Sociological Review, 24*(3), 271–283.

Blackwell, C., & McKee, M. (2003). Only for my own neighborhood? Preferences and voluntary provision of local and global public goods. *Journal of Economic Behavior and Organization, 52,* 115–131.

Branch, D. (2011). *Kenya: Between hope and despair, 1963–2011*. New Haven, CT: Yale University Press.

Bratton, M., & Kimenyi, M. (2008). Voting in Kenya: Putting ethnicity in perspective. *Journal of Eastern African Studies, 2*(2), 272–289.

Buchan, N., & Grimalda, G. (2011). Global connectivity and social capital. In S. R. Thye & E. J. Lawler, (Eds.) *Advances in group processes*. New York: Emerald.

Buchan, N., Grimalda, G., Wilson, R., Brewer, M., Fatas, E., & Foddy, M. (2009). Globalization and human cooperation. *Proceedings of the National Academy of Sciences, 106*(11), 4138–4142.

Buchan, N., Grimalda, G., Wilson, R., Brewer, M., Fatas, E., & Foddy, M. (2011). Global identity and global cooperation, *Psychological Science, 22*(6), 821–828.

Chua, A. (2002). *World on fire: How exporting free market democracy breeds ethnic hatred and global instability*. New York: Doubleday.

Collier, P. (1998). *The political economy of ethnicity*. WPS/98-8. Oxford: Centre for Study of African Economies.

Dawes, R. (1980). Social dilemmas. *Annual Review of Psychology, 31,* 169–193.

Easterly, W., & Levine, R. 1997. Africa's growth tragedy: Policies and ethnic divisions. *Quarterly Journal of Economics, 112*(4), 1203–1250.

Eifert, B., Miguel, E., & Posner, D. (2010). Political competition and ethnic identification in Africa. *American Journal of Political Science, 54*(2), 494–510.

Giddens, A. (1990). *The consequences of modernity*. Cambridge, UK: Polity Press.

Hannerz, U. (1992). *Cultural complexity: Studies in the social organization of meaning*. New York: Columbia University Press.

Hornsby, C. (2013). *Kenya: A history since independence*. New York: I. B. Tauris.

Kenya Bureau of Statistics. (2010). *Ethnic affiliation*. Kenya: Population and Housing Census Results.

Lancee, B., & Dronkers, J. (2008, May). Ethnic diversity in neighborhoods and individual trust of immigrants and natives: A replication of Putnam (2007) in a West-European country. Paper presented at the International Conference on Theoretical Perspectives on Social Cohesion and Social Capital, Royal Flemish Academy of Belgium for Science and the Arts, Brussels.

La Ferrara, E. (2002). Self-help groups and income generation in informal settlements of Nairobi. *Journal of African Economies, 11*(1), 61–89.

Lassen, D. (2007). Ethnic divisions, trust, and the size of the informal sector. *Journal of Economic Behavior & Organization, 63*(3), 423–438.

Leke, A., Lund, S. Roxburgh, C., & van Wamelen, A. (2010). *What's driving Africa's growth?* McKinsey & Company. http://www.mckinsey.com/global-themes/middle-east-and-africa/whats-driving-africas-growth

Lentz, C. (1995). Tribalism and ethnicity in Africa. *Cahiers des sciences humaines, 31*(2), 303–328.

Morrison, L. (2006). The nature of decline: Distinguishing myth from reality in the case of the Luo of Kenya. *Journal of Modern African Studies, 45*(1), 117–142.

Muuru, J. (2009). *Kenya's flying vegetables.* London: Africa Research Institute.

Ohito, D. (2005). Economic report: Nyanza is Kenya's poorest province. Hiiraan Online. http://www.hiiraan.com/2005/nov/somali_news02_4.htm

Polillo, S. (2012). Globalization: Civilizing or destructive? An empirical test of the international determinants of generalized trust. *International Journal of Comparative Sociology, 53*(1), 45–65.

Putnam, R. (2007). E pluribus unum: Diversity and community in the twenty-first century: The 2006 Johan Skytte Prize Lecture. *Scandinavian Political Studies, 30*(2), 137–174.

Radelet, S. (2010). *Emerging Africa: How 17 countries are leading the way.* Baltimore: Brookings Institution Press.

Reilly, B., & Phillpot, R. (2002). Making democracy work in Papua New Guinea: Social capital and Provincial development in an ethnically fragmented society. *Asian Survey, 42*(6), 906–927.

Roth, A., Prasnikar, V., Okuno-Fujiwara, M., & Zamir, S. (1991) Bargaining and market behavior in Jerusalem, Ljubljana, Pittsburgh, and Tokyo: An experimental study. *The American Economic Review, 81*(5), 1068–1095.

Steblay, N. M. (1987). Helping behavior in rural and urban environments: A meta-analysis. *Psychological Bulletin, 102*(3), 346–356.

Wit, P., & Kerr, N. (2002). Me versus just us versus all: Categorization and cooperation in nested social dilemmas. *Journal of Personality and Social Psychology, 83*, 616–637.

Zerfu, D., Precious Zikhali, P., & Kabenga, I. (2008). Does ethnicity matter for trust? Evidence from Africa. *Journal of African Economies, 18*(1), 153–175.

13 Improving Outcomes in the Trust Game

The Games People Choose in Oman, the United States, and Vietnam

■ IRIS BOHNET, BENEDIKT HERRMANN,
MALIHEH PARYAVI, ANH TRAN,
AND RICHARD ZECKHAUSER

■ INTRODUCTION

Trust has been studied extensively across the social sciences. It has been defined as a component of social capital, "features of social life, networks, norms, trust that enables participants to act together more effectively to pursue shared objectives" (Putnam, 1995, pp. 664–665). It has been argued that the level of trust that is shared in a society is the single cultural characteristic that determines a nation's well-being and ability to compete (Fukuyama, 1995, p. 7). Alesina and La Ferrara (2002) found that high measures of trust or social capital are associated with effective public policies and with more successful economic outcomes, themselves the results of smoothly functioning public institutions and reductions of transaction costs. Trust is also positively correlated with economic growth (Knack & Keefer, 1997), with improvements in institutions (Zak & Knack, 2001), and with reductions in corruption (LaPorta, Lopez-De-Silane, Shleifer, & Vishny, 1997).

Choosing to trust is a dangerous action. If one's trust is betrayed, one loses. Skilled practitioners often find ways to change the game to reduce their risks. Successful companies often are characterized by their ability to improve outcomes in trust situations. For example, eBay and Amazon changed the nature of online shopping by allowing buyers to issue public ratings of sellers. The reputational incentives thus changed anonymous one-shot interactions into the equivalent of repeated games. In a different approach, PayPal created insurance arrangements that protect buyers from nonfulfillment.

We are interested in examining how people—in contrast to firms—deal with situations where trust is at stake. When given the option, how do the first movers in a trust situation, the principals, find ways to improve their outcomes? Reputational mechanisms for the second movers, the agents, would be splendid but are not always available. We consider two possible instruments that increase either the willingness to trust or the incentive to be trustworthy. Insurance protects principals should they be betrayed, thus decreasing the risk involved in trusting. A bonus for trustworthiness encourages the agent to reward trust, thus decreasing the incentive to betray. Both mechanisms should make trust more likely although they work through different channels. While legal remedies, such as insurance or damage recovery through a lawsuit,[1] focus on reducing the cost of betrayal, bonuses for trustworthiness, through reputational and repeated-game incentives or direct compensation, seek to reduce the likelihood of betrayal. These two approaches can be thought of as mitigation and prevention (Bohnet, Herrmann, Al-Issis, Robbet, Al-Yahya & Zeckhauser, 2012).

This chapter uses laboratory experiments to examine whether principals choose a mitigation-based intervention that decreases the cost of betrayal (such as securing insurance) as opposed to a prevention-based approach (such as giving a bonus for trustworthiness) that seeks to decrease the likelihood of betrayal by agents. It assesses how these choices affect rates of trust and trustworthiness. In our experiments, we offered principals a choice between taking insurance and giving a bonus, and agents were informed of this choice. We measured what choices principals made, how agents responded to them, and how both parties' behaviors compared to a situation where insurance or bonus was assigned by chance, with agents being informed that chance made the determination. This setup enables us to assess whether the intentions and expectations that would be conveyed by choosing a certain trust-fostering mechanism affect agent behavior.

Whether a mitigation or prevention approach is chosen in a given context will likely relate to the principal's assessment of the likelihood that trust will be rewarded or betrayed. Other factors, such as concerns about payoffs to oneself and to one's counterpart, and betrayal aversion will also play a role. A significant body of research shows that people care about how their payoffs compare to those of others (e.g., Bolton & Ockenfels, 2001; Fehr & Schmidt, 1999), thus attention to social comparisons matter. In addition, Bohnet and colleagues (Bohnet, Herrmann, & Zeckhauser, 2010; Bohnet, Greig, Herrmann, & Zeckhauser, 2008; Bohnet & Zeckhauser, 2004) show that beyond pure monetary payoffs, people who are betrayed incur psychological costs and demonstrate betrayal aversion. Bohnet et al. (2008) and Bohnet et al. (2010) found betrayal aversion to be a general phenomenon in the potpourri of countries they studied: Brazil, China, Kuwait, Oman, Switzerland, Turkey, the United Arab Emirates, and the United States. Betrayal aversion was generally most pronounced in the Gulf countries and least pronounced in Brazil and China, with the other countries ranging in between. But while there were some cross-cultural differences (Al-Issis & Bohnet, 2016; Bohnet et al., 2012), one main conclusion from our earlier work is that betrayal aversion is a robust phenomenon, relevant in many different cultures. The larger the psychological costs of betrayal, the more likely it is that people will be willing to consider a prevention-based approach, one that increases the chances that their counterpart will reward trust.

One such approach to make rewarding trust more attractive is to give the agent a present, a "bonus," should he choose this action. (For expository ease, principals are female in this analysis; agents are male.) Previous experimental research elaborated the power of positive reciprocity in games like the "gift exchange" game (e.g., Brandts & Charness, 2004; Fehr, Gächter, & Kirchsteiger, 1997; Fehr, Kirchsteiger,

& Riedl, 1993; Hannan, Kagel, & Moser, 2002). In these experiments sending a gift, or an above-market-price wage offer, generally secures positive reciprocity. However, providing a bonus conditional on the reward decision of the agent is not identical to offering the agent an unconditional gift and thus may not elicit reciprocity in the same way. A conditional bonus instead is about reducing the cost for the agent to be trustworthy. It may still instill reciprocity if it was chosen by the principal (e.g., Rabin 1993).[2]

In our experiments, principals have the choice to use a fixed amount for either insuring themselves against the financial loss in case of betrayal through taking insurance or to award the agent with a bonus should he opt to reward trust. If some principals prefer sending a bonus to relying on insurance, this indicates how responsive they believe agents will be to this friendly gesture, its increased payoff for rewarding, and the magnitude of the principal's betrayal aversion. High responsiveness and high magnitude increase the attractiveness of using the strategy "bonus and trust."

Our experiments test for trust and trustworthiness behavior and, particularly, the choice between mitigation and prevention strategies under the significantly different social and cultural contexts represented by three disparate countries: Oman, the United States, and Vietnam. We find some differences among the studied countries, but, overall, our results show strong similarities. About two-thirds of our principals prefer the safety of the insurance mechanism. However, by insuring themselves, they make it less likely for their trust to be rewarded by the agent. The remaining one-third of our principals prefer sending a bonus, making themselves vulnerable to the actions of the agent. This vulnerability pays off by tripling the likelihood of trustworthiness compared to when insurance is chosen. Still, when a bonus is chosen, only about half of the agents reward trust. This fraction is not sufficient to make the principals whole. That is, in terms of expected payoffs, principals would be better off had they taken insurance. Either these principals are too optimistic about the induced change in their counterparts' trustworthiness or betrayal costs indeed loom large and the additional benefits from making betrayal less likely justify choosing the bonus option.

This chapter is organized as follows. The next section presents a conceptual framework. The third section reviews the experimental design and procedures. The fourth section reports the results, and the last section concludes.

■ **CONCEPTUAL FRAMEWORK**

In a standard binary-choice trust game (e.g., Camerer & Weigelt, 1988; Kreps 1990), the principal first decides whether to Trust or not to trust his counterpart (i.e., chooses Not Trust). Table 13.1 illustrates with the payoffs used in our experiment, but the ordering of payoffs is the same as in any trust game. If the principal chooses Not Trust, that effectively ends the game and both earn the same payoff, here $10 each. If the principal chooses Trust, the agent must decide whether to Reward (i.e., be trustworthy) or Betray trust. If the principal chooses Trust and

TABLE 13.1. *Payoffs in the Standard Binary-Choice Trust Game*

		Agent (Second Mover)	
		Reward Trust	Betray Trust
Principal (First Mover)	Trust	15, 15	5, 25
	Not trust	10, 10	

the agent chooses Reward, both parties earn the same payoff, say, $15. If trust is betrayed, then the agent earns $25 and the principal earns $5.

Positing that the players are self-interested money maximizers, if the principal chooses Trust, the agent's best response is to Betray. Hence, the self-interested principal will choose the Not Trust strategy. Hence, the Nash equilibrium is found in the lower box, where the agent has no move to make. Therefore, if self-interested behavior is posited, the players will never reach the Pareto superior outcome available in the upper left-hand box (Trust, Reward Trust).

However, besides monetary concern there are also potentially emotional payoffs associated with each action and outcome. The agent may experience a feeling of guilt if he Betrays trust or a warm glow if he Rewards trust. We denote these feelings as G (for guilt) and W (for warm glow) in Table 13.2. A rational self-interested principal will take these emotions into account and will make her decision according to her expectation of the distribution of such emotions in the population of agents (we return later and consider emotions of the principal). This attention to emotions helps to explain why the principal chooses Trust and the agent chooses Reward Trust in a large proportion of trust games played.

In the real world, trust games usually do not end here, and people often make efforts to change the payoffs or the distribution of outcomes of the game they are playing. Schelling (1980, pp. 173–187) studied very familiar practices that involved making promises or threats. These actions are taken by the agent to affect the choices of the principal. Schelling considered the realistic case where second movers can lower their payoff, given an outcome. Our study is in the spirit of Schelling, but we focus on the principal and ask what she can do to change the outcome of the game. In the real world, the principal often has an ability to reward the agent for cooperative behavior, that is, to send a "bonus," or mitigate the damage incurred by an agent's betrayal by choosing "insurance." In this study, we create these possibilities by giving the principal the ability to add an amount ($5) to any one payoff in the matrix. We then assessed how agents responded. Our choice of trust-fostering mechanisms is inspired by the earlier literature in psychology on

TABLE 13.2. *Trust Game Payoffs, with the Agent's Emotions*

		Agent (Second Mover)	
		Reward Trust	Betray Trust
Principal (First Mover)	Trust	15, (15 + W)	5, (25 – G)
	Not trust	10, 10	

TABLE 13.3. *Trust Game Payoffs If the Principal Chooses Insurance*

| | | Agent (Second Mover) | |
		Reward Trust	Betray Trust
Principal (First Mover)	Trust	15, $(15 + W_I)$	$(5 + 5), (25 - G_I)$
	Not trust	10, 10	

"fear" and "greed" (Rapoport, 1967; Snijders & Keren, 1998; Van Lange, Liebrand, & Kuhlman, 1990; Yamagishi & Sato, 1986).

In this "extended" trust game, the principal's first decision is whether to use insurance or offer a bonus. Given that decision, she then must decide whether to Trust or Not Trust. In the case the principal chooses Trust, the risk inherent in trusting can be affected by decreasing the cost or the likelihood of betrayal; this is exactly what the two alternative strategies accomplish in this study.

If the principal chooses Insurance, she reduces the cost of betrayal. If she chooses Bonus (delivered to the agent if he Rewards), this choice makes betrayal less likely. If Insurance is chosen, the principal is "made whole" in case of Betray. That is, an amount of $5 is added to her payoff in case of Betray, where 5 + 5 = 10. Insurance thus removes any financial risk from trusting, leaving the principal with a weakly dominant strategy to Trust, given that the agent may choose to reward Trust. The Nash equilibrium is now in the upper-left-hand box (Table 13.3). Note the subscript I on W and G, since we think the magnitude of the agent's warm glow and guilt will depend on whether the principal chose Insurance or Bonus. We speculate that both magnitudes would be smaller for Insurance than for Bonus.

If a principal chooses Insurance, how might that change the likelihood that the agent Betrays? The fact that the principal chose Insurance could be perceived as indicating a lack of faith in the trustworthiness of the agent, as well as being a less generous gesture. An intention-based model such as in Rabin (1993) would explain such behavior. Therefore, when Insurance is chosen, apart from monetary payoffs, this would make the agent less likely to Reward Trust.

If Bonus is chosen, the principal sends a bonus by adding $5 to the payoff of the agent, should he choose to Reward Trust. We chose the payoffs so that even with the bonus, Betray still offered a higher monetary payoff to the agent than Reward: that is, 15 + 5 < 25 (Table 13.4). In choosing the Bonus, the principal has two goals: to make Reward less costly to the agent relative to Betray and to encourage reciprocity represented by Reward. Hence, when Bonus is chosen, the warm

TABLE 13.4. *Trust Game Payoffs If the Principal Chooses Bonus*

| | | Agent (Second Mover) | |
		Reward Trust	Betray Trust
Principal (First Mover)	Trust	15, $(15 + 5 + W_B)$	5, $(25 - G_B)$
	Not trust	10, 10	

glow and guilt feelings of the agent would become W_B and G_B, respectively larger than W_I and G_I, which would make the agent more likely to Reward Trust.

Additionally, we explicitly introduced a control treatment, where the choice between Insurance and Bonus was randomly assigned. Comparing outcomes between the experimental and control (random assignment) treatments will show whether the agent's perception of the principal's intentions mattered.

As we mentioned earlier, there may also be some emotional experience for the principal. Past studies have shown that individuals incur a psychological cost when they are betrayed (Bohnet et al. 2010; Bohnet et al. 2008; Bohnet & Zeckhauser 2004). We represent this cost as k and calibrate this psychological cost at its monetary equivalent.[3] The principal's decision will revolve around her assessment of the likelihood that the agent will Reward Trust. Let that assessment be p for the original Trust Game, p_I if she chooses Insurance, and p_B if she chooses Bonus. We hypothesize that $p_I < p < p_B$. That is, relying on Insurance makes one less likely to be Rewarded; indeed, that action itself shows doubt about the agent's trustworthiness. By contrast, a Bonus is thought to foster reciprocity and is given to encourage reciprocity.

Whether the principal chooses Insurance or Bonus, she should Trust. With Insurance, Trust has become her weakly dominant strategy. With Bonus, the only justification for the Bonus was to encourage reciprocity once one proceeded to Trust. If these were the only two available strategies, as they were for many of our principals, which should she choose? The expected payoffs for the two strategies are

$$\text{Insurance} \qquad\qquad \text{Bonus}$$

$$p_I(15)+(1-p_I)(10-k) \quad p_B(15)+(1-p_B)(5-k)$$

A Bonus will be preferred to Insurance if $(10+k)p_B>(5+k)p_I+5$ This inequality will be satisfied when there is some combination of large values for $p_B - p_I$ and k. As a result, the Bonus is attractive if it substantially increases the probability of Reward or, if it only increases it modestly, if betrayal aversion is substantial. Whether the principal chooses Insurance or Bonus along with Trust, the sum of payoffs for the two players is the same, regardless of what the agent chooses. Hence, given that the principal Trusts, the efficiency of the game is unaffected by either his or the agent's choices.

The next section reviews the experimental design where we allow for insurance and bonus and assesses the impacts of those instruments on Trust and the probability of Reward.

■ EXPERIMENTAL DESIGN AND PROCEDURES

Our experiment had two different treatments. The Choice treatment, described earlier, gave the principal the opportunity to add 5 points to alternative payoffs in the game. The Chance treatment added the payoffs at random to produce the

Insurance or Bonus outcomes. The goal of the comparison was to see if the principal's intentions, as revealed by her choice, affected the agent's actions.

Choice Treatment: What Game Do Principals Choose to Play?

Subjects started with a binary-choice trust game. The payoffs were given in points and presented to subjects in a matrix and graphic form with neutral terminology (summarized inTable 13.5). Each player was identified as "X," the principal, or as "Y," the agent. Each principal was offered a choice to play or end the game. If a principal decided to exit (choice A) and end the game, both subjects earned E = 10 points. If she decided to trust (choice B) and the agent rewarded trust (choice 1), both would earn R = 15 points. If the agent betrayed (choice 2), he would earn B = 25 points and the principal would be left with C = 5 points. For each point earned, in the United States subjects were paid US\$1, 0.2 Omani rial in Oman, and 5,000 Vietnamese dongs in Vietnam. The price of a modest dinner in a restaurant was used as a benchmark to control for purchasing power of average earnings from the experiment.

Before the game was played, each principal was offered a choice to change the game by allocating 5 points to any one of the payoffs, which would be earned if she were to Trust (i.e., one of the payoffs in row A in the Table 13.5). The 5 points could not be divided and had to go to one payoff. The agent was subsequently informed of the change. The possible changes to payoffs were presented to subjects in a matrix and graphic form with neutral terminology. It was hypothesized that principals would use the points either for Insurance as the principal's payment for the Betray outcome (A,2), or to give a Bonus as the agent's payment for the Reward outcome (A,1). That is, they would not give themselves 5 points extra for the Reward outcome, nor the second movers for the Betray outcome.

Neutral language was used to determine how the game would be changed. The principal, Player X, was asked: "To which payoff do you add the 5 points?" The payoff table was then modified accordingly and shared with player Y, who became aware of the changes made to the game by Player X (Table 13.6). Once the game was changed, the principal had to decide whether or not to trust: "Which alternative, A or B, do you choose from your modified Payoff Table?"

If the principal, player X, chose A, the agent, Player Y, was then asked whether he would choose 1 (Reward) or 2 (Betray).

TABLE 13.5. *Trust Game*
Payoff Table

		Player Y (Agent)	
		1	2
Player X (Principal)	A	15, 15	5, 25
	B	10, 10	

TABLE 13.6. *Insurance Payoff and Bonus Payoff*

Insurance Payoff		Player Y (Second Mover)	
		1	*2*
Player X (First Mover)	A	15, 15	5 + 5 = **10**, 25
	B	10, 10	

Bonus Payoff		Player Y (Second Mover)	
		1	*2*
Player X (First Mover)	A	15, **15 + 5 = 20**	5, 25
	B	10, 10	

Chance Treatment: A Control to Determine whether Intentions Matter

To observe if the principal's intentions and expectations about the agent's actions matter, we created a Chance treatment where the Insurance and Bonus structures were assigned at random (e.g., by drawing a red or black playing card from a deck). The Chance treatment thus served as our control experiment. Once the new payoffs were determined by Chance, players continued the game as described previously.

This allows us to compare the results of the Choice and Chance treatments to see if the intentional choice of Insurance or Bonus, as opposed to a random adjustment of the game, affected either trust or trustworthiness.

Procedures

This study was conducted with 606 student subjects in Oman, the United States, and Vietnam, with 180 subjects participating in Oman, 176 in the United States, and 250 in Vietnam. Demographic and summary statistics of subjects are presented in Appendix 13.A. About 55% of the participants were women, and the average age was approximately 22 years, with no significant differences among countries. Twenty sessions were conducted in total, seven each in Oman and the United States and six in Vietnam. Table 13.7 presents the number of subjects in our control treatment (Chance) and in our treatment condition (Choice) in the three countries.

TABLE 13.7 *Number of Subjects in Choice and Chance Treatments*

	Oman	US	Vietnam	Total
Choice	108	94	126	328
Chance	72	82	124	278
Total	180	176	250	606

Subjects were randomly assigned to principal and agent roles and were randomly matched. All were identified by code numbers and were anonymous to other players. There was no communication among the participants, and the experiment took approximately one hour. The English version of the experimental instructions is included in Appendix 13.B. The instructions were drafted in English and next translated into Arabic (Oman) and Vietnamese (Vietnam). To ensure consistency, instructions were translated forward and backward. Experiments in all locations were conducted manually using pen and paper.

The experiments were in the native language of the location. Participants first read the instructions. Next, the experimenter summarized the instruction orally. To control for understanding, all participants had to solve some quizzes before the experiment started. In the United States, students were invited to participate from the CLER Laboratory subject pool at Harvard Business School in Cambridge, Massachusetts, which includes students from the greater Boston area. In Oman, experiments were conducted at the Sultan Qaboos University in Muscat, and in Vietnam the experiments were conducted at the Foreign Trade University in Hanoi. In Oman and Vietnam, students were recruited across the campus from all faculties and schools several days prior to the experiments, ensuring that participants would not know each other.

At the end of the study, subjects were informed of the outcomes of their decisions and, by presenting their code numbers, received their cash earnings in sealed envelopes. The next section presents the results from our experiments.

■ EXPERIMENTAL RESULTS

We first present results for the principals and then for the agents. Before each result, we discuss the theory involved. For some results, only the Choice treatment is of interest. For others, the comparison between the Choice (experimental) and Chance (control) conditions is important.

Principal Behavior

Insurance versus Bonus

Theory makes no prediction as to whether principals will choose Insurance or Bonus. Which option a rational self-interested principal will choose, as discussed earlier, will depend on their assessment of the likelihoods that agents will Reward in the two cases.

Result 1: Most principals chose Insurance rather than the Bonus option.

Across the three countries, among the principals who chose either Insurance or a Bonus, 68% chose a mitigation-based intervention and thus protected themselves in case of Betrayal; the other 32% sent their agent a contingent Bonus.[4] There are no significant differences in allocation patterns among the countries; principals in each preferred to rely on Insurance rather than send a Bonus ($p = 0.53$). Table 13.8 presents the results.

TABLE 13.8. *Choice Treatment: Share
of Principals Choosing Insurance versus Bonus*

	Insurance (%)	Bonus (%)	N
Oman	73.7	26.3	38
US	62.2	37.8	45
Vietnam	68.9	31.1	45
N	87	41	128

Trust Depending on Insurance or Bonus Choice

Principals choosing Insurance have a weakly dominant strategy to Trust. A principal would have no reason to choose Bonus unless he intended to Trust. Theory would thus predict a very high level of Trust for Insurance and a high level for Bonus. This prediction leaves aside a principal's potential betrayal aversion, which would diminish levels of Trust.

Result 2: Principals trusted overwhelmingly in the Choice treatment, and their Trust rates were not affected by whether they chose Insurance or Bonus.

Choosing either the Insurance or the Bonus option produced an extremely high and virtually the same rate of Trust across all three countries. Table 13.9 presents the breakdown of these Trust decisions by principals' Insurance and Bonus decisions; it also shows no significant differences in rates of Trust between the two strategy choices in any of the countries. There were also no differences between countries (results not shown).

Trust with Chance versus Choice with Insurance and Bonus

Theory would predict high levels of Trust with Insurance for both Chance and Choice, given that it is a weakly dominant strategy. We should expect Choice to lead to less Trust, since when the principal chooses Insurance it conveys a negative signal about low expectations for Reward and/or lack of generosity.[5] Bonus, on the other

TABLE 13.9. *Choice Treatment: Percentage
Choosing Trust in the Insurance and
the Bonus Games*

	Insurance (%)	Bonus (%)	p-value*
Oman	92.9	90.0	0.774
US	85.7	82.4	0.763
Vietnam	83.9	85.7	0.874
N	87	41	128
p-value*	0.555	0.862	0.757

*p-values are determined using chi-squared tests comparing principals' choices within a country (horizontal comparison) or across subject pools (vertical comparison).

hand, presents a different story. With Choice, the principal has put herself at risk by choosing Bonus, presumably with expectations of reciprocity (Reward choice by agent). Also, there was a selection effect: principals who are more (less) optimistic about Reward would differentially choose Bonus (Insurance) and then Trust (Not Trust). With Chance, by contrast, the Bonus choice is less likely to win Trust for two reasons: First, the principal did not allocate money in a manner that would win reciprocity. Second, there is no longer a selection effect among the principals.

> Result 3: Compared to the Chance treatment, principals in the Choice treatment were less likely to Trust if they chose Insurance and more likely to Trust if they chose Bonus.

Given Result 2, outcomes in the three countries were added together for this result. Principals were significantly less likely to Trust when they chose Insurance (87.4%) than when Insurance was randomly assigned to them (100%) ($p = 0.003$). It appears as if a random assignment of Insurance evaporates potential betrayal aversion or social comparison. In contrast, principals were significantly more likely to Trust when they had chosen to send a Bonus (85.4%) than when the Chance treatment assigned it to them (59.5%) ($p = 0.004$). We reiterate the two plausible explanations. First, principals believed that the intentions behind sending the Bonus would increase trustworthiness (likelihood of Reward) of the agent. Second, there was a selection effect at work. Principals who chose to send a Bonus revealed their confidence in the trustworthiness of their counterpart, at least if he received a bonus for Reward. Table 13.10a summarizes these results.

As can be seen in Table 13.10b, principals in all countries responded in the same direction to the Chance versus the Choice treatment: They Trusted less when Insurance was chosen and Trusted more when Bonus was chosen. This is quite in accord with the theory, since both a selection effect and the indication of intentions to the agent work in the same direction.

The differences, however, were not significant in all countries. While the effect sizes were relatively comparable in the Insurance game, whether a Bonus was by Choice or by Chance had by far the biggest impact in the United States. Eighty-two percent of US subjects Trusted when they could choose to send a Bonus, whereas only 30.4% Trusted when the Bonus was randomly assigned ($p = 0.001$). The Trust rate in the Chance treatment was significantly lower in the United States, 30.4%, than in Oman and Vietnam, where it was 63% and 78%, respectively ($p = 0.002$).

TABLE 13.10A. *Percentage Choosing Trust in the Chance versus the Choice Game*

	Insurance (%)	Bonus (%)	p-value˙
Choice	87.4	85.4	0.757
Chance	100	59.5	0.000
p-value*	0.003	0.004	

˙p-values are determined using chi-squared tests comparing principals' choices across allocation type (horizontal comparison) or treatments (vertical comparison).

TABLE 13.10B. *Percentage Choosing Trust in Chance versus Choice Game, by Country*

Choice	Insurance (%)	Bonus (%)	p-value*
Oman	92.9	90	0.774
US	85.7	82.4	0.763
Vietnam	83.9	85.7	0.874
N	87	41	128
p-value*	0.555	0.862	0.757
Chance	Insurance (%)	Bonus (%)	p-value*
Oman	100	63.2	0.005
US	100	30.4	0.000
Vietnam	100	78.1	0.007
N	65	74	139
p-value*	1	0.002	0.000

*p-values are determined using chi-squared tests comparing principals' choices across allocation type (horizontal comparison) or subject pools (vertical comparison).

Agent Behavior

Result 4: In the Choice treatment, Reward rates were higher when Bonus rather than Insurance was chosen.

Agents were significantly more likely to Reward Trust in the Bonus game than in the Insurance game, with 46% Rewarding Trust in the Bonus game and 14% Rewarding Trust in the Insurance game ($p = 0.000$). This is as we would expect, given the effect of Bonus versus Insurance on both payoffs and in indicating the principal's intentions and beliefs. Although directionally supported in all countries, at least doubling the Reward rate, given the modest sample size the effect was only statistically significant in Vietnam (Table 13.11), where Bonus had a Reward rate 2.8 times that of Insurance.

TABLE 13.11. *Choice Treatment: Percentage of Agents Choosing Reward in the Insurance and Bonus Games*

	Insurance (%)	Bonus (%)	p-value*
Oman	11.5	33.3	0.135
US	20.8	42.9	0.149
Vietnam	11.5	31.8	0.002
N	76	35	111
p-value*	0.564	0.504	0.000

* p-values are determined using chi-squared tests comparing across decision type (horizontal comparison) or across subject pools (vertical comparison).

TABLE 13.12A. *Percentage Choosing Trustworthiness in the Chance versus Choice Game*

	Insurance (%)	Bonus (%)	*p*-value*
Choice	14.5	45.7	0.000
Chance	26.2	47.7	0.020
p-value*	0.083	0.859	

*p-values are determined using chi-squared tests comparing across allocation type (horizontal comparison) or treatments (vertical comparison).

Result 5: Compared to the Chance treatment, agents in the Insurance game were less likely to Reward in the Choice game (but this effect was exclusively driven by Omani agents). Agents in the Bonus game were not affected by whether the Bonus was sent to them by the principal or allocated by Chance.

Agents were less likely to Reward Trust when principals chose Insurance (14%) rather than having it assigned to them by Chance (26%) ($p = 0.083$). This was significantly less than the 46% of agents who Rewarded Trust when principals actively chose to send a Bonus ($p = 0.000$). In addition, the difference in rates of Reward when Bonus or Insurance was randomly selected by the Chance lottery was also significant (Table 13.12a).

As can be seen in Table 13.12b, agents in all countries were more likely to Reward Trust when their principals had chosen Bonus versus Insurance, although the effect is not significant in each country. In the Chance treatment, the picture is more mixed, with agents more likely to Reward with a random Bonus than random

TABLE 13.12B. *Percentage Choosing Reward in Chance versus Choice Game, by Country*

Choice	Insurance (%)	Bonus (%)	*p*-value*
Oman	11.5	33.3	0.135
US	20.8	42.9	0.149
Vietnam	11.5	58.3	0.002
N	76	35	111
p-value*	0.564	0.504	0.000
Chance	Insurance (%)	Bonus (%)	p-value*
Oman	52.9	25.0	0.132
US	0.00	57.1	0.000
Vietnam	26.7	56.0	0.027
N	65	44	109
p-value*	0.002	0.181	0.020

*p-values are determined using chi-squared tests comparing across allocation type (horizontal comparison) or subject pools (vertical comparison).

Insurance in the United States and in Vietnam but not in Oman. Generally, agents' responses to the Choice versus the Chance Treatments varied by country. Under Insurance, Omanis were less likely to Reward Trust ($p < 0.01$), Americans were more likely to Reward Trust ($p < 0.05$), and the Vietnamese Rewarded Trust roughly equally often in the Choice and Chance treatments. In the Chance treatment, the Reward rate was significantly higher in Oman than in the United States or in Vietnam. Whether the Bonus was due to Choice or Chance had no effect on Reward rates in any of our countries. The Reward rates were about the same.

With the exception of Omani agents, our results suggest that agents were little affected by how the final outcomes came to be, by Choice or Chance. In contrast to the implications of an intention-based reciprocity model, agents were not more likely to Reward Trust when Insurance was randomly assigned, nor were they more likely to reward Trust when Bonus was chosen by the principals. This suggests that agents were largely driven by outcome-based considerations—because the bonus decreased the temptation to Betray.

Our results say nothing about two factors that could be significant, betrayal aversion by the principals or inequality aversion. We made no direct tests of the potential roles of these forces. Betrayal aversion, as mentioned, might eliminate the weak dominance of Trust given Insurance. It would increase the argument for Bonus, if the principal thought that gains in reciprocity were likely.

Inequality aversion would produce a much more complex story. For the agent, its application would have to be modified by the fact that the principal had already made two choices that directly affected the inequality of outcomes. The principal who was inequality averse would have to assess the likelihood that the agent would Reward in order to know the structure of inequality. A further consideration, if the principal were Betrayal averse, would be how inequality aversion factors in the loss that comes with Betrayal. Though it may have a monetary equivalent, it is hardly clear that inequality-averse players would simply value it on a monetary basis. Interestingly, the observed 100% trusting of principals in the Insurance-Chance setting indicates that principals experiencing by chance a manna from heaven like Insurance lose all betrayal aversion and inequality aversion. Future research might show whether experience of good luck makes people less concerned about exposure to betrayal or inequality.

Conclusion

The experiments in this chapter offered people the opportunity to modify a Trust game to increase the chances of a successful outcome. Specifically, we allowed principals to choose between Insurance—a mitigation-based approach that decreases the cost of Betrayal to them—and Bonus—a prevention-based approach—that increases the likelihood of Reward by giving an agent an additional payment to Reward.

We find that about two-thirds of our principals prefer Insurance, to protect against Betrayal, as opposed to Bonus, to make Reward more likely. Still, one-third of principals are willing to forgo the safety of Insurance and take a gamble on their agent's trustworthiness by adding a bonus to their payoff should they Reward. Indeed, Reward rates are about three times as high when Bonus rather than Insurance is chosen. However, in our experiments, Reward rates in the Bonus treatment were still not high enough to make the principals whole on an expected value basis in pure monetary terms.

While possibly too optimistic, principals seem to anticipate agents' reactions to Bonus versus Insurance. Those who chose to provide a Bonus were more likely to Trust than principals who chose Insurance. This is not necessarily intuitive. Given that Insurance fully compensated principals for monetary losses in case of Betrayal, Trusting was a (weakly) dominant strategy. However, if we allow for betrayal aversion, and principals think a Bonus will greatly increase reciprocity levels, then Bonus is preferred.

Trustworthiness—the propensity to Reward—in our experiments was largely driven by outcome-based motivations. It generally did not depend on whether Insurance or Bonus was chosen by the principals or determined by Chance. Our agents were responsive to their personal payoff change that resulted from the Bonus. In short, agents generally did not respond significantly to principals' intentions and expectations of Reward, as conveyed through their choice of Insurance versus Bonus. There was one exception: Omani agents were substantially more likely to Reward Trust when Insurance came through Chance than through Choice, suggesting that they understood and responded to intentions and expectations. This last result accords with evidence from Jordan, another Arab country, where Jordanians cared much more about intentions in Trust situations than did Americans (Al-Issis & Bohnet 2016).

Principals appeared to overestimate how responsive Reward would be to whether the principal made a choice or was assigned an arrangement. Thus principals expected that the intentions and expectations conveyed through their choices would have a more powerful effect than they did in practice. Hence principals were more likely to Trust when they had chosen Bonus and less likely to Trust when they had chosen Insurance as compared to a Chance assignment.

Overall, our results suggest that at least some principals want to make Trust work. They send a Bonus to encourage trustworthiness (Reward) rather than insuring themselves against the losses from Betrayal and/or merely choosing Not Trust to avoid exposure to potential betrayal. Given our results, it appears that these principals are too sanguine about the likelihood of Reward given proven intentions.[6] About half of our agents Betray despite being offered a Bonus. Mostly, agents seem to care about outcomes independent of how they came about.

Our chapter contributes to the larger debate about the relative importance of processes versus outcomes in determining how players will behave. Equally important, we suggest that in addition to studying how people respond to given environments, the laboratory lends itself to questions of institutional design. What games would people play if they could choose? And are people "good" at choosing? Do they have a good sense of what will work best? Our results raise some cautions. A prime dictum for choice in interactive situations is to place one-self in the other player's shoes. Unfortunately, that may not tell in which direction he would walk.

■ NOTES

1. Of course, in situations where damages likely follow after a betrayal, that will also deter betrayals.

2. Note that it could also prove counterproductive if the agent regards it as a bribe and betrays so as to turn down the bribe.

3. For this analysis, we posit that the cost of betrayal is the same in the original trust game as it is when the principal relies on damages or sends a bonus. Future analyses should test for differences among these costs.

4. The corresponding fractions for all principals, including those who allocated the additional money to the two other payoffs (i.e., to themselves in case their agent rewarded trust or to their agent in case he betrayed) were 54% for Insurance and 25% for Bonus, with 21% of our principals making choices that did not make intuitive sense. The difference between Insurance and Bonus allocations remains significant.

5. The disparity might arise, despite the weakly dominant strategy because the principal did not fully understand the game but did understand that a reduced reward probability was bad. Alternatively, principals may have been betrayal-averse, which would remove the weakly dominant property of Insurance trust.

6. Obviously, for slightly different payoffs, this optimism might be justified.

■ REFERENCES

Alesina, A., & La Ferrara, E. (2002). Who trusts others? *Journal of Public Economics*, *85*, 207–234.

Al-Issis, M., & Bohnet, I. (2016). Risk mitigation and trust: Experimental evidence from Jordan and the United States. *Journal of Economic Psychology*, *53*, 83–98.

Bohnet, I., Herrmann, B., & Zeckhauser, R. (2010). Trust and the reference points for trustworthiness in Gulf and Western countries. *Quarterly Journal of Economics*, *125*, 811–828.

Bohnet, I., Greig, F., Herrmann, B., & Zeckhauser, R. (2008). Betrayal aversion: Evidence from Brazil, China, Oman, Switzerland, Turkey, and the United States. *The American Economic Review*, *98*, 294–310.

Bohnet, I., Herrmann, B., Al-Issis, M., Robbet, A., Al-Yahya, K., & Zeckhauser, R. (2012). The elasticity of trust: How to promote trust in the Arab Middle East and in the United States. In R. Kramer & T. Pittinsky (Eds.), *Restoring trust in organizations and leaders: Enduring challenges and emerging answers* (pp. 151–169). New York: Oxford University Press.

Bohnet, I., & Zeckhauser, R. (2004). Trust, risk and betrayal. *Journal of Economic Behavior & Organization*, *55*, 467–484.

Brandts, J., & Charness, G. (2004). Do labour market conditions affect gift exchange? Some experimental evidence. *The Economic Journal*, *114*, 684–708.

Improving Outcomes in the Trust Game ■ 253

Camerer, C., & Keith, K. (1988). Experimental tests of a sequential equilibrium reputation model. *Econometrica: Journal of the Econometric Society, 56*, 1–36.

Fehr, E., Gächter, S., & Kirchsteiger, G. (1997). Reciprocity as a contract enforcement device: Experimental evidence. *Econometrica: Journal of the Econometric Society, 65*, 833–860.

Fehr, E., Kirchsteiger, G., & Riedl, A. (1993). Does fairness prevent market clearing? An experimental investigation. *The Quarterly Journal of Economics, 108*, 437–59.

Fehr, E., & Schmidt, K. M. (1999). A theory of fairness, competition, and cooperation. *Quarterly Journal of Economics, 114*, 817–868.

Fukuyama, F. (1995). *Trust: The social virtues and the creation of prosperity.* New York: Free Press.

Hannan, R. L., Kagel, J. H., & Moser, D. V. (2002). Partial gift exchange in an experimental labor market: Impact of subject population differences, productivity differences, and effort requests on behavior. *Journal of Labor Economics, 20*, 923–951.

Knack, S., & Keefer, P. (1997). Does social capital have an economic payoff? A cross-country investigation. *The Quarterly Journal of Economics, 112*(4), 1251–1288.

Kreps, D. M. (1990). Corporate culture and economic theory. In J. E. Alt & K. A. Shepsle (Eds.), *Perspectives on positive political economy* (pp. 90–143). Cambridge, UK: Cambridge University Press.

LaPorta, R., Lopez-De-Silane, F., Shleifer, A., & Vishny, R. W. (1996). Trust in large organizations. *The American Economic Review, 87*, 333–338.

Putnam, R. D. (1995). Bowling alone: America's declining social capital. *Journal of Democracy, 6*, 68.

Rabin, M. (1993). Incorporating fairness into game theory and economics. *The American Economic Review, 83*, 1281–1302.

Rapoport, A. (1967). A note on the "index of cooperation" for prisoner's dilemma. *Journal of Conflict Resolution, 11*, 100–103.

Schelling, T. C. (1980). *The strategy of conflict.* Cambridge, MA: Harvard University Press.

Snijders, C., &. Keren, C. (1998). Determinants of trust. In D. V. Budescu, I. Erev, & R. Zwick (Eds.), *Games and human behavior: Essays in honor of Amnon Rapoport* (pp. 355–385). Mahwah, NJ: Lawrence Erlbaum.

Van Lange, P. A. M., Liebrand, W. B. G., & Kuhlman, D. M. (1990). Causal attribution of choice behavior in three N-person prisoner's dilemmas. *Journal of Experimental Social Psychology, 26*, 34–48.

Yamagishi, T., & Sato, K. (1986). Motivational bases of the public goods problem. *Journal of Personality and Social Psychology, 50*, 67–73.

Zak, P. J., & Knack, S. (2001). Trust and growth. *The Economic Journal, 111*, 295–321.

◼ APPENDIX 13.A DEMOGRAPHIC AND SUMMARY STATISTICS OF SUBJECTS

Demographic Variable	Oman	United States	Vietnam
Gender	41% Male 59% Female	47% Male 53% Female	45% Male 54% Female
Race	100% Arab	57% Caucasian 24% Asian 7% African 6% Hispanic 6% Other	100% Asian
Age Distribution	NA	70% between 18–22 years 13% between 23–26 years 17% older than 26 years	79% between 18–22 years 14% between 23–26 years 7% older than 26 years
Religion	100% Muslim	37% None 26% Protestant 14% Catholic 13% Jewish 10% Other	46% Buddhist 46% None 8% Other
Education	99% Undergraduate 1% Graduate Studies	82% Undergraduate 18% Graduate Studies	96% Undergraduate 4% Graduate Studies

■ APPENDIX 13.B EXPERIMENTAL INSTRUCTIONS
WELCOME TO OUR RESEARCH PROJECT (X-C)!

How the study is conducted. The study is conducted anonymously. Participants will be identified only by code numbers. There is no communication among the participants. In the experiment you will make decisions that earn you points. At the end of the study we will pay you in cash according to the amount of points you earned in the experiment using the following exchange rate:

1 point= $1

In this study half the participants are randomly chosen as a Person "X," the other half as a Person "Y." *You are a Person "X."*

You will be randomly paired with one Person "Y" now present in this room. You will never know that person's identity nor will that person know your identity. In addition, your choice will not be known to other participants or to the researchers.

All information provided in these instructions is commonly known by all the persons "X" and all the persons "Y."

About your decisions. First we present the basic problem to you (Payoff Table 1 and Figure 1). Your first decision is which payoff to increase in the problem (Payoff Table 2, Figure 2). Your second decision is to choose between A and B from the modified Payoff Table 3. We will ask you to make these decisions and will then determine the points you have earned.

BASIC PROBLEM

The basic problem is described in Payoff Table 1. Figure 1 presents the problem graphically. You have to choose one of two alternatives, A or B:

A gives you a payoff for sure and Person Y takes no action.
B gives you an outcome that depends on Person Y's behavior. If you choose B, Person Y has to choose between options 1 and 2.

Payoff Table 1

You choose	Nature of choice	Earnings to you	Earnings to Person Y
A	Certain outcome	10	10
B	Person Y chooses 1 2	15 5	15 25

The payoff table reads as follows:

> If you choose A, you and Person Y will each get 10 points.
> If you choose B and Person Y chooses 1, you and Person Y will each get 15 points.
> If you choose B and Person Y chooses 2, you will get 5 points and Person Y will get 25 points.

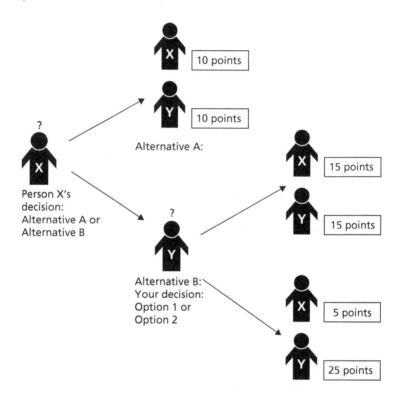

POSSIBLE CHANGES TO BASIC PROBLEM

Before you decide between alternatives A and B, you are asked to allocate an additional 5 points. You can add these 5 points to any of the payoffs in Row B of Table 1. The 5 points cannot be split. All must go to one payoff. Your person Y will be told where you put the points. Payoff Table 2 shows all possible changes to the payoff structure you are allowed to make. *You need to choose one of them.* Figure 2 presents your options graphically.

Payoff Table 2

You choose	Nature of choice	Earnings to you	Earnings to Person Y
A	Certain outcome	10	10
B	Person Y chooses 1	15 + 5 =20?	15 + 5=20?
	2	5 + 5 =10?	25 + 5=30?

Choose one

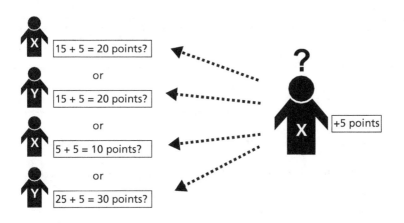

Conduct of Study

(i) We will distribute YOUR ANSWER FORMS to you, where you can indicate your decisions.

(ii) First you will be asked to decide where to add the 5 points, then you will be asked to choose either alternative A or alternative B.

(iii) After you have made your two decisions, we will collect all answer forms.

(iv) Answer forms will be randomly distributed to Persons Y.

(v) If you chose alternative A, your Person Y will not have a decision to make. If you chose alternative B, your Person Y will choose between Options 1 and 2.

(vi) After Persons Y have made their decisions, we will collect all answer forms.

(vii) We will calculate your earnings.

Completion of Study and Earnings

- After conducting the study, we ask you to complete a post-study questionnaire.
- You can collect your earnings by presenting your COIE NUMBER FORM at the end of the study. Your earnings will be in an envelope marked with your code number.

YOUR ANSWER FORM (PERSON X-C) Your code number is: ....

QUESTION: To which payoff do you add the 5 points? Please indicate your choice in Payoff Table 3 below. Remember, you can only add the 5 points as a whole to one of the payoffs in Row B.

Payoff Table 3: YOUR ANSWER

You choose	Nature of choice	Earnings to you	Earnings to Person Y
A	Certain outcome	10	10
B	Person Y chooses 1 2	**15 + ...** **5 + ...**	**15 + ...** **25 + ...**

Before you decide between alternatives A and B, please answer the following questions:

1. Based on the modified payoffs in Table 3, how much do you earn if you choose alternative A? _____

   How much does Person Y earn in this case? _____

2. Based on the modified payoffs in Table 3, how much do you earn if you choose alternative B and Person Y chooses option 1? _____

   How much does Person Y earn in this case?_____

3. Based on the modified payoffs in Table 3, how much do you earn if you choose alternative B and Person Y chooses option 2? _____

   How much does Person Y earn in this case?_____

FINAL QUESTION: Which alternative, A or B, do you choose from your modified Payoff Table 3?

YOUR ANSWER: I choose _____

WELCOME TO OUR RESEARCH PROJECT (Y-C)!

How the study is conducted. The study is conducted anonymously. Participants will be identified only by code numbers. There is no communication among the participants. In the experiment you will make decisions that earn you points. At the end of the study we will pay you in cash according to the amount of points you earned in the experiment using the following exchange rate:

$$1 \text{ point} = \$1$$

In this study half the participants are randomly chosen as a Person "X," the other half as a Person "Y." *You are a Person "Y."*

You will be randomly paired with one Person "X" now present in this room. You will never know that person's identity nor will that person know your identity. In addition, your choice will not be known to other participants or to the researchers. All information provided in these instructions is commonly known by all the persons "X" and all the persons "Y."

About your decisions. First we present the basic problem to you (Payoff Table 1 and Figure 1). Then we explain to you how a Person X can make changes to the basic problem (Payoff Table 2, Figure 2). Finally, you will make your decision based on the modified Payoff Table 3.

BASIC PROBLEM

The basic problem is described in Payoff Table 1. Figure 1 presents the problem graphically. Person X has to choose one of two alternatives, A or B.

A gives you and Person X a payoff for sure and you take no action.
B gives Person X an outcome that depends on your behavior. If Person X chooses B,
you have to choose between options 1 and 2.

Payoff Table 1

Person X chooses	Nature of choice	Earnings to Person X	Earnings to you
A	Certain outcome	10	10
B	You choose 1	15	15
	2	5	25

The payoff table reads as follows:

> If Person X chooses A, you and Person X will each get 10 points.
> If Person X chooses B and you choose 1, you and Person X will each get 15 points.
> If Person X chooses B and you choose 2, you will get 25 points and Person X will get 5
> points.

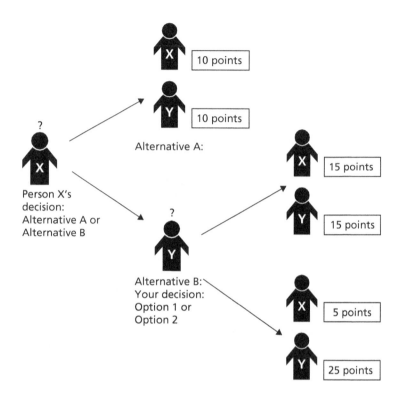

POSSIBLE CHANGES TO BASIC PROBLEM

Before Person X decides between alternatives A and B, Person X is asked to allocate an additional 5 points. Person X can add these 5 points to any of the payoffs in Row B of Table 1. The 5 points cannot be split. All must go to one payoff. You will be told where Person X put the points. Payoff Table 2 shows all possible changes to the payoff structure Person X is allowed to make. *Person X needs to choose one of them.* Figure 2 presents Person X's options graphically.

Payoff Table 2

Person X chooses	Nature of choice	Earnings to Person X	Earnings to you
A	Certain outcome	10	10
B	You choose 1 2	15 + 5 =20? 5 + 5 =10?	15 + 5=20? 25 + 5=30?

Person X chooses one

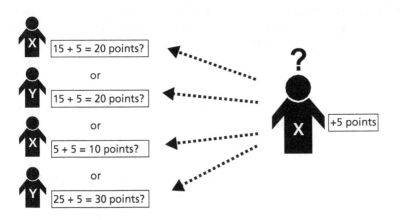

Conduct of Study

(i) We will distribute answer forms to Persons X, where they can indicate their decisions. They make two decisions: to which payoff to add the 5 points and what alternative, A or B, to choose. First Person X will be asked to decide where to add the 5 points, then Person X will be asked to choose either alternative A or alternative B.

(ii) After all Persons X have made their two decisions, we will collect their answer forms.

(iii) Answer forms will be randomly distributed to Persons Y. In addition, you will receive YOUR CHOICE FORM to indicate your decision.

(iv) You look at your answer form. You will learn to which payoff your Person X has added the 5 points and which alternative, A or B, your Person X has chosen.
   a. If Person X has chosen alternative A, you do not make a decision.
   b. If Person X has chosen alternative B, you decide between Options 1 and 2.

(v) After you have made your decisions, we will collect all choice and answer forms.

(vi) We will calculate your earnings.

Completion of Study and Earnings

- After conducting the study, we ask you to complete a post-study questionnaire.
- You can collect your earnings by presenting your COIE NUMBER FORM at the end of the study. Your earnings will be in an envelope marked with your code number.

YOUR CHOICE FORM (PERSON Y-C)　　　　　　Your code number is: . . . .

Your counterpart's code number is: . . . .

INFORMATION: Please learn from Payoff Table 3 on your Person X' ANSWER FORM where the 5 points were added. On the Answer Form, you also see which Alternative, A or B, your person X has chosen.

Before you make any decisions, please answer the following questions:

1. Based on the modified payoffs in Table 3, how much do you earn if Person X chose alternative A? _____

   How much does Person X earn in this case? _____

2. Based on the modified payoffs in Table 3, how much do you earn if Person X chose alternative B and you choose option 1? _____

   How much does Person X earn in this case?_____

3. Based on the modified payoffs in Table 3, how much do you earn if Person X chose alternative B and you choose option 2? _____

   How much does Person X earn in this case?_____

MAIN QUESTION: If Person X chose alternative B, which option, 1 or 2, do you choose?

YOUR ANSWER: I choose _____

14 Trust in African Villages

Experimental Evidence from Rural Sierra Leone

■ PAUL HOFMAN, ERWIN BULTE,
AND MAARTEN VOORS

■ INTRODUCTION

Gambetta (2000) writes that

> when we say we trust somebody or that somebody is trustworthy, we implicitly mean
> that the probability that he will perform an action that is beneficial ... is high enough
> for us to consider engaging in some form of cooperation with him. (p. 217)

Trust, in other words, reflects expectations about the behavior of others. Echoing
this perspective, Mayer, Davis, and Schoorman (1995) define trust as

> the willingness of a party to be vulnerable to the actions of another party based on the
> expectation that the other will perform a particular action important to the trustor, irre-
> spective of the ability to monitor or control that other party. (p. 712)

The expectation of fair behavior by others implies trustors may willingly expose
themselves to the risk of bad behavior by the other party—think of defaulting on
loans or supplying bad-quality goods. Trust therefore permits "riskier situations."
One might argue that exposing oneself to such risk can potentially yield higher
payoffs. For example, net payoffs from transacting might go up because of lower
transaction costs, or simply because transactions are possible over a broader range
of actions.

Economic work indeed suggests a positive correlation between trust levels and
economic performance (e.g., Knack & Keefer 1997). In the words of Nobel laureate
Kenneth Arrow,

> Virtually every commercial transaction has within itself an element of trust, certainly
> any transaction conducted over a period of time. It can be plausibly argued that much
> of the economic backwardness in the world can be explained by the lack of mutual con-
> fidence. (1972, p. 357)

For trade to flourish, enabling modes of exchange extending beyond simple
barter or cash-and-carry trade, moral obligations of fairness and reciprocity should extend to anonymous others—not just kith and kin. In other words,
generalized morality and trust should develop and spread (e.g., Fafchamps 2011;
Platteau 1994; Tu, Bulte, & Tan, 2011). But what are the determinants of trust and

trustworthiness? This question has emerged as an important research topic in the social sciences.

The literature contains various conjectures and suggestions regarding the determinants (and consequences) of trust and trustworthiness. A full treatise is beyond the scope of this chapter, but we discuss some important insights, focusing on the three key determinants identified in the literature: (a) beliefs and perceptions, (b) individual characteristics and preferences, and (c) context. For example, Mayer et al. (1995) argue that trust amounts to one's perception of the trustworthiness of one's partner and therefore depends on the assessment of the ability, integrity, and benevolence of others. Trust levels are therefore specific at the transaction level. In contrast, Delhey and Newton (2003) distinguish between trust as a personal and societal trait. At the level of individuals, trust may be a stable personality trait (perhaps acquired at young age) or a trait reflecting the history of interaction with others. Instead, societal theories of trust are based on the structure of a society, including how individuals are linked in various networks. Other community factors affecting (average) trust levels may be community size (smaller communities tend to be more trusting) and wealth, the incidence of violence, or the quality of institutions. Focusing on the composition of the sample population, Fehr and Schmidt (1999) propose that trust can emerge and persist (in experimental games) because of the presence of sufficient inequity-averse players. Inequity aversion implies that noncooperation ceases to be the dominant strategy, and trusting behavior can emerge as an equilibrium outcome.

In this chapter we report experimental and survey data for a sample of African smallholders. Specifically, we visited a large number of villages in eastern Sierra Leone and organized a trust game in each village. The study site is a remote part of the country and one of the poorest regions in the world. It was also ravaged by a protracted civil war (between 1991 and 2002), which pitted rural villagers against each other, and in more recent times—after the collection of our data—by an Ebola epidemic. Formal state intuitions are largely absent, and most village exchange takes the form of repeated, personalized interaction, oftentimes embodied in kinship ties or patronage relations (see Richards, 1986). Community-level activities, including the organization of public goods projects and conflict settlement, are governed by local institutions supported by strong social norms of cooperation. The predominant occupation is farming, and many villagers are engaged in labor-exchanging arrangements based on reciprocity (e.g., Cartier & Bürge, 2011). Understanding the determinants of trust in these communities is an essential starting point for effective policymaking to foster postconflict and post-Ebola reconstruction and development.

In this chapter we empirically investigate the correlations between trust (and trustworthiness) on the one hand and individual characteristics, beliefs, and village context on the other for West African smallholders. We report outcomes for this non-WEIRD (Western, educated, industrialized, rich, and democratic) sample of respondents and contrast measured trust to trust levels as reported in the existing literature. We also probe the key correlates of trust and trustworthiness and ask whether these variables are correlated with individual characteristics (age, gender, income), preferences (whether a respondent is generous, inequality averse, or selfish), specific shocks (resulting from the weather or wartime violence), and village-level variables or "local context" (institutional quality, economic inequality, migrant population, and beliefs).

This chapter is organized as follows. We first introduce the two main methodological challenges researchers in this domain are confronted with and discuss how these challenges are important for the interpretation of our results. In the third section we introduce our subject pool, describe our data, and introduce our (simple) empirical strategy. The fourth section presents the main regression results, and the final section concludes.

■ METHODOLOGICAL CHALLENGES

The literature on the determinants of trust and trustworthiness struggles with several challenges. Two leading challenges involve the measurement of trust and trustworthiness and untangling complex webs of correlations to arrive at evidence of causal effects. The latter issue emerges as a concern because, in a regression framework, trust might emerge both as a dependent and an explanatory variable. Theory suggests trust evolves in response to various factors, but in turn (via its effect on behavior) may also codetermine the evolution of these same factors. For example, market integration and associated "learning" might enable the building of trust (as argued by Heinrich et al., 2010), but accumulating trust in turn facilitates trade. Similarly, higher incomes may enable people to behave in a more trusting manner (i.e., accept greater vulnerability to the actions of others), but trusting behavior may simultaneously be rewarded by rising incomes.[1] To untangle the causal effect of context factors on the dynamics of trust and trustworthiness implies the analyst may resort to econometric approaches—for example, using so-called instrumental variables to identify exogenous variation in the factors of interest—or to a (natural) experimental approach, where exogenous variation is implied by design or exogenous shocks. In this chapter we are less ambitious and seek to establish correlations between measured trust and various variables of interest. Future work should reveal whether or not these correlations imply causal relationships.

The second challenge facing empiricists working on trust concerns the issue of measurement. Trust is not observed directly but may be gauged by either a (standard) survey question or by observing one's behavior in a choice setting. Two measurement approaches dominate the literature. The first common measure of (generalized) trust is based on the well-known World Value Survey question: "Generally speaking, would you say that most people can be trusted or that you cannot be too careful in dealing with people?" The validity of this approach has been scrutinized, and recent work by Sapienza, Toldra-Simats, and Zingales (2013) concludes that trust thus measured indeed captures beliefs about the intentions and behavior of others.

The second common trust measure is based on behavior in the so-called trust game. In this (lab-style) experiment, a trustor receives an endowment (X) of tokens (or money) which he or she can either keep for him- or herself or (partly) transfer part (Z) to an anonymous partner (e.g., a co-villager). The amount transferred is multiplied by 3, so the other party receives $3Z$. The receiver, in turn, can return any amount ($Y \leq 3Z$) to the sender. After the experiment, the trustor has earned $X - Z + Y$ tokens (ultimately convertible into a monetary amount) and the receiver has earned $3Z - Y$. One "socially optimal" outcome is for the trustor to send the entire amount (X), which is subsequently split by the receiver. In this case both players end up with $1.5X$. But in the absence of sufficient trust, the trustor is likely to send nothing. The amount sent in a trust game, Z, is typically interpreted as a measure of trust, and the percentage returned, $Y/3Z$, is typically interpreted as a measure of trustworthiness. The experimental approach to gauging trust and trustworthiness is more complex (and costly) than the survey-based method but has the clear advantage that it is incentive compatible. That is, participants in the experiments have a (monetary) incentive to act in accordance with their true beliefs and expectations rather than, say, provide (politically) correct answers to hypothetical questions. A potential disadvantage of measuring trust via trust games is that sending behavior in the game might reflect other preferences than simply trust, including altruism, inequality aversion, or risk preferences (e.g., Karlan 2005, Sapienza et al. 2013). Possibly, triangulation based on combining behavior in multiple games can help to isolate trust from such potentially confounding effects.

In Table 14.1 we provide an overview of amounts sent and returned in earlier trust games. Across these studies, trust appears relatively high: on average, respondents send 50% of their endowment. However, the studies also display considerable variation, suggesting that context (and perhaps respondent characteristics) may matter. On average, receivers send back 37%, so that the investment of the trustor just pays off (on average). Again, there is variation in return rates, and several studies find that transferring money does not pay off for the sender.

■ SETTING, DATA, AND ESTIMATION STRATEGY

We use data from respondents in 86 communities in rural Sierra Leone surrounding the Gola Rainforest National Park. In each village participants (mainly household heads) were randomly selected to participate in a series of behavioral experiments (including a trust game) and a short survey during the fall of 2011. In total, 1,289 people participated in both the trust game and the survey. Table 14.2 summarizes descriptive data for our respondents.

Our main variables of interest, trust and trustworthiness, are based on the classical trust game proposed by Berg, Dickhaut, and McCabe (1995). Our group of participants was divided (randomly) into senders and receivers. The identities of the sender and receiver are never revealed. The senders receive an endowment of 1000 Leones (about €0.17) in the form of 10 tokens—a small amount but nevertheless a salient incentive in this cash-stricken part of Sierra Leone. As mentioned, senders are invited to send part of this endowment to an anonymous receiver from their community and informed that the experimenter will triple any amount they choose to send. The receiver can send any amount back to the original sender, as

TABLE 14.1. *Overview of Findings in Studies on Trust*

	Bouma, Bulte, & Soest (2008)	Cox (2004)	Schechter (2007)	Buchan, Croson, & Solnick (2008)	Burks, Carpenter, & Verhoogen (2003)	Cochard, Nguyen Van, & Willinger (2004)	Holm & Danielson (2005)	Johnson & Mislin (2011)
Participants	Indian rural households	US students	Paraguayan rural households	US students	US students	Unclear	Tanzanian and Swedish students	Meta-analysis
Sample Size	92 senders	32 senders	188 senders	39 senders	44 senders	20 senders	100 Tanzanian, 55 Swedish	137 studies
% sent nothing	13	19	7	–	–	–	–	–
% of endowment sent to other	49	60	46	68	65	50	Tanzania: 53 Sweden: 51	50
% of received tokens returned	29	27	43	28	40	38	Tanzania: 37 Sweden: 35	37
Return on investment (received back/sent)	0.87	0.82	1.3	0.84	1.31	1.14	Tanzania: 1.11 Sweden: 1.05	1.11

TABLE 14.2. *Summary Statistics*

Variable	Number of Villages	Obs	Mean	SD	Min	Max
% sent in Trust Game	86	657	31.52	22.67	0	100
% returned in Trust Game	86	632	32.73	16.99	0	100
Age	86	1279	38.77	14.23	13	97
Gender (Male=1)	86	1289	0.566	0.496	0	1
Farm size	86	1286	5	5.333	0	60
Social Type, 1=Generous	86	1289	0.137	0.343	0	1
Social Type, 1=Inequality-Averse	86	1289	0.420	0.494	0	1
Social Type, 1=Selfish	86	1289	0.175	0.380	0	1
Social Type, 1=Other	86	1289	0.268	0.443	0	1
Do you hide your harvest? (Yes=1)	86	1288	0.648	0.478	0	1
With how many household do you share your harvest?	86	1288	4.117	3.333	0	60
How many households share their harvest with you?	86	1288	3.130	2.496	0	30
# times asked chief for help, village average	86	1289	1.590	0.809	0	4.750
Do you trust the chief? (Yes=1), village average	86	1289	0.917	0.103	0.381	1
Presence of crop shocks in previous year: rain, drought, or crop disease	71	1051	1.805	0.573	0	3
Gini Index (Farm Size)	86	1289	0.402	0.0844	0.118	0.636
Percentage of migrants in village, 2013 data	86	1289	0.118	0.123	0	1
Donation in public good game, village average	85	1273	9.359	3.103	2.642	17.13
Village size	86	1289	45.29	28.57	4	148
Fraction of people who died in the war	63	932	0.150	0.121	0.0231	0.920
Fraction of people who fled the war and did not return	66	980	0.336	0.213	0.0357	0.940
Distance to main market town (km)	63	942	8.037	4.961	1	23

long as this amount does not exceed the amount that was received. Our measure for trust is the percentage of tokens shared by the sender. On average, respondents shared 32% (*SD* 23) of their endowment (see Figure 14.1a). This is on the lower end of the values reported in other studies (Table 14.1). Our measure of trustworthiness is the fraction of tokens receivers send back (see Figure 14.1b). On average participants returned 33% (*SD* 17), which matches earlier findings.

We distinguish between three types of explanatory variables to explain the variation in trust and trustworthiness that we observe in our sample. First, we collected data on a range of individual characteristics, including age, gender, and farm size (a proxy for income). In addition, subjects were asked about their beliefs and expectations regarding the behaviour of co-villagers. Specifically, we asked three questions (a) "Do you hide any of your harvest so others won't know you have it?" (b) "If you had a good harvest, how many households in your village would you share with?" and (c) "If you needed food, how many households in your village would share [food] with you?" On average, about two-thirds of our respondents say they hide part of their harvest (64%, *SD* 48%). The average respondent would share food with about four other households and expects to receive food (if asked) from about three other households. These data suggest the existence of norms of sharing, which is not surprising in a context characterized by near autarky. However, it is interesting that many individuals seek to evade their sharing obligations if possible.

To proximate social preferences we invited subjects to participate in an allocation game based on Fehr et al. (2008). Participants were asked to make four dichotomous allocation choices, allowing us to classify our respondents into four

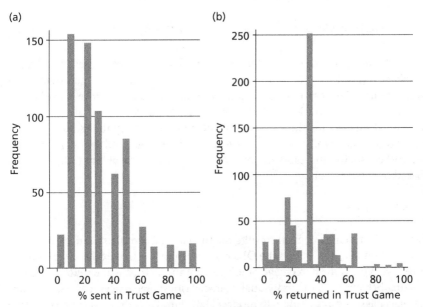

Figure 14.1 Distribution of contributions in the trust game (A and B).

different "types:" generous, inequality averse, selfish, and other. The four alloca-tion choices consist of an egalitarian and nonegalitarian allocation (see Appendix Table A1 for choice options). The majority of our respondents are classified as "inequality averse" (42%). About 14% are "generous," and 17% are "selfish." The remaining 27% are classified as "other."

We obtained data on a range of context variables. First, we used survey ques-tions to obtain two proxies for chief quality, or the quality of local governance ("How often have you asked the chief for help?" and "Do you trust the chief?"). We also collected data on the incidence of crop failure in recent years, due to pests or adverse weather conditions. Based on data on farm size, as mentioned, we com-puted a Gini coefficient to capture within-village inequality. To complement our vector of context variables, we also administered a village-level survey collecting information on the size of the village (in terms of the number of households) and the share of migrants in the village (as a measure of heterogeneity). We used aver-age contributions in a public good game as a proxy for social capital (or social cohesion—the ability to overcome dilemmas). Finally, we collected village-level data on access to markets and exposure to conflict during the civil war. The latter variables capture the number of villagers that died during the war (scaled by pre-war village size) and the percentage of people who had to permanently flee from the village. Unfortunately, these market access and conflict data are only available for a subsample of the villages.

Our identification strategy is very simple. We used ordinary least squares (OLS) and regressed our measures of trust and trustworthiness on our prefer-ences, beliefs, and context variables. Specifically, our main models are

$$Trust_{ij} = \beta_1 + \beta_2 X_{ij} + \beta_3 B_{ij} + \beta_3 P_{ij} + \beta_4 V_j + \varepsilon_{ij} \qquad (1)$$

$$Trustworthiness_{ij} = \beta_1 + \beta_2 X_{ij} + \beta_3 B_{ij} + \beta_4 P_{ij} + \beta_5 V_j + \beta_6 Trust_{ij} + \varepsilon_{ij} \qquad (2)$$

where $Trust_{ij}$ is our measure for trust, or the fraction of tokens sent by player i in village j ($i = 1, \ldots, 1278, j = 1, \ldots, 90$). $Trustworthiness_{ij}$ is the fraction of tokens returned by respondent i; X_{ij} is a vector of individual controls; B_{ij} are beliefs; P_{ij} are preferences; and V_j are context variables. We add the percentage sent into the model for trustworthiness to see if the amount sent by the trustor matters. Throughout, standard errors are clustered at the village level and corrected for heteroskedasticity, and estimates are weighted for the probability to be sampled (based on village size).

■ RESULTS

Table 14.3 presents our main results for the correlates of trust and trustworthi-ness. Column (1)-(3) reports the OLS results of a model that explains variation in trust. We regress the percentage of tokens sent in the trust game (our measure of trusting behavior) on the individual characteristics, preferences, beliefs, and con-text variables—corresponding to model (1). Columns (4) through (6) do the same

TABLE 14.3. Origins of Experimental Trust and Trustworthiness

	(1)	(2)	(3)	(4)	(5)	(6)
	Trust	Trust	Trust	Trustworthiness	Trustworthiness	Trustworthiness
Individual Characteristics						
Age	0.505*	0.468*	0.534*	0.343	0.383	0.652**
	(0.255)	(0.261)	(0.287)	(0.269)	(0.271)	(0.300)
Age^2	-0.004	-0.003	-0.003	-0.003	-0.004	-0.007**
	(0.002)	(0.002)	(0.003)	(0.003)	(0.003)	(0.003)
Gender (Male=1)	2.603	2.244	1.998	-0.408	-0.343	2.126
	(2.348)	(2.258)	(2.042)	(2.292)	(2.295)	(2.650)
Farm Size	-0.174	-0.120	-0.067	-0.119	-0.163	0.070
	(0.278)	(0.282)	(0.275)	(0.185)	(0.185)	(0.294)
Social Preferences						
Social Type, 1=Generous	1.037	1.206	-1.830	-2.554	-2.810	-0.643
	(3.055)	(3.226)	(3.767)	(2.898)	(2.934)	(3.310)
Social Type, 1=Inequality-Averse	-0.097	0.199	-1.629	-4.759*	-4.573*	-3.813
	(2.374)	(2.456)	(2.491)	(2.389)	(2.362)	(2.985)
Social Type, 1=Selfish	-5.314	-5.462*	-1.188	-6.729*	-6.830*	-2.291
	(3.256)	(2.955)	(2.943)	(3.385)	(3.452)	(4.305)
Beliefs						
Do you hide your harvest? (Yes=1)	-2.652		2.090	-0.518		-1.730
	(2.196)		(2.272)	(1.550)		(1.842)
With how many households do you share your harvest?	-1.069**		-1.031	0.043		0.276
	(0.529)		(0.674)	(0.252)		(0.269)
How many households share their harvest with you?	1.501**		0.610	-0.725**		-0.822*
	(0.636)		(0.686)	(0.343)		(0.414)

(continued)

TABLE 14.3. Continued

	(1)	(2)	(3)	(4)	(5)	(6)
	Trust	Trust	Trust	Trustworthiness	Trustworthiness	Trustworthiness
			Context			
# times asked chief for help, village average	-4.045 (2.785)	-3.907 (2.830)	2.262 (2.990)	-2.296 (1.682)	-2.584 (1.723)	-2.584 (2.044)
Do you trust the chief? (Yes=1), village average	23.497 (19.326)	24.697 (19.843)	-3.042 (24.451)	1.049 (11.043)	1.039 (11.068)	14.313 (11.575)
Crop shocks in previous year	-2.994 (4.376)	-2.996 (4.378)	-3.164 (4.867)	-1.651 (2.411)	-1.722 (2.384)	-3.092 (2.600)
Gini Index (farm size)	21.426 (23.566)	19.497 (23.658)	54.338* (28.445)	22.616* (11.940)	23.044* (11.909)	23.152* (11.943)
Percentage of migrants in village	16.464 (21.177)	20.836 (22.231)	1.499 (40.552)	2.442 (9.526)	1.570 (9.705)	-1.836 (14.413)
Donation in public good game, village average	1.198* (0.658)	1.170* (0.671)	1.078 (0.742)	-0.041 (0.383)	-0.053 (0.373)	0.127 (0.320)
Village size	0.016 (0.043)	0.020 (0.041)	0.134 (0.088)	0.082** (0.033)	0.087** (0.033)	0.054 (0.060)
Fraction of people who died in the war			3.846 (39.515)			-19.525 (17.761)
Fraction of people who fled			22.851 (15.085)			9.298* (5.325)
Distance to main market town (km)			0.144 (0.499)			0.013 (0.274)
% sent in trust game				-0.003 (0.063)	-0.001 (0.060)	0.058 (0.070)
constant	-12.604 (18.968)	-14.037 (20.363)	-26.934 (24.156)	24.632 (15.215)	21.924 (15.149)	3.365 (14.470)
Observations	532	533	341	507	507	324

Note. Trust is measured as the percentage of tokens sent in the trust game. Trustworthiness is measured as the percentage of tokens returned in the trust game. Robust standard errors in parentheses clustered at village level. Weighted for probability to be sampled (based on village size). For variable definitions, refer to the appendix.

$* p < 0.10$, $** p < 0.05$, $*** p < 0.01$.

for trustworthiness. We regress the percentage of tokens returned (our measure capturing trustworthiness). Our main specifications are in columns (1) and (4). In columns (2) and (5) we exclude our beliefs variables, and in columns (3) and (6) we add our proxies for war exposure and market access (restricting our analysis to a subsample of the villages).

We find some interesting correlations. Few of the individual characteristics predict trust or trustworthiness. Trust increases with age but does not vary with gender or income. The amount returned is not significantly related to any of these variables, except (nonlinearly) to age for our regression on the subsample.

Turning to our preference variables, we first observe that prosocial types do not seem to send or return more tokens (relative to the omitted category of "other" types). We find that selfish individuals send and return less than others (though this finding is not significant in all specifications). In addition, inequality-averse individuals tend to return less.[2] This makes sense. On average, senders send one-third of their endowment and receivers return the same amount (or 33% of the amount received, after tripling by the experimenter). This leaves the sender better off than the receiver: net payoffs for the former are X and net payoffs for the latter are only $0.66X$. Inequality-averse individuals will therefore return less than the average player, in an effort to restore equality. However, the finding that selfishness and inequality aversion are correlated with the number of tokens sent implies that the game presumably does not capture trust in the narrow sense—defined as the expectation that one will not be exploited by the bad behavior of others. Instead, the trust games picks up a range of preferences (see also Sapienza et al., 2013).

Next, we turn to beliefs about the intentions of behavior of others. Note that we did *not* explicitly ask about expectations with respect to the behavior of the receiver in the trust game (which would have been the closest proxy of trust according to Gambetta [2000] and Mayer et al. [1995]; Sapienza et al. 2013). Instead, we asked respondents about their attitudes and beliefs with respect to (informal) sharing with others in the village. We assume this is related to the quality of social relations, or with social capital, affecting trust and trustworthiness in the experiment. We find, in column (1), that households supporting a larger number of other households in case of need will send less in a trust game.

We also report the puzzling finding that respondents expecting more support from others share more (as senders) but tend to return *less* (as responders). It is an open question why trusting behavior on the one hand and trustworthiness on the other correlate so differently with sharing behavior in real life. The finding that sharing positively correlates with trusting behavior could indicate that beliefs (or expectations) about fair behavior by others spill over from the village context to the experiment. It could also be consistent with the interpretation that receiving transfers from peers invites a livelihood strategy that involves investing in social capital (by displaying trusting behavior). But this finding is not very robust, as it does not appear significantly in column (3). Why are more optimistic beliefs about other households' generosity associated with lower levels of own trustworthiness (column 6)? This could indicate that while people "on the receiving end" of informal sharing networks might invest in social relations (via trusting behavior), they are not used to repay their "debts." These conjectures are food for thought, suggesting that beliefs regarding behavior of others are correlated with behavioral trust—perhaps social capital is a more important correlate of behavioral trust than social preferences.

Perhaps surprisingly, very few of our context variables are correlated with trust or trustworthiness. For example, local governance is not correlated with amounts sent or returned or with the share of migrants in the village, market access, or exposure to crop shocks. In villages with higher levels of social capital (as measured by the average contribution to a public game), respondents tend to trust more, but trustworthiness is unaffected. We also observe that amounts returned are higher in unequal villages, in larger villages, and in villages that suffered exposure to conflict (if conflict caused permanent fleeing from the village). Note that the coefficients are large (but that in some cases the standard errors are even larger). In the absence of exogenous variation in our study, however, it is impossible to infer causal effects from the correlations presented in Table 14.3. We hope future research will allow us to zoom in on the most promising relationships (such as between inequality and trustworthiness).

■ CONCLUSION

Understanding the determinants and consequences of social capital is becoming increasingly important in economics. A recent shift has moved this field of inquiry from the lab to field contexts, as analysts increasingly seek to understand behavior in the "real world." In this chapter, we look at the determinants of trust and trustworthiness in a large sample of rural African villages in eastern Sierra Leone. We organized a series of trust games and empirically investigated the correlations between behavior in the game (our proxies of trust and trustworthiness) and certain individual characteristics, beliefs, and measures of the village context.

This study is exploratory and limited in focus and scope. Due to the nature of our data and sample, we only report correlations and abstain from any causal claims. We do believe the results are nonetheless interesting, if only because this is one of the first studies to measure trust, social preferences, and expectations of individuals in an African setting (certainly on such a large scale). Our results suggest that behavior in the game reflects expectations with respect to the (fair or not-so fair) behavior of others. In addition to this issue, which arguably is at the heart of the concept of "trust," we find that social preferences may also matter. In other words, and echoing insights from Sapienza et al. (2013) for a completely distinct sample of respondents, we believe the trust game does not cleanly measure trust as properly understood.

On average, we find that our sample of respondents send slightly less than respondents in earlier studies. While trust may be lower, we observe that trustworthiness is comparable to other studies.

■ AUTHORS' NOTE

Erwin Bulte is the corresponding author (erwin.bulte@wur.nl).

We are indebted to the Royal Society for the Protection of Birds and to the Gola Rainforest National Park's Gola REDD Project (supported until 2012 by the European Union, Fonds Français pour l'Environnement Mondial, and the Global Conservation Fund), BirdLife International, as well as Paul Richards, Esther Mokuwa, and Martha Ross for their collaboration in this project. We thank NWO (#45-14-001) and ESRC grant # ES/J017620/1 for financial support. We acknowledge the loyalty and hard work of the team of field enumerators and the patience and cooperation of interviewees.

■ NOTES

1. Moreover, "other factors," for example related to culture, might affect both trust and its apparent correlates. Failure to control for such "other factors" in empirical analyses implies that the correlation between trust and its correlates need not be indicative of a causal relation (omitted variables problem).

2. Note that the latter findings do not enter in a statistically significant way in columns (3) and (6). This may be due to the smaller sample size (reducing power of the test), or could reflect multicollinearity with the conflict and trade variables in these columns. Earlier work (e.g., Cecchi, Leuveld, & Voors [2016] indeed suggests that conflict exposure may alter social preferences and behavior.

■ REFERENCES

Arrow, K. (1972). Gifts and exchanges. Philosophy and Public Affairs, 1, 343–362.

Berg, J., Dickhaut, J., & McCabe, K. (1995). Trust, reciprocity, and social history. *Games and Economic Behavior, 10*(1), 122–142.

Bouma, J., Bulte, E., & van Soest, D. (2008). Trust and cooperation: Social capital and community resource management. *Journal of Environmental Economics and Management, 56*(2), 155–166. doi:10.1016/j.jeem.2008.03.004

Buchan, N. R., Croson, R. T. A., & Solnick, S. (2008). Trust and gender: An examination of behavior and beliefs in the investment game. *Journal of Economic Behavior & Organization, 68*(3–4), 466–476. doi:10.1016/j.jebo.2007.10.006

Burks, S. V., Carpenter, J. P., & Verhoogen, E. (2003). Playing both roles in the trust game. *Journal of Economic Behavior & Organization, 51*(2), 195–216.

Cartier, L. E., & M. Bürge. (2011). Agriculture and artisanal gold mining in Sierra Leone: Alternatives or complements? *Journal of International Development, 23*, 1080–1099.

Cecchi, F., Leuveld, K., & Voors, M. (2016). Conflict exposure and competitiveness: Experimental evidence from the football field in Sierra Leone, *Economic Development and Cultural Change, 64*, 405–435.

Cochard, F., Nguyen Van, P., & Willinger, M. (2004). Trusting behavior in a repeated investment game. *Journal of Economic Behavior & Organization*, *55*(1), 31–44. doi:10.1016/j.jebo.2003.07.004

Cox, J. C. (2004). How to identify trust and reciprocity. *Games and Economic Behavior*, *46*(2), 260–281. doi:10.1016/S0899-8256(03)00119-2

Delhey, J., & Newton, K. (2003). Who trusts? The origins of social trust in seven societies. *European Societies*, *5*(2), 93–137.

Gambetta, D. (2000). Can we trust trust? In: D. Gambetta (Ed.), *Trust, making and breaking cooperative relations* (pp. 213–227). Oxford: Oxford University Press.

Fafchamps, M. (2011). Development, social norms, and assignment to task. *Proceedings of the National Academy of Sciences*, *108*, 21308–21315.

Henrich, J., Heine, S. J., & Norenzayan, A. (2010). The weirdest people in the world?. *Behavioral and Brain Sciences*, *33*(2-3), 61–83. doi:10.1017/S0140525X0999152X

Holm, H. J., & Danielson, A. (2005). Tropic trust versus Nordic trust: Experimental evidence from Tanzania and Sweden. *The Economic Journal*, *115*(503), 505–532.

Johnson, N. D., & Mislin, A. A. (2011). Trust games: A meta-analysis. *Journal of Economic Psychology*, *32*(5), 865–889. doi:10.1016/j.joep.2011.05.007

Karlan, D. (2005). Using experimental economics to measure social capital and predict financial decisions. *The American Economic Review*, *95*, 1688–1699.

Knack, S., & Keefer, P. (1997). Does social capital have an economic payoff? A cross-country investigation. *Quarterly Journal of Economics*, *112*, 1251–1288.

Mayer, R. C., Davis, J. H., & Schoorman, F. D. (1995). An integrative model of organizational trust. *Academy of Management Review*, *20*(3), 709–734.

Richards, P. (1986). *Coping with hunger. Hazard and Experiment in a West African rice farming system*. London: UCL Press.

Platteau, J.-P. (1994). Behind the market stage where real societies exist: Part II—the role of moral norms. *Journal of Development Studies*, *30*, 753–815.

Sapienza, P., Toldra-Simats, A., & Zingales, L. (2013). Understanding trust. *The Economic Journal*, *123*(573), 1313–1332.

Schechter, L. (2007). Traditional trust measurement and the risk confound: An experiment in rural Paraguay. *Journal of Economic Behavior & Organization*, *62*(2), 272–292. doi:10.1016/j.jebo.2005.03.006

Tu, Q., Bulte, E., & Tan, S. (2011). Religiosity and economic performance: Microeconometric evidence from Tibetan area. *China Economic Review*, *22*(1), 55–63.

■ APPENDIX 14.1 DATA DEFINITIONS

TABLE A1. *Overview of the Allocation Games*

Game		Allocation A		Allocation B	
		Self	Other	Self	Other
(1)	Costless Sharing	1000	1000	1000	0
(2)	Costly Sharing	1000	1000	2000	0
(3)	Costless Envy	1000	1000	1000	2000
(4)	Costly Envy	1000	1000	2000	3000

- *% sent in trust game*. An individual level measure for trust game senders. Number of tokens sent/total tokens (10) *100.
- *% returned in trust game*. An individual level measure for trust game receivers. Number of tokens returned/tokens received by sender *100
- *Age*. Individual-level measure. Self-reported age measured in years.
- *Gender (Male = 1)*. Individual level dummy. 1 means male and 0 female.
  Farm size. Individual measure for farm size. Measured by asking how many bushels of rice could be sown on the farm. 1 bushel of rice equals about 1 hectare.
  Social type, 1 = Generous; Social Type, 1 = Inequality-Averse; Social Type, 1 = Selfish. Individual-level measure. Takes value of 1 of a person who can be classified as generous (else) (based on Fehr, 2007). *Social Type, 1 = Other*. Individual-level measure. All participants who could not be specified using these types were classified as other.
- *# times asked chief for help, village average*. Village-level measure. Village average calculated from the number of times people in a village asked the chief for help.
- *Do you trust the chief? (Yes=1), village average*. Village-level measure. Village average calculated from whether they stated they trusted the chief, with 1 being Yes and 0 being No.
- *Presence of crop shocks in previous year: rain, drought, or crop disease*. Village-level measure. Sum of answers to three questions from village survey if they experienced agricultural shocks in the previous year (high rain, drought, or crop disease).
- *Gini Index (farm size)*. Village-level measure. Gini index calculated from variation of farm size in a village. A value of 1 represents complete inequality (one person has all the land) and a value of 0 represents complete equality (everyone has equal land).
  Percentage of migrants in village, 2013 data. Village-level measure. The percentage of migrants in a village, based on a 2013 survey. Calculated from the percentage of respondents that said they were a "stranger" in a random draw from the village.
- *Donation in public good game, village average*. Village-level measure. The average amount that was donated over several rounds in a public goods game. Public goods game participants did not participate in the trust game.
- *Village size*. Village-level measure. The number of heads of household in a village, based on a village census.
- *Do you hide your harvest? (Yes=1)*. Individual-level dummy. Value of 1 means they hide some of their harvest so their neighbors will not know they have it; 0 means they do not.

- *With how many households do you share your harvest?* Individual-level measure. The number of households with whom they would share some of their harvest if they had a good harvest.
- *How many households share their harvest with you?* Individual-level measure. The number of households that the respondent expects would share with him if he needed it.
- *Fraction of people who died in the war.* Village-level measure. Data from 2010 survey. The number of people that died in the war. We divide this by the size of the village prior to the war. As there was village growth during the war, this value can exceed 1.
- *Fraction of people who fled and did not return in the war.* Village-level measure. Data from 2010 survey. The number of people who fled and did not return during the war. We divide this by the size of the village prior to the war. As there was village growth during the war, this value can exceed 1.
- *Distance to main market town (km).* Village-level measure. The distance, as the crow flies, to the nearest chiefdom headquarters (in kilometers), which is the main market town.

■ INDEX

Note: Page numbers followed by *f* or *t* indicate a figure or table respectively

Neurosynth, 48n1
Neuroticism, 82
Newton, K., 86, 88, 165, 264
Niemi-Jennings Youth-Parent Socialization Panel study, 80–81
Nishikawa, L., 80, 81
Nonunderstanding feelings, 43, 45
Nordblom, K., 111, 112
Nørgaard, A. S., 82
Nottingham (UK), 163f, 164–67, 164–67t

Ogden, D. T., 19
Olson, M., 14–15
Oman. *see* trust games
Openness, 82
Open online datasets, 19
Open Source projects, 19
OpenStreetMap, 19
Opercular insular region, 43
Oreopoulos, P., 90
Organizational trust research
  antecedents of trust, 176, 185
  betrayal, 186
  bilateral/multilateral extensions, 185
  central underlying dimensions, 184
  construct clarity, 177
  contextual boundary assumptions, 176, 187–88
  contingency factors, 187–88
  data analysis methods, 175–77, 178f, 179–81t
  dynamic diffusion of trust, 182–83, 186
  fragmentation, cumulative research, 173–74, 189
  generalizability/context-specificity, 183
  "how" developments, 185–86
  "how" recommendations, 182–83
  levels, referents of trust, 184, 188
  limits, liabilities of trust, 186
  mediating mechanisms, 187
  multiple parties, 177
  multiple theory integration, 187
  nature and dimensions, 176
  sample, data collection methods, 174–75
  third-party trust, 185
  trust/distrust relationship, 184
  trust dynamics, 176
  trust–performance relationship, 185–86

trust types/dimensions, 177
"what" developments, 184–85
"what" recommendations, 177–81
Orthodox Jews, 14
Oskarsson, S., 82, 90
Ostrom, E., 17–18, 20–21, 25
Otten, W., 113
Oxytocin, 37–38, 60–68

Pain Overlap Theory, 41
Papua New Guinea, 216
Parsons, K., 112
Paryavi, M., 5
Pascoe, J., 112
Paxton, P. M., 24, 88
Personal control, 82
Peus, C., 184
Phillpot, R., 216
Pickles, A., 88
Pituitary gland, 64
Poland, 85
Poulin, M. J., 107
Predator–prey game (PPG), 61–62
Prisoner's dilemma, 10–11, 13, 40, 46, 102, 134n5, 150
Projection hypothesis, 129–30
Prosociality
  age and trust, 112–13, 114n6
  assurance game, 123, 128–30, 134, 134nn4–7, 135n8
  chicken game, 123, 128
  collective best/team reasoning, 129, 134n6
  cooperation/defection, 128–31, 134nn5–6
  dictator game, 121–27, 127f, 132, 134, 134nn1–3
  distribution of wealth, 126–27, 127f, 131–33, 133f
  egocentrism, 131–32, 134n7
  games, types of, 123
  inclusive fitness theory, 125
  individualism-collectivism, 201–2, 201–2t
  mind reading, 130
  profit *vs.*, 133–34
  projective prediction, 130–31
  rationality, 122–23, 128, 131